EARTH WILL BE REBORN

A SACRED WAVE
IS COMING

MARC MARAMAY WITH VAL YOUNG

The Circles of the One Heart
One Heart, Book One

Winchester, UK
Washington, USA)

First published by O Books, 2007
O Books is an imprint of John Hunt Publishing Ltd.,
The Bothy, Deershot Lodge, Park Lane, Ropley, Hants, SO24 0BE, UK
office1@o-books.net
www.o-books.net

Distribution in:

UK and Europe
Orca Book Services
orders@orcabookservices.co.uk
Tel: 01202 665432 Fax: 01202 666219 Int. code (44)

USA and Canada
NBN
custserv@nbnbooks.com
Tel: 1 800 462 6420 Fax: 1 800 338 4550

Australia and New Zealand
Brumby Books
sales@brumbybooks.com.au
Tel: 61 3 9761 5535 Fax: 61 3 9761 7095

Far East (offices in Singapore, Thailand, Hong Kong, Taiwan)
Pansing Distribution Pte Ltd
kemal@pansing.com
Tel: 65 6319 9939 Fax: 65 6462 5761

South Africa
Alternative Books
altbook@peterhyde.co.za
Tel: 021 447 5300 Fax: 021 447 1430

Text copyright Marc Maramay and Val Young 2007

Design: Stuart Davies

ISBN-13: 978 1 905047 80 2
ISBN-10: 1 905047 80 0

A CIP catalogue record for this book is available from the British Library.

Printed in the US by Maple Vail

EARTH WILL BE REBORN

A SACRED WAVE IS COMING

MARC MARAMAY WITH VAL YOUNG

The Circles of the One Heart

One Heart, Book One

BOOKS

Winchester, UK
Washington, USA

Acknowledgements

Val and Marc would like to heartily thank Minette, Maeve, Kay, John, Brendan, BlackJohn, Kath, Ken, Lynette, and also their families and all who helped the miracle to happen, in big ways and small. Their support and their love are deeply felt and appreciated and will never be forgotten. We would like to thank all the beings of every Circle who took part in the great weaving for their contribution, their patience and their trust. Especially, for this volume, the Sisters of the Flame and the Sisterhood of the Web. Thanks to all who have held the threads of the Rainbow Circles!

Most of all, Marc would like to express eternal gratitude to Val, one of the more thinly disguised Angels, without whose love and support, laughter and sacred patience, this book and so many other miracles would never have happened.

Contents

Introduction
Opening the Weave

Welcome to the Circles of Love within the One Heart. In one of these, you have a place, one that has been kept open for you to enter. One that you may be aware of, or that you may even have been looking for, but it is *your* place. You enter your Circle, sit in your place and open your heart, so that all can flow through you. You sit as an equal, in peace, with an open heart. The journey you are about to start on is about taking your place in the Circle and remembering all that goes with re-entering that space. It is a record of a journey that Marc and I went on, but it was always meant to be shared with you.

We had no idea of the enormity of the journey, or the commitment that we had taken on. We simply opened a sacred space and Marc channeled all the beings that came through in the different circles. We did sense that there was an Overlighting Being or Circle, who would gather the beings that sat in the Circle each night, and who would carefully look after us as well. We always felt safe, well supported and deeply loved.

At the beginning of the journey, I felt as if I was an audience to the beings that were coming through, I would listen and respond silently, in my heart and mind. I would stoke our wood fire, which often became very lively, taking on quite a life of its own. The beings each spoke in their own way and it was the words and inflections that I listened and responded to. When we began, I only had an inkling of my star-connections. Then, one evening, Star-Beings energetically landed with a bump in our tiny front room, full of humor, and any unease that I had simply vanished. Later on, a circle of Star-Beings came through that I had a huge heart reconnection with. Tears of joy were streaming down my face when, at last, I remembered our connection, having forgotten for so long. Gradually, I became more energetically sensitive, as my whole system was opening up, and over a long period of time I started to gain confidence in myself. I realized that I was part of the Circles too, not just an audience, so I took my place in my Circle, which had been waiting for me all the time. And that is why I could greet you the way that I did!

Marc would always do the channeling, but as my system began to open up, I was involved energetically too. Sometimes beings would enter my system, sometimes so that they could feel what it was like to be in a human body, other times it was so that I could feel their energies. Although no names were ever used for any of the beings or Circles, we began to recognize certain energies of individuals and Circles, remembering these maybe months later when they returned. The Angelic Beings were an easy energy to recognize and so were the Tree Beings, as they each have a very special feel, but others were far more subtle, or so new to us that we only began recognizing them after meeting them a few times. People are very interested in the names of the beings and who they are, and at first so were we. But soon we realized that all the beings are coming from Oneness (sometimes in rapid succession!) and by listening with our hearts we could recognize them or know who they are.

Each channeling, which lasted about three hours, was recorded and then transcribed, so a chapter came through each night. Before the channeling, there would be a healing session and we slowly realized that during these times our "Higher Selves" were being introduced to that night's circle. Yet when the session began we would have no conscious idea of who was going to come through. Our daily lives became so synchronistic with the channeling that at times we felt an amazing closeness with the circles and such a thinness of the veils. It was often these magical moments, or the silly or humorous ones, that either reinforced what had been said the night before or were preparing us for that evening's meeting. Always, at the end of each session, there was the beautiful energy of a Storyteller, whose stories were always profound, archetypal and heart warming, pulling all the threads of that evening together. We could both really relax when the Storyteller held us in their loving spell.

Sometimes the beings would come in easily and the rate of speech would be a steady pace, other beings took longer to enter Marc's system, either because they were so unused to human form or even so far from physical form themselves. Sometimes it was uncomfortable for us to have such Beings in our systems that were obviously so different energetically to us. During the sessions on the history of the Earth, we came to realize that our bodies' cells and DNA still held memories of those times, which were being released as we remembered, and these were difficult nights. The journey was full of the expansion and remembering, letting go of the debris that we had clung on to. It was painful and exhausting at times, but also full of joy, with many magical moments. Though we were going through this together, we each had to work on our own "stuff," so we just held each other and were held by the Circle in a loving place, in the One Heart, so we could begin the process of awakening consciously.

So enjoy sitting in your circle again, greeting old friends and beginning to remember who you truly are. You will always be lovingly supported and, though it might not feel like it at times, you are never alone. May you have a magical journey to meet your magical self!

The Question

On the night that "the Wave" was first mentioned (Chapter 13), I asked the Storyteller a question and to our delight, we got a much fuller answer than we expected. Here is their reply...

Val: "We were wondering what you would like done with this material that has come through?"

Storyteller: "It is to be read and experienced by the people, yet not in the old passive way, but as part of a wider experience. For the wave we speak of, and the other waves, are real and there will be many ripples to them. These words when formed onto paper and made available will hold potential for learning and remembering – as well as confusion! Many will feel great joy as they read these words, and cry the tears that fill me now, for these are the tears of joy and remembering and Oneness.

The tree we know so well has shed tears with you and she has felt joy at your remembering of her, at your holding of her in your hearts. [Referring to a particular tree we came to know and love] For she had been damaged and was in need of healing. You came to her as friends, you gave her great gifts, and for these she is grateful. She knows herself now in a new way, as other beings of other trees know themselves too. They will have the tears running down their barky faces and their old hearts will be warmed. And they will welcome you, and welcome others they once feared. For not all come with love in their hearts and the forests have wept many tears over the centuries.

And now we come to tell you that that time is ended. The forests will hear the voices and the songs, the whispers and the cries; they, too, will rejoice. They, too, long to be joyful and long to know themselves more deeply. For they know the difference between love and hate, between joy and fear, even as you do, though in a different way. So we say to you to bring forth these words into the light of day and into the shadows of night; out into the bright spaces and the dark places. For, as you know, your work continues and your joy will increase.

So, yes, these words will be bound together and made one in themselves. And then there will be a book whose cover will perhaps be like bark, like of the ancient books. And it will carry something special inside it for, though the trees do not read in your way, they can truly read in many other ways. They can read the heart more clearly than many Humans and they welcome a loving heart into their heart, as any Human would. For they are like Humans with deep roots and with a great task to fulfill as you do. And the trees long to be remembered by all the Tribes and by the great Tribe. For the Tree Tribe is also remembering itself; it is gathering itself, its senses and its memories. Amongst the trees are many teachers and wise ones, and though every tree is a teacher, there are some who are more gifted in this respect than others.

These will spread news of this opening and this gathering and the wisdom and the knowledge will be spread in the forests. And from forest to forest, from tree to tree, from stone to stone, something will flow that is difficult to describe in Human terms. It is beyond the knowing of most Humans at the moment, yet it is real. It is a special form of Love. This will be a wave in itself and it will reach some Humans too who are attuned to it. And our sisters and brothers in bodies of bark and stone – tree flesh and stone flesh – as of human flesh and animal flesh, will again know themselves to be made of one flesh, all. Every creature great or tiny – even the most invisible – is a vital part of Creation, part of all, and as loved by the Creator as any other.

We thank you from our hearts, which are One Heart with yours. We are truly a little sad to leave, but we know we are welcome to return. And we will bring the wisdom we have gathered and the stories we have shared to you again. In the meantime, just enjoy the love as much as you can. We float in a warm bath of love, which is an ocean overflowing, and is yours to dip into at any moment..."

From heart to heart, within the Circles of Love,
Val Young

The 2012 Overture

The One Heart is the Universal Heart Space we all share, and we can enter it through the doorway of our own heart. Within the One Heart, a vast spectrum of Beings has come together from all realms, meeting as equals within Circles-of-Circles. Many of those we met are Elders-in-Spirit from the Indigenous traditions of Earth, who share their experiences and wisdom, telling stories to open and heal the heart. We had the very real experience of being part of the Circle, like sitting at an ancient Council Fire or a Weaving Circle, sharing their stories and insights.

One of the biggest surprises was how diverse the Circles were, ranging from Shamans and Spiritual Elders of many spiritual traditions, to Devas, Elementals and beings from many of Earth's realms, to Star-Beings and others who do not have physical forms. And when we heard the tones that signaled the Circles were coming in, we never knew who was going to come to the Circle round the fire that night.

Part of the journey of this book involves tracing the "Rainbow Threads" through human history. These living threads carry the original Earth wisdoms and have been held – often through very traumatic times – by women and men who have largely been forgotten by history. In fact, history never knew them at all. They are the ones who held this delicate and vital web of human life together. Their names are mostly unknown and their work went unrecorded, so their achievement is seldom recognized. But without them, the connections of the human community with the Earth and all her life-forms, and with other realms would have snapped long ago. In return for holding this web together, they have often been accused of being primitive, evil, ungodly or uncivilized. Over the centuries, for many reasons, it has mostly been women who have held these sacred Rainbow Threads that hold the very Web of Life together. These threads create a "Golden Rainbow Light," the unified light of the whole spectrum that flows from the Source through all realms.

One important aspect of human nature is that we can communicate with, and travel to, these other realms. Shamans and Wise Ones of all cultures have been doing this for countless centuries, and those in the Circles remind us we all possess these abilities and we need only remember our true nature for the Universe to open up to us. Science is now catching up with the "primitive" Shamans and discovering that we are part of a multi-dimensional Universe. So, by our very nature, we are multi-dimensional beings. We can touch these other realities though the One Heart, and we can communicate through this Heart Space in a safe and sacred exchange.

We began our own process of opening a space by making a large Crystal Mandala of many dozens of crystals (which included two Archangel Michael crystals). Then the Circles suggested transforming it into a crystal mountain. (The significance if this only became clear later, and you will see it as you go through the book) So a crystal portal was created that soon became very busy... Having a multi-dimensional portal in your parlor might not sound ideal, but it soon became a major part of our life.

In the sessions that followed, each being had a very definite arrival and departure, and usually each one would speak their piece and pass the thread onto the next with a short pause in between. Sometimes the beings would flow through in the Circle so fast, they would move on mid-sentence and the next speaker would finish it. Having a storyteller tell a story through you "live" is quite an experience when you have no idea where the story is going, but even more so when a circle of storytellers tell one story, with each taking the thread of the story further along to god-knows-where.

After the first book came through, the waves went on, so 13 moons later, we had three books. Then, over the next 13 months, two more came through, which included well over a hundred stories from the storytellers of the One Heart. We were also receiving hundreds of images running parallel to the words, so it was a rather busy time! The divine order behind all of it goes way beyond our comprehension, while the synchronicities, twists and surprises, emotional ups and downs packed into such a small period would fill a book in themselves.

In the midst of it, we got the surprising message that a wave of energy – Earth's inner creative essence – will emerge from her core to renew life here. Out of the gray, manmade chrysalis that now surrounds the planet, Goddess Earth will emerge like a butterfly, reborn. We were made aware early on that the Earth is entering a new phase, one that is foretold in Indigenous traditions around the world. Many would agree that we are coming up to a major shift or event around the year 2012. It seems we are experiencing the build-up to this opening in the awakening and creative outpouring that is taking place around the world, and strange phenomena on the Sun and on Earth herself. Maybe all of these are part of "The 2012 Overture."

So we pass these visions and insights on to you, as we promised to do. The book is a journey with 19 different Circles through 19 Spheres of experience. It is not really the words themselves that are important, but what is flowing through them. As we were well advised by one in the Circles, "Let yourselves sense the other languages that are flowing, the music behind the words, and you will sharpen your senses." These are the Languages of Light, the Heart Languages, that we hope will flow through the weave of the words.

As with all channeled material, be aware that everything is colored by flowing through a particular person, so use your discernment to sense what is true for you, take it all lightly and, above all, enjoy the journey!

Marc Maramay

Prologue

We are seeds of the Star Tree.
We are fruit and leaf,
Root and branch.
We are Crystal Seeds
And we grow as a Crystal Tree.
One become Many,
And Many,
One.

The Serpent and the Tree of Love

Long ago, in a great forest, there were a serpent and a tree who were truly sisters of the heart.

The fruit-tree was very broad and ancient, her fruit was beautiful and delicious, and the wise, old snake was her friend and guardian. The tree and the serpent were both storytellers who knew and shared many ancient tales, so creatures did not come to their home only to fill their bellies, but to listen and laugh, to remember and dream and, sometimes, they came there to heal.

In their time, they thought they had seen at least one of every kind of creature in the forest. But one morning, the snake heard, through the earth, that a creature with two legs was approaching. The snake looked up to see a creature that was new to her step through the leaves. She was a being with two legs, who stood tall and straight on two long legs, had two arms, and a head with no feathers and not much fur. Her long hair was dark and her skin was the color of the earth.

Then another of her kind stepped through the veil of leaves and he saw the fruit-tree. She could see them making sounds to each other and pointing at the fruit. They were doing a little dance of delight and she was happy for them, as she knew they would enjoy the fruit. Then they beckoned with a sign, and others of their kind came out of the forest. Soon, around the space there were many two-legged creatures jumping, dancing, laughing, celebrating their find, and the snake smiled widely and enjoyed their joy. When they had eaten their fill, they gave thanks to the tree and said goodbye to the serpent, then they disappeared back into the forest. But, every so often after that, they would return for a feast of fruit, and the snake slowly learned a little of their ways.

There came a time when the creatures in the forest began behaving strangely, acting agitated, as if they were in danger or afraid there would not be enough food to go around. The tree and the serpent did all they could to calm them in those days and nights. One afternoon, however, they heard a creature coming through the forest, making a sound that the forest had not heard before, a sound that shuddered through the leaves and echoed from tree to tree. When she stepped into the circle where the tree grew, the snake recognized her as the first to find the tree, and knew that she was one of the kind called women. It was a long time before her great emotion allowed her to speak, but finally she told the serpent that the man she loved would no longer walk with the tribe and had grown cold to her and to all. It was as if something had him in its power and he could not break free.

The woman led the serpent to the place where the man spent his time. The snake looked up and saw a man sitting on a branch of a dead tree, staring, fixated on something in the distance. When the snake climbed up the trunk of the tree to the branch, she could see what the man had fixed his gaze on. It was the great tree in the center of the forest, the oldest and tallest one of all, rising high above all other trees, and its branches stretched beyond the clouds. The old ones told stories of it that were ancient when their ancestors were learning to walk. It was said that it had grown from a seed planted on the Earth's first day. Surrounded by light, the tree was an astonishing sight, with its fruit and leaves of so many colors and shapes, circled by whole flocks of birds, a truly generous giant feeding countless thousands of creatures each day. Yet the man was not looking at it with wonder, but with a kind of desperate hunger. His mind was set on what was out of reach and out of sight, the very highest fruit of the tallest tree - the fruit that shone like stars. The man told the serpent that if only he could taste one of those star-fruit, he would be happy again.

Then the man asked if the serpent would climb the tree and pluck one of those special fruit. She could not tell what was the wise thing to do, but she wanted to help somehow. An image flashed within her of a serpent spiraling up a tree towards the stars. She agreed to make the journey, if the woman would stay with her old friend, the fruit-tree, while she was away. She did not know if it was possible to reach these fruit, but she promised to climb as high as she could.

The serpent made her way to the center of the forest, to the great Tree of Life, whose every fiber was shining. She felt herself in the presence of love, abundant and overwhelming. The trunk of the tree was as broad as a mountain, and stretched higher than the sky, but the snake had made a promise and she began climbing. Hour after hour, she climbed the trunk in a spiral, moving through the fruit-laden branches until, below her, she could see the patterns and colors of the treetops. When she was tiring, a broad-winged eagle who was circling the ancient tree came to her aid. Carrying her, he flew as high as he could, close to the roof of the sky. From there, she climbed on, moving through the edge of the sky into the space beyond. There, far away in the darkness, were the shining fruit, beyond reach. She made her way towards the distant stars, feeling her way, guiding herself by touch and intuition. Deeper and deeper into the night, she traveled, and when she looked back, the Earth was a dark disc, far below her. The only lights she could see were the campfires of the Human tribe, scattered like stars across the face of the Earth.

Meanwhile, in the forest far below, the old fruit-tree missed the embrace of her friend, so the woman opened her arms and stretched them around the trunk, singing to soothe the troubled heart of the tree. As she held the tree in her embrace, she softly sang a song of her tribe, the race of Humans. In the silence after her song, the woman heard the voice of the tree in her heart. In return for her song, the tree began to tell her an ancient story, one that told of a time before people walked. When the tree had told it, the woman thanked her and promised that she would tell the story to her tribe when she returned. The tree realized that her people did not know these ancient tales, so she began to tell the woman another, and so the nights and days passed.

And, for days and nights, the serpent journeyed on, watching the sun and moon rise and set behind the Earth. The speaking tree told story after story and, in the silences between, the woman digested them, as one would a piece of fruit. Each story nourished her, and each had a special seed within it that would emerge and then seem to disappear, as it planted itself somewhere within her. In return, the woman would sing the songs and tell the stories of her own tribe to the tree, so the circle around the tree remained, as it always had been, a space for sharing songs and stories.

When the woman would look up through the branches of the fruit-tree to the sparkling stars, she would wonder where the serpent could be. There were lonely moments, when the tree and the woman held each other, holding also a distant friend in their hearts. They both told stories and listened deeply, and the seeds of so many stories planted themselves within the woman, that day by day, night by night, she became a keeper of countless stories and a teller of ancient tales herself.

The shining fruit seemed to beckon the serpent on, for they glowed brighter each time she looked. Yet the moment the serpent reached the star-fruit was a surprise when it finally came. The trunk of the tree had been getting thinner and thinner - as the snake had too - so she kept her focus firmly on the ever-narrowing path. Then she came to a point where the path narrowed to the width of a single thread. When she looked along the length of the thread, there, hanging from its slender end, was something startlingly bright – a star-fruit in all its ripe and bright glory!

Suddenly, she sensed a great light rise behind her and turned to find a great, winged figure shining there, a giant being of dazzling brightness, with high, arching wings. As he came nearer, she could even glimpse his shining face, though to look on it was like trying to look into the face of the Sun, and she could feel the full gaze of his face blazing upon her. One of the star-fruit fell from its thread and landed in his giant hand. She heard his voice, then, which seemed to wrap around her like the warm breath of a breeze.

"This tree grew from a single seed, a star planted deep in the heart of the Earth. It grows so high because it is rooted in infinite love. And this fruit is the fruit of love. Now, it is for you to taste that fruit, if you wish."

The snake reached out and took the shining fruit into her mouth, feeling a delicious tingle. As she swallowed it down, she felt a sense of excitement, and closed her eyes to savor the experience. She made a pulsation like a wave as the fruit traveled down her body. Suddenly, she felt the fruit burst open inside her and light coursed through her. When it reached her heart, she felt her heart burst open, so that great light poured out around her, opening as wide wings of brilliant light. She was bathing in an ecstasy of love and, in her bliss, she let go of the thread, but instead of falling, she sensed herself being held by the shining one. She felt as one with the winged being who held her and she knew the one light flowed through them.

Far below, a woman sat on the roots of a fruit-tree, telling a story. She looked up to see a remarkable sight in the clear night sky. Among the stars was a serpent of starry light, gently held by a winged and shining giant of the sky. And that night, across the forest, a new story was told. In a certain place in the forest, a sleepless man, who had kept a lonely vigil, saw the sign in the sky and wondered how much longer his wait would be.

The serpent could not tell how long she was held there, whether it was days or years beyond counting. She was dreaming, but she was more awake than she had ever been. Her eyes were filled with a new light, and she could see the light within everything. With surprise, she noticed the roots of another tree traced out in light around her, and these roots were entwined with the branches. She realized that these star-fruit were also growing in a much bigger tree of light, one that stretched out further than she could know. Suddenly, it seemed that she had been traveling through a web of roots, though she could not tell which were roots and which were branches, yet it did not seem to matter, as they were all connected in this web of light around her. When she looked back along the path of the trunk of the tree, it was crowned with the most beautiful fruit she had ever seen, the Earth herself. Within her, the Earth was full of seeds, and across her body, starry seeds were scattered.

The shining one still held her in his love, and the serpent thought she was outside of her body, watching him holding her, until she realized he was only holding her old skin, which she had now shed. She looked down at her own body, which was newly shining and shimmered in pulsating, lively patterns. She knew the moment had come for her to return. The winged one gave her a message to pass on, and she promised she would. A bright star-fruit fell like a crystal tear, to land in his open hand. The serpent picked it up in her mouth, and with a final look into his shining face, bade him farewell. Then, she slowly turned to Earth and wished herself there.

A moment later, she was at the edge of the sky, stretched out on a broad branch, as the Sun rose over the rim of the world. She watched this wonder, as if for the first time, while the Sun unfurled brilliant wings of cloud in all the colors of the rainbow. Then, from her own heart, the serpent unfurled her own bright wings even wider and stretched them out in the light. A great eagle rose up from below and landed on the branch beside her, with a deep cry of joy. The eagle and the winged serpent then flew together over the wakening Earth, gliding over the rivers and mountains, the plains and the forests. Soon, they were skimming the treetops, side by side, and they dipped down through the canopy of leaves, to find a large fruit-tree standing there in an open circle.

A woman with sleepy eyes looked up to see their silhouettes in front of the rising sun and wondered if she was still dreaming. But the serpent had returned and the tree rejoiced, while the woman sang a song of homecoming. That day became a day of celebration and great light filled this circle in the forest. Creatures gathered in the circle to share the songs and witness the marvel of the star-fruit. When the snake placed the glowing fruit into the open palm of the woman's hand, it illuminated her face as she held it, as if the Morning Star had come to the Earth. She received the gift with gratitude, and she looked forward to giving this precious gift to the one she loved.

News of the event spread, and there was quite a gathering, unlike any that anyone could remember, with so many creatures arriving to celebrate and none seeming to leave. The celebrations continued late into the night, with the star-fruit illuminating them, as they danced and sang. And few slept in the forest until the morning light was already in the sky.

The moment came when the woman knew she must go to the lonely man who had waited and waited. The serpent gave her the message from the winged one to pass on. The woman felt a little sorry to leave that joyful place and so many friends, but as she made her way through the forest, she dreamt ahead of all that could be, now, and the future began to fill her thoughts. By the time she reached the place where the man waited, she was in a state of high excitement.

She found him, there, sitting on a low branch of the dead tree, thinking and waiting.

With her hands outstretched, she came to him, holding the golden fruit, offering him all from her open heart. He jumped from the branch and ran to her, his eyes wide and hypnotized by the sight of the fruit. The woman spoke the message then. "The seeds are already within you. All you seek is within." But the man heard nothing. With a shaking hand, he took the fruit, placed the fruit on his tongue and closed his mouth around it. The woman tingled with anticipation, wondering what wonder was about to take place.

To her shock, the man spat the shining seed into his hand and held it tight in his fist as he spoke. "I have been thinking hard about what I should do with this seed. It would be foolish to simply swallow it. I will plant it here and grow a tree from it. In time, there will be a whole grove of these trees of wisdom. No one will need to travel halfway to the stars to receive a seed of light. Of course, I will have to stay here to guard the seed and I will have to watch over the sapling as it grows. So, I cannot leave now."

He saw pain and disbelief in the woman's face. She slowly turned and walked from that place, and, though her pain was great, she did not return there in all the years that followed. She returned to the Human Tribe, hoping that, in her time, she would find love again. With her stories and songs and the wisdom of her years, she came to comfort and guide many, and her days became happy ones once more.

When the woman had gone, the man looked at his fist with the light held inside it. Bending, he pulled up a handful of grass, and made a hole in the bare earth with a stick. Opening his fist, he dropped in the seed, covered it, watered it and watched the spot all day and slept on the spot by night. Day after day, week after week, his patience was tested, as there was no sign of anything making its way through the soil, and the man's world narrowed to this small patch, for he had focused all his hopes there. Finally, when he had almost given up on hope, the tiniest of tendrils appeared. Slowly it grew, yet it seemed so weak that the man feared it would not survive. The lightest breeze seemed strong enough to pull it from the ground; any creature walking on it would have crushed it, and all his hopes with it. So the man made sure to keep all the animals out of his patch, and he chased away any that came near, while he waved away any birds, in case they tried to tug up the frail tendril. He also cast a suspicious eye on the plants and grasses that grew around the patch, so he pulled up and dug out every growing thing he could, until he had made a big patch of bare soil.

Month after month, he carried on this practice, until he finally had a very thin young tree that reached almost to his knee. A year passed and, in the spring, the tiniest of buds produced small, pale leaves that struggled to open to the light. He knew his tree would need more light, so he began to cut the branches from all the surrounding trees, until only their trunks were left standing. Still, the thin sapling did not thrive, so the man, in deep frustration, cut every surrounding tree down to stumps. By now, most of the creatures were afraid of the strange man who danced an angry dance when they appeared, but sometimes, the bigger animals had walked through and ignored the angry man with his spindly sapling. Now, looking at the high pile of tree-trunks, he had an idea - with furious energy, he began to dig holes all around the space and then into every one, he placed one of the tree-trunks, until he had made a high and forbidding stockade. Behind it, he remained for the years to come, climbing out only once a day to find food and water. He did not know how many years had passed when the tree finally bore its first fruit. But, to the man's disappointment, they did not look much like he expected. They were small and looked shriveled even before they had ripened. No light shone from them. When he finally plucked up enough courage to pluck one and taste it, the fruit tasted so bitter that that he could not even hold it in his mouth and had to spit it out.

The man cried, then, bitter tears that stung his cheeks and tasted sour, falling to the dry soil at his feet. He told himself, however, that he would not accept defeat, and he planted the dark seed from the fruit just there. He picked every fruit from the tree and planted all their seeds around him. Something would come from all his efforts, he knew, something that would make all the lonely years here worthwhile. So he went on waiting and waiting for yet more years. Those tendrils that did appear were more frail than ever and they only grew into saplings that were ever more spindly. He could feel himself shriveling, too, as if he was shrinking in this narrow and shadowy place.

Then, one year, no fruit appeared on the tree. He waited and wondered if it was simply late. But, each morning, when he awoke and ran to the tree to search it, he found not even a hint or hope of fruit. Even the leaves were shriveling and, one day, he finally accepted that the tree itself was dying. He looked around him at the sad-looking saplings that had not even the strength or thickness of his bony little finger. Their dark leaves hung limp and lifeless. He knew then there would be no more fruit. An end had come.

He fell to his knees, as if crushed by a great weight of grief and disappointment, and his body shook with dry and painful sobbing. Then, in a rising wave, his frustration and anger poured out of him, and for days, his rage laid waste to all that he had tended so carefully, tearing the withered leaves and breaking every branch of the dead tree, then, pulling up every shriveled sapling and trampling them into the dust. He dug up every rotting tree-trunk that had imprisoned him all those years and laid them low. When he had exhausted all his rage, his strength seemed to drain away, and he fell to the earth, his face in the dust, and did not move. The dried-up husk of his heart burst open, scattering the seeds of his love in all directions, releasing all that had been hidden within him. Sleep finally came upon him, and he lay there, as a light rain began to fall. For days and nights, he lay there, as if drifting somewhere on the edge of life.

Then, one day, he painfully turned to face the sky, before slowly rising to his feet. He left that place, and walked and walked, making his way through the forest until he was far from anywhere he could remember. He found a spring rising from the earth between smooth stones, filling a small pool with clear and sparkling water. He sat at its edge to rest and, to his surprise, the creatures gathered here did not fear him and his presence was accepted. They were drinking from the pool and feeding from the trees and plants around, peacefully grooming or playing in the shade. He began to feed himself from the abundance growing around the glistening crystal pool, and soon he could feel strength returning to him and life flowing again within him.

He remained there for days to come, watching with growing joy the creatures who came there and the life that revealed itself around him. All that had once been so vital to his mind had no meaning here. Here was life, a dream that was real and alive, and he was alive within it. He had no reason to hide, nothing to fight, and his own life opened up again, as his heart slowly unfolded.

Now, he felt himself to be one with the circle of creatures who gathered at the crystal pool, and the feeling was one of gladness.

One day, he decided it was time to explore more of the forest around him. And, after saying goodbye to the creatures who lived around the pool, he set off. He made his way through the abundance of life, reminding himself of all that had once delighted him, awakening himself to new discoveries every day. So much that he had almost forgotten, he remembered now. So much beauty surrounded him that joy awakened him each day. He joined in with the songs of the forest and, soon, could answer any call.

The creatures came to know him as the curious being who observed their ways with fascination and delight, who gathered fruits and nuts and seeds for them, who took great pleasure in watching them feed and play. With grasses and leaves, he wove a bag that he filled with seeds gathered from the forest floor. He carried it with him, and if he found a space in the forest where the trees had been visited by fire or felled by men, he scattered some seeds as he passed. Wherever he walked, he scattered the even brighter seeds of his love, so the creatures found it easy to follow his trail. Often, a little procession of creatures followed him on his way and, when he rested, they came to him to be fed and to enjoy his playful ways. At dawn, when he reached up to welcome the Sun, the birds would perch on his arms and shoulders, and he would stand, strong as a tree, to greet the day.

And there were places where the man planted seeds in patterns that were unique and new. And with the help of the birds and animals, these little spaces became gardens within the great, wild garden of the forest. More than once, the woman wandered into one of these spaces, with a sense of delight at her discovery, for she also had planted gardens in which her healing herbs grew. She would sense the subtle presence of an old friend and wonder where in the world he was. But their paths were not yet to cross. The man became beloved by all and his gentle presence became part of the life of the forest. Yet there were moments when he longed to speak to his own kind, and he wondered when others of his tribe would cross his path.

Near the end of one particular day, he walked into a space in the forest and stopped. He realized that where he was, was the one place he had avoided; the place of the dead tree. He recognized the circle of trees around the space and felt a pang of shame, but they greeted him as an old friend. They asked him to stay the night and dream with them, now that he could hear their voices again. The man thanked them and agreed, and lay down in the midst of their circle, which was growing green once more. The curious creatures who had been walking with him gathered there and curled up, and they all began to dream together, deep into the night.

Far off, deep in the center of the forest, a star seemed to fall from the starry dome above. Then, another brilliant light fell gracefully to Earth, and another and another, until the creatures of the night began to look up in wonder. So many were falling, that the sky became ablaze with light, and an astonished silence fell over the forest, a hush so sudden that it woke those creatures who were used to the calls and cries of night. Even a man deep in dreaming awoke, to wonder what new dream this was. Even the sleepiest ones quickly realized that the stars were all falling around the Great Tree. Each star traced a thread of light in the sky as it traveled to Earth, so the tree was soon surrounded by a high column of light that stretched as far as sight could see.

When it was near dawn, creatures of all kinds began to make their way towards the Great Tree. When they neared it, they found it surrounded by a circle of light, made by shining star-fruit scattered in brilliant abundance. And, around this circle, the creatures of the forest assembled, united in awe.

It was not long after, that a man in a forest clearing looked up to see a marvelous sight, a long, lively procession of creatures snaking their way through the trees towards him. A trio of weaverbirds flew to him, carrying in their beaks a basket woven from fine grasses, which they laid at his feet. Leading the procession was an old serpent, who bowed her head and dropped a bright star-fruit into the open basket. "Fruit falls to Earth in its own time," she said. She smiled at him, as he thanked her from his heart.

Around them, the creatures gathered, and each gently held a star-fruit in their mouth, and one by one, they dropped it softly into the woven basket until the basket overflowed with light. Then, a woman who had joined the joyful procession stepped forward and placed a shining fruit into the man's open hand. They stood before each other, each a little older and wiser. They looked deeply into each other's hearts and their healing began. Tears of joy flooded the man's face, which shone in its own way, as he thanked the creatures from his heart.

The woman turns to the hollow tree, and, from her heart, she sings into the heart of the tree through an opening. Her song flows through the forest, echoing from tree to tree and heart to heart, and those of the human tribe begin to make their way to the gathering place. A great celebration begins, a feast of the fruits of love, and the planting of so many seeds of love that the circle of earth shone beneath them.

From that day, these two happy humans left a starry trail on the path they traveled. They walked in peace through all their days, and each day was as their first upon the Earth.

There was once a mirror that told only the truth.

It was very precious, as you can tell. It was said to be a piece of a vast mirror that had broken in ancient times. Someone had once looked into it with such love that it shattered in pure joy. When it burst, the parts of it scattered through the universe as so many stars. Yet each piece of this great mirror was somehow complete in itself. Each mirror was unique, and the truth it revealed was uniquely beautiful. Since there were so many of them, they were once very easy to find. In fact, everyone had one. Perhaps that was why, in later days, they were sometimes not valued highly. They could not be lost, but it was possible to forget about them. Since we all had one, kept in a very obvious place, you may think they would be hard to forget.

Yet there came a time when these mirrors of truth seemed to disappear. Soon, they became very difficult to find, and there never seemed to be one near when you needed it. Some were willing to spend great sums to find one, but found one could not be bought. Others tried making all sorts of imitations to replace what was lost, but without success. Some spent many years searching, in hope of locating one, but it seemed that they were now rarer than dragons' teeth, and soon they became half-forgotten and mythical. But the mirrors were no myth, and there were always a few souls who remembered them. There were even a rarer few who remembered where to find them. So their memory was not totally lost, though they seemed to be hidden somewhere, out of sight, as if hidden behind veils of all kinds, buried beneath dusty cobwebs in locked rooms, near impossible to find.

What if, after a great search, you finally found a chamber where one of these precious mirrors was hidden? You try to open the door, but it seems firmly locked and bolted from the inside, and no pushing or pulling, no frantic banging will budge this obstruction. Even if we happened to have a key handy, this door does not have a keyhole. So we stand at the door, which is dusty and neglected, with its locks rusted, its paint peeling. We feel frustrated, for we can sense the presence of this wonderful mirror very near; we know it must be within. Yet there seems to be no way we can enter the chamber, and the door does not look like it will open itself, even if we wait until the end of time. So we give up the struggle and sit on the threshold, wishing we could have a glimpse of such a wonderful mirror. We might seem rather forlorn, outside the door, but we can still dream...

We want to see this magical mirror so much that we begin to imagine it, as if in a daydream. We imagine the door opening and all the veils melting away...and the mirror is revealed to us! We see what seems to be a shining disc, a golden plane of light, and, as it glows, its light fills us. Yet, when we look closer, we notice that this mirror is not flat, but a perfect sphere, so it reflects all around it. We raise it up and hold it close to us, and we notice it seems to have countless flaws, but each is sparkling uniquely, and we understand these flaws are, in fact, its facets. It is clear this mirror is not broken, but beautiful and whole in itself. We hold this crystal moon before us, and we breathe in its soft, golden light. Rather than just look at the moon, we look deeply into the heart of it. Immediately, it grows brighter, because it is reflecting our true beauty. We sense great space within it, because it is revealing our hidden worlds within, still undiscovered.

And now we step through the skin of the crystal mirror, into its shining heart, moving into the great light beyond, to find ourselves in a bright and familiar place. We sense love all around us, and vastness opening up within the light. We have stepped inside our own heart, and its loving light surrounds us now. This is our heartlight, the light of truth within us, pouring from a sacred source. We sense the great scale of our inner world, and we feel the space open within, as inner veils melt away, revealing new spaces. The light within us seems boundless, and we glimpse unknown realms within, waiting to be explored.

We have boldly stepped across the edge and a whole world has opened up. We have moved through the illusion and found the truth within. We stand in truth, not the truth reflected, but the light of living truth. In its glow, all within us opens, all is revealed in its true colors. As you breathe in this light of truth, you move your awareness fully within, back through your skin to the light that is alive and breathing within you. This is your breathing space, where peace always awaits you. And here we rest.

☯

We begin with one thread, as all begins.

Draw a thread of light forth from deep in your heart, and spin it out in a golden spiral. Breathe your love into it, and this heart-thread will sing into life as it spirals out, brightening the web of the world as it emerges. It moves in a circle around you and returns to its source in your heart, before the thread loops out again and again, reaching out and returning, moving at the speed of love. You relax and enjoy the light as it dances, and the more you open its source, the more light is released.

Now so many threads are stretching out around you that the very air lightens. Your heart lightens even more, and circles of light are opening from within you, ripples pulsing from your center. From a point of peace and stillness deep inside you, love is rippling out in rings of light, and you are at the center of the circles. These pulsations change the space around you, and it becomes a place of peace. All these circles are creating a sphere of light around you. From your core, a perfect sphere is opening, as beautiful as a full moon, and as radiant as a sun of love. As your light flows out, it forms a dome of light over you, and a bowl beneath you. You open this golden sphere of shining love, a Sun of the Heart.

You are at the center of the sphere, with a bright spine of light rising through its center. From this spindle, the light-threads stretch out, reaching down into the Earth, connecting us to her heart, and rising up to connect to the stars. We relax and rejoice in the beauty that surrounds us, we sense the patterns and colors in the crystalline light. We take time to appreciate and absorb the subtle, glowing colors of this shining sphere.

Like a spherical lens, this all-seeing eye of our heart can look out in every direction. We see then that ours is not the only sphere, that it is connected to others, which appear to be all around us. We realize that they are all connected within a greater globe, which encompasses them all, and embraces them in its living light. This Rainbow Globe is a world of love, flowing and abundant, and your sphere is within it. Here, you see through the eye of your heart, and so you slowly adjust to the brightness of its light. You notice that within the great Globe are many shining circles flowing with different colors and energies, united in a circular flow of life. As you look into each circle you see the blending and melding of energies in living threads of all colors, which make up the Rainbow Circle. As you look more deeply into the weave of the living threads, you see glimpses of bright bodies of light, with radiant faces, and eyes that shine in every color. Within each circle are diverse beings, flowing in Oneness, and each circle you look into seems so different, filled with fantastic, flowing colors, and luminous, moving forms that dance in waves within the weaving circle. Each circle seems to be weaving itself together as you watch, creating a unity of all its energies.

You see life expressed in a multitude of hues, in mingling colors, woven into a harmony that seems impossible, but is real and alive before you. The unique flow of living light in each circle creates the One Light, the golden glow within this globe of love. You realize that you are flowing in one of the Circles, though you feel still and at peace. On each side of you, stretches a circle of living light in every hue you could imagine – and some you have never seen before. You look more deeply into the open weave of the light, and you see you are one of a Circle of beings of astonishing diversity, of many different origins, natures and wisdoms. Yet they are *you*, all aspects of your One self, the spectrum of who you are. Your hearts are connected, and you sense, flowing from heart to heart, a wisdom that unites you all. In this Circle of unity, your many ways and wisdoms flow as one, the many forms and faces shine as one; the light you share creates one Rainbow Circle of Light.

Remember your place in the great Circle.

You take your place within the Rainbow Circle, the Circle of unified life, where every being has a place of equal esteem. A Circle of evolving Creation, through which great waves of creativity flow; a Circle of creators, of weavers, of dreamers. A Circle of dreamers, wide awake; a Circle of weavers, wise and bright; a Circle of creative hearts, open and overflowing. Reach out on each side of you and feel the flow of Love in the Circle. You are welcome here, the space is open to you, you create with us; you add your ways to the way of the Circle. Your voice joins the Circle of voices singing as one, in a harmony of diverse voices. Your threads are welcome in the weaving of the great pattern. Your unique way of weaving is welcome here.

You express your growing perfection in the growing Circle. You weave with us now as you have always done. Your heart knows the ways, the ways of reverence and respect for life. Here in the Circle of life, all are held sacred, all receive the gifts of life and give their gifts freely into the web of life. We weave a web of wisdom between us, woven of our many ways and wisdoms, of our many dreams and visions woven as one. We observe life through our eyes of love, and we see in the Circle how love flows full circle. It returns to the one who gives in the circle of return, so all flows in a living circle of love beyond time in the endless circle. We hold the sacred space open, so that all may enter as they remember, and return to the spinning Circle of wisdom.

We have waited for you, and we rejoice in your return to the Circle you never truly left. We sleep and we dream, we rest and we wake, and we awake now to find ourselves in the space that has waited for us. We awaken to our place in the weaving of life around us. We remember we are part of the weaving and we are always weaving, even as we live and breathe. As we awaken, we breathe new life into the weave, the flow of life brightens, and the light in the Circle rises. We open more of our selves to the flow, to the growing love between us, and the Circle of wisdom widens.

We are here in our places of honor in the sacred Circle. We are here in the Circle, as we have always been, and in the Center, the point from where the Circle flows.

We are the weavers and weaving is fine work, but our eyes never tire. Though our eyes are ancient, they are clear, not cloudy. They see far in every direction. We see what is called past, present and future. Our eyes shine brighter than firelight, they see to the ends and to the beginnings.

We see, not in a straight line, but in a circle, just as we weave in a circle. And in our circle, the threads flow, rippling out like tree rings through the Universe. These are rings of time, though each would hold within its hoop more centuries than you could count, and they circle out beyond time and space. From the center, we pull the threads; from the spinning center, out they spin, through our hearts and our hands, and we add our love to the love that is within them. Though they are full of love, there is always room for more... We add our hearts' desires in patterns of love that sing through the galaxies. We breathe bright life into the colors of the singing threads.

Life then evolves its way through Creation, creating anew through its evolution. We are spinning through spaces in the revolving wheel of the spinning circle. We are its arms and hands and fingers, delicate and clever... and we are spinning too! We spin as we shape and design from the skeins of creation. There is wisdom in our fingers; we never make a mistake...not so you would notice.

Is there a mistake in Nature? Ah, what a question! The mistake you make is part of the design, as you wend and weave your way through your lives, and lives wend their ways through your weave. And if we have to mend the web, we make sure not to obscure *your* designs so you will recognize them when you look back at the patterns of the path you wove, the tangled path or the open one, the overgrown or the clear way. It is yours to choose.

We do not try to unpick what is perfect, the way those who meddle with the threads do, for they make tangles others must undo. We let Nature breathe and weave, and we make space for all to grow. We create space between the threads, for the finer threads of life, for the details to be stitched in, with your choice of embroidery. Choose well and the patterns of your life will seem to weave themselves, without you needing to work too hard. For you can make life a misery by trying too hard to make a perfect design, with no missing stitches, no loose threads, with a flawless surface pattern. Remember that what is behind the outer pattern is what really matters, for when you flip it over, you see the truth of what lies behind. In the tapestry of Creation, even the hidden side is truly beautiful. There, where the threads are tied, there are the knots *we* tie, the invisible connections behind the weave you perceive.

Soon you will see glimpses of what lies behind the outer weave, the hidden face of Creation, the beauty behind the images and forms you think you see. We will turn down an edge of the tapestry for you, and give you a glimpse of what lies behind. And you will recognize the Grand Design even from a fleeting glimpse. Even this tiny corner contains hints of the greater truth. So don't blink or you might miss it! Try to keep your eyes open, especially the eye of the heart, for when the moment comes that Nature awakes and reveals hidden things, who wants to be still asleep?

In the dream-weaving of sleeping and waking, we weave the dream between us and our dreams thread together into the One Dream of which each one of us has a glimpse. This is the dream that wakes us up, the dream that shakes us out of our sleep. So bright and vivid is it, that all else fades. We find ourselves revealed in the dream, all of us together, in the one woven Living Vision. We stand in the full light of this day dream, this waking dream, and we see ourselves as we are, all of us, moving through the Light in our garments of living color. Our threads extend through one another, we move through each other as our lives connect and intertwine. We see the connections revealed, and know we *are* the web; the weavers of the web, the weavers *and* the web. We are creating, we are creation, we are our own creation, and the creator we are.

Are we ready to accept this? We know it deep down, so we cannot deny it; we cannot hide from the truth, the truth of who we are. So weave out the doubts, pick out the tangles, find where the mind has hidden old broken threads. Find the frayed ends and the tight, constricted places where the weave cannot breathe. Sing out the doubts, the fears, like the birds who weave frequencies through the trees. When they sing their web-songs, their connecting-calls, they sing their hearts out and All hears. Creation has as many ears to hear as throats to sing. It listens to itself, it sings to itself. So sing to yourself and you will be surprised by what you hear; birds might reply, the trees might too. They might trill a note for you or shake a leaf or two. Or maybe your reply will be more dramatic, but you will get a response. Life is listening to you. It is responsive only when it wants to be, but it hears you, never fear. For if Creation did not listen to itself, what else would it listen to?

Keep your frequencies clean, make sure they shine. Make sure the threads are bright enough to see yourself in – to hear yourself, too. Open the weave and blow in fresh air and life. Do not forget any corner of your own tapestry, check it often to see if it seems dull or faded. Look beneath the surface of the pattern to the patterns underneath, then to the ones under these, to the deeper ones. You need not be afraid to dig down, to let your fingers dig deep into the weave, because you will find the deeper you go, the brighter it is, the more alive.

The liveliest patterns are not on the surface, but in the deep weave. There you will find, revealed in the weave, the who and why of you. And if you tug the threads, you will sense the connections to all the other you's who make the spectrum of the you's who are the One.

You are at home in the Circle and, within, you feel a sense of homecoming. You recall that part of you has never left here, that some ancient aspect of you has been here from the beginning, holding your place in the Circle of Light, from the moment that the first Light flowed. Through all the forms, all the faces, all the colors of diversity, one Light shines. And in the stories that flow in the Circle, the Light flows too. There is, within the Circles, a harmony of histories, for all the stories that have been lived by the beings of all the Circles form one story. Through every story, runs a subtle thread of Light; through every history runs a hidden thread of love.

In each sphere, there are songs flowing, and the harmonies of the spheres arise between them as they dance. Within every sphere, the Circles ring with songs, and their singing tones compose its own harmonic song, in tune with the love song singing from its center. There is a point of Light at the center of all the Circles, and at the center of every shining orb of Love. This point of Light is seemingly tiny, yet of intense brightness, and all the threads appear to be flowing from it or flowing to it. All the countless viewpoints converge at this one point of brilliant clarity, all the sightlines emerge from this one viewpoint, the Eye of the Creator. It is the point of origin, the eternal moment from which all moments flow, the opening where all life-stories appear from and disappear to. All of the Light flowing around us in this woven web of color, this golden sphere of unified Light, emerges from this one point, at the center of all. You flow towards it now, along the single thread, which you drew from your own heart. You flow along this golden thread, as it brings you to the center point, and you flow to the center of All. You enter the center where All is Light.

We are here in the Heart of Love. All begins and ends here. All flows from here and returns to here. Here is the source of life, the source of Love. We feel we could stay here forever, in this place of peace, of stillness, from which all movement flows – and we know we have been here forever, also. Soon, we flow on, we feel ourselves move, and we realize we are moving in a spiral, again flowing into the Circle of Love.

We are once more in our place in the Circle, yet we have not left the Center. We know now that the center is within us, shining in our own heart. In this new vision from the center, we are looking out and looking within at the one time. Here is the point of peace and stillness, the creative point, the weaving-point of Creation. Here, at the center of our heart, is the center we all share, the point we all hold in common, the meeting-place of all our threads. Here, is the center of all hearts, the Heart of the One, the One Heart we all share.

We feel the Light flow more strongly in the Circle now, it feels stronger and more real to us, as the Circle does too. We see more clearly the vivid diversity of faces, the light in the eyes, and the shining hearts of the wise beings who share this Circle. Each of them shines as a great light, and amongst them, we shine, too. We are here in our full wisdom, we are present as the wise being we truly are. We feel our wisdom flow within us, flowing on into the Circle, to return to us in brighter revelation. Here, in this Circle of the Rainbow Heart, we feel the circle of our heart open wider to the living wisdom. We feel our light flowing into the Circle, enlivening it and returning to us even brighter. We feel all within the Circle united in the one Love. We feel whole, a circle within ourselves, and the circle of our many selves forms the Circle of One. And we are that One, within the Circle of Love.

We love as One, in a Circle of many Circles become One, a woven globe of flowing spheres, an orb-web of living wisdom, with One Heart at the center, animating and creating All. Together, the Rainbow Circles create the great Golden Sphere, the Sun of suns. Within its core, is the central spindle of living threads, a Tree of Light, with ascending and descending spheres. Orbiting it are the Circles, holding the forms and patterns, holding the whole in form.

One thread of love runs in a perfect Circle from heart to heart, spun from One Heart forever opening, creating a universe of love that knows no limits. One that expands forever, filled with endless worlds, woven with endless love. Through all the worlds, flows one thread, which creates all form and being, woven from One Heart, which knows no other but its own infinite reflections, mirroring its Oneness.

We are none other than the One. The One we are. The One I AM.

The Golden Thread

Once, a woman found a thread that led her to a new life.
When she had looked out the window first thing that morning, the day had not looked promising. Gray clouds that she did not like the look of hung low overhead, and a few drops of rain fell on the pane to confirm her suspicions. Since then, the sky had not brightened, and neither had her spirits. The old woman was looking out of the window, yet again, in the hope that the day might lighten up, when she noticed a loose thread at the edge of the carpet. It looked untidy, so she tucked it under the carpet and went to make coffee, as she was still trying to wake up.

A little later, her black cat tried to attract her attention, as she had just got a great idea for a game, but the woman turned on the morning news on the TV. She sat and, from then on, her eyes seemed stuck to the screen, to the gloomy news and the stream of fearful images. Meanwhile, her nervous fingers were busy knitting, making a dark scarf that was getting longer every day. She was drinking black coffee because the milk had run out again, but she still couldn't seem to wake up. Her eyes were becoming very heavy, when a high, curious sound from her cat jerked her fully awake.

She looked around, to find that the cat was playing with something. Her cat always seemed to find something to amuse herself, and she seemed to be having a fine time. The woman couldn't see what her plaything was and she suspected the worst, but her curiosity had been awakened, so she flicked off the TV and went to investigate. The cat had something wrapped around her paws, and when the woman bent down, she could see it was a dull and dusty thread. It had obviously been pulled out of the carpet and more was coming out as she watched. She quickly grabbed the thread and began to scold the cat, but stopped suddenly when she saw a glint of gold between her fingers. Where she had touched the thread, the dust had rubbed off and she saw that the thread glinted gold. But she had never noticed any golden threads in the carpet before. Maybe they had been buried under layers of dust and dirt, she thought. It was true that the carpet had seen better days, and was worn and frayed in places, with a few patches and repairs. But its intricate design was still fascinating and it must have been quite spectacular in its heyday. Still, she couldn't remember there being any gold threads in it.

The cat happily went back to tugging the thread, which ran through the woman's fingers and seemed to glint a little brighter. It looked nice, the woman thought, but it was still an untidy, loose thread. It didn't seem to belong there, so she gave it a few tugs to try to pull it free. The thread just got longer, so she gave it a bigger tug, but it got longer still. She suddenly became worried that she was unraveling the carpet, that this thread had some important job to do, unknown to her. She unwound it from her cat's paws and dropped the thread, wondering if she could get it back into the carpet. She looked at the patterns of the carpet, then at the thread, but couldn't see how it fitted in at all. Lifting up the carpet a little, she examined the back of it but, no, there was not a sign of this perplexing thread. Yet there it was, just stretching out into nowhere, and it seemed to be coming from nowhere as well.

She wondered if it was possible to get the thread back into the carpet somehow, so she got down on all fours and looked closely at the weave of the carpet. Closer and closer she looked, examining the ways the threads fitted together, their intricacy, their complex beauty, the way the little patterns fitted within the greater pattern. She couldn't remember ever looking at it so closely – and then she did. She suddenly remembered when she had last done this; as a child, playing on the carpet when it was fresh and new, its colors bright and vibrant. Wriggling and crawling across what seemed like a vast expanse, a whole world in itself. Then, as she had grown up, she had played her games on its soft surface, and when her friends had come, they had played games together and scattered their toys across it. It had coped with their rough-and-tumble, with snags and spills, and the wear and tear from lively children and family life. And her own children had played on it in their turn. Oh, it had known plenty of dramas… What stories it could tell! All of its history was somewhere in its threads, and some of hers was, too. So many times, she had walked on or rested on it, sat down or lain on it. And she had dreamed here, she had imagined so much, yet had she ever seen such a golden thread? Perhaps, in the distant past, if only she could remember…

The cat was watching the grandmother with renewed curiosity in her green eyes. How cat-like the old woman looked, all of a sudden. The cat went to her, purring, and looked up into her face. The woman had a distant look in her feline eyes as she smiled at her old, furry friend. She took up the golden thread again and began to wrap it around her fingers in a cat's cradle. As she did, more of it began to appear, so she began to wrap faster until she was making a figure-eight, which was growing thicker by the moment. The thread was still coming thick and fast, and seemed to be growing brighter, too. The woman's face was brightening as well, as she began forming a golden ball of thread between her fingers. It really seemed like the more she wanted to get to the end of it, the more of it was appearing, as if by magic. It wasn't long before this glowing globe had grown as big as a football. It was certainly big, yet so light, and its glow lit up the whole room. As she wound the thread onto the ball, she considered what she might do with it. She couldn't exactly roll it under the carpet now, and it was too large to fit on the mantelpiece. Perhaps she could give it to someone who could make something from it. They could weave a golden fabric, maybe make a golden veil…though, at this rate, there would soon be enough to make a full-length robe. Well, she still had a figure in there, somewhere, but she wasn't sure if she'd ever dare to wear it and, anyway, she hadn't been to a party in a very long time.

She was reeling it in as fast as she could, but this thread seemed to have no end to it, and she wondered how long she could go on. Could she keep drawing it out forever? Should she just cut it and that would be the end of it? She decided to stop for a while and have a well-deserved drink. Then she could have a think and try to decide what was best. She laid the shining sphere on the carpet and went to the kitchen. Meanwhile, her cat started to play with it, rolling it this way and that, leaping on top of the orb and balancing herself, then making it travel across the carpet's complex design, lighting up the patterns on the way.

Then the woman heard her cat make a very strange sound, and she hurried back to the room. But the golden ball was gone! She felt disappointed and checked if the globe had rolled away into a corner, but, no, there was not a sign of it. And the window was closed, so there seemed to be nowhere for it to go. The cat was looking about her with very wide eyes, and the woman noticed that the room was filling with a soft glow. Yes, the room had this definite glow to it and, when she looked out of the window, everything outside seemed more golden too. As if, all of a sudden, the Sun had appeared, yet there was no sign of it, either. She told herself this must be a trick of the eyes. She had felt a little dizzy earlier and maybe this was one of the side effects, a kind of afterglow.

But the whole room seemed to have lightened up and, when the woman looked down, the carpet looked different too. Its colors looked livelier and the patterns had a new life to them. Both were beginning to flow, as if something new was moving through them. This old carpet had a glow to it now; it seemed to be coming to life. And then she suddenly glimpsed the golden thread in the weave of the carpet, glinting subtly in the midst of it all. Not only that, she noticed it shimmering in the air in the room, moving through the walls, stretching up through the ceiling...and moving through her, too! The eyes of her cat had a golden glint in them and so did her glistening fur. When the woman looked into the mirror, there were golden threads glinting between the silver threads of her hair and shimmering between the lines of her face and the fabric of her skin. How had she not noticed them before? They seemed so obvious now.

Then her attention was drawn to a particular thread that led out of the little room. She followed it, and her cat followed her, down the corridor to the front door. And when she opened it, what a sight she saw! There were shining threads everywhere, connecting everything that she could see, and every person in the street had threads of gold reaching out of them and stretching back to them, connecting them to all. She felt almost overcome by the wonder of it, and sat on the threshold with her cat beside her, looking at the play of the subtle light that shone through everything. What a web it was, shining through the trees and the people, moving through the world before her, from the tumbling clouds, down into the ground beneath her. It wasn't just the clouds that had a golden lining, everything else had, too; this golden web didn't seem to have any end to it. And it had all kinds of colors shimmering within it, more than she had ever seen before. She wouldn't have believed it, if she hadn't seen it with her own eyes. And when she looked down, there were golden threads pouring out of her own heart, spiraling out in all directions. No wonder her eyes had brightened up!

In the distance, she saw a bright ball rise up in the sunshine and wondered…but then it passed through a hoop and an echoing cheer went up. She remembered the playground in the park was only a block away and it sounded lively right now. She hadn't even stopped to look into it for so long. She grabbed her coat and went back to the little room for her bag of wools and needles. The scarf she had been working on looked so dull to her now that she left it behind and decided to start a new one. She walked to the park on this day that seemed so dull to most everybody else, but so golden to her. In the middle of the park was an old oak tree with benches all around it that gave a perfect view of everything. She sat on one and began to knit a new pattern, and it wasn't long before the Sun just had to come out and join in.

The children were surprised to see her there. Some of them had been a little afraid of her, this strange one wrapped in dark colors, who always kept herself to herself, who didn't seem to smile or speak to anyone much. She certainly looked happy about something today, but none of them could tell what it was. Maybe it was her birthday, suggested one girl, who was smart about these kinds of things. When a balloon-seller passed by, the grandmother couldn't help buying one of every color, and when she tied them to the bench, the bright spheres floated in the breeze amongst the branches. The girl was sure then she'd guessed right. Though it looked like nobody else was coming to her party, the old woman looked as happy as can be. Her hands were whirring away and something colorful was appearing between them. Before she left that day, the woman let one of the balloons go and it floated up through the branches of the tree, surprising more than a few birds on its ascent. She gave the other balloons away, one by one, and when the girl walked past, she got one, too.

Every day after that, the grandmother came to the park. The young girl became intrigued by this woman and her ways, sometimes watching all the activity of the playground, sometimes feeding the birds or watching them do their hopping games. The girl would watch the woman's fingers as they whirred, surprised by their speed and dexterity. The old woman didn't talk to herself or anything weird like that, but she did sing to herself sometimes, though no tunes that the girl knew. They must be from some other time, she realized. Most of the time she knitted and, every day, the pattern of the scarf she was creating became wilder and the colors more vibrant. It would be curled up beside her on the bench under the tree, like a sleeping snake. Every day, the old woman and the girl said hello, but neither could think of much to say after that. But, one day, the woman's black cat came to check on her, and the girl couldn't resist coming over. As the girl played with the cat and chatted, the woman cast off the last stitches of the scarf, which had grown longer every day. Then she had an idea. The rainbow scarf was complete, and the old woman asked the girl if she would like to have a scarf made especially for her. Of course, she said yes, and then, after a moment, the child asked what it might be like.

The grandmother looked into the child's smiling face and into her clear, crystal eyes. The woman wondered what colors would suit her unique beauty, what patterns would reflect her perfection, what possible creation would be beautiful enough for her? She looked into the worn and battered bag she had by her side. One glance at the wools there, and she realized that her present selection wouldn't do at all, even though it had seemed quite colorful a moment before. So, that very day, she went off to the wool shop, and found all kinds of colors she had never noticed before. Iridescent fibers, pearly and opalescent ones; oh, the options seemed endless. How could she resist? From then on, when passers-by glanced into her bag, they saw these shimmering away and a whole rainbow of different colored wools: azure blue and kingfisher, fawn and foxy red, ice white and raven black, deep indigo and bullfrog green, sunny gold and quicksilver. Now that she had expanded her palette, the seams of her bag were stretched to their limit by the colors bursting to get out!

The girl watched her scarf taking shape and coming more to life each day, until the morning came when she came to the tree and the old woman sat on the bench with a finely wrapped parcel on her lap. When the girl opened it, it was as if she had never laid eyes on the scarf before. It had transformed now, and taken on a life of its own. Interwoven in its graceful flow of colors, there were exquisite crystal patterns, and bright diamond designs that somehow seemed to mirror her. There was fine sewing too, with beads and sequins that glinted and hinted. The grandmother had revealed a whole hidden rainbow of potentials, mapped out in patterns that seemed to speak her name. She wrapped the scarf around herself and then wrapped her arms around the woman and thanked her from her heart. She did not know what to say after "Thank You." But, at that moment, the girl heard tinkling music by the park gate and ran off, soon returning with the biggest ice cream she could buy. They sat in the sunshine, side by side, while the girl sweltered happily in her scarf and they shared ice cream and the wisdom of the day. It was not long before the girl asked the grandmother if she could try her hands at the craft. So the old woman guided the girl's fingers through their faltering phase, until they began to move smoothly and they found a rhythm of their own. The old woman could see the girl's face brightening as she watched the patterns appear between her fingers. Soon, the stitches seemed to fall into place all by themselves. She had a gift, that was plain to see.

One day, when it was raining everywhere but under the tree, the girl's friends found shelter there. They watched her and the old woman knitting away, while they swapped stories, and it wasn't long before curiosity got the better of them and they tried a stitch or two. They put their phones and games away, gave their sore thumbs a rest and began to use their other digits in new ways. Soon, the old woman had quite a few youngsters in her close-knit circle under the tree and, between guiding their fingers and guiding their lives a little, they were busy times beneath the tree. Her stories kept them entertained, and the tales of her wild youth, even suitably edited, held them spellbound. She would hum to herself in the music of her heart and this went into the patterns as well. She sang strands of old songs and some shiny, new ones she had learned from her young friends. They didn't notice the other ball of wool that she was knitting with, the one that was spooling out of her loving heart. It was a vibrant, singing gold, a color that you can't buy in any shop, but one that is always available and never runs out. So, in between the fibers, was a lot of love.

By the time the acorns started falling, the little circle had quite a few creations to display. When the autumn winds blew in, the grandmother had already finished scarves for them all. Now that she had got to know them, she was able to make a scarf for each that reflected their true colors, the ones that she could see, sometimes better than they could, and expressed the bright potentials she saw in them. So the children could be surprised by the colors of their scarves, but they were always delighted by them and how they somehow seemed to fit them perfectly.

When winter came, each child wore their scarf with a kind of pride that warmed her heart. With her new friends, she knew winter would not be as long this year. One winter day, she was sitting by the pond in the park, feeding the swans and ducks, when a bright ball of wool rolled from her lap and bounced down the path. It rolled up to a pair of feet, and the old man, whose feet they were, picked it up and knew exactly whose it was. When he came up to her bench, she murmured her thanks, then looked up from his shoes to find his bright eyes and warm smile, with kindness in the lines of his face. She had noticed him before, from a distance, and he had noticed her over the months.

Soon they were sitting by the pond, watching the birds floating on its surface or diving below it, taking flight or landing with a splash. And in the chill winter air, she noticed that he had no scarf...

When the space has been prepared, the Circle opens.

A new flow begins, bubbling up from the depths in a burst of liquid light and fresh inspiration. Where once the earth was dry, crystal water flows, feeding the seeds sleeping in the soil. Life awakens and the desert blooms again. New insights and visions come, new sounds and songs, new pleasures and hopes. The sky seems wider, the air clearer and the Earth, broader. The heart is lighter now, yet we are still walking on, and with, the Earth.

The Light increases now, the space expands as more enter it. The dome of Light reaches up higher, the central spindle of Light stretches up like a spire through which new Light pours, Light from the Source and from the stars. Each star sends us its blessing and its connection. We scan the skies, and each star has a place in our heart. Now each star will shine brighter for us. And deep in our heart, the stars will shine in their constellations and galaxies. The Universe will be within found our heart, and all we see will be like a mirror of the perfection within.

Together we will reveal secrets, open the doors, unlock the portals together. And when we play together, "great and small" will be seen as one, there will be no borders or divisions. At times there will seem to be no up or down, no right or left, but we will not be disorientated. We will always know where and who we are and we will be in awe of All. We will not feel lost again.

This becomes, not a grand crusade, but a gentle procession into the Light which all are free to join. The process will continue until there are no leaders, no followers, until each reveals their own creator within, and each creator acknowledges the other, until Oneness is realized on every level. Light to light, heart to heart, fire to fire, peace to peace, body to body, soul to soul; the growth will be exponential. If we start with a peaceful heart, we can find the still-point at its center. From this point, stillness creates activity, by radiating ripples of Light through the Universe, which can become waves. And then the dance begins!

As we release the Light within, each being reveals themselves as a star, as a living Star Heart. So we will see in each galaxy, galaxies of beings moving amongst each other, whole constellations of souls that flow and interact, families of stars, each weaving amongst the other. In these star families, you will see patterns: the star patterns, the crystal patterns, the patterns of the past and future. And they will recombine and re-orientate, from small star patterns of five or six, up to patterns of hundreds, then thousands of stars, lighting up the face of this globe. All of these Star Hearts will then illuminate the Earth. All who watch from the stars, these other Star Beings, will see clearly that the awakening continues. The Stars of the Earth will shine as brightly as those of the night sky, each burning with a crystal purity, as they dance on the face of the Earth.

When satellites look from space, they see the lights of the cities and civilizations. So, soon, those who look on at the Earth will see new constellations arise. Together, these fiery lights, these bright hearts will make the patterns of the future, the New Earth.

The Crystal Age will truly begin.

A Sword of Light rises from the deep lake of our heart. This Sword of Peace has been forged in the fire of our deepest love. A Sword of Unity, reaching up into the heavens and pointing down into the Heart of the Earth, its blade is a tall flame, a flame of love.

This Sword is not a weapon, but a wand, a tool of transformation. Now the edge of this Sword of Truth is sharpened and made ready. The cutting edge of our vision is being sharpened. Soon, the veils of illusion will be parted more easily, and you will be able to slice through them with a wish, with a thought. The Light of this Flame of Peace will illuminate for us the new lands, the new worlds to be discovered. Its sharp edge will cleave through the veils of illusion, the thick, gray cobwebs of the past, those that are woven to clog the vision and block the way of the Light. They will be burnt away by the Sword of Truth and new threads of Rainbow Light will replace them. For this sword is a spindle, too, and threads of light flow from it; threads of every color, every hue that can ever be imagined, and others that can never be imagined, yet are you, and part of All, and are One.

When this spindle rises from the Earth, it is a pillar of light, like a towering tree growing from her. And your Wand of Light is a branch of this sacred tree. Where you plant this branch, a Tree of Peace can grow.

Now a higher, deeper connection has been made. You will connect more closely to your Higher, Deeper Self, and to your aspects seeded in all realms, who are threaded together, woven as one and working as one. Your facets are being revealed, your hues are brightening, the relationships between them are clarifying anew. All will seem clearer, sharper, more intense. The light will increase slowly to what may seem like a blinding intensity, but your inner vision will adjust. Your bodies, also, will adjust and change with these new experiences: they will, in a real sense, expand and open inwardly.

The "outer world" will not narrow, nor will you lose your interest in life. In fact, it will expand in new ways. It will open up, achieve new depths, new levels of meaning and knowing. In the new hope you will feel, you will experience heart-burst: the opening of intense joy, bursting within the breast. This will bring a vivid intensity to your everyday experiences, and those around you will notice the changes and wonder at their source. Some will think it has to do with what you are eating – perhaps popping! – but soon they will realize that this is a natural joy flowing from the inner heart.

There is no other source than the Living Light, flowing through the universes like a Rainbow River, sparkling in its intensity, shimmering around corners; in its depths, multi-layered, deep colors and on the surface, opalescent. The eye of the heart may first be attracted to the surface layer, but then it will begin to notice the flow beneath. If the inner ear listens to the bubbling and murmuring of the river, it will hear the Song of the Rainbow flowing through all life. This living River is moving though life in all realms, weaving its way through the worlds, through the dimensions, its Rainbow threads snaking their way through the veils of the worlds. And if you follow it, you will be taken on a journey through the universes. This Rainbow River flows not only on one plane, but in many directions, sometimes looping back on itself, but always searching, seeking out the new turn, a new way to flow.

If we pull back, we see the river on its journey flowing out like a rainbow woven through space, flowing forever, looping, swirling and dancing, further than the eye can see, yet beginning within us. For we are part of it, following it or leading it, carried along by it or guiding its flow. And where does it end? Where it began: at the weaving-point of the threads, which is also the gathering-point, the center of our sphere of being – our hearts.

This very point is the portal to infinity, to worlds beyond, the point from which we can open our own portal, one of our own devising. We can take the threads and weave them as our will desires, or as we are guided, or as we envision. Though we must be aware of why we wish to open a portal and why we wish to enter it. Or why we wish the world on the other side to come into ours. And we must know whether this is wise and whether we have the wisdom to cope with the consequences. We can, in the beginning, use the point merely as a peephole – a tiny porthole where we can view the other worlds, glimpse the other dimensions and see what life is like on the other side. Where we can see what the other worlds are made of, and what their beings look like and live like. Then we can use our discernment to see if we wish to go further and make contact – to put the key in the lock, as it were.

It is time now for Humanity to view more of the other worlds, for them to know the greater design of which they are a part, to know more about the cultures and ways of life of the other races and groups of beings who fill the universes. This will indeed expand the world-view of humanity. In this expansion, of course, there is room for new fears to be created by those who wish to profit from these fears – or they may be self-created. While it is necessary to acknowledge these fears, if they govern our future together, all will lose. All beings will feel diminished in the long run by the loss of these experiences. For these potentials contain within them hope for all the beings, all the races and species of the universes. We are indeed a spectrum wider than the mind can allow, even the greatest mind of the greatest being created. Only the Creator knows the full spectrum of what life is, of what is beyond us all. Yet at the time of re-unity, we will remember All, and All will be One.

Hope rises in the human heart when doors open and light-filled opportunities arise. The opportunities ahead will, indeed, be shimmering with color and light, and new visions of unity, which will be woven by you and others, will open up portals within beings of all kinds. These inner portals are all connected through the One Heart, and there will be a real chance for greater openness between beings to be created. These tiny portals of light, if united, can illuminate the universes, for within them is infinite light from the Source. They will seem like stars shining out in the darkness, into the seeming voids, and others from afar will marvel at them. They will create constellations, new families of Light in all its hues will be revealed and will form themselves, happy gatherings and creative comings-together will forge a new unity across the old divisions. Once the unity begins in the heart, then true hope is there, and the old hatreds of the mind, the old, dark patterns will fade.

The peace within is infinite, while conflicts end; they are finite and soon burn themselves out. Meanwhile the peace is always there, waiting to be rediscovered. It is patient beyond knowing and it will wait through the wars, through the times of conflict and division, the dark days when armies are raised and borders are fought over and defended. These borders, which have cost so many lives, are themselves illusions and they will lose their meaning very rapidly when the veils begin to be opened. When the new worlds are revealed, these divisions will seem meaningless for it will be realized that movement – true freedom of movement – cannot be contained in such a way. The new universes opened up will attract travelers who wish to explore these new places, these new worlds of adventure and experience. As on old Earth, they will attract the wise and the foolhardy, the unprepared and the seasoned traveler; also the true explorers, those who wish to learn and to know, who wish to listen and then –when they understand – to participate. These will be welcomed by those of the other worlds, for they have been waiting for the time when the veils could be opened and the portals unlocked.

They will welcome with open arms and open hearts whose who come with open arms and open hearts; those who leave fear behind, who discard the old weapons, the mistrust and greed, the old hatreds and fears. Those who come with the open heart of a child beating within their breast will be known for who they are and recognized. They will be made welcome and guided through the new worlds. They will be guided on their journeys through the newly discovered realms by the dwellers of those realms. In return, these new travelers will uncover old paths for them, paths they themselves have forgotten, and they will look with fresh eyes on their own "home" dimensions – then they will go on to discover new paths together. So both sides will learn and they will share the joy of discovery. The new worlds discovered together will become a common universe, a shared space, which will itself be new. In the coming together, there will come into being a new universe, a co-creation, in this meeting of worlds and world-views. This melding of dimensions will create a universe that we cannot as yet anticipate in its new forms, for it will be something that has not yet been seen in Creation. It will be a new weaving, a new tapestry and in the breaking of the old threads, a new space will be created. A new universe that will seem to have expanded in every direction into new spectral hues, into new depths, and opened up to new heights, further than even the soul can see.

For some, this will be disorientating in the beginning, yet with trust and help, soon all will adjust. This new universe will become a haven of peace, for there we can be cleansed of the old wounds, and the old scars can be washed away. The wisdom of the past will be expanded and reintegrated, while that which is not needed anymore can be assigned to the museum of history.

Together, we will face a new horizon, a horizon which will know no end and over which many, many stars will rise – so many that the sky will blaze at midnight. These new constellations of stars will be mirrored in new constellations of beings who live amongst them, with suns and moons in their hearts and the light pulsing within, radiating in every direction. Joining with the Light of every brother and sister and all the other "you's" who make the One Rainbow, the One River flowing, the One Light and the One Unity. The One who is the Heart of All. The tests will be given soon and, when passed, the portals will appear and then the true weaving will begin. We wish you all the Love in the Universe and pledge all our help, all our trust and love and the joy of the journey ahead. Namaste.

The coming time will be a phase of great changes. You will witness the birth of a new world. The outer changes will be as dramatic as the inner, and the rebirth of hope will be spectacular and colorful.

It will sweep the world in a great wave, cleansing many who have felt lost in the earlier waves and ripples of darkness and it will wash away much pain and much that is no longer needed. The brightness that is to come will be a surprise to many and the playfulness that is part of it will be a new learning experience for many who have become very high-minded and serious. For we come first of all to play, to rejoice in the wonders of the Earth in all her aspects, in her magic, in her wonder and bliss, in all the gifts that she so generously bestows. There will be many more awakenings, and those who are opening will be found in all corners of the Earth, and they will find each other in many strange and dark places, often places that have been forgotten. Sometimes forgotten by time and by change, sometimes by "progress" in all its forms. The Old Ones of the Earth will be waiting to be rediscovered in all their manifest forms. In all their manifold forms they will reveal themselves, in stone and wood, in plant and earth, in water and shell, in crystal and color, in leaf and tree, in cloud and mountaintop. In fact they will be hard to avoid! Eager will they be to speak with us again, with all their wandering children. The Old Ones will feel a new burst of life and joy and vitality. Along with their "new" old friends, they will be part of a new time of play.

The first phase of the new times is about play, about discovering the inner knowing, the life of the child within and the rebirth of the child within. By playing together, we will be creating new places of sacred exploration, zones of new learning, new circles of weaving. Weaving with color and light, and earth and darkness, weaving ourselves together too, creating greater unity between the realms and within each realm. Many ancient divisions will be healed, old tangles will be unpicked and new bright threads woven in. Then the older threads will be cleansed and uncovered in their true brightness, their true color and richness. And new colors will be found for the first time, and their brilliance will be astonishing! They will manifest in all areas of life, in the colors within the home, the streets and the workplaces, also in clothing and, most importantly, in the faces of those we meet; the new old friends – and those we have never met before.

For there will soon be a coming together of realms that have not yet met face to face. This will be a moment of great discovery. In the seeming unfamiliarity of the mutual aspects there will be room for great learning. Each, after a while, will recognize themselves in the other and the strangers will become familiar; and the most strange, the most familiar. The new friends will weave new circles of healing. In the new Play Spaces there will be time to re-weave ourselves and between ourselves, according to our intentions, wishes and desires. And those less visible who come to play will also have a chance to learn, interact and be part of the weaving.

These new threads will indeed reach to the stars and into the heart of the Earth. They will seem like a Rainbow Road, stretching in each direction to infinity and into the infinities of the heart. A road along which we are free to travel simply by following the threads. Along these threads, we can send messages to our sisters and brothers of the heart, of the light and darkness, and we will get to know them and they us, and we will each heal and find a new unity. They will see the new hope rising. In these new colors, the spectrum itself will seem to have extended as if others had been added – and in a sense they will have been. People will discover new colors that they have not noticed before; these will reflect their inner changes, the new feelings and sensations they will experience. The threads themselves will tell part of the story as they are woven and weave themselves into patterns. They will reveal the new relationships, weave the meanings of the new patterns and reveal the meanings of the old patterns, while they reweave themselves before our very eyes and in our very hearts.

From our inner hearts we will spin out threads, spooling out to the universes, out into pasts and futures, into the new realms and back into old realms, pulling them together into Oneness, back into Unity. In the threading and in the weaving is woven the new future: the fabric of time and space in all its new colors and brilliance, in all its new densities and textures, in all its new stories woven through the old stories. And when the one cloth is revealed, there will be the realization that we are all of the One Cloth, of the one Grand Design, the One Grand Pattern made of patterns innumerable, extending out in every direction, into every space and time. Yet this cloth is not a flat piece of fabric, it extends to every dimension.

This is the tapestry of Creation, and each movement we make moves the threads subtly. Each tiny movement creates a reaction and Creation reacts accordingly. Each time we notice a new thread, a new hue, we extend ourselves and our vision. We weave that thread back into our own hearts and become more of the Oneness that we are. For all forms part of the Grand Design woven from our inner hearts in which is the Heart of Creation, the Heart of the Creator.

The more we weave, the more free we will be to grow, to expand and to extend our colors out into the universes. And we will see those colors return on other threads and our color reflected in other threads. Even in a single thread, we realize the whole rainbow is there – even colors we have never noticed in the rainbow before. With our new eyes we will see the one thread that extends seemingly in one dimension, in two directions. Yet we will realize that, through the Universal Web, this thread is connected to every other thread of the worlds, so that *every thread* is connected to every dimension and every one of the universes. So in a sense there is no one thread, for each thread has endless connections and extends to infinity. Each thread *is* the web, the unbreakable web of Creation and as we touch one thread we touch all Creation.

And we can trace that thread back to its source deep in our hearts, seemingly in one direction, and in the other direction into the Heart of the Creator, only to realize that we have made a circle, as the thread will also be connecting to the Heart of the Creator within. So all directions flow into one direction, there is only Oneness, and all ends and begins in the One.

The Great Game

We take our place on the field of play and the game begins...
The crowds cheer, the dancers dance, the watchers wait to see the outcome.

This is a game played on many levels at the same time. Many of the players are not aware the game has begun or even that there is even a game to be played. The few who do find they score easy goals – especially when they discover they have no opponents! They are only playing against themselves. So the goal is open, no one defends it. Everyone is too busy stumbling over their feet, kicking themselves, staring at their surroundings or waving to faces in the crowd.

The game goes on around them and they do not realize they are being swept up in its strategies and machinations. The players of the game wear many different colors from many different teams. They find it difficult to recognize each other, let alone recognize themselves. They really want to locate their own team members, so they look for a flash of the same color, some familiar hue; a glance, a knowing look, anything that will tell them which side they are on. Meanwhile, they stumble and fall over their own feet. They pick themselves up and walk backwards into obstructions, banging their heads into goalposts. Even now they do not realize that the goal is there, staring them in the face – if only they were facing the right way. They wander into the net and are caught up it in, like struggling fish. They desperately try to escape, not realizing that they have already reached their goal. So busy are they in trying to free themselves, they have no idea where they are.

If only they were to cease struggling and look around them they would realize... They would feel the peace of arrival, of completion. This could be so simple, yet they struggle and fight, caught in the mesh, pulling until their fingers hurt and their hearts bleed, and they cry out for help from those around them. But all the others can see is someone trapped in a mess of their own making. So the tangled ones wait for someone to help them, some kind soul who will unravel them. Or perhaps the day will come when they can free themselves and calmly realize where they are – standing in an open goal surrounded by the open space of the playing field and, above, an open sky.

The fall from grace that others feel as they stumble about the field of play is humiliating and confusing. They feel disorientated, lost, finding themselves on all fours, stumbling on the grass, trying to stand again, to regain their dignity. They want to find their place in the game again, to catch up with the pace of play. Desperately, they seek another team member who can show them which is the direction of play, where the goal is, who they have to defend themselves against. So they make it to their feet, compose themselves and look around, only to be knocked down by someone else stumbling backwards, looking for their way back into the game. Each is tangled in the other's anger, as they blame each other for their predicament.

Eventually they untangle themselves from each other, make it to their feet again and march forward across the playing field, trying to convince themselves that they know where they are going. They are becoming bitter now, full of blame and hate, believing they could find their back into the game, if only they were not surrounded by fools. Frantically, they look for clues as to where they should be, what they should be doing, who they should be impressing amongst the onlookers. And so they wander amongst the other apparently lost souls, trying to avoid bumping into each other. Some try to make eye contact, in the hope of finding a team-mate, a soul-mate, a friend; someone who can help them out of the mess.

As each person makes their way around the field of play they weave patterns that crisscross and interlace each other. As the patterns they make become more complex, they create greater confusion, piling up in layer upon layer. Some of these patterns entangle themselves in each other, to make their makers feel even more lost.

Then for no apparent reason a few will notice a thread – and grasp onto it. They follow it for a while, hoping it will lead them in the right direction, if only they can follow it and not be distracted by the apparent chaos around them... Perhaps then they will make it out of this human labyrinth of their own making, with its dead ends and blind corners; this invisible labyrinth, with its walls that seem to be there, but cannot be seen or touched, only felt, cold and hard against the heart.

Some also realize they are not simply playing on a level playing field. There are others moving amongst them who are playing at right angles to them, and diagonally across them, passing them by at unexpected angles, shooting past them, appearing around corners that do not seem to be there. Other players materialize right under their feet, or seem to fall out of the sky, to land in front of them, nose to nose. Some of these others seem familiar, yet it is hard to comprehend their presence or to fit them into the vision of the game. The players feel there must be a pattern or a plan somewhere; a set of strategies that might explain all this activity. They search for hints of this hidden meaning in the faces of those they encounter, and in their actions as they try to decipher them. But most of what they find there confuses them even more.

The behavior of the others seems inexplicable; it appears foolish or childish or just plain crazy. Yet those who are being observed believe their actions are the correct and appropriate ones in this situation. They believe they have found the meaning of the game and they are pursuing that meaning to its end. They believe they have found a way out of the chaos and if only they pursue their own game plan, or copy one that they believe successful, they will eventually be free.

What of those few who are still grasping onto a thread? And those even fewer who are faithfully following it, wherever it leads. They too are trying to work things out, too, but at least they seem to have found a guide, a thread to lead a way out of the labyrinth. Some of them even make a trail for others to follow. Some discover that others are following on behind them, thinking that they have found a way out of the game. This often makes the leaders uncomfortable, for they do not recall wishing to become a leader. They do not want to be responsible for the welfare of others or hold the fates of others in their hands. But some relish the opportunity to take the lead. They hope they will help others out of their predicament.

Sometimes a sort of team emerges, a group of like-minded players suddenly finding each other, realizing that one is following the other, slightly relieved to find others following the same way. The one who finds themselves in front, though, feels they are in a dangerous position. What if they are to stumble into a hole or crash into a wall? What if the earth opens up or they find themselves on a cliff edge? What then – which way will they go? Will they follow the thread that leads across the abyss? Will they trust its sense of direction? Will they believe in its strength, that it can carry them across the chasm? Will it hold all of their combined weight or is it just for one?

The reluctant leader will have to face their own fears in trying to answer these questions. And the fear itself poses the biggest question – are they a leader or are they a follower? Is it enough to be responsible for oneself and to leave others to find their own way? Is it right to abandon them there at the cliff edge?

For that is what they now face... This is where the thread has now led them, to the edge of a cliff. They gather there and peer over at the sheer drop below them, wondering how high they are, how far they could fall. They will find themselves asking almost as many questions as the leader. Are they truly a follower? Can they follow the lead of this person who seems to know the way, or should they turn back and find another way, choose another fate, and, hopefully, a less risky route? The pressure on the leader will increase as the moment of decision comes near, and the fear in the eyes watching them will add to their own sense of fear and indecision. What would you do, try to cross the chasm on a single thread? Would you volunteer to cross on your own first, so others can follow, if you make it safely across? Would you ask another to take the lead, or would you turn back from the brink?

But what if you knew that the thread that led the way was unbreakable, that it would support your weight and the weight of all those who chose to use it. That they could make their way on it across the deepest abyss, trusting in themselves and in the strength of the thread. This is a thread of Light they have found, a golden thread of many colors spun into one. All they need do is follow where it leads.

So a leader makes the decision and inches out slowly, testing the thread, making their way cautiously and then with growing confidence, realizing the thread will hold. And then the others begin to follow, one by one, or they choose another thread and make their own way. A few who cannot take the step out over the void, watch the others setting out across the abyss, some crossing slowly, hand over hand, others using the thread as a tightrope. And so they go on, with a vast open space around them on all sides, following their thread, inching along, keeping their spirits up, encouraging each other to keep moving. They feel, after a while, a kind of peace, perhaps brought on by the by the fact that they have made a choice; a sense of exhilaration and freedom, enhanced by the openness all around them. They feel they have chosen the sky and the air and the spirit of freedom.

Those on the threads over the abyss are making some discoveries. They find there are a lot more threads than they first thought. They can step from one to another and the threads will still hold them, almost as if they were glued to them. The only thing that makes them part company with a thread is their own choice. But they find another, and another within easy reach. They find, in fact, an unlimited number of threads to follow, each leading somewhere, maybe out of the chaos forever, perhaps leading them to peace. They discover these threads radiate in every direction from the point they are at. As well as the one they are following, there are others radiating around them in every possible direction. They need only to choose one or another, or another... All the threads seem to be coming from them, but who knows where they lead?

After a long time, they find another cliff approaching them. Increasing their speed, they make their way towards it. When they finally reach it, they step gratefully on to solid earth, or help each other to clamber up, all relieved that their journey is over and their trust was repaid. And those who tight-roped across, who strode confidently, and those who came more cautiously behind, all end up in the same place. They look back at the way they came and suddenly notice the connections between the threads across the chasm, and how many threads were there, unseen.

In front of them is open land, rolling away from them to unseen horizons. And the open sky above, doming over them, and the Sun warming them while they rest. They rest on the cliff top and survey their surroundings. And there, in front of them, they see a mountain rising up, up towards the clouds. And they wonder why they had not noticed it before. To some it is frightening, intimidating, to others it is exciting. They all look up to the spiral path that winds its way around the mountain, snaking its way to the top, and some decide to climb it. Others decide to ignore it, they choose to walk around the mountain and head onwards across the open plain. So the group divides and they set off on their separate ways. The group that set off up the mountain had forgotten the thread until they noticed that the thread ran along the path in front of them. And so they began climbing, soon breaking into a sweat in the hot sunshine, for the Sun itself seemed to come closer with every step. But still the mountain rises up before them, and they soon stop looking up to make climbing easier. Up and up they go, around and around the spiral path, climbing higher and higher, seeing the view now on all sides. Some are marveling at the vista in every direction, they feel their hearts open to the beauty around them, the sense of intoxication in the clean air and the height. All that others want to do is reach the top, and they climb on, oblivious to their surroundings. These seem to tire earlier, but still they climb on, past the point of exhaustion.

Then finally, the peak of the mountain is sighted and they make their way up the last few coils of the spiral path to the very, very top. Here the mountain seems to come to a peak above them that is sharp as a quartz point. From this point, there flows light inwards and outwards, up and down, then spiraling around the mountain, from the top to the base, the base to the top. When they have overcome their surprise, they step forward, one by one, to touch the point, believing for some reason that it will relieve their exhaustion. Which it does... They feel themselves fill with light, they feel their bodies drink in the light and peace. Those in the small circle on the mountain-top feel united. The see the light shining in each other's faces and wonder is it the glow reflected from the mountain-peak lighting up their faces, shining in their eyes...? In the center of the circle is the light, and they realize that the thread they have been following comes to the point of light, then seems to disappear.

For some reason, they stare at the point until it grows brighter, as if the whole world was concentrated into this point of light the thread has led them to, after such exertion and sacrifice. They seem to know that it is an opening; that the end of the thread is a point of light that is also the thread's beginning. And the point shines like a star. They watch it as darkness falls, as the Sun slides behind the horizon. The star on the mountaintop shines on, and still they watch, illuminated by its glow, held there in peace, warmed and unified by its light. Into the night they watch, until one after the other, they close their eyes.

When they open their eyes, they all seem to do so simultaneously. They are no longer on the mountaintop, but in a place they do not recognize. Around them is nothing they know, no familiar sights – even the colors seem strange. The only recognizable things they see are each other, and they wonder how they got here... Are they all dreaming the same dream? Or is one of them dreaming and they have all somehow found themselves inside their dream? But around them, everything seems real, though odd. They see things for which they have no name, objects whose purpose escapes them; they see views and visions that flash and change, which seem to flicker, become transparent, then solid again. Within this space, all the forms and spaces seem alive, they seem to empty and fill with light, or turn inside out and transform into something else.

Those gathered feel disorientated, yet not really lost. They know they came here together, so surely they came somehow by the same route, through the same doorway...? Then they remember the point of light which fascinated them for so long. Perhaps it hypnotized them in a way, then they awoke in this strange place, though one which seemed safe in its vivid, peculiar way... So perhaps they are inside the very mountain itself! Yet this is not what they would expect to find there.

Each one of them is beginning to feel rather strange, even to themselves; their bodies feel different, and seem to move in a new way. Now, even their images of each other – which had seemed constant and fixed – are slowly changing before their eyes. Those around them are beginning to change in form and, apparently, in nature. They are each beginning to transform; they are, in ways, becoming more like their surroundings. Yet, they are also somehow becoming more like themselves...

They gradually acclimatize to their new environment, and now these forms become more familiar. Things start fitting into place and they work out the meanings of spaces and objects. Places seem almost recognizable now, as if once seen in a dream, or remembered from another time or place, or another place in time – or somewhere beyond it. As they grow in confidence, they look at each other, and at themselves, with new eyes. They begin to enjoy this expanded world of new shapes and forms, colors and textures, new spaces that seem to live and breathe around them. These shimmer with living light, they softly pulsate and radiate light in all possible colors. Forms seem to grow, to take on lives of their own, to coalesce and come together in different combinations, shapes and forms, then divide and recombine in a different way. They come to comprehend how everything around them is alive and changing, shifting and re-patterning. After a while, they realize that sometimes they can see the same things as others, yet at another moment, in another space, they each see distinctly different things.

They grow quickly here, they seem to expand in all directions, in all senses. Time itself seems to have expanded and lost its usual meaning – or found a new meaning. They have found new space and freedom, and they find themselves playing constantly, becoming more child-like, exploring their ideas and giving form to their thoughts. They are finding that their ideas themselves take on forms. More surprisingly, they discover that, depending on their thoughts and feelings, their own bodies react visibly, and shimmer. There are moments when they can feel a thought of fear pass through them as they wonder if they can comprehend or even accept such freedom, such possibilities. They and their surroundings shiver at fearful thoughts, until, somehow, they are reassured, and they find their calm and peace again. Breathing easily, they then relax, expanding as the world around them expands. They discover that they and their environment are intimately connected; apparently almost indivisible. Their very thoughts change the world around them; their every feeling and action seems to change their environment instantly. It seems to anticipate their thoughts, waiting to respond to how they feel, how they think or wish to interact.

Seemingly in no time, they are all playing on a grand scale, weaving wonders around each other, surprising themselves with their new sense of freedom and possibility, impressing each other with their new creations, brought forth from a moment's thought or feeling. Now, they seem to have forgotten the struggles – and the curious question of how they got there – as they revel in their newfound joy and sense of liberation. All else seems trivial when all they feel is expansion; breadth and space, light and form, color and movement.

They feel they have become artists whose palette is a universe, and they create grand, moving murals and giant, living sculptures in the blink of an eye, the flash of a thought. As their palette expands, they find themselves weaving a world together out of their new freedom, finding new ways of creating together, discovering new possibilities by working as one. They pool their freedoms to create an ocean of greater freedom. Then their universe expands still further; they sense new space around them, as if new space is created with every loving thought, every beat and feeling of the heart. They learn that love is the greatest creator. They find their joy in expressing their love, they find their love creates the world around them, and the more they love, the more their universe expands, the greater the space created. Now all their trials are distant memories, here in this new world; a universe of love and creation, of color and joyful discovery, of expansive learning. Yet their journey, their experience is just beginning. All around is open space and, within them, a space even greater that fills more and more with love.

Then each one sees a brilliant light in the distance in the distance, of scintillating crystal beams. Each seems to see a different light, as if beckoning them. They are drawn gently towards it by some inner impulse; such is its beauty, they feel impelled to explore it. As they near it, the beams seem to reach out to them, and they find themselves reaching out, too. The broad beams seem to enfold them in their brilliance and they give themselves to the embrace of the Light.

Once more, they all appear to open their eyes at the same time. They blink and take a deep breath, or shake themselves to see if they are really there. They are again in the circle on the mountaintop, around the glittering star. They look different to each other now, and they know each other more deeply and truly. They stand up and walk around the summit, enjoying the spectacular view in every direction around them. Yet, soon, they all feel the desire to go back down the mountain to the world below. So, together, they begin their descent. They make their way down the mountain in silence, but something is passing between them that communicates all they need to.

Their journey now is an easy one, and their steps are light and sure. They come down the mountain in a state of high anticipation – they know a new world awaits them.

This is the time of the quickening.

Humankind is in the womb of the future, awakening to its inner potentials. The pace of change within Earth and humanity is speeding up, for below the surface of events, beneath appearances, human evolution is accelerating.

Your face will open up new facets and reveal glimpses of your other selves, the other you's. In the blink of an eyelid, the shape of an ear will seem to change, the color of an eye will flit between one hue and another, the line of chin or brow will redefine before your eyes. Your own face will seem less familiar, yet become more familiar in other ways, as the family of you is revealed. If you look deeply enough into the mirror, beyond its surface reflections, it can become a mirror of your heart. Your face will become more illuminated from within as your eyes grow brighter, as your heart lightens and relaxes into the changes. You will see your face like a gently flickering flame and, in the movement within the moment, the shimmer and flicker of other faces, other lives.

You will begin to reveal the multiplicity that you are, some of the many faces of the many souls that are One Soul. The soul-connections between your selves will become clearer when you understand yourself as a living matrix of many lives, of many soul-spheres connected in a living web. This web is not static, but flowing; it orbits around a center that is the heart of you, and the heart of All. It flows like the turning wheel of a spiral galaxy spinning in space, made up of countless stars, each unique, yet connected. All are part of the one great movement, with many far-reaching arms spinning round the center. You are many-armed, like the ancient deities. You have as many arms as a god, as many facets as a diamond, as many faces as a gallery of souls.

This is your spiral-galaxy of souls, your whirling world of identities, composed of fragments and wholeness, jigsaw pieces of unity spinning through the Universe. All flow from the original whole, and now are moving through infinity, spiraling through the seeming void, the many facets flashing as they dance through space, reflecting on each other. These pieces of the original

One may seem disconnected, yet all are still moving as one, all are flowing towards Oneness again.

Now that the pace of the spinning is increasing, the whirling spiral galaxy will accelerate and pull its pieces closer into the center, recombining them, condensing them, bringing them nearer to the Light at its heart. The sense of compression will increase as the pressure intensifies, with the center exerting a stronger pull, like a powerful magnet, drawing the fragments into a new Unity. New, because it will be different from the Oneness from which they first exploded.

For in the expansion, the "Big Bang" at the heart of every soul, the illusions of disunity and fragmentation were created. From this point, arose the illusions of disconnection and division, of distance in space and time, of separation from the very source of love, the Heart of the Creator. From the same original expansion, came the strongest illusion: that of separation between hearts and souls. Here, in the sense of distance from the Source, was the beginning of loneliness and isolation.

In the illusion of separation from the Love of the Creator, was born the sense of distance from the divine, the loss of God. Hidden in the mental concept of God is the sense of separation, in the idea that you are not God or Goddess or the Creator, but something other and lesser. Hidden in the concept of the divine is the sense of the un-divine. In this sense, the search for the divine can become a fruitless quest, leading one away from one's own heart, from the Heart of the Creator within. Here, in the heart, is the heart of the problem, the question and the solution.

In the sense of loss of Oneself was created the long separation, as the many you's seemed to separate and split from Unity. As the illusory space between your selves became greater, they seemed to flow further and further away from the Light at the Center, often becoming heavier and denser and darker. This was also, of course, a new opportunity for experience and learning. With the birth of so many you's, there was an opportunity for the greater gathering of experiences, the deeper learning of lessons and for the clearer distillation of meanings.

So the original fragmentation was not an accident or a disastrous mistake.

It was not a violent explosion at all, but a moment of opening to All, an unimaginably vast expansion of love into form, a moment of creative awakening for the Creator. New patterns were created in the expansion of these many facets, in the relationships woven from soul to soul, woven through the great illusions of space and time. The Great Game had begun. The great weaving began between soul and soul, and within each soul, opening One Soul into many. In the great weave of the whole, is the most complex tapestry ever created, stretching through worlds beyond your knowing now, woven of beings beyond counting or comprehension.

Within the weaving of this one great Web, a new unity could be glimpsed; a creative web of greater complexity, yet of even greater unity. Within the shimmering web could be glimpsed the future unity, when all souls would weave back through the illusion, back into Oneness, into the Unity that *is* and waits to be rediscovered and rewoven through the illusions. So the roots of the illusions of separation actually form the web that allows us to know there is no separation!

When we peel back the veils of illusion, we can get a glimpse of the whole in the patterns of the web that connects All. And if we look deep into the weave, we can make out a glimmer, like the glimpse of a distant candle on a stormy night. Hope rises in the heart when we notice the distant glimmer and know what it hints at. That there is a guide waiting there, that someone has a light to guide one through darkness. We will soon realize that the glimmer we see is our own eye – the All-seeing Eye at our center. We can look along one light-thread, stretching into this center, and see deep into the light within our own heart and our own soul. For that is where the guide is waiting to lead us; to lead us from within, to lead us through our own darkness and shadow and lead us into our own Light. This being with the guiding light is the One within us, patiently waiting, lovingly holding the knowing of our own unity.

This Weaver of Light holds the threads that weave out from our own center, to which are connected all our facets, like droplets of dew on a beautiful spider's web hanging in space. Each crystal dewdrop glistening in the blackness, each shimmering like a star, and, within each dewdrop, the shimmer of rainbow colors, the rainbow world within. The light inside shines out, sparkling out into the Universe like crystal tears caught in the web and the web stretching out seemingly without end.

At the center is the Divine Spider, the Weaver of Light, who spins the threads of the Web from the spinning center, weaving them out into space. Among these threads of light she spins are unbreakable heart-threads, which can bend, but which can never break our heart-connection. She holds the unity of all the souls, she knows the wholeness of their experience and wisdom. She sees in every direction, is sensitive to every touch and vibration, senses every message sent, every thought created, every wave of emotion, every ripple of feeling. She is the creative core of our many selves. She holds the matrix, and there will come the moment when she slowly begins to weave the web back in to the center, to weave it back into her heart, to weave it back into Oneness. She will fill her heart with all the wisdom gathered, all the experiences, all the love, all the knowledge; with the memory of conflict; the remembrances of adventure, the souvenirs of the soul, the treasures gathered in the great game of separation. Then the illusion will be ended, and the Sacred Spider, too, will fold her legs, and melt into the Heart of Love.

All the hearts will congregate, becoming more attracted to each other, condensing in the fiery intensity of love, gathering back into the One Heart. All the souls beyond counting will coalesce into the One Soul that they are. The Great Illusion will be crushed by the gravity of love, the strongest power in the Universe. For in the Heart of Love, there is always the One.

The journey back to Oneness begins in the present moment, in Now. At the point of opening, of discovery, of play, it begins. When the heart is opened, the inner eye is unveiled, the fabric of illusion is peeled back a little and we see the glimpses of the other side, of the other realities through these little openings like windows. Within these windows, we may see the playthings and toys we desire, like a child looking into a window filled with toys, who sees glittering within all the wonderful playthings they wish they could touch.

Their heart leaps, but they are separated from these objects of desire by the window, and so, outside, they dream, imagining what it would be like on the other side of the window, with all the toys to play with. The child believes the shop is not yet open, that the shutters are down and they must wait for the owner of the shop to appear. Like the child, we do not yet realize that the shop is always open to us, so we already have all the toys we could ever play with, and the ability to create more than the greatest toy-maker has yet imagined....

Within our heart, in our sense of play and discovery, we have a key to opening a new world. To truly play is to open a space and, as we open this world, our reality suddenly expands. Life takes on new arrangements, new colors and patterns appear, familiar objects transform, and we reveal the possibilities hidden within the forms of the world around us. They spark off old associations and memories, and we can suddenly create new connections and possibilities. In that creative moment, we create a space and we expand the Universe. We move beyond the constraints of time; in a single second of clock-time, we can imagine an hour or a day. Just as a child can create an hour and fit it in a minute, or it can live a day within an hour.

Play expands, opens and extends. The child playing on a beach, in a tree, in a little room, can discover new universes and stumble on lost worlds. Playfulness fills the Universe and then stretches it to make new space; it moves everything on, affecting the whole Universe in its ripples. That opportunity is open to us, too, no matter what apparent age we may be, for we all have a sense of play and we each have within us a playful heart. It may be buried deeply, but there is still a glimmer down there, somewhere. It may be hidden under heavy layers, but it is there, shining behind the veils. Once this playful flame is found, it can be taken out of the heart, and brought out into the world to shine. It will light up our faces with joy and wonder, it will brighten our lives and the spaces around us. In the flicker of the flame, things will come alive: in the shapes and shadows, we will see the creatures and the faces, the dancers in the threads.

As we watch the dancing shadows, our heart, too, will begin to dance, and in the silhouettes we will see living beings and characters of all sorts. Shadow-play will develop, made up by these characters given life from the heart and the imagination, brought to life before our very eyes. These become our new friends, this spectrum of characters of all sorts: the beautiful and the ugly, the friendly and the fierce, the strong and the weak, the hopeful and the downcast, the healthy and the wounded, the dreamer and the cynic; all interacting and playing with each other so that new stories emerge.

Then, suddenly, they have taken on a life of their own, and as they play or fight with each other, we watch their stories take shape. We watch their lives with amusement and wonder, learning and watching without judgment. With close attention, we can discern the patterns; we note the outcome of actions, we see the results of the courses taken, of corners taken sharply, of roads that are walked down or turnings that are avoided, of doors that are opened or left unopened.

We watch the Great Play take shape, in its many phases of action and inaction, of exits and entrances; we watch the players move amongst each other, loving each other or avoiding each other, weaving their lives around each other. We watch as the tapestry is woven before us and soon we realize we too have been woven into it. Its threads seem to flow from the ends of our own fingers. Though we thought we were just an observer, we realize that we are the weaver: we have given animation to these characters, they have flowed from us. We are creating the costumes and the scenery, we are inventing the dialogue and the silence. The threads can sometimes seem to be the strings of puppets, but at other times, the puppets tug us and we are pulled after them.

Yet we feel a sense of responsibility, for if they are our creations are we not responsible for their lives and the outcome of their actions? Are we to control them or to let them learn from their own mistakes? We begin to worry and fret over their fates: we wonder if we can help them, whether we need to assist them to guide them through life, whether they will become lost. Whether they will take wrong turnings and pull us along or simply step over a cliff, pulling us down with them into the void.

For a moment, we want to detach from them, to cut their threads and leave them to their own devices. Far safer, it seems, to fold our arms and let them get on with the Great Play; we will be a detached observer. And so this we do. Then we find that the play goes on without our direction! All seems as before, the general patterns and textures seem basically unchanged, yet we feel different; we do not feel the highs and lows, the worries and the fretting, the pain and the passion, the loss and exhilaration. Instead, we find we can still discern the patterns; we can observe all with a sense of compassion and interest, but not be tugged headlong into the play. We stay centered in our seat and watch the action unfold around us.

And when the characters speak to us, we answer, and when they do not, we keep our silence. If we feel we must applaud we do so, if we feel the need to cheer we do, but still we keep our seat and let the action circle us, and ebb and flow around us. As the action seems to grow more complex, more densely woven, we notice details we did not see before: the patterns within the patterns, the weaving within the weave. Then there comes a point where it seems the action increases in its urgency and pace. Now the characters seem to interact more closely and their stories knit together more intensely. We notice patterns that seem separated, yet mirror each other exactly; words and actions that echo each other across time and space. We are able to see the greater pattern within all the patterns, a flow within the flow.

We look around at the great circle of life flowing about us, and see the players starting to move as waves that make more waves, their actions flowing together in ripples that create eddies, which spiral away. We observe the concentric ripples that shiver out from one action connecting with others, and then their interaction weaving new patterns; the ripples of thought or emotion crisscrossing, then communicating out to influence others, seemingly separated by space and time. As we watch the flow of the waves, we suddenly receive glimpses of the Grand Design, the Divine Pattern, the unseen unity woven by all the patterns and hidden within the whole. All the living patterns of the actions and reactions become one movement, one flow, one cycle. This spiraling wave is moving in close around us, until the flow of the spiral encloses us.

This creation that flowed from us now returns to us. We again sense our connection to the characters and their lives, and the whole living flow. All is gathering into one great wave of Oneness, and we are part of it. We feel ourselves spiral in, now, spiraling into our own center; we realize we are pulling this wave into our own heart, into the center of our being. All the characters return to their source, to become one with their creator, and all know love again.

As the pace of change increases, you can bring yourself back into a sense of Oneness, rather than let it fragment your sense of wholeness. If you stay with your own sense of unity, no matter how fast-changing life becomes, you will not lose your sense of connection to your core. You may feel like you are being spun in a centrifuge, being pulled away from your own center, and parts of you may become dizzy and disorientated, as if they are being pulled along too fast.

At these moments you need, most of all, to feel the stillness that is always there somewhere within you. No matter how hectic activity is around you or how rapid change has become, you need not allow the overlapping of illusions and the friction between them to distract you from peace. When the pace of life intensifies, let the peace within increase also, then you will be able to embrace the changes or allow their effects to pass you by. You will not feel the need for external armor or grand strategies of protection. Let yourself love the illusion as it passes by, where once you would have been pulled into it, to become part of the illusionary game. The coming days will see the pace of change greatly accelerate, but you will be able to cope with the changes for, truly, you have created it and allowed it to be, and the Creator has given you the strength to see you through these events. If you see them as opportunities for growth and expansion, they will be sources of ever increasing joy.

If you allow it, the more childlike side of you will be reborn, and venture out to play again in this beautiful planet filled with its richness of wonders, its magic waiting to be discovered behind leafy veils or in forgotten corners. This natural magic will become more obvious to you, as part of the playful awakening. Some of your aspects may be slower in catching up with the pace of change, and you may need to be patient to allow these to catch up with the rest of you. After all, we are all flowing in the same direction, and ripples need not race each other, for they know they all end in the ocean.

In the time of play that is beginning, each moment can be an opportunity for play and discovery, if we open to its hidden hints and colors, to its little glimpses of the greater worlds beyond. Creative play reveals the potentials concealed in each moment and play awakens us to the other realities that interweave with our "normal" illusory reality. So, despite what you may have been taught, play allows us to be more in the real world! It is time to release the creative whirlwind of the playful child within, and help them clamber out into the light again. Feel free to create, to be silly, to be colorful. Your inner child, when released, may make quite a mess and leave a trail of apparent chaos behind it, but, after this phase, will come the clearer patterns. In these, there will be echoes of the future. Those who peer into those patterns will see the weave of Creation, will see the weave of which we are made, our own nature and texture.

If we put our eye to the veil and look through, we will see flashes of those on the other side. They may not see us at first, but there will come the moment when they glimpse us. Then there is the joy of mutual discovery; two worlds meet, divided only by this thin veil of illusion. And, if we unpick the threads of the veil and create a space, we start to see the bigger picture of the other worlds beyond. They, too, will get a greater sense of who we are, and we will realize that we are looking at each other looking at ourselves. The face in the mirror will, for once, be us. Not just a reflection, but a facet of us, another face of ours. Then we can truly make faces at ourselves and see how our other self responds, stick our tongue out and see what reaction we get, be playful and see if the other you wants to play.

If so, the barrier will be down and play can commence between dimensions; between the different dimensions of you. You can reach out your hand and touch your other hand, clasping your other hand in peace. In this point of contact, there is the hope for the new world; the starting-point of the new unity of which we speak. As the two hands come together, we realize the veil is no longer there, and there is contact skin to skin, face to face, body to body, reality to reality. After the first flutter of excitement and fear, when you realize that you are dealing with yourself and facing yourself – another you –

together, you can relax and explore the potentials in this meeting-place of your fears and your hopes, your desires and your dreams, your thoughts and emotions.

Yet within and between the two hands there is indeed something; there is a *shared dimension,* and it is here you will meet and play in this shared world, this world that was brought into being by your meeting. It is a place of peace and creation, which will open out before you. As your hearts open to the One in one another, the space will grow wider and there will be more room to play, to discover each other. And there you will meet others, other you's, who will enter the space, and in this gathering and reunion, you will create nourishment for all the facets of yourself; each individual facet will expand and all of you will expand.

As each facet expands and grows in the knowing of itself, and its related facets, the expansion of love and light will create a gathering of all the facets, and the attraction of the love within them will bring them closer together; the magnetic attraction of their own love will bring them into Unity. They will be pulled together by Love, the greatest force, the strongest energy there is and the expansion will continue until suddenly the force of love brings together all the fragments spiraling back into Unity.

The many hearts will become the One Heart they truly are, and, from these constellations of starry hearts, there forms one great Star Heart, one great condensation of Love, brilliantly shining out into the darkness around it. And its love begins to attract all the other Star Hearts as they are attracting it, pulling each other together all the scattered hearts, all the stars falling back into each other, all gathering into One. All the galaxies of Star Hearts, spiraling back into Oneness... And then all will know Love.

The new dimensions we have spoken of are very near – nearer perhaps than you can now imagine. Even when you reach out a hand, you stretch through unseen dimensions. Of course every new world, every new beginning of this kind, will raise new questions and resurrect old fears, for many will feel fear when they even think of such new possibilities. In a strange landscape, we feel wonder, a sense perhaps of overwhelming beauty. But we may also in the sense of wide, open space feel perhaps a rising of fear that there may be hidden dangers, that we may wander off and get lost, that we may not be able to find our way out, or back to the road we knew. In the new landscapes, in the new spaces, we need to remember that if we go within and stay centered within our own hearts we will not and cannot get lost.

Yet if you hold your inner sense of peace, you will know you have the inner strength you need to see you through the new phase. You will be able to hear the inner guidance needed to bring you through the new landscape. Our inner wisdom and guidance is there within our inner heart, beyond the illusions of the mind. Within the heart, we find our true guide, and there is our greatest protector and strength because the true path is within, waiting within the heart. So how could we lose our way? As long as we are in our heart, the path will always be there waiting for us, we need simply to turn and find it. So we will not stray from the path and the path will not stray from us....

Within our heart is, in fact, a map of these spaces. It is a holographic map that will be a guide through these dimensions that are new to us. It is not like the maps that we are familiar with yet we will, given time and patience, be able to read it. We will read it with the eye of the heart and know its meanings, we will learn its topography, the patterns of the landscape. This map will be our true guide to these dimensions that we can access from our heart. They grow from the One Heart and the map within our heart will change and grow with us as we grow in experience. So it is constantly updated and will guide us as we change, and as the dimensions expand and grow with us. Those that we encounter there will be following their maps, also. We will find that they overlap and that we will be able to orientate each other, as long as they are following the map within their heart.

As these different maps come together, overlap and intersect and these hearts begin to interact, they will become one, a common map which can be followed by all. This will change and grow as the beings meander and wind their way through the space, meeting each other and expanding sections of it. Some may cordon off a section of it, as others will open new ones or create expansion. If some start to believe that they can possess or control a part of it, they will soon realize that they are in a shared space, a space where love rules, a space where hearts meet.

In the great space where hearts come together, there is no ownership or control, there is no possession except self-possession, self-control and ownership of one's own heart. This will become the commonly understood way of being and living in these dimensions and those who venture within them will learn the wisdom. So we wish you joy in discovering you own map, hidden there within your heart and we wish you peace in the whirlwind of change. We ask you to nourish your roots and sink them deep into the loving Earth. She will hold you in her heart as you hold her within yours, and there will come a time when you will meet her in your inner heart, and you will play within each other's heart.

The heart of the Earth can be as light, and *is* as light as the heart of a child. For the heart of the Earth *is* Light, as you are within your heart, and there you are One.

The unfolding of the moment reveals the many hidden within. Within each moment is hidden unlimited potential, within the moment lies power greater than that within the atom, greater creative and destructive potentials whirl within the moment, whirling into the center, enclosed and enfolded on each other, within each other, spiraling in to the Center of All, hidden within each moment.

Which is the One Moment, the Center Point of all, the point of Light, the point of Oneness, the portal through which all time must travel, all points enter and depart. The point of weaving, the spool of thread from which the worlds are woven. All is within that Now, whose loom is like a grid of the Infinite, a Universal Loom stretching in every direction; omni-directional and omni-present. And on this loom is woven, with a thread of Now, a tapestry that is the Universe and all the universes within it and within each. Therein is contained all the colors we see and experience, the threads of universal light in varying hues, of densities and darkness all woven together into the tapestry of life and each thread is unbreakable and can be traced back to the center as if following the labyrinth to its center. We can find the center from the point we are now because it is *within* the point we are now. From its center will weave out all that is and all that will be and was, within the is-ness of now.

And *we* are the weavers, we are the dancers with the threads, we are the spiders dancing through the webs of all the universes. All the interwoven webs of all our worlds make the One, and the dance of each one affects the dances of others; it trembles the threads, sending out ripples along the threads right to infinity. As we look out from our center, we see the celestial sphere around us, each point of it sparkling like a star, while we are within the shining point of Creation from which all extends, from which point all threads are spun out into the Universe by we, the weavers.

Finding our still point can seem a difficult task when forces around us seem to pull us away from the point of stillness within, the silence at the center of the whirlwind. From this point of silence, all sound flows, all song begins there. From this point, come the dances and the songs of life, all the movements spiraling out, the galaxies shooting their arms out into the infinities and the stars spilling and tumbling through the seeming voids. From the center of the spiral, returns the peace, as we travel back into the point of light. From here, we can travel out in any direction we wish, in order to undertake any adventure, any experience. As long as we can return to that point, we will still feel the connection with our own center, the stillness in our busy life.

The Earth will be a busy place, but with a new kind of busyness. Cooperation is growing between realms, as unity is being woven again, and already, a greater unity exists. Earth's Devas of all her realms are already working as One, and their grand "team" is cooperating with more and more awakening human beings. The great weaving continues, the reweaving of the Earth as one world. In the sharing of this vision, the unity is born. In the language of Light and Love we are reminded of our unity, we find our high guidance, our inner wisdom.

The pace of events will quicken, so you will need the stillness even more.

You will need the laughter and the silence, the walking and the dancing even more to make Earthly that which wants to be manifested. Excitement will grow on all planes as they see more clearly that they all interlock and inter-weave, for there are those on all planes who sometimes forget their connec-tions for a moment. The trust will grow and the love between the realms will grow and familiarity and trust will breed new ventures, new projects and the hearts of many will be lifted and brought forth more clearly into the world. They will be able to manifest their love more clearly and bring their creative energies out into the safe spaces that will be created. In the pouring forth of this love in new creation, many old borders and divisions will be dismantled, the temporary fences between the realms will be dissolved as new portals are created. Many will learn how to cross the portals in safety and ease and we will enter each others' realms, visiting each others spaces and each others homes, though of course we will remind all to knock first – as there are times when one is not prepared for visitors…

In the growth that manifests, people on this plane will feel an inner expan-sion as they connect more to the other worlds that are woven within and which interpenetrate and weave inside each other. They will see more clearly the overlay of the worlds, the layering of realities. In the new visions that are created, they will also find a new vision of humanity. They will see the true potentials of human nature and they will expand their now limited view of these, because within humanity is a range of natures still waiting to be recog-nized and allowed to pour forth.

The common divinity of humankind still waits to be witnessed, and there is the unity that can end division, for true divinity can heal division. To many, this concept will seem strange, when they witness the divisions created by religions, but within every sacred circle of human beings, there is the point of Light shining at the center, waiting to be witnessed. For that is all that needs to be done.

And when the knowing comes, the circle flows as one, and from that one moment, unity is woven. The threads all seem to pull together, knots untan-gle, the tapestry takes on new brilliant colors; hidden shades noticed and rec-ognized for the first time. More of the images of the tapestry are revealed, its connections seem to be pulled together, gaps close up and the image of Oneness then becomes clearer. Oneness is the starting point and the end point and they are themselves the one point, the point of creation and uncreation, the point of stillness, the point of One, the point of it, All. The Light will flow thicker and faster, it will come in greater waves which will at times seem to wash away that which you needed, but the Light will simply be cleansing and that which it washed away was no longer necessary. You will feel clearer and cleaner, lighter and brighter as, in the washing, more of your true face is revealed.

This is the face of Light, the face of Love that shines beyond all the faces and shines through the shadows that are part of your tapestry. The mirror of your heart will each day reveal new possibilities, new moments of growth. In the revealing of new aspects, the point is not to confuse or to disorientate, but to unify and integrate so as each new aspect is allowed and accepted, it integrates and weaves into the Oneness. All seems to fall into place as the pieces of the jigsaw present themselves and they will each find their place, slotting into the greater picture, a single image that is you, that is All, that is One. The more unfamiliar the aspects seem, the greater the need to integrate them, to welcome them home, to weave them back into the Oneness. The more strange or unacceptable, unfamiliar or unwelcome they are the more they will need to be welcomed and healed; then peace is achieved in the internal conflict.

From the peaceful heart, all the aspects can be reflected clearly in the circle of unity of the heart, the unbreakable circle. At the center of the circle there is a still point, a center point from which all the aspects radiate like the spokes of a great wheel spinning in space, reflecting the light of the center out into the cosmos. The myriad facets glint in the light from the Central Source, the Center Point at the Heart of All. From this center radiate out all the points of the Universe, and all of the countless points can be traced back to this one point.

Expanding from this one point come all the galaxies, the spinning-wheels of stars, the scattered constellations, all the wide weaving of the universes… All Is, born within the One Moment.

The Rabbit and the Wonderful Warren

There was once a rabbit who got lost in his own warren.
It was no ordinary warren, it must be said, because this was no ordinary rabbit. This warren was more complicated than any maze, since it was made by a very complicated rabbit, indeed. He was a white rabbit, but he didn't look it, because he was always so covered in earth. You see, he loved digging, just loved it, and there was nothing else he would rather do. He didn't just dig deep, he dug in every direction, in search of interesting things and new experiences. So his warren, which had started off as a couple of tunnels and a place to sleep, became, in time, an amazing creation. From every tunnel, he dug upwards and sideways and down, branching out in every direction until he had created a more complicated network of tunnels than any rabbit, before or since.

Along the way, he found lots of intriguing things; old bones, strangely-shaped stones and the tangled roots of ancient trees. Sometimes, near the surface, he found something to eat, too, but mostly he didn't think of food, he was too busy digging. He would follow his nose to sniff out something interesting in the earth, or follow his instincts to lead him in a new direction, digging with a passion, digging in the dark for hours until he was too tired to dig anymore. Then he would sleep a little, but the moment he awoke, he would be off digging again.

He could wander for hours through his warren, running down one tunnel, then another, taking this corner or that, as if following an invisible trail, then always adding a tunnel or two, just for the fun of it. In time, he felt justly proud of his work. Surely no rabbit – or gopher, fox or mole – had ever created such a fantastic labyrinth. Maybe he could invite the other rabbits to drop by and look around his great creation. He could be their guide, leading them through the network, showing them the most interesting places, the funny or mysterious things he had found. His rabbit friends hadn't seen him much for a long time, so at least he could show them what he had been up, or down, to. Of course, there were so many tunnels now in different directions that it was getting difficult to find things when he wanted to. But he felt sure that, over time, he would learn where everything was.

While he was digging, he often felt like he was looking for something, but he was never quite sure what. Sometimes, with a burst of joy, he would think he had found it, but it would turn out to be another interesting root or bone, not whatever it was he was always looking for. After a sniff and a nibble, he could tell a lot. Most things he discovered were found in complete darkness and his greatest discovery had been that, sometimes, things spoke to him as if they were alive. Or, maybe, he just listened harder than most. He did have big ears, after all, and he knew how to use them. But, either way, he got to know things. He could pick up a bone and know what kind of creature it came from. And, often, old objects had lots of memories, so they were happy to tell him their tales.

One day, he found something hard in the dirt, something that was too tough to eat and didn't have a scent of anything. In fact it smelt very clean for something down so deep. And when he held it in a beam of light, it sparkled. Well, he sat with it between his paws and it made him feel so good that it seemed to take his tiredness away. Pretty soon, he began to see a picture of where it came from, and he saw that it was part of a tree that grew underground; a crystal tree growing up from deep below him.

He thought it would be lovely to find more of these crystal fruit and show them to his friends, so off he went down the warren to dig up some more. After he had been digging for hours, he finally realized he was very tired and hungry. He thought he had better make his way back out of the warren to find something to nibble on before taking a nap. He wandered this way, and then that, then tried another and still another, before trying a few more. Until, after an hour in rabbit time, he realized he didn't seem to making much headway in making his way out of the warren.

He raised his nose and sniffed, trying to scent a flow of fresh air, but could sense nothing. He had to accept that he must be pretty deep in the warren, maybe near the very center of it, so he was going to need some real luck to find a route out. He set off again with a great spurt of energy, sure he would find a way out if he set out confidently and with determination. But as the hours rolled by, and he had stumbled over the same old bone for the fourth time, he realized he had been going in circles. He had also been going in spirals, parallelograms, tetrahedrons and octagons, but none seemed to have brought him any nearer an exit.

Then he had a thought that seemed quite brilliant. He would do what any self-respecting rabbit would do – dig his way out! He started digging straight away, first one way, and then another and yet another. He burrowed a few more tunnels until, with the last of his strength, he dug one final tunnel. His paws were raw and sore, but this brave rabbit kept on digging, because he felt sure *this* was the one. Just a little more digging, just a few more inches and then he would make the breakthrough.

So he pushed himself on and on, without a pause, telling his tired heart that soon he would be free. On he dug, until the pain from his paws and his fevered brain began to overtake him. He finally stopped digging, and the depth of his predicament began to register, and suddenly he felt a sense of hopelessness move through him. How could he have been so foolish, to create a rabbit labyrinth from which he might never escape? He had no signposts and no map and no way of knowing where in the earth he was. His great creation, that he thought would bring him joy and pride, had become his own prison. He called himself every unkind name a rabbit has ever been called, adding a few new ones to the list. This tired him even more and dragged his spirits even lower, so eventually he collapsed onto the soft soil in sheer exhaustion. It was with relief that he slid into sleep, welcoming the velvet embrace of the void. Soon, he was in a different darkness, dreaming, playing and far away.

But he awoke with a start some hours later, wondering where he was. He had been having a wonderful dream about tunneling his way through the biggest carrot in the world, and having to eat his way out. He woke up very reluctantly, for once. For once, also, his first thoughts were not about digging. Slowly, he was remembering his predicament. He wondered if his friends were missing him yet. Maybe they would come and find him!

But how likely was that, when he couldn't find his own way and he had created this place? For a start, they didn't even know it existed. Of course! He would attract their attention by drumming on the earth with his back paws.

Then, they would follow the sound right to him. So he began to drum and drum and pound and pound. But no reply came. He started drumming again, even louder this time, building up into a frenzy of sheer frustration. Didn't those rabbits have ears, couldn't they hear a cry for help? He pounded his paws as hard as he could in hope of a response, but the only other sound he could hear was the rush of hot blood pumping through the tunnels of his brain. Soon, the rabbit's back paws were sore too, and he gave up hope of escape by percussive means. To add to his gloomy mood, he wondered what would happen if he couldn't find his way out. How long could he last down here? There were just a few dried roots to be found, and he wasn't going to last too long sucking stones. On the other paw, surely there were creatures who spent most of their lives beneath the earth... maybe he could make friends with them...?

But, he thought, what if they weren't friendly – what if they didn't like rabbits burrowing into their underground world on such a grand scale – what if they weren't quite ready for the creation of the greatest rabbit brain there ever was? Suddenly, the darkness around him didn't seem so familiar and friendly. Who knows what lives down here, deep in the darkness? Maybe all kinds of creatures he wouldn't like to meet... He felt as if the darkness was suddenly closing tightly around him, making it even harder to breathe. He began to imagine the fearsome creatures that could be there, lurking around every corner, the rabbit-eating monsters that he had helpfully called to himself. There was only one thing for it – he would have to escape...but which way?

In his panic, he froze into a state of rabbit paralysis, unable to move, unable to decide, unable to think at all. This state lasted for quite a while until, in the silence and stillness it created, it was as if room was made for something else, apart from his fears. His imaginings gradually faded away, and the rabbit gradually realized there was nothing around him but the dark and the earth and his own tunnels stretching through them. It was like a new space had been created – in which, all of a sudden, he had a moment of clarity. Yes, he was lost and disorientated, true, he didn't know if it was night or day, but at least he knew one thing – or maybe two. He knew Up and he knew

Down. Up was up and Down was down, and, surely, that was all there was to the matter. Just to prove his theory, he took a few steps back then tried to run up the wall of the tunnel. Sure enough, he soon landed on his tail in the dirt – and he was delighted!

So there were two directions he could dig. He could burrow down, and go deeper into the Earth, down towards the fire that some creatures said was there. But, interesting though that would surely be, it was a journey for another day (and maybe for another rabbit). Or else, he could dig straight up and, sooner or later, he would reach the air and the light. It wasn't a very difficult decision to make. He knew it was going to be a tough journey, but it seemed to be the only sure way out of the labyrinth. It was the most difficult way to dig, but he knew he would eventually escape and that was all he wanted right now.

So he started straight away, slowly and methodically, digging up through the layers of tunnels, scratching at the dirt, spitting out the soil, breaking through the floor of tunnel after tunnel, level after level. Breaking also through the many levels of pain, but knowing he had to go on, telling himself that every painful pawful of dirt was bringing him closer to the surface. He still could see nothing, but he knew he must be climbing a little higher each time.

On certain levels, he stopped, breathless and exhausted, and rested for a while. He was astounded all over again at the scale and complexity of his own creation. He had no idea he had dug down so deep – he'd never guessed he would have do dig up for so long. But he couldn't give up now, there couldn't be much further to go. So he set about burrowing upwards once more, telling himself over and over that he would never ever dig again. He must have done more than a lifetime's worth recently, so after this he would deserve a long, long rest.

He had just reached the point when his spirit had stretched to breaking-point, his paws were aflame with pain and his heart seemed about to burst with the effort of it all, when suddenly a thin thread of light pierced through the earth above him and shone through the gloom. With both paws, he broke through the thin crust of soil and the light poured in. He had made it! The Sun was directly above him and its beams shot straight down the shaft he had dug, into the center of the warren.

The rabbit clambered out of the hole into the noonday Sun and stood gratefully in the fresh air; with the last of his energy, he did a little dance of joy, then dropped wearily on the ground and looked about him. He could see nothing but the light for quite a time, so bright it seemed after his incarceration. Slowly, he began to make out clouds and then blue hills.... Then, to his growing surprise, he could see treetops – and they were below him! He wiped the last of the dirt out of his eyes and blinked as hard as he could, then he could see as clear as day that he was flopped on top of a great hill of earth, with fresh blades of grass starting to grow on it. He knew that hadn't been there when he started digging, all those months before. It suddenly dawned on him. Over the many weeks and months of burrowing, all that earth had to go somewhere, and *he* had created this hill! Then he had gone on digging into it, without knowing it was there. No wonder his friends had told him to get out more often. The rabbit felt a mixture of feelings now, a type of pride, a sort of stupidity and a kind of wonder at it all. True, the hill looked a bit bare at the moment, but he knew that, in time, it would be covered in deep grass and scattered with flowers, and, some day, there might be a tree or two. They might even name the hill after him, some day.

He felt justified in retiring from burrowing, now that he was at the top of his game. But he didn't give up digging, of course, he enjoyed it too much. Now, however, he made sure every tunnel was connected to another tunnel that led to the outside, so you could find your way back to the light of day, and the Sun could flood in when it shone.

It's a popular place to visit among rabbits, nowadays, and sometimes even other creatures come too, to witness this wonder of a warren. Some bring a carrot or two, to say thank you for the experience, so the rabbit never goes hungry these days. In fact, I'd say he's getting a bit too wide around the middle to fit down some of those tunnels anymore. But that's okay, he knows well what's in them and, anyway, there are always more tunnels to be made – bigger ones, wider ones, two-lane tunnels, tunnels with archways and little windows... Maybe he'll get carried away, one of these days, and there'll be another story to tell.

The Crystal Cave of your heart opens, revealing your hidden space within; your precious place of peace and healing.

Here, the walls sparkle with hints of your inner truths, the crystallized lore of your earthly experiences, slowly flowing or frozen in past patterns. Deep seams of meaning run through the glowing walls of this treasure chamber of untold stories, which pulsate with potentials of the future. The multifaceted surfaces reveal flashes of the many faces of the Crystal One you are. This chamber of our heart may seem smaller than we expected, but it holds the open doorway to many worlds. Here we find the portal of the Heart Space, the opening that reveals the infinity beyond. Through the doorway of the cave, we glimpse the spaces beyond, we hear the flow of liquid light, the rivers and cascades of crystal waters flowing.

Out beyond the cave, many suns are shining, all born of the One Sun, the Central One. The suns shine on many inner worlds, the Heartlands; landscapes rolling and smooth, jagged and hard, dry and dusty, lush and moist, oceans green and deep. All the worlds are there, waiting within to be explored and the life within them waits to be witnessed, to be befriended.

All the creatures and aspects within wait to be witnessed in their freedom and approached in friendship. Some of them we are afraid of, others we have never dared to think of or look upon. Yet they too have their beauty, they have their role within our inner eco-system, the habitat of our heart. They inhabit us, they have their own place within our inner habitat and they too are curious about us, about where they are, about what their role is, how they relate to the greater whole. They wonder why they sometimes feel hunted, sometimes free; sometimes hungry, sometimes sated. They wonder where they are, and what is beyond the apparent boundaries of their world. They, too, wish to explore the greater "you," the you of which they are a part.

Their courage is tested too, when they have to face their role within the greater scheme of things, when they have to imagine the scale of the world around them, when they realize how small they seem, yet how connected they are to something greater, something of which they can only catch a glimpse. They too live their lives as fully as they can, eating and drinking, sleeping when necessary, trying to enjoy themselves and make fun. They cry, they laugh, become lost and find themselves again. They lose themselves in forests of their own making then help themselves out into a clearing, which they created long before and forgot about. So, they save themselves only to lose themselves again.

As they wander through their world, they search for others who are also of their kind, who seem somehow related, to have a likeness to them. Someone who can end the inner loneliness they seem to feel, the unquenchable longing that their routines cannot erase or help them forget for long. So they wander into new territories in hope of finding the other, another part of themselves or another part of the greater whole, something or someone that can give meaning to their life. In searching, they do encounter scattered aspects of themselves, mirrored all around them in a landscape of their own making. When they encounter their other aspects their surprise is matched by a sense of familiarity, the mystery is matched by the feeling of somehow looking at oneself.

The image is unfamiliar and so is the mirror, yet somewhere in a flash of the eyes, or in a turn, a mannerism of the body, one sees oneself. One realizes that this "other" is oneself reflected and there is a contact, like a handshake that connects heart to heart, a connection across time and space; a recognition of connectedness and a glimpse of Oneness. We see these two meeting, perhaps falling in love, perhaps meeting and mating, or perhaps frightening each other away, repulsing each other, sending each other scurrying away in search of another more to their liking. We see there the potential meeting of hearts, or the "breaking" of hearts, the opening and closing, shattering and uniting.

When these patterns are repeated, we can learn from them. If we can step "outside" of ourselves a little, we can begin to discern our patterns within the greater pattern. We will then see the mirrors glinting in the undergrowth of our forest, ones that we had not noticed before, flashing in the light like waxy leaves. In these flashes of light, we see aspects of ourselves illuminated. In these partly-concealed mirrors, we get glimpses of sides of ourselves we are avoiding, have lost track of, or forgotten long ago.

If we take our courage in our hands and push away the undergrowth, pull back the creepers and cut away the dead matter that covers the image, a reflection of the original image will shine out in brilliant clarity. We may think it ugly, malformed or misshapen, or we may think it wonderful, strange and beautiful. A face we would never have guessed was ours, a body we would never think we owned. If we can accept these images and bring them together in our hearts we will feel ourselves recombine, we will start to melt through the illusion, to meld the fragmented images into one. We will see the hard edges soften and blend into unity. Then from this kaleidoscope of ugliness and beauty, horror and hope, laughter and tears, the familiar and the forgotten, we will discern our true face shining back at us in its true beauty, pouring out its light. Then the many faces will melt into one face and this one face expands to fill all our field of vision, until there is *only* one face. This One Face will be recognizable to all, for all will see the One Face, the face of the Unknown, the Unseen, the Indescribable. The Face of the Creator, the One Face behind all.

Now we hold the space open, for others to enter within the Circle of Oneness. A Dance of Creation is performed before us…

We dance and dance as one, spinning the spirals around us, through us. We carve the Light with our dancing limbs; with our dance we shine our thoughts out into the ends of darkness. We dance and our hearts soar high, we leap up and spin among the stars, setting them trembling! Our skirts twirl, and scatter stardust into all the corners of all the worlds. We spin our dreams for all to share. We leap, we soar, we sing, we shimmer – we are the spinners of the living threads and we are the living threads too. We spin Light into rainbow threads and weave a rainbow fabric, then with the rainbow, we clothe ourselves and dance.

We take our time to dance and make our time a dance. Time spent dancing is never wasted! Time given to dance is given to Creation, to renew itself and spread its light and color through the worlds. From our fingertips, we spin our threads to the stars. We paint the heavens, we weave new patterns and swirl them with our fingertips, so that the stars dance with us, we through them and they through us. And all dance and the spiral becomes one as the dancers become one. Curving, arcing out into darkness, then back around, in towards the Light, spiraling, spinning in towards the center. Oh, how we dance!

We call all to join us, to take their place in the Spiral Dance and dance their special dance, unique to them. For no one can dance the dance of another, and yet all dances are one. And that's where the fun begins. The big and the small, the tiny and the terrifying, the graceful and the grisly, the happy and the grumpy; all the creatures, great and small, in the one dance. Following the leader that they are, and each leading themselves back into the center, into the One Heart which dances within now and always, which is the Heart of the Dance of Creation, the heart of the Living Dance. So why not dance with us, for when you dance with the stars, the Earth's heart dances within!

We take our place, to find our space waiting for us. It knew we would come someday, so it waited, patient as a rock, until we found it again. It knows we could have chosen another place, yet it waited all the same, in hope. In the waiting and hoping is the knowing that, one day, the unknown will arrive, the hope will manifest. There is wisdom in the waiting, there is knowing in the patience, that what was envisioned in love will, one day, come into being. The place we chose was offered once and we were free to choose it or refuse. From our unlimited freedom we were given the choice of restriction for a time and a space, so that we could learn again what freedom is.

So we chose a place of learning, wherein our lessons would be made and unmade, forgotten and remembered. A school of living, a place of discovery where the learning amounts to one lesson: to find what is within our own heart. What is the truth within our own heart, and how do we enjoy its freedom in a place of apparent restriction, a place where it seems difficult to fly, where our thoughts seem bounded by common sense and old habits, where our ideas seem fenced in by the rigid ideas of others?

We batter our wings against the cage and hurt our heart. We seek freedom, to break the fences, to climb the walls and fly from their summits. We try to hack our way through the veils so we can live in freedom, yet sometimes it seems the harder we fight against restrictions, the more firmly they cling to us, the tighter they suffocate us, the stronger seem the fences and walls. So sometimes when we rest, we realize there must be another way. If we cannot cut through, or knock down or fly over these barriers, perhaps there is another way around or under them? Or perhaps a new direction is needed; maybe we can take a different route to find we have stumbled on a path towards freedom, towards the liberation we know is waiting for us, somewhere.

And, as we rest, perhaps we close our eyes and look within or, through our open eyes, look more deeply at that which is before us. Now we look more intensely until the wall seems to dissolve, until the very fabric of its existence seems to thin. Until it seems to be transparent, made of layers of veils, not the solid object we thought we saw at first. Hope now rises in our heart and our mind prepares to fly. Our heart unfurls its wings, in the hope that a doorway is near, a way of escape. We look again and feel the freedom beckoning, but then we feel the fear tugging in the opposite direction, gripping us, holding us in this spot. We feel paralyzed in sight of freedom. We can feel the veils grow thinner, we know they will dissolve at a touch, like old musty fabric, yet something holds us back.

The love of freedom and the fear of freedom come face to face within our hearts. Love and fear begin to move around each other, spinning around our center, trying to balance each other, yet somehow over-balancing the other. They each seem to spin, trying to find an equilibrium, and we seem caught in between. We wait for the situation to resolve itself but we notice the fabric seeming to grow thicker, the wall more solid. Hope seems to dim. In desperation, we reach out to grasp the fabric and strike solid brick.

The pain wakes us up and we wonder: should we ever have hoped to be released? Was it too much to hope for? Could we ever have made it through?

So we settle back to wait for another glimpse, for the moment when the veils thin. The moment when solid obstructions seem to lose their strength, their overpowering solidness, when they do not seem to tower over us with such deadening weight. This moment does eventually come and, to our surprise, we feel hope rise again. We concentrate all our effort and attention on this one point, trying to pierce a hole through the barrier with our mind, to burn an opening through to the other side with our eyes. In our determination, again we over-exert, concentrating all our attention on our mind which becomes overpowered. Again the image fades, the wall seems to seal itself up again and all returns to "normal." We feel the opportunity slip away. Yet still, hope lives within us.

Finally the moment comes when we have almost given up hope; we have given up on all the tried techniques, tossed away the old strategies, ruses and tricks, discarded the illusions of the illusions. Now we have only love left, only our old heart, tired now it seems. But still we know that we can love, still we know that our heart can open. And in its opening, we discover that it can open a door, that it can create the portal. We realize that only the heart knows the way through, only it knows the way to freedom. The wider it opens, the wider the walls open; the deeper we breathe in freedom, the deeper we can enter the portal. For this is the mirror of the heart, the doorway into love, the opening into light.

When it seems that all is opening and expanding within us, around us, we flow through the expanding love. The light grows before us, around us, within us and through us. We see the colors take shape and dance around us, take on forms and faces – come to life! Creating the form of every creature we have ever seen or imagined, then creating the forms of creatures we have never imagined, yet wish we could have. Still the universe expands, and still the threads stretch further and further out, deeper into infinities.

Now we are climbing up the threads, scaling the heights. And as the threads expand into thick ropes, and we grow and open out, we are carried further and further, deeper and deeper into the Heart of Love. There is no effort now, we realize we are swimming through the threads, through this ocean of color. Surrounded now, but unbounded, we know that we are the colors and the threads and we are connected to all. The pattern of our movement is reflected in the threads, rippling out in every direction around us. We play, we swim like a dolphin through space, through the living color, flipping our tail, shrieking our joy, laughing with the Creator!

We swim in the spiral currents, riding the spiral wave, moving into the point of stillness. And we have forgotten our fear, our paralysis is no more. The walls seem far away, but we know now what restriction is; we celebrate its end and its wisdom. We swim through the currents in this infinite ocean of freedom....

Take heart! The signs of the coming days are becoming clearer to you, the signposts are easier to read. The glimpses are easier to catch, the hints are caught now, rather than dropped. All becomes more fun, more creative, closer to the true life. The coming lightness will dust off your wings and lift your legs higher, it will make it easier to hope. It will be a simple task to be yourself as your love for yourself will have increased.

You will be able to measure your progress by how much love you feel for yourself, as well as those around you. For you cannot feel too much love, for love itself is infinite. Once it does not create obsession or dependency or misplaced pain, then the love will help you grow and expand. Your heart itself will find new room to grow in the coming expansion. All will seem different, even look and feel different. You will learn to accept the "strangeness," and then it can become "normal." Then the new wonders can come and you will find yourself living in an ever-expanding universe where discoveries seem to come, without fanfare, in every second moment. It seems around every corner is a sight more surprising and wonderful than the one before.

You will even see the darkest places begin to change, just a little at first. You will notice things you have not seen before, a glimmer of something in the corner of your eye, a flash somewhere amongst the shadows. You will know that something is shifting and changing. Even in the deepest dark, the light is always there, awaiting the moment of re-discovery. From the dark can flow the greatest surprises, so we will need to be aware and patient, then the change will come and the waiting will have been worth it. For light will find a way and love will snake its way somehow through the undergrowth, then start to climb up to the light and find the warm sunshine. For the cold-blooded know well the warmth of the sun and the nourishment it gives them. So those who seem cold and indifferent are also searching for the light, seeking out the warmth, hoping in their inner hearts that they too will be warmed and comforted. Then they will be able to shed their cold skin and feel the warmth rise within them – the heat of the sun within – until they feel they are at one with the sun, united with the light.

The coldest and the hottest entwine and are combined in the light, bound together in unity. The shadows wrap around the light, and the light around the shadows; the darkness enfolds the day and the day embraces the darkness and all are made one. The blinding light and the blinding darkness become inseparable and each is as the other; the darkness, light and the light, darkness, until there is no dark or light, only the one Light from which they both flowed. Until there is the one life from the one source, the unity of heart, and separation ends. No day or night, but eternity, an eternity of love.

All flesh is one flesh, every body is divine. Every word is the word of God, every thought comes from the Creator. Every hope flows from the one hope, every day is but the One Day. Every passion springs from the One Fire of passion, every dance but a step in the One Dance.

We call ourselves by many names, but we are all One. We all carry the words for naming the beings and things of the worlds. We spend so much time searching out the names, finding out their meanings, divining the truth in what we are told and seeking what we believe lies hidden in the names.

The names and the words multiply and the books grow thicker, the libraries larger and the databases expand. It seems that our knowledge is growing, it seems we are becoming more wise, yet all we are doing is accumulating more versions of the same name, more ways of saying the same thing, more images of the same illusion. So we pile them up, higher than we could ever climb, we stack them higher than the highest peak. We marvel at the wonder of our work, at the mountains of wisdom we are accumulating, at the lakes of knowledge we are filling by the day, so wide and deep. The mountains and the lakes grow greater, yet still we want more. So we pour more effort into filling them and into building them higher, searching for more information, more names, ideas and definitions with which to fill our libraries and our heads. Until they become stuffed with the stuff of knowledge, in the great illusion of apparent knowing.

But under it all, we have buried the pearl of true wisdom. It is there, deep down at the bottom of the lake. There, hidden in the heart of the mountain. It seems insignificant, tiny, scarcely to be noticed by the hurrying mind, by the busily scurrying seeker of knowledge. Around it, is a circle of ancient souls, of open hearts, who hold it in their patient gaze, waiting for the day it is reclaimed.

And those whose buried us, who built a mountain over our heads, who threw us deep into the bottom of a lake, those who cast us away, would wait a long day, until, when the mountain had reached as high as it could go and the lake had been dug as deep as it could be, when both had been filled full, they would cease their labors and rest. Then, perhaps, they would ask themselves what it was they were seeking in the first place. What was there at the heart of this great endeavor? What was within the heart of the mountain? What rests in the depths of the lake?

Then some would begin to dig, not to dig the lake deeper, but to tunnel into the mountain they had created. Others would dive down, down into the lake, into its dark depths. They would tunnel or swim through the darkness, keeping their hope alive with the distant glimmer they sometimes glimpse in the distance. They would have to face their own fears, which seek to crush them, to push them back into the light and apparent safety, but in reality, further away from what they seek. So they go on, tunneling and swimming deeper and ever deeper, until after a great labor, they would reach the bed of the lake, its murkiest depths, and they would reach the darkest heart of the mountain. There, where it seems all light is extinguished, looking about them with the last of their strength, they would discern a tiny glimmering point of light, almost too small to see.

So they would go closer and there they would find a tiny shining pearl. Something inside them would know this is what they seek. They pick it up and hear, softly, the whispers of hidden wisdom. In this little pill of wisdom, they would have found the truth of the Universe, Within this pearl, they would have found their own wisdom.

If they look deep into the center of this tiny sphere, into its seemingly tiny heart, they find a glimmer like sunlight or moonlight shining out. There they find a glimpse of their true selves, of their own inner wisdom, of the inner light of Creation. They find, illuminated, their true face and the faces of any who gather to look into its heart. The pearl can be held in the palm of a hand, even in the palm of a child, yet, they have found the Heart of Creation hidden within, and revealed within. Open within it, is the truth of the Universe,

They enclose it in their palm and give thanks. When they open it again, the pearl would seem to be gone, but it would have turned itself inside out and they would find ourselves inside the light of the pearl, within the world of the pearl of wisdom. All around us would be illuminated. We would have found the Heart of Wisdom. We would find ourselves in familiar surroundings, in our own Heart Space. And we would find others there in this great shared space of the One Heart. Those who tunneled and dug, those who swam deep, those who waited patiently, all united there in the Light, in the wisdom of Oneness. We would know ourselves to be within the Heart of the Creator. Wisdom is all around us and we find All waiting there. All wisdom, all the light and dark of Creation, all the hidden Oneness, revealed.

I am Darkness, yet I come from the Light, for I am created by Light. I am shadow, yet I flow from the One. I am coldness, for I shun the warmth, even

as I seek it. I am hate, born of a wounded heart; I am bitterness, born of disappointment. I am narrowness, who strayed from the wide path. I am sorrow, grown old in a young heart; I am grief given with love; I am love lost. I am sadness, I have no friends. I am loss, I come after.

I bring no comfort... yet I bring a gift. I bring no warmth, yet I bring a wisdom. Though I am not easy to be with, I have a beauty too, if only you, or I, could see it. But I am blind to myself, so I am Darkness. Yet I have my place and that is my comfort and, somewhere in the darkness, I know that I am loved. But my coldness is that I cannot feel it, I do not know its warmth. I know not its light, but I have my time, and within my time I shine, darkly. I illuminate the light with my bright shadows. I am the hidden sister of the Light; I am the other hand. Each hand senses the other in the dark and when they reach out, they touch each other, yet know each other not.

For one sees but the darkness, and the other is the darkness. But there is One who knows both, who knows their wisdom; that is the One I seek. For light seeks light, light seeks dark, dark seeks dark and dark seeks light. And in the dance is time made; in their movement is space created. I am your sister, as all are one and I make no greater claim. But I ask to be known, to be recognized and remembered. For I am loneliness, most of all.

I am a sister of the Darkness, a Priestess of the Light. I am guided by the Light, and I guide my light through the pools of darkness. I have known the darkness, as I have known the light and I know each seems equal in the points between, when we have darkness on one side and light on the other. When we are at the center of the scales; on the one hand darkness, on the other hand, light. We wonder which will over balance us, as we begin to topple one way, then the other. For the darkness can seem so heavy, so almighty, so deep and powerful; its majesty and strength can seem unconquerable, its mystery unfathomable, yet somewhere we know that a small candle can illuminate the darkness; a beam of light can reach out into darkness and find what lies hidden there, though it seems but a weak beam. So we know, deep within us, that light can find what it wishes to find in the darkness. Darkness can be a sister or brother, a companion or friend; then it too can be guided through the paths it has created. We can find the star-lined path picked out in the dark of space. And the burning stars shine all the brighter for being surrounded by the dark; for the darkness is illusion, as all is illusion.

We can see, with the eye of our heart, through the darkness. We can pierce its depths to find our way through it and thank it for its guidance as we go, as we wander through the shadows with the stars to guide us above, or beneath our very feet; or we peer ahead to a pinpoint of light that will guide us through. We are also learning to know the darkness, to know its velvet depths that conceal the light. There, hidden within its deepest depths is the source of the light itself. When you tear away this fabric of illusion, this dark veil, you will be dazzled by the light that was there all the time, like the Sun behind the clouds. You will laugh at your own fears and terrors, knowing now that you created these illusions so that you could learn to discern, to guide yourself through the valleys of darkness out beyond, into the infinity. For beyond what seems like boundless night is the infinity of infinities; the Life of Forever, the Love everlasting of the Creator of Light and Dark, of you and I and the One that we are.

The Man By The Lake

There once was a man of infinite patience who waited by the circle of a lake.

He hoped to catch a fish he knew was there, somewhere in its depths. He had heard the stories of its breathtaking beauty, of its wonderful colors, of its grace as it swam and its great size and strength. If only it could be caught, he often thought, how delicious it would be. What a wonder of a fish! And well worth the wait. It was said to be the only one of its kind and had fallen into a deep sleep long before. There it rested, safe and dreaming on the bed of the lake, its beauty hidden in the murky depths. It was said this magical fish would rise to the surface one day, but only if the right person could awaken it.

Only one thing could attract its attention in those murky depths, the lure of a colorful feather. Only then would it be reminded of the forgotten world waiting above, and it would begin to rise and shine, awakening as it rose to the bait. So the story was told, but only a few believed it now. And only one of those few was willing to wait long enough to be a witness to its truth. It would take one with rare dedication and patience, but now one such man sat on the bank, his mind fixed on a single purpose.

So he waited, day in, day out, with a rod of wood, an unbreakable thread and a baited hook. At his belt, was a knife to gut the fish. The hook was baited with a bright feather, which he hoped would attract the fish's attention and spark its curiosity...someday. He had attached a heavy weight to it and flung it into the water, sensing it sink down until it was touching the very bed of the lake, its muddiest depths, where no other fish could live. At the lake's edge, he waited, day after day, through the long days and longer nights, forgetting his family and his friends, losing interest in the rounds of daily life, waiting for the fish to rise to the surface. He waited at the ever-shifting edge to catch a glimpse of its beauty, for the flash of a fin to break the surface, for a hint of something moving in the depths, some movement to give him hope. But there was never even a tug on the line. Never once did he catch even a glimpse of the fish. Crouched there, as if ready to pounce, he stared into the waters until his eyes grew bleary and tired, until he would lose consciousness and fall asleep.

By night, he tied the thread to him, so that if the fish awoke while he slept, they would awaken together. Whenever he woke up, the man would at once be on the alert, resuming his duty, waiting for the fish to appear. Standing amongst the reeds, holding the rod, with the thread twined between his fingers, waiting for a tug, a sign of life, he became sensitive to every subtle current. Yet, still, the sign he expected never came. But something seemed to keep him there, to keep his hope alive. Sometimes he did feel trapped, and a feeling came that he must escape this place and give up on his quest. He would start to think the stories were fanciful lies, that he had been hoodwinked, that there was no fish there at all. Yet, somehow, he could not leave because he still believed, in spite of everything, in spite of catching nothing.

Days and weeks passed and, as he grew paler and thinner, others worried about him. Friends brought him food, while his family came often to plead with him to leave and come home with them. Others tried to entice him back to the old social life he had lived, but, still, he stayed and waited. The presences of the big, mossy rocks that stood above the surface of the lake had become as familiar as old friends and, with them and the trees that ringed the shore, he seemed to have all the friends he needed. But there were lonely moments and he was often stiff and tired now. He knew, nevertheless, his belief was stronger than fatigue. Yet he doubted himself often. Why did he want to prove this mythical fish existed? He could not explain why to anyone, even himself. His muscles ached, his clothes had become dusty and ragged during his long vigil, waiting through all weathers. Every day, he had tasted disappointment, and he was afraid that it would make him bitter.

Then, one morning, he woke as he had done on so many mornings before and again looked into the lake expectantly, with hope rising in his heart. He scanned its surface and its depths until, once again, every inch, every ripple and tiny wavelet was examined. There was nothing to see but the lake and its reflections, the pure beauty of the lake he had come to know so well. He let himself relax then and began to enjoy watching the lake, as he had watched it each day and so come to know it deeply. In the gentle whispers of the waves, he followed the conversation of wind and water, reading their messages written on the writhing surface. There had been special moments that the man and the lake seemed to have shared. Moments when it felt, just for an instant, as if he was part of the lake, or the lake was part of him. As he sat there, gazing at the lake, he slowly came to realize that what had been keeping him there was not the fish, this fish he had never seen, but something else that made the hope rise in his heart. Something burned within his heart, which had sustained him through his lonely vigil.

He realized, with a start, that it was love. Was it a love of something he had never seen? A love of something he knew to be there, beautiful and strong, unique and wonderful? He looked again into the circle of the lake and saw no fish, but the lake itself, the lake he had grown to love, rippling and shimmering with light that glinted off its surface. He was thirsty now and he bent down to drink, to quench his thirst as he had done every other day. He dipped his hand into the lake, making his hand into a bowl and took from it enough water to slake his thirst. But, as he brought the water to his lips, he saw his own face reflected in the little lake in the palm of his hand. For a moment, he did not recognize himself, it was so long since he had seen himself in a mirror. He knew that he looked different now – or looked at himself differently. Yet he could see himself as the lake saw him; for the lake saw him with the eyes of love, with a deep peace. The lake saw him as a lover sees the beloved, as one who is beautiful and patient, one who would wait long, long hours in search of something never seen, but only known within the heart.

He found he could not bring himself to drink the water, so he stared at the reflection in his own hand for a long time. Finally, thirst overcame him and he drank. His reflection disappeared and the crystal water flowed down into him, refreshing him. When the water of the lake entered him, he felt, for the first time, truly at one with the lake. Now, when he looked again at the lake, he saw himself reflected in its movement, in its surface and its depths, in its inner life, its peace and stillness. He was one with its waves. When the wind blew across its skin, it also caressed him; each wave that flowed through the lake flowed through him too. Now, the ripples on the face of the lake were the wrinkles in his own smiling face, each silver flash was a glimmer in his own eye. A single tear of joy fell from his eye and melted into the waters with an almost invisible ripple.

The man untied the thread from the rod of wood and planted the rod in the soil amongst the reeds. He looked down at the thread, which he had held onto so tightly all that time. He loosened his grip on the thread and opened his hand, letting the gentle waves of the lake take it from his fingers. He breathed a deep sigh of relief. His body relaxed, his mind widened, his heart opened to the beauty all around him. He stood up and looked out over the lake, feeling free and content. He took a step to the very edge of the water then he stepped into the circle of the lake. He waded in deeper and deeper until he began to float and the lake embraced him. With his face to the sky, he stretched out beneath the blue veil, resting on the surface of the lake like a dreamer on a soft, watery bed. Far below him, in the murkiest depths, something stirs. Deep within the heart of the lake, something shimmers into life, something glows and flashes into living light.

The man floats in the bowl of lake with the Sun high above him, warming the water. He feels a sudden pull from below. He takes a deep breath and disappears beneath the waves. In the swirling waters around him, light is rising and colors are appearing, taking the flowing form of a great fish, yet the man can sense so much more within this light that has risen from the deep of the lake. Her form is more beautiful than he could ever have imagined, and her shimmering scales flash in the sunlight as she circles him, making a circle of light in the clear water. Her movement creates a liquid spiral, with him in the spinning column of water, like the spindle in the center. He is spinning slowly, enjoying the beauty of this moment, with her colors reflecting on his skin, feeling like a fish-man himself. She touches him with her fins that wave like wings through the water, their bright feathers caressing him. Together, they dance in a flowing, spiral dance, deep into the lake. The knife he has carried falls from his belt and disappears into the murk and mud.

Finally, he rises to the surface for air, and he notices her glow in the water swimming out in a circle around the lake. A bright wave ripples through the lake then all is still. The man slowly drifts to the shore. He walks from the water and stands on the bank, looking with new eyes now, more awake than he has ever been before.

That day, he returned home. As he turned to leave, he knew that, though he was turning his back on it, he and the lake were one and he would hold it within his own depths forever, as the lake held him in its heart. And the secret held within it would live within him. As they moved apart, love brought them together, and there was no distance between them now.

The opening of the heart opens up the new universes.

The spaces so created multiply and interconnect, and movement from space to space becomes easier. Each space itself expands, growing in scale and dimensions, opening up new spaces within itself, so that all grows and connects in crystalline patterns. The crystal universes so created become living playgrounds of color and form, light and dark, unknowing and discovery. As they expand outwards from the central point of light, they would, when seen together, be recognized as a piece of sacred geometry, expanding and growing before your crystal eyes.

The forms and patterns created will themselves be unique to each individual, and each form will grow into further unique forms as determined and discovered by you, their creator. These new spaces will be great in number, and they will add to the multiplicity of spaces already available, which await discovery in every direction and dimension. They each conceal new wonders and will reveal new worlds.

This is when you will fully realize the continuum that exists between each creator and that which is created. You will see that the forms – and the living forms – that you create are part of you, an extension of yourself and yourselves. Just as you are an extension of the original Creator, who works through you, discovers through you, while you are in the midst of discovery. When you become relaxed and expanded in these new spaces, the growth will be exponential and accelerated. This is when you will realize the worth of your deep connection to the Creator, as the wisdom of the Creator will flow through you, and your activity will be enlightened by the Creator's light. Your actions will not be distorted by the old ego and the little will, but be guided by the greater wisdom. You will be nourished by this, you will drink from the source, and your spiritual health will be determined by how deeply you drink from the well of the One Wisdom.

As your vision expands, you will see the greater patterns that make up the new life, the brighter living spaces, the wider breathing spaces. Your Heart

Space will have expanded beyond anything you have previously experienced. For it is from the heart that these new experiences will flow, rather than from the narrows of the mind. The heart holds the wisdom. In its flow of love, it can bring together that which seems separate, those forces that seem disconnected or antagonistic. It can unite the divided, bring peace between warring aspects, establish a creative truce between the dark and light facets. When these truly come face to face, they will meet in the Heart Space, that vast safe space, where they can know each other's wisdom, and experience each other's light and dark, each others love and learning. They can truly meet there, blend their wisdom into one unity and, in the meshing of these seeming opposites, they will help weave the universes back together.

All will come closer from one small act of coming together. When these blendings of energies and meldings of dimensions occur, their effects ripple through multiple universes. They echo out into all the dimensions, the Web of Life itself pulsates with the news, as the message is sent in every direction, out into the infinities of space and time – and beyond even these. The wisdom is sent along the Web in pulsations of light and color, carried into every corner of every dimension to which it is connected. The Living Web itself learns, expands and strengthens; rips are repaired, gaps are bridged, separations are sewn together.

What were once holes can become portals through which new energies flow. Gaps become doorways when, across these gaps, the Rainbow web is woven; the hole is closed, yet a portal is opened. In the closing of the old, ragged rip, a portal to the new is created. Stepping through this Rainbow veil brings one through to a new universe, where one meets a new aspect of oneself, waiting to be found, awaiting reunion.

Within the Heart Space, the light will burn brighter, the heart will open wider, and, in the marriage of energies, the fire of love melts and alchemizes the old, the heavy and transmutes it into the new, the light. In the blending and melding is the purifying, in the meeting of two flames, the one fire burns brighter than the two separately, and in their marriage, a sacred flame is born. A new space is illuminated, a new universe revealed. In the shared space, they dance as one, they heal through their dance and heal the space around them.

And in their sacred dance, a single truth is made from the many, though it holds the many open within and does not deny their specialness. In the Circle Dance of many truths dancing as one, the greatest flame is created, the flame that contains all the colors, reflects all the possibilities, has all the passions and potentials burning within it. Within it, is the fire of love and anger, the flame of hate and forgiveness, the light of every life lived, the heat of change, the warmth of desire, the radiance of transformation.

Even from a distance, its glow will light up the worlds. When this great flame dances upon the Earth, it will be visible through the galaxies. The flame of hope, of new creation, the fire of the unity of opposites, the grand alchemizing flame of a great candle that the Earth becomes. This sacred flame will burn away so much that is no longer needed, that has been gone beyond. So much of the old deadwood, debris and rubbish will be burned away, then the new green life can burst through. The face of the Earth will be transformed, and the faces of her people will glow brighter as they watch the flame arise. This time, they will not fear the fire in the sky, since they will know within them that it heralds the new beginning, the new Unity.

It is the great Heart Flame, made of many hearts burning as one, in the One. Then the great cleansing and healing will have begun, and will continue until all dwell within the Heart Space and none are excluded or forgotten by their brothers and sisters. All will be given the opportunity to dwell there. Within this freedom, all will make a new dwelling within their own heart and find themselves welcome in the greater space of the One Heart, the Heart of the Creator.

WE ARE FIRE!

We are the dancing Fire, we dance through the worlds, and we scatter our light. We are living firelight, we burn, we dance on our feet of flame. With our limbs of firelight, we stretch out to caress you, but you pull back, amazed, for we are fiery, we are flame! We are hearts on fire and dancing; with our skirts of flame, we dance the transformation. We rise, spiraling, to the stars and fire is our life, our nature, our fuel. Our hearts' desire lifts us where our hearts desire. We wear wings of fire, we singe the leaves as we fly through the trees – we cannot help it, we are fire, we are free and we are flames, alive!

We are the living Heart of Fire and we come to warm your hearth. And our heat will dance through your rooms and keep you company in the cold nights. For we are generous, we are happy to share our warmth. We give birth to the tiny flames and we teach them to dance like their fiery mothers. Whether their lives are short or long, they dance as brightly as they can. They, too, hold the Fire Wisdom; they carry the memory of the first fire, the first flame created. Within their little hearts is the Flame of Creation, the Creation of which they are an honored part, for they are the fires of cleansing and healing, of togetherness and comfort.

We keep the lonely warm while they wait by their fire for a friend to come and warm their hearts. We warm the cold bones of the old and help them to heal. In their lonely moments, when their hearts seem frozen, we help them remember their times of passion, their days of youthful fire, their days of light and sunshine. And those winter days too, when the fire sang and danced just for them. So we are loved as well as feared, but the love is greater, because we give much more than we ever take.

For we are the Creative Flames, we bring a gift from the Creator. And the fire of the gods and goddesses still dances through the world in many forms, known by many names. The Fire of Creation never truly burns out, but only changes, and the flame transforms and reappears elsewhere. The Eternal Flame burns on, and it is One Fire, one great flame of infinite flames. We truly dance for Joy, for the Fire of freedom lives in our hearts, and is our gift to you.

Did you see the proud and naked flames? How they love to dance! They seem tireless, their fiery legs never seem to flag, though sometimes they dance away just when we wish them to stay... Oh, Fire can be fickle, it is true. It has a will of its own and its fiery character is difficult to judge; it will not be bound for long and cannot be held or restrained easily. It is our friend and it wishes us no harm, but it needs respect, the respect due to all created natures. If we honor fire, we honor an element that can help us to understand our own natures, the character of change and the potential for transformation. We can each dance a Fire Dance in our own way, feel fire flowing within us.

So remember you carry the Rainbow Flame within your heart. Remember it is there waiting to flame forth into the world, to fill your aura from within, to make you a bright flame in a world that can seem dark. Then you will gather together with the other dancing flames – and then begins the Fire Dance of Creation. Why not have a merry Fire Dance tonight... Let us see your legs fly higher and your hearts dance higher, and we will share your joy, one in love. Fire Hearts, unite!

Soon, we will find ourselves at the portals of entry to the new spaces. A moment, perhaps, of trepidation, of doubt and expectation. We will have a hint of the great potential that lies within, yet we may doubt ourselves, wondering whether we have the wisdom to venture in, in case we become lost, or so enamored of our new surroundings that we will not want to return to the world of 3 or 4 dimensions. Maybe we will not trust ourselves, so we will decide to wait for a guide we can trust, but such can be difficult to find when one's fear is greatest. Fear creates fearful masks that we place on the faces of potential helpers and guides. So we end up seeing our own fear reflected, and we cannot see the face of love behind the mask.

Ultimately, we will simply have to trust ourselves and our inner wisdom. This heart wisdom is our true guide, after all, and the other guides, if they are true, will only remind us of its existence and alert us to its constant presence. They will not seek to bend us to their will or thoughts; they will allow us to rediscover the wisdom within. So, as we peer through the open portal and gather our courage, it is the connection from heart to heart that will sustain us from our heart to the Heart of the Creator, from each individual to the many and the One, from the One to the many. Once we know that there is an unbreakable thread of light linking us to the Creator's Heart, we can venture forth and make our way along the threads of light. Even if we let go of it, it will not let go of us!

Our connection cannot be broken, so feel free to open the heart and see what is revealed there. For there is the true portal; all others open to us from there. And as we enter through them, we enter deeper into our own Heart Space; as we explore them, we are exploring our own inner wisdom and all that is hidden within. These spaces will, indeed, seem strange to many, with no familiar landmarks. When we reach our hands out into them, we will realize that the movement of our hands is changing the space, sending ripples through this environment, as if through liquid.

As we venture out fully into the space, we will find we are swimming within an ocean of creation. Its colors will be even more wonderful than the myriad colors of coral or opalescent shells or the iridescence of crystal. As we begin to sculpt the space, we will find ourselves creating forms, playing with shapes, making patterns. If we watch the patterns we are creating, we will see our own creative force at work. We will observe if these forms are rigid or tightly-structured, or free-flowing and fluid, and we will learn which aspects of us they reflect. We will discover whether we are afraid to be free, whether we want to create a small space or a large one, notice whether we swim freely, like a dolphin, or whether we are cautious, moving a finger at a time, making a single movement, then watching its effects before we dare move further.

Some will take their time to explore the colors, others will rejoice in their freedom of movement, but others will feel restricted by the patterns of the past, and may find themselves re-making these very patterns before their eyes. Yet, if they can move on through this space and push these patterns aside, they will find a new space behind – a greater space. They will have revealed new spaces within their own heart, where they will feel free to play and create. Some will begin to feel the new space as forming a vast musical instrument which responds to their every touch and thought. They will be fascinated by the music that fills them and flows from their lightest thought. Their most delicate touch will create a ripple of sound, which will build and grow as they move. If they dance, they will create a symphony of heart music. They may hear their own voices in this new space, and wonder at how strange they sound, how different to what they expected, and how they echo…!

In the new dimensions, there will be unexpected results as we learn the different effects of each action. And as the play expands, the heart will open more, relaxing into the open space, feeling free to fly on wings of music, or swim through waves of form, or make ripples of color, weaving novel patterns into this world of infinite color and space. After each time of play, it will be good to return to a state of rest, to return back to the more familiar dimensions, in order to give time for body and mind to absorb the experiences, to integrate the new energies. How well this is progressing will be seen by the state of health of mind and body, which should be flourishing and clarifying. There should be an increasingly crystalline clarity of thought and physical health. When development is balanced, all elements remain in balance, and no one element is harmed by the developments flowing through. In fact, one should be a picture of health – but a new picture, a holographic image of the new self, healthy and happy within the body, content to be of the Earth. The human body, also, will soon reveal its wonders, its hidden worlds and dimensions. It is not something to be cast off like an old shoe, or discarded hastily. The body has its own wonderful wisdom and wishes to be part of the new experiences.

As we ground the changes within our bodies, the Earth will also absorb them into the very earth beneath our feet and the air around us. Our heart-expansion will be reflected in the Heart of the Earth and registered there as increasing light. You will each bring new light onto and into the Earth. As you grow, as you root and ground yourselves, the greater Light will flow through you into the heart of the Earth, making new space for play there, too. Who knows, you may find yourself soon playing in the Heart of the Earth….

She will welcome you there as one of her children, playing in her safe space, basking in her light as you give her your light; so both will heal and grow. Millions will do this healing "work" in the coming years in their own way, and many are doing it now, in greater numbers by the day. The Old Ones will always be there to guide, the Elders who have waited patiently to be of service again will give freely of their wisdom to those who are ready to receive it. So, perhaps, we will meet soon and dance together in the Heart of the Earth, and play together in her Light. I am sure we will recognize each other, and I will be sure to save a dance for you. And our laughter will echo out as the Earth rings with it, like a great bell echoing our laughter out to the stars...

We spiders dance so well because that is our way of weaving. The spider dances as she weaves and weaves as she dances, and the web is made as the world is made. And all the busy spiders that we are, we weave our webs through each other's webs and we dance with each other as we weave. Sometimes we tangle them, since sometimes even we make a slip, for not all spiders are elegant, as not all dancers seem to dance divinely – to the human eye. Though, to the Creator's eye, all dances are divine, and all dancers, too – even you.

For your dance is beautiful and true, as you are; that is what makes it special. The web you weave is a special space, and you do not scare away the spiders, nor do they scare away you. Though sometimes the bigger ones take up too much room for comfort... But we all share the one space, after all, and all of our webs are connected. The wonderful weavers with artistic flair, the fine skills, are all weaving the same web as those whose fingers seem more clumsy, more prone to dropping a thread. Yet the knots and tangles are part of the web, and they can always be disentangled, if we are patient – or it may be that this little knot is there to remind us of something we would otherwise forget.

We spiders have more eyes to see with than you humans, and we see differently, for we see in different directions and dimensions simultaneously. We can see connections that have not been revealed yet to the human race. But, of course, we have been weaving a lot longer than you, so we will wait patiently for you to catch up! Though we appreciate that your skills are developing, and the joyful human weavers are increasing in number, these conscious weavers around the Earth who know themselves to be part of the Web and of the weaving, who are busily spinning out their connecting threads. So we spiders see the special connections being woven over the Earth by you Humans between each other. A little clumsy still, but we will not be picky, for we can see them glinting in the moonlight and sunlight, and we see the flashes of the Rainbow there. So we know the Rainbow Web is growing! Word is getting round, since we spiders are very well-connected and speak to each other all the time. Our World-Wide Web is very sophisticated and ancient...

We could tell you some tales, some ancient creation tales, that we have not forgotten. For we hold the wisdom of the Web, and as we spin out our threads, we manifest the connections between all. Of course, we can see a little more than you as our eyes outnumber yours. But, I'm sure you'll soon find you have eyes in the back of your head...and around the sides. As you feel your senses develop, you will feel your vision less restricted. Many of you have already "seen" someone coming up behind you and wondered how you knew they were there. So perhaps you are more spider-like than you think! Of course, you may not dance as elegantly as we do, but we have more legs to choose from. In time, I'm sure you will learn a spidery dance or two – perhaps you could do it in fours, sharing your legs to make eight. Then you can make a happy Spider Dance! And we won't laugh...much.

And we wish you well in weaving with your feet, for we have had millions of years to learn the tricks, so we will be patient while you catch up. Your Spider Sisters will watch and applaud, and one may tap you on the shoulder and ask to join in the dance, maybe teach you some of the old web-weaving skills. We can see much fun ahead! There will be many happy spiders watching from the corners, hanging overhead, watching the show and swaying to the spidery rhythms. You will weave with your feet; you will dance a Tarantella and we will all join in. And the men too, with their hairy legs, like ours, will be welcome! For web-weaving is not solely for women and we will share our wisdom with all those who wish to grow.

We will spin a few tales for you, too. You will enjoy the ancient tales, for in the old days, spiders were more familiar than now, more of a close friend and companion. Except for the occasional nibble – but what is a bite or two between friends? And we are all old friends and all one in the Web, are we not? So watch out for the Rainbow Webs, perhaps across the corner of a doorway, or hanging between the branches in the woods. And we will watch your webs grow and connect into one, watch the threads thicken and grow in strength. Then you will all feel as connected as we do. Oh, what a web it will be! Once it is woven of love, every thread will be connected to love, and at the center of the web will be the Weaver of All.

So, happy weaving, Rainbow Makers...World Weavers... Spider Sisters and Brothers. See you soon!

The Fox's Dream

There once was a fox who was wiser than he seemed.
He looked like an ordinary fox, but he was a very creative one and quite a daydreamer. He was a good hunter and ate well enough, but most of all, he liked to play and to dance. He had always been a playful fox, from the time he played with his brothers and sisters as a cub, carefree in the warm sunshine, rolling in the soft, silky grass. Even now, when he had a life and a home of his own, he let his imagination out to play whenever he could. He could make up a game at the drop of a leaf, transforming a fallen leaf into a delicious morsel, clamping it in his jaws like a juicy snack; or make an odd piece of bark or a twig into a playmate. He saw every tree and creature as a friend he hadn't played with yet, though he was doing his best to get through them. Sometimes it was difficult for other creatures to appreciate that he might want to talk with them, rather than stalk them. Even when everyone seemed too busy or reluctant to play with him, he could always rely on his imagination to brighten the day.

Sometimes he would imagine he could climb the trees, like the squirrels did, way up into their branches. He often felt he could climb to the very top of one, if he really wanted to, and look out over the landscape. He was light and agile – like they say, nimble as a fox – so who better to be up there than him? Though, when he had tried climbing, he found it was not as easy as he had imagined. Trees were tricky to climb and obviously not designed with foxes in mind. So he found it better to sit at the base of a tree, in the silence that sometimes comes in the forest, and imagine himself climbing up with ease through the branches of the tree, muzzling through the leaves to the very top. There, he would pop his head out through the top-most leaves and feel like one of the birds.

At other times, he even imagined himself to be a flying fox, happily flying through the trees to taste the fruit that dangled on the branches. While resting himself in a treetop after a long flight, he would feed on a few fruits or berries, enjoying the wonderful view. He would look down at the nests of the birds and feel protective towards them – even towards their eggs, which are normally a delicacy for a hungry fox. But he would not feel inclined to eat one, because he felt like a brother of the birds. So he was a very unusual fox, as you can see!

But there were times when he would not let himself play or dance, moments when he remembered the tribal tales told to him when he was growing up, about the strangers who came to the forests and meadows to hunt, terrible tales of what some humans did to their cousins of the Fox Tribe. Sometimes the warnings would ring in his ears so loudly that he could hardly hear the music of the forest, and when he looked around him, the world would seem less safe. Humans had strange ways, he knew, and one might want to hang his tail up as a trophy, so he would stay well away from their haunts and out of their vision.

One day, when he was still young, he had heard the sound that the foxes dreaded, coming towards him on the wind. It was the sound of many creatures calling and people shouting out, of barking and baying; the voices of many dogs and humans on a hunt. He was being hunted, though he did not know why. He had run with all the speed he could muster, and he had youth and an agile mind on his side, so he easily outfoxed them all by his complicated changes of direction, his loops and double-backs. He ran with the wind, and it carried his scent ahead of him, so soon his trail was lost. But it was as if a seed of fear had been planted in him that fine day. Years later, that seed would germinate.

From that day on, he listened more intently to the fearful stories the others told, and they seemed to take hold of him. He found it hard to be at ease, the way he used to be, and the world seemed different to him now. When he ventured out of his den, he was often on the alert for danger, rather than looking for the next adventure. He tried to keep alert for eyes that might be watching, for a sign of anyone who might be observing him with harm in their heart. There were moments when he suddenly felt vulnerable, and he would do everything he could to be less visible. He slunk low to the ground, and even his bright eyes that once flashed with fire, he kept downcast, and he only held his head up in places where he felt absolutely safe.

But, in wanting to be invisible, he knew he was missing out on life. There were times when he wanted to play and dance in the wide, open spaces of the forest. He would peer from the shadows into the clearings when the Sun was filtering through the trees, with glittering shafts of sunlight making the leaves glow golden and lighting up the open spaces. Once, he had felt free to be himself in these places. Within them, he could play, gambol and scamper; he could dance and discover new moves. The only time he had ever left all fear behind was when he began to play. But it was as if he had forgotten how to be playful now. The fear of being caught in the open held him back and he kept to the shadows. So now he never danced in the clearings. He only dreamed of doing so, while he hid in the safety of the shadowy leaves. He dreamed in the daylight, these days, because he did not want nightmares to disturb his moments of peace in the darkness of his den.

One night, years later, after wandering through the woods and meadows all night, he was on his way back to his den, when he stopped to rest. Suddenly a strange sound made him shiver, though he didn't know why. Drifting on the wind was a high sound coming nearer that sounded like some mysterious creature in pain. He hid in the undergrowth, to let this strange something go by, but as the sound grew louder, he realized what it was. He heard the garbled voices of many dogs and humans, and under it all, the thumping of muddy paws and the drumming of hooves. This terrible sound surrounded him, growing louder and nearer, and when he poked his head out of the undergrowth, he could see, in the distance, the most frightening sight he could imagine. Coming towards him was a gallery of furious faces of hunters and dogs, and their eyes were all focused on him, their minds all fixed on catching him.

He turned and ran, and they began chasing him across the open country, through and over hedges, racing through thorns and dense patches of nettles. As the dogs neared him, he wished he could just fly away. He ran and ran until the sound could be heard no more and the exhausted fox slowed down. Running blindly into the undergrowth, tripping over brambles and falling into the tangled growth, catching his coat on thorns and trying to tear himself free. But he felt trapped, without the strength to escape...

Suddenly he opened his eyes and woke up. He knew then he had been dreaming, though it had all seemed so real. When he tried to move, he realized he really was stuck in brambles. He must have run blindly into them when he was asleep, in the midst of the fearful dream. He slowly untangled himself from them and made it out into the soft grass. He felt so foolish now. Why had he let those old stories take such a hold on him? Even though his fears had been imaginary, his wounds and his pain were real.

When he looked about him, he did not know this country at all. He could recognize no landmarks around him and the scents were different to those he knew. He found himself in a place of rocky hollows and low hills with deep shadows between them. He made himself move through the pain, and he began to search for some safe place to hide away and recover. Finally, walking between two hills, his eye was drawn by a glint of quartz in the grass, and he found a small opening in the hillside. He sniffed and scented nothing but stone, so he made his way inside, to find a space that was a little cave, just big enough for him to curl up in. He gave in to sleep gratefully and drifted away. Every so often, nightmares of being chased woke him up abruptly, his body shaking and his mind seized by fears. But, each time, he quickly recalled that he was safe in the little cave and he let himself succumb to sleep again, and his terrors slowly faded away in the velvet darkness. Then there were moments when it seemed like there was a gentle light in the cave. He would have healing dreams in which he enjoyed watching delicate crystalline patterns taking form around him and changing.

He could not sense how long he spent in the cave, but when he eventually woke up, he had a burning thirst. Still, he was relieved that he did not feel the pain of the stings and scratches anymore, and he seemed to have healed quickly. When he came out of the opening, the sunlight outside seemed intensely bright and everything looked a little different to him. He searched about for something to drink. The best he could find was a muddy puddle, but before he could even wet his parched tongue, he stopped at the sight of his reflection. He was shocked to see how pale his face looked – until he realized his fur had turned completely white!

Staring at himself, he wondered how it had happened. The mystery of it held him, until he told himself he had best get home to familiar ground. And so he set off making his way through the undergrowth until he reached his old hunting ground. It was not far at all from the place of the cave, and he was surprised that he had never found the cave before on his rounds. By now, hunger burned inside him and he was even starting to acquire an odd taste for leaves. He was walking along a subtle path through the grass, when an egg rolled into his path. It was the color of the sky, as blue as can be, and for a moment, he imagined it had fallen from on high, right out of the blue to land before him. Maybe it was a gift from the sky to him! Maybe the sky knew how much he would love to be one with the birds and had sent him an egg to look after until it hatched. He could roll it into his den and keep it warm until then. Wouldn't it be a surprise to see a bird fly out of the earth! What a pair they would make, the fox and the fledgling...

But, after a moment or two, he came back to earth himself from his flight of fancy and thought it best to look for a more likely source for the egg. When he looked up, right overhead was an overhanging branch, but there was no nest on it. At the side of the path, however, was a bush, and when he poked his snout into it, there was the empty nest. When he looked down at the egg, it seemed so delicate, and he sensed there was something alive and moving inside it. He knew there was no way the parent could return it to the nest and there were hungry mouths hereabouts. So he picked up the egg in his jaws, as gently as he could, and placed it back into the nest. It was just a short way to his den from there, and when he came to the little hole hidden amongst the trees, it had never looked so welcoming. He slid down the entrance into his little home, into the den that he had dug out with his own paws. And he felt warm and safe there, he curled up to sleep and dream, for the earth felt warm to him and he found the darkness a comfort.

From then on, the patterns of his life were very different. His old fears seemed to have dissolved and he had a new vision that he was slowly getting used to. But there were moments when he felt rather out of season with the world. With his snow-white coat, he felt very conspicuous because, in daylight, it stood out against the green and, at night, it shone out against the dark of the forest and the bark of the trees. In the moonlight, he glowed. Some confused creatures, sighting him, would think he was the spirit of an ancestor who had come back to visit their old haunts, others would be convinced that snow was on the way. The wiser ones knew that he was a living sign that something very special was to happen in the forest, and they asked themselves what it was. And so they waited...

One morning, the fox awoke from a dream in his den, one of his rare dreams in the darkness. In the dream, he was dancing in the biggest clearing he had ever seen, a great circular open space. He was happily dancing there and, to his great surprise, there were humans there with him. They were dancing too, and they looked at him with eyes unlike any he had seen before, or even dreamed of. They were eyes that were not hard or full of anger or any kind of hate. These people smiled at him and danced with him. In fact, they were so beautiful that they looked a little like foxes! So he felt happy in their company, and they were obviously happy in his. They danced around and around the great clearing, in this great circle and he could see at the center of it, a glowing, radiant fire.

He was no great friend of fire, as he had heard tales of what it could do and how people sometimes used it to create damage in the forest. He knew that if you were chased by it and it caught you, it could consume you. So, in the dream, he wondered why he found the fire so beautiful and welcoming. But it seemed to be a very special kind of fire, and he found himself dancing around it and did not feel any fear within. As they danced round and around, he realized other animals were joining them and their circle was growing. The small animals came first, and these little ones wove their way between the legs of the people. And each of the creatures thought the humans looked a little like them, so they felt happy in their company.

Then the larger creatures arrived, including a deer who danced with the others. And then, to their surprise, a wolf appeared and did not lick his lips, but seemed to wear a wolfy kind of smile. He, too, entered the circle and joined in the dance around the fire. The wolf looked about and noticed how wolf-like all the creatures looked, and he was happy to dance with them. Finally, the shadow of a great bear was seen at the edge of the clearing. Some of the animals shuddered a little as they saw the tall silhouette. But, when the bear entered, she was already dancing! All the creatures laughed for joy as the great bear joined them and space was made for her, amongst all the other animals and humans. And all danced their own dance in the great circle, in this bright clearing with a radiant fire at the center. Up above them all, his brothers and sisters, the birds, circled like a turning wheel.

Suddenly, he woke from the dream, in the darkness. It was the first time he had realized it was a dream, so real it seemed. How vivid it had all been! He slowly stirred himself and uncurled his body, then went up the short tunnel. But this passage did not lead out; he found another tunnel at its end, then another turning and another. This was all so strange, and he felt quite odd and disorientated, so he was deeply relieved to see a glow of light up ahead. At last, it was an opening to the world outside.

He poked his nose out into the air and sniffed. He felt light on his eyelids and he stretched his head out into the cool air to wake himself. He came up from the tunnel and looked about him. Everything around him looked different. He had been careful to make his tunnel in a secret place in the forest, well camouflaged with undergrowth and leaves. The opening was hard to see, even to the eye of another fox. But now, as he looked around, he was in a great circular clearing! He wondered, how could this be? Had the humans come in the night and cleared away the trees? No, as he looked about he could see grass and plants growing with no sign of disturbance, as if the space had been here a long time. He felt a shiver at the mystery of it all. With great relief, he decided that he must be still dreaming, and he relaxed a little. For if this was all a dream and he was safe in his den, even if anything frightening happened, no harm could really come to him. He looked around, but could see no hint of danger, there were only the trees with their glowing leaves, and the sunlight filtering through them. And, under his feet, were leaves of gold and brown and red – including the familiar tones of a fox's fiery coat. He stepped out into the clearing and noticed a small hole like a bowl in the center.

It reminded him of his earlier dream. He began to walk around the space and then to skip slightly. Soon, as he felt the lightness in his feet, he started to dance and to roll on the earth, to spin and chase his own beautiful tail, waving it high, without a care. And then to leap high in the air, skipping high like a young lamb. His leaps became higher and higher and he began to yelp and make noises he did not know he could create. His own voice sounded strange to him now, but wonderful. Round and round he went, and only then did he realize that he could see many eyes – eyes all around him, in amongst the trees. Eyes of all sizes and colors, at different heights and behind the eyes were shadows of different shapes and dimensions; there seemed to be a whole gathering behind the veil of leaves.

He stopped dancing, frozen to the spot by the old fear. He could not move a muscle until he remembered that this is *his* dream and they are sharing it with him. So he releases the fear and starts to dance again, the creatures all stepped forward, one by one, into the clearing to join him. The small animals first, coming through the undergrowth. The squirrels skipped, the frogs hopped and all the little creatures came out to dance. Then the larger ones, including the deer, stepped forward. All seemed calm, gentle and peaceful. Even when the wolf stepped forward, he seemed to have a foxy look in his eye. None of them seemed frightening to him now. Even when the great big bear stepped out and cast her giant shadow into the clearing, he was surprised he felt no fear.

So he slowly began to move and then to dance again. And, to his joy, the other animals joined in, the smaller animals first, then the deer and the wolf, and then they made a big space for the bear and she joined them. Above the circle, the birds of all kinds wheeled, weaving in between each other, their songs harmonizing in a glorious chorus. The fox felt great happiness in his heart, that he was able to dream the same dream twice. He felt them all united and the circle seemed to be one, going round and around until, all of a sudden, the creatures in front of him stopped dancing. They looked around them to see, amongst the leaves, another circle of eyes watching. These were all around the same height this time, and the shadows they knew were those of humans. Some yelps of fear went around the circle, and a murmur that became louder when the people stepped forward into the clearing. But they seemed different from the humans they had heard of or imagined. In their faces, they looked a little like the animals. They somehow seemed friendly and familiar now, their eyes seemed soft and the creatures found their fear fading away.

The fox remembered again that this was *his* dream and they were all sharing it, and he began to dance again. Then, the little animals joined him, the squirrels skipped and the frogs hopped, then the larger ones joined in, the deer and wolf too, until finally the bear began to stomp her way around the circle. And these unusual humans smiled, then they laughed out loud and they cheered even louder. At that moment, the great big bear made a space in front of her for one of the people to enter. The human stepped forward and took her place in the circle, and then the deer made a space in front of her, and another of the people took his place. Then each of the creatures made a space, until all of the people had joined the circle and were dancing in their own way. Not as gracefully as the animals, maybe, but in their happy, human way. And the animals thought that some of the humans must have been watching them and learning their dances, for they did have some of their animal grace and elegance. Round and round they went, and the circle became more lively, full of laughter and joking, songs and chants, the cries of the creatures and their yelps of joy. The fiery leaves fly around them, whipped up by the whirling wind they create.

Then they noticed a small glimmer of a flame rising in the center of the circle. Like a tiny candle-flame, it flickered up from the earth. Then it grew, opening out into a small handful of dancing flames, which began to fill the hole in the earth until it was a bowlful of bright fire. And the animals marveled at the beauty of the fire that they had shunned in the past. They were entranced by the beauty of its joyful dance, its grace and power, and the warmth it gave them. They felt no fear as the flames danced higher and the animals and Humans leaped higher, too. Their hearts danced even higher, as all became one great circle around the fire in the earth, the flame at the heart of the circle, the heart of the dance.

Some wondered who had made the fire and why was it so healing. And why had it suddenly come to life? They only knew that they were healing together, as the circle grew stronger and the fire grew hotter and danced higher with ever-greater energy. The fox was pleased to see that even he looked fiery red again and he waved his tail high, like a flame. Then he realized he really had transformed! His coat, once more, was as earthy red as the fieriest leaf, in fact, even fierier than before. Far into the night, they all danced. Until, when finally they could dance no more, they each made a space for themselves and went to sleep around the fire in a great circle, curled up amongst each other, sharing their warmth and the warmth of the fire, which still glowed brightly.

And as the fox drifted off to sleep, he realized that this surely could not have been a dream – he must have been awake all the time. So where was this magical place? Or was this a special daydream, a vision of some kind? Would he wake up in the circle of all the creatures or into another dream? Sometimes it was so hard to tell what was a dream and what was real! But, whatever his future held, he knew he would never feel hunted again. He wondered what he would really dream about, as he drifted into the warmth of the darkness, by the light of the fire…

And when the fox opened his eyes in his dream, he was on the back of a beautiful, brightly colored bird, whose wings stretched out on either side of him. The egg of the Earth was below, rolling past in all her glory, and the fox laughed with such delight that he almost woke himself up!

The Call of the Wild has been heard in the hearts of the city-dwellers.

It is the Cry of the Forest, the Music of the Rivers. In the hearts of the house-dwellers, there are secret murmurings, ancient songs are faintly heard, and whispers of old stories, older than time.

The Tribe is remembering itself, the Elders are awakening. The leaders are being called forth to take their places which have been waiting for them a long time. They step forth from the shadows, they blink in the light. They see the faces watching them and, with a shock, realize that they are the focus of attention, that others are looking to them. Some of them feel they did not ask for this task, which seems such a heavy one. Others feel a lightness in their hearts or a fire, bursting again into life.

They seem to know things they should not know. They see images and wonder from where they came. They see the familiar in the strange and the strange in the familiar. They find the pieces of the puzzle in their daily lives and start to put them together; they see the greater picture. They hold a sense of unity somewhere within them, a unity they feel is forming and which they are part of. After a time, they find they have no sense of separation or isolation. They feel their hearts joining with the hearts of others in the great task. They feel their hearts starting to dance in the rhythm of the great dance of the circles, the circles which make one Circle, the great dance of One, the dance of Unity.

With the animals they dance, with the trees they dance, with the winds and the waters, with the fire and the light. They dance on the mountains, they dance in the valleys, they dance in the streets, they dance in the old places and the new, they dance in the dark places and they dance in the light. They will dance with strangers and make them friends. They will take the hands of strangers in peace and leave them as friends. They will hold no sorrow for what seems lost for they know that more will be gained and more beyond that. For the past was the Now as the now is the Now and the future will be the

Now as All is Now. And nothing is truly lost. Even that which is no longer needed goes to a safe space and there resides in the Heart of the Creator.

And so we are lightened for the dance, our bodies are made light and fire, our minds are made clear air. Our heart beats with the Heart of the Earth and our hearts echo within her, as hers echoes within ours. We will then be One Heart, one love, one body, one spirit, one mind and one wisdom. The one of many, the many of one. We hold no hate in our hearts and we hold no sorrow there, the anger is washed away in the crystal waters of the Earth, and the crystal brightness of the Light.

The Old Ones will be young again and the Elders will be as babes, the children of Earth and Sky. These are the reapers of the new harvest, the harvest of spiritual fruits of every color and flavor. All will be good and all will be One. What is rotten will be renewed and made fresh again, as the One Spirit is made flesh and the flesh is made spirit. And all will dance within the One, will dance the Earth Dance, which is the Dance of the Universes, which is the dance of the shared future. All will Come Home and their homecoming has begun. All will Come Home to the Heart and the homecoming begins there.

❧

Good news! We bring good news. We are happy to be here to bring you news of a gathering, far away it would seem in time and space, but still among neighbors, though distant to you. They, and we, have gathered, for we have heard of the events on your planet in some of its dimensions. For some of the ripples reach us through what some call the Etheric Web. Other events, we observe ourselves from our safe distance. We do not interfere, nor do we pry where we are not wanted. But we watch the unfolding of those events that we feel will have an impact on us at some stage. For as your peoples grow and change, their growth – and sometimes their lack of it – has effects that are sometimes unforeseen in your world, and yet they are real to us. As you have been told, the Web is fine and strong and, through it, all are connected to the One.

We, too, feel the ripples and the waves when they reach us. This often takes what would seem a very little time. Although we would appear to have no direct connection with your world, we have known of it and been interested in its development for a long time. And we hold you in great respect for the strides you have made, and for the learning you have made for yourselves. And the teachings, which you could give to others by your example. For we can all learn from each other, and we can all be teachers in our own way.

We do have much to share for, as worlds, we have been through many parallel experiences, some of which have touched each other through the Etheric Web. Many worlds, as you suspect, observe yours – though this observation has different intents and intensities. Some have but a vague interest, others keenly observe to see how events in your world may affect them. For some feel threatened and others are simply concerned. They hope you will not make the same "mistakes" that they have made in their past. As we are all brothers and sisters in the One, a learning is shared even when it is not intended to be, for minds and hearts are linked across the illusions of time and space. We have no real sense of separation from you; you are next door and we are in the next room. The doorway between us is thin and the lock on the door can be quite easily opened if one really wants to – when it is wise to do so.

We are grateful for this opportunity to speak to you from inside your room for a while as we learn simply by being here; we are also grateful for the peace we feel here and the love that is given to us. We are, in our ways, quite different from you, though such things of course are relative and trivial in the scheme of things, and beyond things. We have no great taste for adventure as the humans do. We are, perhaps, a little boring from your point of view!

We know well the sense of adventure in the human heart and this is one of its gifts. When used wisely, this can open you to new experiences and pleasures. Through this gift, you glimpse the new worlds; you stand on their borders and do not feel the fear that others might. This sense of adventure seems to drive you along, and though, of course, it has led to some terrible events, it is not to be thrown away. It is not something to be ashamed of; it was a gift created for you to explore. It will be useful to you in the future. Maybe we, too, will pick up a little of this sense, and when we encounter each other, we may both meet as adventurers, as mutual explorers – and as friends, we hope – meeting in a mutual sense of peaceful curiosity, meeting in a space of shared love and openness. For as events unfold on your planet, they impact on many worlds.

We wish you only well in your development. There is little indeed that we can do to help you, as it would not be right or wise for us to intervene in your affairs. But we can share with you our thoughts and our love and a little of our experiences. Through this sharing, we will grow to know one another. For we all may sit at the one table as equals and friends as we do now, with many of many worlds. In the Councils of Oneness and Wisdom, in the circles of listening, in what have been called the spaces of play and exploration. In these zones of freedom, we will meet – sooner, perhaps, than you think. Then we will meet again, heart to heart. We look forward to this little adventure that is part of the greater adventure of which we are all a part.

We pledge to play our role honestly and sincerely in a sense of friendship and shared development. There will be no hidden agendas, no hints of domination. There will be togetherness, a brotherhood and sisterhood of unity, no more and no less. And we wait for that day. With Peace.

The Great Rainbow Snake unwinds in her cave deep within the Earth. She uncoils her body and senses the air. The Earth is warm all around her. She is in the womb of the Earth, her Mother in turn, as she, herself, is a Mother. For she guards the egg, which came from the Earth, and, within the cave, she keeps it whole and warm with her body. She gives it the warmth from her heart while her eyes watch for any sign of danger, so that the egg will be safe. So that what it holds within it, will sleep in peace.

She has been a Guardian a long time. Oh, since the Earth was young and green and watery blue. Since the Earth melted and rolled, since her seas rose and fell, since her mountains danced like happy children on the horizon. Since then this Snake has slept and wakened many times, sometimes a long sleep, a deep, deep slumber, when she knew that was what Mother Earth wished. She knew then the great egg was to be kept safe, was to be guarded more closely and its energies contained with her coils, tight around it. For she holds the energy and all the great potentials within. Within the egg, the energies pulsate, they are always flowing, always moving. There are within it, vast stores of energies which, if released, would radiate through the worlds.

There, the great secrets are hidden. There, in the recesses of the great egg, are stories and lores, the knowledge of the worlds before, the Wisdoms of many realms. There are crystal wisdoms, wisdoms of the Earth and her living waters, secrets of all the Star Hearts and of her great Star Heart. Within the egg, all is waiting, all is alive. If you could glimpse in, you would be blinded by the Wisdoms there into an instant Enlightenment.

But, of course, what is there may seem beyond you now. Yet all will be revealed when the Maker wills it. And in the mean-Now, the Serpent awakes... Her long wait is over. She unravels slowly, she reveals more of the egg, and, as she releases her grip, more of the energies within are released, flowing into the body of the Earth. There is more than one great egg and more than one Snake is awakening. So the Wisdom will be returning...

As the world turns on and on, a little more of the light will escape and be released back into the Earth, to radiate outwards to the stars. Those who wish to receive it may open themselves to it. For this too is the great Snake Wisdom of the Earth Keeper, the Deep Dweller, the sleeper beneath the Earth who rises when she is willed, and when the Earth wishes. And she rises through the levels, up through the belly of the Earth, up and up, then through her skin out onto the surface of Her body. Out into the light of the Sun and the Moon. Ah, how she rejoices! Her great coils soak in the light and renew their energy, drinking in the heat and light, the Wisdom of Sun and Moon filling her, and the Earth beneath her, receiving that which flows through her. Across the Earth, she snakes her way, healing as she goes. Healing places of hurt and pain, zones of conflict, places where the Earth has been broken and bleeds. She does her work and lives her joy.

The time when the Serpents return is a time of a great coming, the return of the Wisdom of the worlds half-forgotten. For the Serpent is wise and her path is not straight, but wide, and it returns and returns to the Center. It can lead us on the way back to the Center, to our own heart's center and the Center of the Earth. We can work with her, we can dance with her as she dances through the world. As she slides across the Earth, we, too, can dance the Snake Dance, and feel our snaky side wake up. Feel our muscles and remember their wisdom, their snake-ways. We feel our bodies revive the Snake Wisdom that is buried within them in an egg of light.

For within our body, as the Ancients knew, is a serpent of light. As our body unwinds its Snake Wisdom, our body remembers and we loosen up, we find ourselves making the spiral with our very bodies; our arms, our fingers, our spines, our hips. We feel the snake rise within, uncoiling itself, rising from the egg of Light and, from this egg, it will release the Light, returning it to our heart. We will feel the heat rise within our heart, then the Light rise from our heart. And as the sparks of Light reach our mind, there they spark our memories and we dance the ancient dance.

Our bodies will flow like liquid across the Earth and our old stiffness will be forgotten. We too will do our healing work, our dancing across the face and body of the Earth. And with the Great Snake Mother we will dance as her Snake Children, as Earth Healers. We will again slip into our snake-skins, the shimmering Rainbow scales of the great Snake of the Earth. And we will dance with her in joy, spiraling around and coiling out, releasing the energies, bringing them back to the Earth to warm and revitalize her body. We look forward to dancing with you soon, Sisters and Brothers of the Rainbow Snake, the Great Earth Serpent...

The Snake is awake!

☯

So many Stones of the Earth have slept a long day and a long night. For a long time, as it is measured, many of the Stone Beings have slumbered on the surface of the Earth or beneath her skin. Some have done their work as before, or adapted to the changing circumstances. Some have been scattered, others destroyed; some have forgotten their purpose. For they, too, sleep and dream.

And sometimes, on waking, they forget where they are or how they got there.

But the Stone Beings wish to be useful again, to do their work, to dance their slow dance with the stars and with the planets, with the peoples of the Earth and her realms, and the other worlds beyond. Those that are waking now wish to be connected with and they wish to be reconnected to the Great Work. For the Earth Herself is wakening in new ways, the aspects of the Earth are remembering and playing with each other and their old connections. Just as the beings of the Earth are following a similar process, so they are being united within themselves and with each other. So the Earth is piecing herself back together again. Her fragmentation, the damage that was inflicted, the great calamities are being healed. Many, many beings have united in this work.

You, too, are called to this work and this joy. And if you wish to join the work you will know your own role by looking within and reading what is written within your own heart. For you chose your role before you entered this world, and you chose your freedom, so now the choice is yours. If you choose to work and play here, to be part of the great healing and reconnection, the great re-weaving, then you have chosen well. For the work will bring you a greater joy than anything else you could imagine, and the benefits this work will bring to the beings of this world and others is beyond measure.

So it is with enormous pleasure that we welcome you to the task, if that is what you have chosen. We look forward to playing and co-creating with you in many spaces and lands. For the Stones of the Earth are calling to us again. In greater numbers, they find their voices, their vibrations grow louder and stronger. They can now sing with greater ease; they can hear us, and we, them, with greater clarity. A great choir is assembling on the Earth – the living frequencies are uniting. They are being woven back into a seamless tapestry.

A great choral Song of Joy has begun; a great multi-layered oratorio, a story-telling. A song cycle woven from the cycle of frequencies of all the beings of Earth and all the worlds beyond, a great hymn of the joy of life and healing. By healing our home that is the Earth, we help heal so many other worlds. For as the Earth goes, so go many other worlds. So the great re-weaving brings the frequencies closer together and the harmony of color and tone becomes closer and more unified. You will be able to hear and see the unity in action. We will see the effects of the singing in Unity. A song of Tree and Stone, of Earth and Sky, of human and every creature will unify into one great Chant of Creation, one wonderful Rainbow-weave of Unity, the music of living Creation. What a choir it will be!

If you wish to join, there is a space for you, for we have kept one free – as you asked us to. Your voice will have perfect pitch and the Universes will sing with you in a perfect Harmony. And we will not be in the audience, but on the stage, all of us, for this great Oratorio of Creation. The audience will be the other worlds, the galaxies of sisters and brothers.

Our song will sing through the dimensions, and our song itself will weave the dimensions together. The awareness of Oneness will be manifested in the most beautiful way imaginable. What joy it will be!

The Flame and the Shadow

There was once a flame who danced her way through the world.
Oh, how she danced! When she burst out into the dark, she lit up all around her. She made a delightful, joyous dance of freedom; she leapt and pirouetted, she spiraled and twirled. She flickered lightly through the world, always just keeping her connection to the body of the Earth beneath her, for she remembered this was the home she flowed from.

She had many fiery friends whom she loved, though few could dance as beautifully as she. And they loved to watch her as she danced for them. She was proud of how lightly she could step on the Earth. She loved to invent new fiery steps to impress and please her friends and they would be sure to try them out as soon as they could.

At night especially, the flames loved to dance as they shone out more brightly then. They could see each other more clearly, too, and they would be accompanied by wonderful shadows that were part of the dance. They enjoyed dancing with their shadows, and they became close friends with them. The shadows also loved to dance with the flames, and sometimes they learnt from each other, as the shadows imitated the flames and followed them, and the flames saw themselves reflected. For shadow-dances are beautiful, too, and some of those who watched the fire-dances would notice them, as they added to the beauty of the spectacle. But, over time, our friend, the dancing flame, grew jealous of her shadow, this one who followed her every move so exactly, who always seemed to be behind her, copying her, imitating her every step. And sometimes she would imagine her shadow was dancing better than she could herself, and this would make her angry. Then the flame would make a dance of rage, and blaze out angrily, daring her shadow to dance as furiously as her and be as fiery as she was.

One night, she decided that she would enjoy dancing more if she could lose her shadow and dance on her own. Then she could dance solo for the onlookers, and those who gathered to watch her beautiful dances in the night, or who watched her in the hearth of their homes could see her in her true glory. So she made up her mind to break free from her shadow and dance alone from then on. She knew she did not need that shadow – surely it was the shadow who needed her. For she was fire and she was free and she was beautiful. Her shadow, meanwhile, seemed dark and ugly compared to her. It did not even have the graceful shape that she did; shadow was lightless, lacking form and dimensions, and could only slither over surfaces. She would show that she was the greater dancer and that her shadow was but a crude imitation. So she told her shadow to go and leave her forever – to leave her to dance alone. Her shadow was saddened, for she knew they would both be alone now, but she did as the flame asked her. Darkly, she slid around a corner and disappeared from sight. And the flame made her heart as cold as fire can be, so she would not feel sorry for her lonely shadow. She looked to the future, now that she had broken free. She felt liberated, and she enjoyed the exhilaration of release.

That night she danced in the hearth of a little home where a few people were gathered. One person was huddled over the fireplace, trying to make her appear, but the flame delayed her appearance to create greater expectation. Then in a bright blaze of light, she appeared, showering sparks all around her, dancing so wildly that the people watching jumped back with fright. She danced a wild and violent dance of freedom that entranced those who watched her dance around her little stage. The wood beneath her crackled and banged, in rhythms that excited her and spurred her on.

As the fascinated family watched her, she could see the amazement in their faces when she flashed out her heat and light, and she danced on her wooden stage, climbing ever higher, burning the wood away beneath her with her fiery presence. For she wanted to dance like a Rainbow Flame, the brightest of all living flames. She danced and danced, until she began to tire a little, but still she did not want to leave, for she could see she held the audience enthralled. She could sense the surprise of the onlookers at every new color she displayed, every new movement she made. So, on and on, she danced until her wooden stage was burnt away into ash.

She began to feel her strength flagging, but she did not want to leave. She could feel the fatigue overcome her and those who watched saw her seem to fade and die. She summoned all her strength and danced on as best she could, still flickering and moving, making her weak flame of a body dance as beautifully as she could, though her heart was weakening. She felt herself begin to faint and, little by little, she began to lose consciousness. She could feel herself sinking down into the black ash. She felt her colors fading, the faces of those in front of her disappearing into darkness. She felt the dark wrap around her and she could not fight it for her strength was gone, so she had to surrender to it.

Gradually, she felt a kind of peace, knowing that she had danced to the end of her strength and danced perhaps more beautifully than any flame ever had. She had shone more brightly and created more spectacular colors than any other flame. She had given more warmth than any flame of her slender size ever had, but now she knew she must rest so she felt herself sink into the darkness, which welcomed her. Though she was sad to know she could no longer even see herself, and her form had disappeared, for here there was no form, only darkness.

She seemed to be there a long time before she could feel herself changing, and it seemed she was transforming slowly, becoming something other. She felt differently now; she felt at peace, though she no longer felt like fire

– she felt like something new. After a while she began to enjoy a new sensation, a new freedom she seemed to have, now that she had accepted where she was and what she was becoming. Then she realized that she was beginning to dance again. She felt herself dance within the darkness. She knew then she had not disappeared, but only changed her nature. Here she was still dancing, still expressing herself, feeling the pleasure of the dance. Though no one observed her, she did not need anyone to watch her now. She danced for the pleasure of the dance and enjoyed exploring its possibilities.

After a while, she felt another change take place. This time, she was aware of sensing something around her, something that was familiar swirling around her. It seemed to be forms and colors, like those she had once known. The forms slowly took on shapes and colors that she recognized very clearly. The moment came that she realized where she was. This was the world she had once been part of, and here she was again, renewed. Now she was a living shadow. She felt the urge to dance rise within her and dance she did, out into the world, expressing herself again, turning and leaping, a pirouetting silhouette.

As she danced on through the world, she sensed that she was searching for someone or something. Though she felt her freedom within herself, she wanted someone to dance with, for she was a shadow and she longed to dance with a flame. So she searched and searched, but each flame she came across already had a shadow and she knew she would have to find another. She searched on until, one dark night, as she made her way through the other shadows, she came to a windowpane that had a lovely glow on the other side. She looked through the glass, and she saw a flame dancing in a hearth. It was a single Rainbow Flame, very bright and dancing in rainbow colors, shining out a fiery light. And she noticed it had no shadow!

Watching the lively flame was an old man and woman, who were warming themselves, and enjoying the bright display as the flame shared its gifts. The shadow made her way to the door and slid under it. Unseen, she moved through the small room to stand beside the fire, so she could enjoy its dance, too. How she longed for even one dance, since she could tell they would move well together. She was fascinated by the beauty of this flame, and when she could no longer contain herself, she began to dance by the fireside. To her surprise, the flame beckoned her forward, so she stepped up onto the logs. She began to dance with the flame, and they moved in a perfect harmony, as if they had always been partners. They danced for joy and life and togetherness. And the old grandmother and grandfather noticed the new arrival and how well the two moved together, the fire-flame and the dark-flame.

On into the night, they watched their dance, the flame and the shadow dancing as one. Sometimes embracing, sometimes joining at their base, and when they touched, sparks flew. Theirs was a dazzling, passionate dance, and the earth became heated beneath them. Suddenly the shadow felt something burst open, and a spark ignited within her. She felt a fiery love for life flow through her, and she begin to transform, as colors poured out of her and light blazed from her heart. The two who watched had never seen such a beautiful flame – such colors she had! Oranges, blues, violets, a hint of pink; amongst the reds, a deepest crimson, and a pure, white flash amongst the gold. Her partner grew taller and brighter, too, and they danced on as twin flames, making the one light together.

The old ones watched the lively dance in their open hearth late into the night, until their eyes closed and they fell into sleep. The last image they held was the beauty of unity in their dance. And, as they drifted into dreaming, their old hearts were warmed.

We call to you from the crystal hills.

We of the Faerie Realms sing to you from the hollows of hills and the hearts of mountains.

You may have heard our hearts calling to you. You know us better than you may remember. Even if you seem to have forgotten us, we know who you are. When you have seemed shattered, we have held the pieces of your deepest dream. And when you know you are whole, we celebrate. We hold the knowing of humanity's inner dimensions and Earth's hidden worlds, her inner realms. Like us, they exist just beneath the surface of human awareness, just beyond the veil of popular perception. We have a reality beyond the images painted by the human imagination, one that is ancient and pre-dates the appearance of the human form and being.

There are places where our worlds can meet. These can be created or found, or they might find you! If you wish to find them, you may discover them off the well-worn tracks in quiet corners. What appears to be an insignificant corner of the world might hold a deep secret. Most will walk past, unaware, but a few will hear the call or sense a presence. Of course, they may be seeking you and you may find them waiting nearer and sooner than you expect. Through the flower-portals, one may enter the inner realms. The being of a tree holds a doorway to the deep; the heart of a tree holds open secrets.

Most portals have become veiled through lack of use, or sometimes intentionally, but even when they are exposed as plain as day, human perception will usually not allow them to be recognized. Yet human beings hold the keys within them, though few have used them in a long time. The key to them all is hidden in your heart, which holds all keys, codes and combinations. With a truly open heart, you can enter and be welcome anywhere. You can travel the realms of Earth as a free spirit.

We will hold the doors open for human beings; we welcome all who come with honesty, love and good intent. We have nothing to hide from the peaceful heart. To the open mind, we hold no secrets. The awakened human has access to all areas of the planet, while those who are not awakened and clarified will not find what they seek in the first place. If they are too dense to move and flow, they will not make it through the barriers of their own illusions. Any heavy agendas will weigh down the seeker and make the passage almost impossible. The overloaded mind or the swollen ego will not fit through the opening, so they might not hold a mental memory of the event, since they are simply left behind. There are no forbidden, secret places except those deemed so by humans themselves. If you are unsure of how to behave, remember you are going to meet relations... We hold no animosity towards humanity, despite the tangles and trials of history. Some of us are cautious when it comes to individuals, as it can be difficult to read their intent for hidden purposes. Yet the hand of friendship is the greatest bridge between worlds and the look of love crosses all barriers of understanding.

Portals are more than gateways or revolving doors; they can hold many purposes. They can be the crossroads of pathways of light, the weaving point of the light-threads, gathering places for beings of many realms. Here, the dimensions knit together, so they are the meeting-places of the planes, points where space and time turn corners, where worlds meet and merge together, or shift into another reality. They can be places of transformation, for all that enters through such a portal is transformed by the experience, subtly or dramatically. Often, the traveler will unravel the puzzle as they move through the maze, for they activate the space as they approach and then pass through it. They, themselves, were the key that the space was awaiting. The portal will recognize them, as will those who hold the space, and they will be able to help the traveler make the transition. A light, playful approach works wonders, coupled with a sense of openness and collaboration.

To communicate with those who may hold the portal, make your intentions clear as you approach. Once fear is left outside the door, the passage is easier and what is experienced can be truly enjoyed. The light within the inner worlds is revealed clearly, once we take off the dark glasses of the past. Then we can step beyond fear and misunderstanding into the unknown realms. These are places to enter only with love and wonder.

Some of the portals appear like closed or sleeping flowers, petal folded upon petal. These are the petals of each dimension folded within the others, each one unique and separate, yet connected at their source. They may seem wrapped up tight, yet they hold great light within. If you wish this light to be released, release yourself from the constraints of the mundane world and leave old belongings and baggage outside the entrance, where they can be collected later, if need be. The portal itself may seem a tangled maze, an unsolvable puzzle. The unfolding and unwrapping of dimensions seems a complex mental task, a truly mind-bending one, but it is child's play to the heart. Returning into innocence awakens the inner knowing. We need the lightheartedness of a child opening a gift, blended with the maturity and wisdom to know why we wish to enter a portal and reveal its potentials. Then the portals will seem to unravel themselves. And a human can move through even what seems a thin crack or a tiny opening, once they have lightened themselves enough.

We of the Fae, we of the Shee (Sidhe) flow together in the Crystal Circle with many beings of the Inner Earth. We connect the surface and the depths, we bridge where there are gaps in the flows of life and communication. We can be the bridges between human beings and those who dwell deep within. We can introduce you to old friends in deep places.

We, who dwell within the Earth's crystal realms, greet you. We bring you the Light of Inner Earth.

Mother Earth does not deny her own children. She welcomes them all and awaits their return to awareness of her. Within her body are forgotten places, gathering-spaces that await the return of the human presence, that wish to resonate again with the heartbeat of joyous human souls. There are chambers made for celebration, which have been silent too long; great caves carved by the water and fire of love, which have too long stood empty. There are forests of countless crystal trees that stretch through the inner worlds, which will echo, once more, to human laughter and the songs of homecoming. These are deep-rooted crystal forests of old growth, nurtured by the light from Earth's Inner Sun and the filtered light of the Sun above, so they are doubly nourished. There was a time when humans walked though these crystal groves and swam in streams and lakes of crystalline water. Soon the vitality of the inner ecosystems of the Earth will be revealed

Now the crystal web of the planet is opening, and life-flows from deep within are rising to the surface. As the crystal lattice opens its weave, more of the inner light will be released to mingle with the light of the Sun. As these two solar energies meet and blend with elemental energies in the crystal web, they will create a new vitality. Life will revive where it has been damaged or exhausted and ancient seeds will be reawakened. Now the very soil is lightening and the Earth-energies are awakening so that new life will rise.

Within the crystal realms, beings are meeting face to face and heart to heart for the first time in a long time. We have entered a phase of revival and reunion, and there is a letting-go of old rivalries and conflicts with a few of humankind. As the inner weave and the outer world connect and grow closer together, new patterns of communication will emerge. New ways of living will be possible, more in tune with the deepest yearnings of the Earth for harmony between all. The ancient sacred sites are being joined by numerous new ones, which are connecting in new patterns, releasing exciting potentials for global communication and healing. Many sacred sites are related to formations within the planet, as well as reflecting those of the stars, so they embody earth's inner patterns as much as the star patterns. More people are remembering how to make places peaceful and sacred again, if these have been abused or damaged. This is another reason for our rejoicing.

Even we, who are lighter in nature, are opening in new light, while more humans every day open a little, so that the delicate and subtle voices can be heard. Those people who begin to feel the rays of the Inner Sun touch them will awaken to ancient memories and find themselves drawn to discover their source. More people, instead of looking out into space and its mysteries, will look into the mysteries beneath their feet, into the neglected depths of their home planet. Just as divers are discovering unknown life deeper and deeper in the oceans, so those who remember how to dive into Earth's inner dimensions will find even greater surprises and return with news of even stranger discoveries.

To explore hidden dimensions, it is not necessary to reach into the depths of space, invent expensive machinery or use elaborate instruments. These realms are much closer to home, and you are already equipped for the task of unraveling their secrets. They surround you, they exist beneath you and within you, so one does not have to quest elsewhere, one does not even have to reach out or take a single step. Simply open your awareness to your true nature, to your own multidimensionality. Your educated personality may have difficulty with the concept, but this is such a miniscule, superficial aspect of your true self that it need not be a barrier to discovering your unseen dimensions. It may limit your expression of the truths revealed, but at least you will have had the experiences, and more of their flavor may filter through over time, if you remain open.

You will reveal hidden dimensions within your own being, as well as in the shared reality of Earth and beyond. By healing any rifts within your being, bridging any gaps in your awareness, you become closer to knowing your own wholeness. And humanity, as the one being it truly is, moves closer to knowing its own nature. A fresh vision of humanity's potential will arise, one that recognizes its unity with the source of all life and its divine role as a unifying agent between all realms. For the awakened human being, in their global view of reality, recognizes the connections and relationships between all forms of life. This was a divine gift, one that is not yet truly remembered, yet not fully forgotten either. Once old egos, personas and roles are thrown away, there is so much more to be enjoyed in real life! The real world waits beyond the inherited inhibitions and social illusions. We wait at the doorways for your approach. We listen for the beating of your heart.

Now, if you lighten yourself, we can enter through one of these portals. What ~~A SPECIAL~~ appears to be a beautiful flower bud on a long stem reaches up from within the Earth. It turns to face you, reaching towards the sun of your heart. If you unfold your own heart's delicate petals, the face of your sun within is revealed as your heart opens. Now the heart of the flower before you opens to the sun shining within you. This unfolding flower opens its petals in radiant patterns while, at the center of the glowing geometries, its heart shines.

Face to face, the two heart flowers are beaming with love, reaching out threads of light into each other. As our love flows down these threads of light, we flow also, moving now towards this sun-heart. Its love enfolds us and its patterns of light surround us as we flow into it. We begin moving down its long stem, into the Earth, flowing down a crystal tube that grows wider as we move through it. Our body of light unfolds its form around us, and we open like a star, unfolding our inner patterns. We move at the speed of love through this glowing tube until we notice an opening ahead of us.

We flow through it into a realm of living crystal. We arrive in a landscape of breathtaking beauty, and we look out of our crystal eyes at this strange, but marvelous realm. Everywhere, we see crystal in formations and patterns, within a landscape suffused with crystalline light. Its rivers flow with liquid crystal, shimmering with light from above that filters through layers like crystalline clouds. The very air here is crystalline; if we reach out into it, it reacts subtly to our every movement, making gentle ripples and swirls. The air seems alive with a shimmering music and the air, as it caresses us, even seems to be aware of our presence. At the edge of a trickling stream, we take a drink from these waters. They enliven and refresh us. What a magical realm we have found! We know we will return here in the future.

Fabulous beings, who glow with inner light, move through this world. In the distance, a bright being beckons to us to follow them. We find ourselves following a path laid out before us. It leads towards a large doorway in the distance, beneath an archway. As we near it, we notice the door has a pearlescent shimmer and, before we reach it, it opens wide to us. Beyond it, is another, smaller door of a different iridescent pattern that also opens to us. We find a brighter door behind it, just taller than we are, that opens to reveal a long corridor beyond. Its walls glow with crystalline light and, while we move down it, we realize every surface acts like a mirror. We find ourselves reflected in our dazzling form of crystal beauty. As we pass through the corridor of mirrors, facets of our many reflections are shown to us. If we reach out to these reflections, they stretch out to us and our light returns to us. Some surprising forms smile back at us when we smile, and we marvel at the diversity of our reflections. Down this gallery of our aspects we move, until we find our guide before us, standing before a door of black obsidian.

Our guide steps back, passing through the wall, so we are alone before this door. Yet we notice no reflection in its surface; it reveals nothing to us. For a moment, we ask if there is a door there at all or simply a void. But when we stretch out to touch it, there is something there that even our light cannot penetrate. Then, very slowly, our living light begins to make an image on this door until, like a photograph appearing, an image emerges from the darkness. It composes itself into a reflection we may or may not recognize, one we may not want to see. Yet it reaches out to us and we reach out to it and, as our fingertips touch, suddenly the image is transformed to become a true reflection and we see a mirror before us. Then the mirror melts away as the door opens. Beyond is a MISTY space and our light reaches into it, searching. In the distance, there is a bright point of light we know we must move towards.

So we step into THE MIST, WHICH FEELS LOVELY, to find our every step is supported as we pass through it. Our light stretches ahead of us, towards our destination, which has grown into an opening from which light pours. As we move close to it, our shining image is reflected in its surface. Now it is as if our light melts the door for the way opens to us and from the opening, light pours out. We move through the opening into an open space, a domed cave of great height, arching above us.

Crystalline arches are stretching up, rising above us, into a high, majestic dome. At its center, is an opening from which light is pouring, flowing down in a broad beam, while light flows up from an opening in the center of the floor. Around the walls, bright beings are appearing, who we feel are ancient guardians. As we move towards the column at the center, we notice the light is spiraling up as well as down, the light-spirals are mingling and exchanging flows between them. Within the beam, the energies spiral and circulate; these are the essences of human life, flowing in liquid light. Now, from the open circle below, multicolored light floods up to the ceiling, stretching out in

every direction, lighting up the space. The walls reflect this light until the
sacred space is transformed into a radiant rainbow dome. The light itself is
filled with singing tones, so the dome is ringing now with light and sound.

Now we notice what seems like a glittering diamond seed suspended in
the flow of light. Its brilliance grows until it becomes like a large egg-shaped
gem, glittering with facets. Then its light pulses out even more brightly and a
new and familiar form emerges; a shining skull of brilliant, crystalline light,
a Mother Skull of ancestral love and ancient memories, a Keeper of Dreams.
Rainbow beams reach up from her crown like a fountain and reach high, the
light inside it intensifies in brightness until we see a face and a form beginning to emerge within the light. As the light crystallizes, a being of true beauty reveals her radiant face; the face of an Angel in human form. A glowing
body of light begins to take shape and a being of crystalline light is revealed.
Her face is shining with tender love as she smiles and greets us. She knows
who we are and we recognize her by her deep love. She reflects to us our original essence. Within her, she holds the divine light of the sacred Human
Rainbow. She reveals the true hues of divine human nature, she releases the
majestic human music to flow through us. An ancient being, forever young,
her hair glows in the radiance of rainbow colors, her eyes shine with diamond
purity, her heartlight blinds us in the intensity of its flame. We feel the flame
within our own heart burn stronger, a Rainbow Flame of eternal love.

We see a path shine out before us, leading us to the Mother, so we move
forward along it. Her crystal eyes look into ours. Within each bright iris is a
circle of colors and, at its center, a circle with the blackness of night. Within
this, is a point of light as bright as a star, which sends out its light-threads.
She opens her arms to us, reaching out, and her love embraces us. We know
she has a message for us, and a song beyond words in the language of   her
heart.

Her heartstrings reach to us, glistening golden threads that shimmer with
her song. We feel the urge to follow them, and we flow along them as they
braid together. We follow a line of   light reaching back, leading us into the
light within. This spiral of light is leading us back to a point of origin, to a
distant beginning. It is a living connection, like an umbilical cord we once

traveled along from the womb of Earth. Its fibers whisper and sing with hints of ancient stories still living, still flowing in this life-stream that leads us deeper to its source. The living threads are bringing us to their weaving-point within the core of Mother Earth. We are not alone in this flow, which is woven of soul threads, shining with the love they hold within them, singing with their wisdom. We spiral deeper into the light, its patterns brightening all around us. The flow grows in strength and intensity until, with a rush of love and a blaze of light, we enter into the Inner Sun, the Heart of Earth.

We travel deep into the Heart of the Mother, from where the threads of life flow. We spiral into this Mother Sun, blazing with abundant love. Her warm love surrounds us in this golden ocean of light. In the Light of the Goddess, we are bathed and cleansed; we dance our joy in the radiant ~~flames~~ LIGHT, the love of the Goddess.

Within us, we hear the voice of Mother Earth. She celebrates our return. Her song of love sings itself into your heart and enfolds you. Solo, she sings a symphony of living tones, her Heart Song of life. Within this, flows your soul song; Mother Earth sings your story, entwined with hers, from your beginnings within her. You know this song, flowing from the heart of the one who birthed you. A song singing from the heart of your Mother Earth, who bathed you in her love, who held you as you grew, who fed you from her loving breast. This song has held you as she has held you; it has connected you with its chords of love to her radiant core, the source of your Earthly life.

Within her ancient lovesong, she sings new tones now, the tones of her own rebirth and emergence. Within us, we hear clearly the voice of the Mother. She is to be reborn from her core, as you are. With her, you will rise to new life. This is her promise to you now.

I love you beyond your knowing. I hold you always in my love.
You are known wholly, you are remembered perfectly.
Your return was eagerly awaited.
You are welcome into my heart, as you have always been.

You have never left my heart.

From me, did you come into human being.

You were conceived in my heart, you grew in my womb.

In the birthing time, you danced out of my body.

You rose to new life in a body of true human beauty.

The cycles since then have been many.

Yet all life cycles pass through me. Now the spiral of life is rising.

We will rise together.

We will emerge in true light. We will rebirth s one.

All beings of the Earth Circles join their voices with hers to create a chorus of celebration, rejoicing in her rebirth. They celebrate the future birth of a new humanity and the regeneration of all life.

You rise now on a spiral of her heartlight, rising in the bright fibers through the patterns of her love. You move up though her body on this radiant pathway until you feel yourself returning to the great cave and the loving embrace. There, you rest until you feel ready to move, and a familiar face of pure love appears before you. You glimpse other faces within this face, generations of faithful love. You feel yourself moving out of the beam, and the light of the Mother intensifies until she becomes a blaze of rainbow light, a singing flame that bathes you in its radiance. The song of the Rainbow Flame pours through you, filling you with deep peace. Then this fire of love flows down through the opening into the Earth.

In the silence after, peace is a sacred presence. The opening still shimmers gently and you move slowly towards it. You find it is a pool of liquid crystal with ripples like tree rings within it. You look into the crystal pool, where the gentle ripples and waves create patterns that form into flowing geometries in shifting relationships. You watch these living patterns move in mandalas that pulsate out from the center in rings of light, flowing from one beautiful form to another. In the rhythms and relationships, stories of life are told. The meaning of each of the life-stories resonates within us. It reflects the inner patterns of your being in formation. Then the movement slows and begins to still itself, settling into a pattern that we know within us. The surface now is like a skin of ice crystal, and we feel we should step onto this circle with its sacred pattern. We do so and light flows up through us, awakening our inner wisdoms.

An ancient seed opens within you and germinates. It reaches a root down to the heart of the Earth, to the Mother Sun below. When it touches the light, your roots begin to web wide and spread out. Then this seed stretches up a tendril to search for the Father Sun above. When it finds the light above, you begin to rise in the spiraling light, still webbing out your roots while stretching your stem high. You grow in awareness in both directions, feeling yourself open to a new relationship with all life on this sacred planet.

You reach the surface in a burst of light and joy, raising your arms high to the Sun, stretching branches into the sky. You stand firm on the Earth within the broad trunk of a great tree, the crystal tree of your ancestry, the living tree of the future. Reaching up, aspiring to the highest and reaching to the deepest, growing stronger in love. Within the ancestral web of roots and branches, you will move through the world.

Just as you live within and through Mother Earth, so she lives within and through you. And all who dwell within her, live deep within your own awareness.

The World beyond the Field

Once, there was a lost lamb who found a forgotten world.
When he was born, he sounded and looked like any other lamb, but for one unusual thing. His wool shone with what seemed like an inner glow, so he was surrounded by a soft, golden light. When his mother saw him, she was astonished, but delighted. The shepherd, who was attending the birth, was lost in wonder, running his fingers through the glowing wool. He had never set eyes on anything like this wool, which grew in golden spirals and illuminated his face. For months, the shepherd had been wondering about the mystery of the lamb's conception, as this one was not just a late lamb - there had been no ram

in the field when his mother became pregnant. But the mystery of his impossible conception, and its possible ramifications, was almost forgotten now, in the light of his miraculous appearance.

It was so late in the year that a light snow was falling, so the shepherd had led the heavily pregnant mother to an old barn on the hillside for the birthing. It was warm and dark and dry, and, there, the lamb took his first tottering steps. Later, when the mother had recovered, the shepherd carried the lamb down the path to the field where the rest of the flock was waiting eagerly. He opened the gate and the mother went nervously in, to be met by bleats of greeting. But, when the shepherd entered and placed the shining lamb carefully on his four shaky legs, all the excited bleating and chewing stopped. The mother could feel the flock's disbelieving eyes on her and her strange offspring - and it was not a comfortable feeling.

She looked down at her hungry lamb when he was suckling and wondered how he would blend in with the rest of the flock. The other lambs would crowd around at times to admire the light of the shy, shining lamb. But the grown-up sheep were not as enchanted by this strange phenomenon in the flock. Theirs was a flock of impeccable breeding that spent their days moving from one field to the next on the bare hillside, which was treeless and windy, its only feature being the network of low-walled fields that covered it. Life within them had been as quiet and predictable as could be, until now. Once the lamb was steady on his legs, he began gamboling around the field and making friends. He took some time to explore his new home and found that three sides of the field were bounded by thick hedges, and the fourth, by a stone wall. When the lamb noticed a gate, he eagerly popped his head through, but all he saw was another wall on the other side of a narrow path. He looked both ways, but could not see where the path led. The mossy stones, at least, had fascinating faces and strange shapes, and in between them, were tiny flowers that, rather like him, shivered a lot.

Most of his time was spent tirelessly bounding and leaping around the field, or playfully livening up the other lambs. The ewes disapproved of his ways and used to complain endlessly to his mother. This luminous lamb was turning their well-ordered field into a playground, inventing games for all the lambs to play, or racing around the field, impersonating birds and other creatures and dancing in odd ways. The sheep were increasingly worried about his carefree attitude and boundless imagination. Even at night, the other lambs gathered around him, their faces lit up by his glow, listening to his silly stories. He was a bad influence on the older lambs, showing them things they hadn't noticed and telling them things they didn't need to know.

Finally, the ewes put their hooves down firmly and forbade him from playing and leading the other lambs astray. Without any playmates, he began to get to know the birds and bees that visited the field and listen to their songs and stories. And when he looked into the faces of the stones that formed the walls, it seemed as if they were looking at him, too. In the grooves and lines of their faces, there were stories written, and he began to listen to them, spending hours with an absorbed expression on his face and a distant look in his eyes. His worried mother did not know what to do. Yes, he was quiet now, but she had hoped that when he gave up his playful ways he would join the other sheep and be obedient. Now she couldn't fathom his behavior at all. "What are you doing?" his mother asked him.

"I'm listening to the stones," he replied, "And they remember all kinds of things from long ago." Some of the sheep began to bleat with nervous laughter. "They told me there were no walls here, then. The stones used to stand up straight in circles and lines, and the people came here to dance in between them! And the stones were all joined up to the stars and the Sun and Moon…"

Most of the flock joined in the mocking laughter, but the oldest ewe of all had overheard and something stirred within her. "He's right you know; my old grandmother told me about that more than once. And we sheep used to wander the hills, feeding where we liked and drinking from the streams. Oh, it must have been a sweet feeling to be free." Her eyes became wistful and misty as she told him about their ancestors, who roamed the hills, high and low, with no walls to hold them. Then came the time when this peaceful land became a battlefield, when the stones were laid low and broken, the trees were cut down and cleared, and the walls were built. The lamb could see it all, as if were yesterday, and wondered if that was why he yearned to be out of the field, why he loved to leap and dance so much…

But the others had heard enough and his wondering was interrupted by an angry voice. "That was all in the past and we know better now! Who wants to be wandering the hills, getting muddy?" The lamb, with difficulty, held his tongue. "We need these walls; we are civilized sheep. Those old sheep were dirty and half-wild. Even the shepherds weren't very clean," she sniffed. Another ewe declared, "Ours is the finest wool there is and it fetches the highest prices, so only the best people can wear it." The lamb opened his mouth to ask a question, but he was met with a barrage of sheep sayings. "Sheep don't ask questions! Just follow the flock! Keep your head down and eat! Bleat when you're bleated to!" When everyone had had their say, they walked away and left the lamb and his embarrassed mother standing there. "Listening to walls, indeed!" she spluttered, "You'll be talking to them next." (The lamb thought it best not to mention his interesting conversations with rocks and stones) No more was said on the subject, but the lamb had got the message. The next day and the one after that, the lamb didn't leap at all and scarcely uttered a bleat. Now he kept all his questions for himself.

One morning, he awoke before the rest of the flock and was the first up on his feet. The clouds had lifted and it felt so good to have no eyes upon him that he felt a little excited and frisky. He even had the urge to have a secret leap or two. He knew it was risky, but he was all ready to take a gamble when he noticed something strange near a corner of the hedge; a bright glow of light. On the tips of his hooves, he quietly went over and saw, to his great surprise, a hole at the base of the hedge. It was small, but so was he. So, before anyone could wake up with some weary saying, he popped his head through the hole to see what he could see.

The sight stunned him with its unexpected beauty. A great, wide valley was filling with morning light and colors that seemed impossibly lovely, while the distant hills blazed in dawn's rays. And there were trees, just as the birds had described them, but even more magical than he had imagined. The waking birds were stirring in the branches and making their morning music, so it seemed like every tree had its own special song. There were running streams and rivers flowing with what looked like thick, liquid light. Oh, if only he had known how beautiful it was! The Sun was just out of view, around the side of the hill, and the lamb stretched his neck, leaning forward to catch its rays, but couldn't quite reach far enough. He had stretched out a little more, when it suddenly seemed as if the world was spinning around him. It took him a couple more tumbles to understand that it was him who was doing the tumbling. By the time he finally stopped, the world had to keep spinning for quite a while, just to catch up.

When he could stand up and see straight, he looked around at the marvelous view of the valley, which seemed even more vast, now that he was part of it. Then, through the other sounds, he heard his mother anxiously bleating for him. Other sleepy ewes began bleating as well, as it seemed the right thing to do. It was a long way back up the hillside, but, if he made it, maybe he could explain to his mother and the other ewes what truly lay beyond the field. There were lots of rocks and hollows on the hillside, and the ground was slippery from the last day's rain, yet slowly and painstakingly, he made it up quite a distance. When he stopped to rest, he looked up at the long climb that still lay ahead. He wished he had some of the skills of his uncivilized ancestors just then. He began the ascent again and had climbed quite some way when his rear hoof slipped and, suddenly, he felt nothing but air beneath him. Down he went, until he felt the edge of a rock strike his flailing leg and then he was at the bottom of the slope. He baa-ed in agony for a while, until he was too breathless to continue. It was quite a while before the muddy lamb could rise to his feet and finally limp off across the meadow, hoping to find a way back to the field. By then, the bleating in the field had died down, with just his mother's hoarse voice to be heard once in a while.

The limping lamb began searching for the path that would lead him back to the gate of the field. He didn't find any sign of it, but he discovered hundreds of other fascinating and beautiful distractions from the path. Even if he wasn't leaping, his heart was. Soon, his swiftly-beating heart felt healed and happy, and he later found that he had even left his limp behind him somewhere. He had wandered wide and drunk deep of the delights of freedom, when he noticed that the Sun was sliding towards the horizon.

He realized he had no idea where he was. He went one way and then another, but he couldn't even see the hill, let alone the road. He kept searching until the Sun was long gone down and the first stars had appeared. By the time the last of the birds had quieted down, the lamb seemed all alone in a strange land-scape. The deep, night sky had crowded out with stars and crowned itself with a bright Moon, almost full. She was shining down on the whole land with her love, and the lamb was glowing, too. He had not realized the night could be so beautiful, so he set off to explore the delights of a moonlit night.

On the way, he met a very creative spider who told him he had to find a twisted tree, one that grew in a spiral, to find his way home. She even created a map to it with shining threads in the air that showed him the way. Now he just had to follow a thread, so he was soon merrily skipping through the meadow in the moonlight, following the invisible thread in his mind. But then a strangely-shaped shadow crossed the meadow, and the lamb looked up. Above him were dark clouds, looking like a whole flock of black sheep the wind was driving across the sky. A moment later, the moon disappeared from view, and darkness surrounded the lamb in an instant. He turned this way and that, but in the silence and the dark there was nothing he knew, and he could see no clues to which direction he should go in. And, after all his turning, he wasn't even sure which way he was facing, so he could not use his mental map.

In the darkness, there were strange sounds and eerie screeches he could not decipher, and the sounds of creaking trees and night-birds began to be trans-formed by his imagination. And when he felt a fluttering right by his ear, he jumped in fright. He was attracting moths who wondered what his wool tasted like. (Some things are conspicuous by nature, and a luminescent lamb is one of these) Those fibers of light looked like a perfect meal for a hungry moth. By this time, there were a dozen moths around the lamb and, no matter which way he turned, they stayed with him. Then he realized why – he remembered his own light, which was enough to illuminate his next step or two.

"Oh, thank you!" bleated the lamb to the moths, who were a little confused. The light around him lit up his next step or two, though beyond that he could see nothing. He knew he could keep from tripping up, but he had no idea where he was going. A sudden fluttering above his head made the lamb jump again, but this time he saw the dark wings of another night creature. The bat started fluttering in a circle around the lamb and, in a moment, all the moths had scat-tered.

"I've seen you before," said the bat. "I've noticed your glow in those fields." The lamb was delighted. "Maybe you could show me the way back there!"

"Is that your home?" asked the bat. "I don't know if it is my home anymore," answered the lamb. "I don't think I can be happy there now. But I have to go back, even if it's just to say goodbye." The lamb told the bat about the spider's map and the twisted tree he was to find.

"I can find that tree with my eyes closed," laughed the bat. "I don't need light to see my way; I can find my way in the dark as well as the light, so it's not dark to me at all." They came to a broken wall and the lamb jumped over it. When the lamb looked up, there was the twisted tree, its trunk like braided fibers growing in a spiral, its branches raised to the sky.

"Thank you," said the lamb. Nearby was the path back to the field and the end of his adventure. A question rose in him that he spoke out loud. "But how will I find my real home?"

"Well, you'll need a map for that. I'm sure there's one inside you somewhere. Try looking inside your heart," suggested the bat. "But," he added, "We've got all night. You have hours before the Sun comes up, and there is something special beside the twisted tree." The lamb looked and, beside a smooth stone, he noticed a cleft in the hillside. The bat flew through the opening and the lamb poked his head in after, but could see only darkness. The hole was small, but so was he. Carefully, he climbed inside and found himself in a narrow tunnel. He was glad his glow could light the way, as he inched along it on his knees. When the tunnel widened, he stood he sensed that the darkness was far from empty. The shadows seemed to be alive, and the lamb heard the sounds of creatures scurrying around him.

"Don't worry," came the voice of the bat, "They're just wondering why you're here." At that moment, the lamb was asking himself just the same thing. When they went a little further in, the roof of the tunnel reached higher and higher.

The dark-dwellers were a little overwhelmed by this living light in their midst, so one of the oldest moles was the first to come forward and welcome him. Apart from the sightless eyes of the mole, there were others there, more lively. The obsidian eyes of the rats sparkled in the radiance, and one of the braver rats greeted the lamb, offering to show him some of the secrets within the hill. So off they set, the bat, the mole, the rat and the lamb, down a winding tunnel, deeper into the rocky body of the hill. The light of the florescent fleece spilled out all around, so they were surrounded by glistening crystal whose facets flashed into life. The further they went in, the higher the ceiling of the tunnel reached, until they came to a cavern with a high vault. The lamb could hear the swish of wings and high-pitched singing, for the air above them was alive, swirling with the wings of bats. Before he could even be asked where they were going, the rat was off, down another tunnel, with the lamb in his wake and the bat's high singsong echoing around them. Then down tunnel after tunnel, making slow curves and sharp turns, past falls of water and alongside trickling streams, up paths and down passages, going deeper and deeper into the heart of the hill.

When they finally stopped, the lamb stood in a passageway, wondering what was next, when a bright figure stepped through the solid wall! Before the lamb knew what to do, it was coming down the tunnel to meet them. The being looked almost like one of the two-legged folk that lived up above, but much brighter. Not that he could see any legs; the being appeared to flow from place to place and seemed to be wearing a kind of long, glowing robe – which shone just like his fleece! The lamb was fascinated by its fibers of light that glowed like his own, and began to feel more at home here. And when the being opened their arms wide and welcomed him, he was sure he did. Stepping aside, the being beckoned for the lamb and his companion to continue down the tunnel. At its end, they found it opened into a vast, crystal cavern that was filled with flowing light.

They entered the space in a state of amazement, and the glare was such that they could scarcely keep their eyes open, as if the Sun was hidden within the hill. The power of love was palpable here and its presence pervaded everything. Here was a cavern full of golden, crystal love, and the companions bathed in it. Crystals sparkled all around and their light was flashing and reflecting in all directions. The lamb could see himself reflected in them, as if there were many of him, and they all looked very happy to be there. He could sense they were at the center of the web of tunnels within the hill. And, at the center of the cavern, crystalline light flowed in a slow spiral – and the light was alive!

A great and ancient being was there, within the crystal light. This flowing being sensed their presence and she welcomed them in closer, so they could discern more of the forms within the light. As she moved, the rich, crystal colors were subtly shifting, in flows that trickled through each other, mixing and melding, yet never still. Her shimmering serpentine form was wrapped around an egg of brilliant light, beaming out golden rays that filled the space. Power moved in waves through the body of the ancient mother, who raised her head and looked lovingly at her visitors with her crystalline eyes. The light around her seemed to be rising, higher and higher, and the lamb could feel his light blending with hers, loving and warm. His heart beat stronger and his fleece shone brighter than it had since the day he was born.

Around her, flowed liquid golden light, like the delicious honey that the bees had told him about. He could not tell how long he was held in the ecstasy of that light, but there came a point when he could see the form of a familiar figure beckoning, and the light began to change and thin. In another moment, he was moving through an opening and traveling down a tunnel. This became narrower until he emerged into a world of a different, dimmer light. When he could feel something solid, it was the smooth face of a stone he was resting against. Somehow they were back at the cleft in the hillside, and the mole was waiting there, with a knowing smile. The lamb came to his feet, unsteadily, while, above him, the sky was brightening and dawn was not far away. Nor was the field, so, when the lamb could walk without wobbling, they made their way down the path to the gate. But, though it seemed a little late, when he looked through the bars of the gate, no one was stirring, and no lambs were trying to rouse their long-suffering mothers from slumber. A low cloud of silence seemed to hang over the field. Then he realized why the silence was so heavy - all of the lambs were gone.

The lamb bleated in surprise and his mother replied, suddenly awake. She leapt to her feet when she saw the little figure standing at the gate. She thought, for a moment, she was dreaming. But, even before she touched the lamb with her lips, she could tell this was real and she greeted her lost one warmly. All the other ewes awoke and came to crowd around the gate, to see the first lamb ever to return from beyond the field. He began breathlessly telling her the tale of his day away, while the other sheep listened, their eyes widening and their minds beginning to spin. He could tell it would be best to help them see for themselves. How he would love to get the flock out of there…

"I wish I could open the gate," he told them, " But it's tied up with thick rope." The rat laughed and scrabbled up the wall, where he began gnawing through the rope. When the lamb asked the sheep if they would like to venture out of the field, they reacted with a well-bred sense of horror. But his mother said she believed him and would come with him, now, to witness some of the wonders for herself. As the rat spat out a mouthful of fibers, the lamb and the sheep watched the gate swing open. The mother took a deep breath and stepped through the gateway, and her lamb ran up to nuzzle her. As they turned to go, there was the sound of many feet behind her and she looked back to see the flock nervously leaving the field and following her. So they all made their way down the road, gathering speed, until they came to the broken wall and the lamb and his mother jumped through the gap. The flock followed in a woolly flood that flowed out into the meadow, and soon that sea of green was dotted with sheep on their own journeys of exploration. The ewes were swimming in the beauty of it all, and their old moods and attitudes were gently washed away, and even their grieving faded a little. The lamb's proud mother watched her flock, which had seemed lost in sadness only hours before, come to new life. One ewe, usually the sternest and harshest of critics, was standing beneath an oak tree, shoulder-deep in grass and Autumn flowers, with tears in her smiling eyes.

"Are you glad that he came back?" the lamb's mother asked her.

"I am," the other ewe said with sincerity.

The meadow stretched for many miles and they had wandered far, enjoying a few glorious hours, when they heard the sound of barking in the distance. It was a familiar sound and they knew the shepherd was searching for them. Some began to become afraid, and the sheep flocked together again and headed for the hills. The lamb and his mother went with them, trying to calm them on the way. When they came through the broken wall, back onto the road, the lamb and the mother told the shocked flock that they would not be going back to the field. Tearful farewells were said, but when they turned to go, there was the sound of footsteps and the shepherd came around the corner with his dog. The walls that bounded the road were too high to leap and the flock blocked the other way, so the lamb knew that day's adventure was over. The shepherd couldn't believe his eyes. As his dog drove the sheep up the road, he picked up the lamb and looked it carefully over. The lamb looked as innocent as only a lamb can, but the man could not see the sorrow in his eyes.

The flock was driven into a more secure field with four walls that no one could leap over and nothing could burrow through. Their old field had a high fence placed around it, so there would be no more wandering. But, now, any field seemed like a prison to the lamb. He could not forget the world beyond the field and his experiences within the hill. The fields were quiet now, since all but one of the lambs had been sold for slaughter. Sometimes, when the silence in the field became too much to bear, they would look to the lamb to raise their spirits. No one complained about his leaping and dancing any more. They saw him as a cloud of sunshine in the gloomy field. They even asked to hear the stories of his adventures, unbelievable though they seemed to be. At times, it was like having more mothers than any lamb could handle.

Meanwhile, the shepherd had been making plans. He would start breeding these sheep as soon as possible and, who knows, one day he might have a whole flock of golden-fleeced sheep. All of his worries would be over. But the shepherd soon began to worry if word of his remarkable lamb had got around. The locals might have spotted him on his travels. What if someone came and sheared the lamb's special wool? Worse still, what if someone stole the precious lamb itself? Hard as he tried, he could not stop worrying. So, one sleepless night, he came to the field and lifted the bleating lamb under his arm, avoiding the gaze of the dumb-struck mother. When the gate of the field banged shut, she cried out, but as the bleats of her lamb faded away into the distance, she had to accept that the moment she had feared had come and passed. The other ewes came to console her, but she knew her special lamb was gone beyond her help.

The shepherd lifted the lamb gently by his legs and laid it across his broad shoulders. As the shepherd headed down the narrow path, a glow surrounded his heavy head, but he hardly noticed it. He felt only a great weight of guilt upon him. He wondered how a gift of such lightness had become such a burden. The lamb, meanwhile, looked at the world from the man's vantage point, looking out across the network of walls that crisscrossed the hill and the countryside. They came to the barn where he had been born, and the shepherd placed the lamb inside and locked the door. At least the lamb had his light to see where he was, though it was just a bare space with four walls, some straw, food and water. The shepherd would come each day to feed him and check on his health, but would never catch his eye. At times, the lamb felt lonely and forgotten but at other times, he was sure he heard sounds beneath him, sometimes like the low buzz of a busy beehive, sometimes like the high chimes of bell-like birdsong.

The day came when the shepherd came into the barn with his shears at his side. He lifted up the lamb and began to shear him. As the fleece fell to the ground, the lamb felt strangely relieved. Now that he was shorn, he looked once more like a newborn, skinny and pink, shivering with the chill in the air. The shepherd left with the golden fleece and the door closed behind him. The barn was dark now and he could see no light around him, but he somehow felt lighter and freer. The night was cold and he found it difficult to sleep. He held himself close to the earth beneath him for warmth and comfort. He was troubled by strange sounds and sensations and fitful dreams. Late into the night, he opened his eyes suddenly to see a thin beam of light from the earth pierce the darkness, and he wondered if he was actually awake. But the beam quickly widened as the ground fell away, and there was a definite sound of scratching and scraping. Two paws appeared on the edge of the fresh hole and the head of the mole popped up, sniffing the air, followed by the rat with the twinkling eyes, and finally, with a flutter of wings, the bat flew up out of the ground.

Warm, loving light flooded out of the earth to fill the cold room, and the lamb leapt for joy. They celebrated their reunion until, all of a sudden, the trio disappeared down into the light and the lamb knew it was time to approach the opening. The lamb came to its edge and looked down a long tunnel of light, deep into the hillside. The mouth of it was small, but so was he, and without his thick fleece, he could easily squeeze down the tunnel. So he made his way down the steep tunnel and, when he reached the end of it, he stepped out of the shaft of light. To his wonder, he found himself in what seemed to be a vast, dark chamber, where he could see nothing and no one at all. He called out, but his voice simply carried away into a void. The space seemed to be without edge or end. The darkness was so intense, that he felt like he was floating within it. To his surprise, he could see his own light once more, beaming out around him. Then, within the dark, he saw a point of light come to life. Then another and another appeared, until they were flashing into life in dozens and hundreds. Light began to flow between them and flow into form in a living circle.

And there, at the center, was the brightest point of all. The circle of light widened and brightened, while forms and faces started emerging within it. Faces that he somehow recognized, forms that were familiar and beloved. So many dancing and weaving forms, so many eyes, bright and alive, so much love flowing in the whirling circle. Within the light were the glints and glimpses of wings and beaks, hooves and horns, claws and paws, fins and flippers, scales and tails, hands and feet; all moving in the one dance within the shining circle. One bright being in particular stood out for the lamb. His face blazed with love while, from his head, two spirals of light rose, like the horns of a ram, radiant and graceful. His gaze was strong and gentle, and his heart reached out to the lamb, who ran to be held in his loving embrace. A special space opened up in the circle, waiting for the lamb of pure love to enter. He felt his heart drawing him towards the circle and the center, and, in a moment, he had entered the dance. The loving light embraced him and blazed around him, as he danced in joyous ecstasy, as all became one light spinning in the vastness; a single ring, golden and whole.

Next morning, as the Sun rose, the shepherd opened the door of the barn. He found only an empty space, some straw and scattered soil; it was as if the earth had opened up and swallowed the lamb down. And the mystery of his disappearance stayed with the man for the months to come. Some time later, the shepherd was walking with his dog through the open meadow beneath the hill, lost in thought, still pondering what to do with his prized fleece. Spring had come and carpeted the land with wild flowers and brought the buds back to the trees, which had been bare so long. The warmer winds of Spring were making waves that passed through the tall grass and set the new blooms dancing. The

Sun warmed the shepherd's spirit until it brightened, and he felt the urge to let the sheep out into the meadows to feed and wander a little. Soon, the flock was coming down the hill into the meadow with the man and his trusty dog behind.

The ewes, pregnant with new life, had not been grazing long when one of the mothers looked up to the hill, over which the Sun blazed. The dog, who had been circling the flock, suddenly stopped and cocked his head, giving out a strange sound. The other ewes raised their heads as one and looked up, and the shepherd followed their gaze. His heart leapt like a lamb's – there, on the rim of the hill, was a fine, strong ram surrounded by a gentle, golden glow. And in his eyes was a light the shepherd had never seen before, and he was touched by the majesty of purest love.

The Circle opens wider, as the heart opens wider.

The Oneness is woven wider and the weave is more open.

More are invited to enter and more choose to do so. Truly, none are woven in without their choosing. For freedom is part of the weaving. And we weave the threads as we wish, open or tightly woven, loose or looping, snaking and dancing or making their way in seemingly straight lines. All weave their own part of the tapestry and their weaving is respected and honored as unique. For they weave the tapestry in their own image and the tapestry weaves them in as they wish to be woven in. They lose no freedom; they are not trapped in a mesh, not held in a net of others' making. They are free to weave and re-weave their own past, present and future.

The weaving is the dance of the fingers, of the feet and body, the dance of life and the living heart. The dance of the world and the worlds beyond, the waking dance, the sleeping dance, the great heart-weave. And weaving through the heart come all the colors of the emotions and feelings, the pains and aches, the joys and the laughs, all the longing and the lettings go. For all flows through the heart, in the end and in the beginning. There it begins and there it ends in the cycle, from heart to heart, from one to one. Within and without, the heart is the one space. All else is necessary illusion for the game to be played out, for the play to be created.

Through the heart weave all the words and deeds, all the knowing and for-getting, all the ancient stories and the brand new ones, all the shocks and hor-rors, all the bright, jeweled moments of love. The moments of strength and tenderness, golden moments and the moments of every color and nature that make up the One Moment. The folding moments, which weave in on each other, fold through each other, looping their threads through each other, weaving them through the dancing fingers, snaking them through each other to make a tight weave that holds the Web of the worlds together; the Web of Love and Oneness, of close and open Unity.

The threads that spin out in every direction, which make their way through and around each other, enfolding and interlacing, are forming a calligraphy of thread in lines of color, of light and dark. A language that speaks to and from the heart, for that is where the weaving begins and from where the busy hands weave the willing threads. As our hearts desire, as our mind allows, through our bodies follow the threads, through our veins and muscles, nerves and bones, our very cells. They trace their way through all that we are, for they are so much of what we are. They wake us up as we wake them up. And we wake them up as we go along.

These are the threads of the great story; the infinite threads of the infinite stories. All spool through our hearts, as infinity flows through our very hearts. Does this not prove how large they are? How great and full of space, how expansive? If we can hold the Universe there, what need have we to fear restriction, to cling to empty ritual, to fear being trapped or crowded out?

For we have a Universe within that is our playground, our place of pleasure-making. In there, we form ourselves and inform ourselves of our own nature, its infinite variety and possibility. For it is without boundary, without borders of any kind. It was made by the Creator in its beginning and it was given the blessing of freedom to expand and grow, to fold outwards and inwards, to go beyond any artificial boundaries – and it was made of Love. It was and is Love manifested. In the gift of freedom, we have the opportunity, duty and pleasure of exploring our own potential, our own who-ness; the truth of who we are in all our multiplicity and infinity. As we explore ourselves, inner and outer, the worlds expand, learn and connect more closely.

The Creator, through us, weaves back the Oneness, moving through the illusions. The back of the tapestry is revealed: the hidden side, in its true depths. There we find the map of our actions, the weave of our deeds, the flow of our own thoughts in the patterns we each create. As we see the tapestry in its hidden aspects, we glimpse the greater patterns, the patterns woven into the Earth, our bodies, minds, and hearts, between us, through us, between all life and all worlds. We see the living tapestry of Creation, and know that we, too, are busy weaving it.

Time flows through our lives in its complicated way, seeming to flow forward or backward, seeming to unravel itself – or suddenly run out. We feel the thread shorten, the spool seeming to run empty or, maybe, we discover a new spool and happily spin out more time for ourselves, so allowing us to unravel more of our story, our history, our many meanings. Time can seem to trip us up with its threads, or choke us with its constrictions. Sometimes the spool of time seems to run so fast that we fear we can never keep up with it, and we grab hold of a thread, to try to slow it down, to hold it frozen long enough to give us rest and peace. But time seems to run on, unhindered by our efforts, and, in our desperation, we may try to cut the thread of time, to be free of it. We may yearn to break its power, somehow, to give us room and space to breathe freely, free from its ever-running spooling and spinning.

But time can also give us a clue to our freedom for it can be gone beyond and transcended. We all know those moments of our lives when we seem to escape time, when the moment seems to open into infinity, and we feel time expand. The thin thread of light seems suddenly to be a thick glowing rope, then a wide bridge, then a road…and then its boundaries and horizons are lost to our sight as it expands. As it did so, we saw that it had no end, for it could expand in every direction, into infinity as all can, as everything can. There, we glimpsed the way out of and beyond the limitations of time, for if we can expand one moment, we have expanded the whole Universe. We have made an opening, through which we can travel, and through which, in fact, others can follow.

For one moment holds within it the infinite possibilities of the universe, its innumerable potentials, all held and hidden in that precious moment. That one moment holds the key to Oneness. For as it expands, Oneness is touched on and the edges of Oneness are sensed, then the endless edges dissolve to boundless space, to borderless infinities.

That one moment holds the key, the lock and the portal. It holds the secret of wholeness, for one whole moment can hold the Universe, can hold all the universes, can hold infinity within it. Just as the cell of a creature can hold its whole history, so one moment can hold the whole history of the Universe; pasts, presents, possible futures, the woven wholeness of all. That one moment is a gift from the Creator, more precious than any other you could imagine. Like a golden orb held in the palm, it slowly expands to contain the one who holds it and then the room in which they are sitting, then the country in which they dwell and the world of which that country is a part; then the galaxy in which that world spins, and the constellation in which that galaxy spins and then the universe in which the constellation spins.

In the orb of that One Moment, the whole Universe is waiting to expand, waiting to be born again, to be reborn as the One, which was the beginning. And the Universe is held in the palm of the One.

We have no time to play, we tell ourselves; no time to waste, to throw away on frivolous matters. We must be serious, focus on what is vital in our life or we will be left behind in the race of life. The crowd will hurry on and we will be left lingering, and all because we did not keep our eyes on the important matters, because we were playing or doing silly things, being creative or day-dreaming. Such things, of course, can have no real importance. Surely they are just diversions from the real substance of life, the weighty matters we must absorb ourselves in? We must not be distracted by our childishness in wanting to play, dream and create.

So we stick to the subject at hand. We take our place in the world and wear its masks, and leave play until some other day; one when we will have some time to waste. A distant, rainy day when we will give ourselves permission to do all the things we wanted to, but would not allow ourselves to do. In the meantime, we do not let regrets get in the way of our seriousness, our sustained focus. For we know there is no profit in playing; it can only lead to us looking silly or trivial. We are here for weighty matters, we have no need of childish fancies. We have outgrown them, we have matured and grown wise in the ways of the world.

We will save our play until that ever more distant day when the world gives us space to recreate ourselves. And we swallow the regrets and we stop ourselves wishing and we suppress our dreams, our wondering. We tame our wandering mind and train it to follow a straight path, for meandering will only get us lost. We will walk streets that are straight and narrow. For we know what is important – we are the wise ones, the ones who have worked out the way the world works. We need only act out its many roles and our success will be assured. We will get there at the same time the crowd does – maybe even a little before. We will not stay behind to play, or we might miss out on the action. So we will take our place in the lengthy queue, and wait for the day when we can recreate something wonderful: something we saw once as a child, something we glimpsed, briefly.

A playground we once saw, a place of adventure, with its swings and slides, its playthings of all shapes and sizes. And all there for us, as if someone had given it to us as a big gift. Our heart wanted to play, to try out every delightful experience available, but something seemed to stop us, to hold us back from running into the playground and leaping onto the playthings with a whoop of joy.

We were not sure what "it" was, but "it" seemed real. Something held us there with an invisible hand, an authoritative hand with a serious intent: the cold hand of duty. And we felt the moment go, the colors of the playground dim and the gates close before our faces, with us still outside looking in. And so we went home our usual way.

Then, many years later, that moment came back to us in all its potentials and possibilities, and we faced it again; the same moment, a different playground. We knew we had to choose... would we be stopped yet again? But this time we knew the cold hand that stopped us belonged to us. It did not hold us – we held it. We knew by then that if we opened the hand and released its grip, we would find there something within it. A flash of something, small and golden, nesting in the palm; a gift perhaps, something that seemed to hold something else inside it.

So, this time, we take the gift and enter the playground. It seems bigger than we remembered, bigger even than we could have visualized – and getting bigger by the moment, it seems. So we run and play. We lose ourselves to duty and find ourselves in the golden moment of play, a moment of peace and of creation. We know the One Moment and, within it, we are happy.

☯

We take our time, as much of it as we wish, for there is always more and we can have as much as we wish. The shortage of time is truly an illusion, woven out of the illusion of time itself. Though a wonderful illusion it is and useful…at times. For the times hold other secrets; they hold secrets woven within them. Within the threads of time, are held echoes, faint or strong, of the wisdom that once seemed lost. If we can be silent and listen to the wisdom singing along the threads of time, we can reconnect ourselves, and we will hear a song singing within our own hearts.

The song will sing on from heart to heart, from time to time, coming down the threads, vibrating through the strings of the great instrument that is time. We, also, can pluck its strings, we can pick out a song or a tune of our own and send it down the threads of time, into the past or future, across all the Now's and through all the Now's, above and below, into all the universes. Our little song will be singing its way through Creation, singing in its rippling joy, its little waves of wisdom winging through the Web.

We each have our own wisdom, and there are many who would wish to hear it if they could, if we were willing to share it. If we sing from our heart, the threads of the Web vibrate and the song expands and shimmers along the threads, pulsing out from our heart's center into the Web, where it will be heard in the hearts of others. Just as a bird sings out and touches the hearts of others, so can we. We can touch the hearts of those we cannot see, those we cannot even visualize. Simply because we choose to sing out from our heart and sing into our own heart's center, expanding in both directions, then all directions.

A song growing out like a great egg of sound and love pouring out, filling space and time with love, to become a great egg of Creation. Out and out it grows to touch the edges of the original Egg of Creation, to fill the infinite. Then we will have sung our Heart Song and we will have filled the Heart Space, the space of Creation. This creative egg would fill the apparent emptiness of space until the wonderful Egg of Creation is filled with its sweetness. What a gift to the Creator, what a gift from the Creator Within. And we can only wonder at the chick that will hatch from this marvelous egg...

The Fledgling and the Egg

**There was once a bright egg in a nest perched
on a ledge in a high cliff.**
It didn't just rest quietly there, as you might have guessed already. The nest was in an opening high up in the ancient face of the cliff, where many generations had been born and raised. The egg had been warm and safe, nestled in amongst soft feathers and grasses in a nest woven of twigs that its parents had collected for it. It had been looked after there for many weeks by the mother who laid it and her partner, while a bright new life formed inside it. Still and silent, the egg lay in the shade, apparently doing nothing.

Then one day, the voice of the chick was heard calling from within the egg. A high chirp echoed from the cliffs, and, soon, the parents knew, it would be time to hatch. But there came a particular moment when both parents were away looking for food, and in that moment, the egg started to move. It started to shudder and wobble from side to side, and, after a while, it started to roll around the nest. It was as if the egg had decided to come alive in a burst of activity, to move and make a new space for itself in the nest. So lively did it become, that the egg rolled out of the shadows and left the nest, to teeter on the edge of that high shelf of stone. While the egg shone in the brilliant sunshine, the chick inside the egg was slowly coming to its senses and waking up. The chick wondered where it was and looked about itself, trying to make things out. There was a kind of soft golden light around it, which illuminated the inside of the egg. The chick could see something of its own form; its furled wings, its wet feathers, and even catch a glimpse of its own feet.

"I am beautiful," he thought to himself. After he had minutely examined everything he could see of himself, he wondered what he could do next. He realized that there must be something else for him to see and experience, something else in the world other than him, wonderful though he was. After all, that light must be coming from somewhere, and he wondered what was out there in this bright world, what marvels awaited him there. He pondered how he could make it out into the world.

After a time, he grew impatient and decided he would use the intriguing beak he had found on his face; perhaps it would help him make his way out into the light. So he began to peck at the hard shell that surrounded him. He pecked and pecked against the shell, almost giving up at one point, when it seemed the wall of his little world was too hard to break through. But the light outside was too enticing to resist, and he knew he would have to make it through. His curiosity drove him on until suddenly there was a crack and he realized he had made a breakthrough – a thread of light appeared. The fledgling's heart leapt at the sight, and he began to peck even more strongly.

But, suddenly, the egg rolled right off the ledge and fell towards the earth below. It passed through the branches of the small trees clinging to the cliffs on the way down, slowing its descent slightly and deflecting it from the hard surfaces of stone. The chick inside felt the sensation of falling and wondered what it was. The egg headed down towards the river flowing beneath the cliffs until it landed with a splash. The impact cracked the egg and down it sank, almost to the bed of the river. Just a thin membrane kept the world of water outside. The light dimmed within the egg and it rested a moment, before it began to rise again and the chick felt another new sensation. Then the egg came to the surface and began tumbling through the waves, so the chick's next feeling was one of dizziness. The confused chick wondered why he felt this way, as the egg rolled and flowed on. All around him, golden light beamed in through a latticework of fine cracks, surrounding him with a web of light that reminded him of why he had wanted to break out of the shell.

So, he began to peck again, until an opening appeared above him and a beam of light entered, exciting him and giving him a burst of new energy. With new strength, he pecked the top of the egg off, to reveal blue sky overhead – and now light poured in all around to dazzle him. With an effort, he popped his dizzy head out of the hole to see where he was. He squinted and blinked until, bit by bit, he could discern shapes of so many different colors, of moving things of all kinds, shadows and strange patterns on every side. Everything was flowing and he felt part of the flow.

The whole world still seemed to be flowing past, and moving pretty fast

– and getting faster. Then a sort of roar began to fill his ears, and when he looked around, he realized that this river seemed to come to a sudden end, just up ahead. He felt a little disappointed, but told himself that maybe if he could be still for a while his dizziness and confusion would go. Then he realized the ride was not over yet, as the egg reached the edge of a waterfall and he looked down from a great height. The sheer drop and empty space below took his breath away and he began to paddle like a terrified terrapin. But, over they went, bird and egg, and he pulled in his head and limbs and hoped for the best. He felt a sense of lightness, tempered with a slight sense of doom. For a long time, he thought they would never hit the water, but they finally did.

The impact smashed the egg into tiny pieces and the chick sank into the water beneath the fall, which swirled and tumbled him into even greater confusion. In his panic, his whole life flashed before him. He wondered how such a short life could be so eventful. It wasn't what he had been expecting at all. But he saw that there were other creatures down here who were greeting him by waving their fins. As well as making him feel at home, this had the extra effect of propelling them through the water, so he began to flap his fins too. It wasn't as easy as it looked, but he had come to expect that now, so he kept at it. Suddenly, he sensed a current under him that raised him up and propelled him towards the surface. Before he had a chance to say farewell to the fish, he bobbed onto the surface and deeply breathed in air and sunlight again. Then, the current gave him into the hands of a wave, and a moment later, he landed on the bank.

All was still, at last, and he let himself recover from his adventure. When he raised his head to look around, he was astonished by the wonders of the world that lay in every direction. The river was lined with tall reeds, while, beyond, were taller trees and beyond them, high mountains and sheer cliffs in the distance. He felt a little weary and very wet, but he felt a good kind of dizziness now, as he was simply dizzy with the beauty that was all around him. For a long time, he was content just to breathe in the beauty of this new world and bathe in the brilliant sunshine.

When he could make it to his feet, he set off through the mud to find his way home. He followed a stream that led away from the roaring waterfall and the tumbling currents of the river. With his short legs, it was slow going, and every step was hard work. But he was determined, and he trudged along the boggy bank, until he reached a place where the water was quite still and slow-moving. Here, there were plants and beautiful flowers that grew out of the water and leaves that floated on its surface. His legs ached by now, so he stopped to rest.

A green creature with big webbed feet came along, hopping from leaf to leaf. The fledgling jumped to his feet with excitement – that was much better than trudging through mud! After watching the frog for a while, he leaped onto a leaf and copied the frog's hopping with great success. Walking on water was a much more sensible way to travel, he decided, and he made great progress through the tall reeds. Well, he did fall off a few times, but he clambered back onto a lily pad and carried on.

On one occasion, he climbed up a handy reed onto a lily pad and discovered that some of the reeds were actually the long legs of birds with bendy necks. The slightly offended bird looked down its beak at the fledgling and commented on the cheeky ways of chicks, these days.

On the lily pad, the fledgling wondered if he was going to grow up into one of these long-legged, long-necked birds… How beautiful they were! They looked busy, all bending over the water and looking in the river for something, so he didn't want to disturb them, but he couldn't keep his question in. "Do you know what I am? he asked. One fisher bird had a sprat in its mouth and said nothing. But the other said, "I think you're lost."

"Can you show me the way home?" wondered the bird.

"You're not a river bird, so go inland and you might find it," advised the other fisher, who had swallowed that sprat. He pointed his long neck in the direction of the distant trees. "A lot of birds make their homes there. Try a tree."

"What's a tree?" asked the fledgling. They looked at each other and both shrugged their drooping shoulders and went back to fishing in the river.

Undeterred, the fledgling hopped three floating leaves onto the bank and started squelching his way through the mud towards the trees. He was relieved that, quickly, the soil seemed to go solid and his feet worked better.

He knew he must be closer to home, now. When he reached a towering brown pillar with lots of arms, he wondered what it was. It had skin like a crocodile and lots of green feathers. How fine it was! He thought it would be a wonderful place to have a home, but he knew he had to go and find some trees.

He began searching amongst the pillars, to see if the trees were in between them, but there were so many hundreds of pillars that he could tell it might take a long time. Just then, a green centipede rippled past.

"Can you tell me where I can find a tree?" asked the bird.

'Yes. I'm just about to climb one," said the centipede, so the bird followed her, at speed. The centipede wasn't sure she wanted to be chased by a bird with such a sharp beak, so she chose the nearest tree and she began to scuttle up one of the roots and snake her way up the bark of the broad trunk. Oh, the little bird became very excited and began to hop up and down with joy. Maybe he was home already!

He was just about to squawk with delight when he remembered that behind that tree were a hundred others and even more behind those. Suddenly, it seemed nearly impossible to find the one tree that was his home. Sadly, he sat on a stone and looked up at the broad red-brown trunk that stretched above him. Like a great wooden road reaching into the distance, disappearing into the clouds, it seemed, so tall was the tree. It went on and on and on, further than even his sharp eyes could see. How he yearned to make his way up this road to see where it lead, to find out what was up there at the top of the tree. Maybe it wouldn't lead him home, but he knew he would discover more wonders there, perhaps ones that would make those down here on the ground seem small. He made up his mind – he would follow the route of the centipede up this broad red road and see where it led him. He ran to the base of the tree, hopped onto the root and began to run up the bark, the way he had run up the back of the crocodile.

A moment later, he was on his back in the soft grass, staring up at the tree. It took him another moment to understand how he got there. Maybe, he thought, you have to have lots and lots of legs to walk up a tree. But a moment later, an ant passed him by, nodded hello and scuttled up the tree. The fledgling counted the ant's legs and his own and resolved to give it another try.

A moment later, he was flat on his back in the grass, staring up at the tree. It took him another moment to understand how he got there. This time, he scuttled fast as he could, but, just as fast, he was flat out on the grass below. When the shock wore off, he set out again to walk up the tree. This time, he clung on tightly with his feet, digging them into the thick bark. To his delight, he climbed an inch or two, but, just over a moment later, he was flat on his back again, his little wings spread out, his feet in the air.

He rested a while, as the ant came down the trunk, casually carrying a neatly-cut leaf. What was so special about the ant's legs? They looked spindly and weak, while his felt strong, with sharp claws. He felt his determination was being tested, so he decided to have one more try. This time he would use everything at his disposal. He dug in his sharp toes and began to climb, holding on to the rough bark with his little beak. Even his stubby, weak wings helped out, as they tightly clung on to the bark. He climbed one inch and after a great heave, another inch then, after a great struggle, another inch. He felt pleased and proud for a moment at his progress and rested to catch his breath. He gazed up at the climb ahead and his heart sank; above him, the tree seemed to stretch forever and his strength was almost gone already. The last of his energy drained away and he fell from the tree, bouncing on a root and landing on the soft grass.

Of course he had not climbed far, so the only thing hurt was his determination, which felt defeated by too great a task. The ant, meanwhile, had been leaning on his leaf, taking a well-earned break and watching this strange behavior. A shadow suddenly passed over the little bird, and he sat up with fright. "What was that? he asked.

'Just a bird flying over," answered the ant, as the bird landed on a branch.

'What's flying?" wondered the fledgling.

'That's what birds do," the ant replied and, as if on cue, the bird took off from the branch and soared into the air. The fledgling leapt to his feet with joy.

'I'm a bird, too, so that's what I do – fly!" With a big burst of enthusiasm, the fledgling did a little run, a little leap – and landed in a heap in a tangle of grasses.

"I was going to say you'll have to wait a while before your wings will work," came the patient voice of the ant. The breathless bird was lying flat on his back in a soft nest of wind-woven grasses, gazing up at the clear blue sky, and he thought maybe it was time he took a rest. He had never guessed a new-born bird would face such complications. Maybe he should just enjoy the view for a while. At least he could lie here and fly in his imagination... The ant – who had a busy schedule – made his excuses and left the little bird to his dreaming.

He imagined himself flying up the trunk of the tree to see what surprises it held in its branches. He saw himself searching for his home, while he wondered what it would look like and how he would know it was *his* home. He tried to imagine the faces of his parents and his own joy at finding them. He lay there a long time, as the Sun moved across the sky and bathed him in its light. His strength came back and he realized it was time that he made a move to find his home for real. So he came to his feet and began to walk around the broad tree, to find out what lay on the other side. He made his way, ducking under its roots or clambering over them, until he reached the other side of the tree. To his amazement, there, at the base of the tree, was an opening with light pouring out of it!

He shook himself to make sure he wasn't still dreaming, then he slowly went forward to see what the source of the light was. The opening was like an open doorway filled with light, and the fearless fledgling stepped through it. When his eyes adjusted to the light, he realized that the great tree was hollow inside, yet it seemed to be full of light and life. The sun was overhead, beaming down this tall tower, while the inner walls of the tree were filled with the nests of birds of all kinds. This tree of great age had been struck by lightning long before and its heart had been opened. Now it was a home to all who came and its name was known throughout the forest and beyond.

The fledgling walked, a little dazed, into the center of this space. He raised his face up to the Sun and felt its rays fill him with new joy. Yes, he was still homeless and he couldn't yet fly, yes, he had disheveled feathers and a dirty face, but he felt beautiful again in spite of all. He opened his beak and began to sing a song he didn't know that he knew, in a voice that he didn't know he had. He sang out in tones of pure joy that amplified and echoed in the great space of the tree and the echoes rang out over the forest and beyond, carrying high in the clear air. The fledgling sings to the sky and to the bright face of the Sun above, and he sings out the love that is within him. The notes flow out of the tree, as if it was a huge flute, and creatures far-off stop to listen to this new song. The joyful bird sings on until the other birds, young and old, join in and a chorus forms from all the diverse voices.

As the bird listens in his turn, he looks up and realizes he can see a spot on the Sun, and it is moving in a circle. He watches as the speck becomes larger until it takes the shape of a bird, silhouetted in front of the sun. The familiar shape comes closer, until the bird is circling around the opening to the sky. With a swoop of her strong wings, she lands at its edge. Her bright eyes pierce down into the depths of the tree. She raises her broad wings and her form almost fills the bright disc of light above. Silence falls over all the birds there. Then, from her heart, she gives a joyful cry, which echoes down the hollow body of the towering tree and touches the young bird. He knows within him it is the call of his mother. The song of his heart had been heard.

He looks up to see this winged one soaring down the threads of light towards him, growing bigger and more beautiful in his eyes as she nears. When she lands on the earth, her eyes are alight with joy and her face was shining with bright love. From her face shone the happiness of seeing her newborn standing up on his feet, here within the ancient tree. She remembered the moment she had returned home, just after the fall, to find her precious egg gone, and the nest empty and lifeless. Her cry of anguish had echoed from the cliffs and rung out over the plains and forest. She had begun to search, and kept on searching, though there was no sign of hope. Together, the parents had searched the surface of the Earth, calling from the empty sky, hoping for a sign, waiting for a reply. Then she had heard a song that had touched her, even at a great distance, and she knew it held hope in its tones.

The mother bird now reached down and lay her head gently against the head of her chick, wrapping her wings around his little body. He felt warm and happy and peaceful inside. The little bird felt safe as so much stirred inside him and he knew he was loved and almost home. Then he heard another cry that echoed in the vault of the sky, and he knew it to be the call of his father. He looked up to see his form with outstretched wings circling around the Sun. He knew these winged ones loved him and would protect and teach him and he would love them in turn. Something told him that, one day, he would be as fine and strong as these great birds and have wide, shimmering wings like theirs. He, too, would have these feathers with their flashes of gold. Some day to come, he would stretch his strong wings and fly, soaring up into the wide sky, as high as he wished.

He knew that moment might be a long way away but, some day, it would come. In the meantime he would be patient and enjoy this moment, standing in the pillar of light, while his wings were folded inside his mother's wings. They held each other, heart to heart, and dreamed the same dream.

When the Raven and the Swan open their hearts to one another, their wings open and enfold.

As the Swan and the Raven embrace, a Circle of Love is made.

When Light embraces Darkness and Darkness embraces Light, they become the One Light they truly are, and Oneness is revealed. There is no struggle between True Darkness and True Light. They are united in the One Light, the Light of Truth. Within the Light of Truth, we find True Darkness is that which spins from the Heart of the Creator, from the Great Mystery from which we come, of which Dark and Light are born. Within this Circle of One Light, now, the old fears fade away, transmuted into truth.

Darkness defines Light, and Light defines Darkness, but it is not so simple to define the nature of Darkness. There is between both energies a dynamic relationship; in fact, a cosmic dance is at the heart of it. Rather than a struggle, there is, instead, a necessary tension between the threads to hold the natural balance. This is a relativity founded in love, a relationship that shifts and flows in every moment, creating the nature of realities and times, defining the experience of what is real or unreal, exposed or concealed, visible or invisible.

Like the relationship between silence and sound, it is not simply one of presence and absence, fullness and emptiness. Silence is not simply the lack of sound, darkness is not just the absence of light. True Silence is a sacred presence in itself; True Darkness is such a sacred presence, also. Its presence held open the sacred space of the Universe before the creation of Light. In this Dark Age that was, Light had yet to emerge into being, had yet to be born from the heart of the Creator. It could be said that the Darkness of the Divine Void was the Mother of the Light, for from the womb of Divine Darkness, the Light emerged and still emerges.

Behind the Light, the Dark is and between the Light-threads, the Dark threads are. Long ago, from between the threads of Darkness, the first thread of Light emerged, and a frail thread it would have seemed with which to weave a Universe. Yet, with this slender thread, the story of Light begins, as the first Circle of Light was formed in the Void. From such a simple beginning, the Universe you are within and the Universe within you are woven.

From the darkest, deepest wombs of the Universe, the brightest, most abundant light is born, and rivers of stars flow endlessly. What appears as a black hole is a birther of galaxies, a Dark Weaver who brings worlds into being and holds them in galactic balance, a portal into the Heart of Divine Darkness. This Divine Darkness is as full of love and as rich with potential as Light is. Yet, seldom are its gifts explored or comprehended. To those with Dark eyes, it is easier to see such potentials sparkling there. But, all can discover this hidden divinity, for the eye of the heart can see as well in the Dark as the Light.

When we weave with the divine filaments of Dark and Light, we co-create a sacred space where infinite possibilities are unveiled, an open space where love welcomes All.

We are the Dark Weavers. Our hands are busy too. We weave the Dark Web, the Web of Night, of living Darkness.

We are Web-Weavers, through and through. We spin from our Dark hearts and we weave with love, as we dance in the deep, dark places. We draw forth the darkest threads and spin them out to dance around the Light. We make the Dance of Balance and, with our weaving, we hold the worlds in a sacred balance. Though few know us or welcome us, we are a vital part of Creation. Spiders appear from the deepest shadows, veiled in the shade. So, now, do we, spinning out our finest threads from the deepest Dark. And only when the Moon kisses them will they glint silver, only when the Sun loves them might they shine. We make our webs to catch the Light and win it for the Darkness, we swallow Light down and keep on weaving. From our Dark wombs, in the fullness of time, new Light emerges, and a sun is born.

We were made as you were made, and we are connected to you by the finest thread of Darkness a Dark heart can weave. You need not fear us, for we know no harm and mean none. Here, in the Darkness, our hearts are at home. We hold no argument with the Light, and, here, we have our say and we have our space. One Light we make between us, One Web we weave between our hearts of Dark and Light. We are at peace, and we are at one, in the One. From the One, we come and to the One, we return in our time. To the grand tapestry of life, we add our threads, we weave from our hearts. We spin the threads of Dark connections and we weave them in between Light and Light. In the spaces in between, you can find us busy, making the links. We fill in where no Light is, so there will be no gaps in the plan, no tears in the tapestry. If the Light Weavers leave a space, there are we to weave it whole. So, we are busy weavers!

Before the dawn comes, the spiders do their work in the night silence. Just as, before the dawn of Light, long ago, we wove the Dark Web of Night. Since the birth of Light, we have co-created whole worlds and universes together and learned much along the sacred way. Now, we take our time and do our dark work, so Creation is the richer and the Light shines still brighter. We wait within the sacred Darkness, if you wish to find us there. For we know many secrets; we are Wisdom-Weavers, too.

We do not forget and our wisdom is to be shared. We hold the secrets of the Web of Night, we hold the stories of the deepest, darkest places. And we hold them open to you, now…

We, who weave with Light, have no quarrel with the Dark Weavers; they are Brothers and Sisters, too.

They are the Dark Dancers, the ones who hold the Web of Night and we love them as we love ourselves. For they are part of the One Love, the One Heart. And all must deal with Darkness, all must walk or dance with Darkness. All must hear its murmurs, all must witness its dark flame and face its truth. Its wisdom needs to be listened to, for the Dark can illuminate the Light as the Light illuminates the Dark. We weave Light between the Dark threads, we trace the outlines of the shadows, spin a veil across the Dark places, not to hide them but to reveal them; not to conceal their wonders, but to show the way to them.

We Light Weavers know the Darkness from the beginning. So we have no fear, for we know the velvet touch of Darkness and we know it is tender in its way. As we weave the peace between, we weave through Darkness into Light and weave the Light through Darkness, so that the Oneness is maintained, and the balance holds in place. For we all weave the One Fabric, we create the One Cloth from all the threads of Creation. And all have their place in the Grand Design, the pattern of tomorrow and of the days beyond.

I come from another galaxy, in the constellation of The Snake. I bring more good news, news of the Circles' widening, of new members being added and the forming of new Circles, beyond the Circles. The great Unity is being woven and we each play our role in weaving the threads.

And we, who find each other strange, are in some ways the most important at the moment, for in our acceptance of each other, we allow new love to enter the circles. For in the healing of the old struggles, the circles bind tighter together, until they spin through space, stronger than chains, stronger than a metal web. A Web that will be hard indeed to break and easy to repair. Many of us will seem strange to you, for we are forms that seem unfamiliar, but of course, this is a two way process, and we might find each others' strangeness quite amusing. Sometime soon perhaps you will meet us face to face and know us as friends. And there will be a healing there, for we each have a history, subtly inter-linked and sometimes more closely, going back through the centuries.

We were there at your beginnings on Earth. Some might be counted as midwives, others as observers. Some came to stay and were hard to persuade to leave when the time came to do so, for they had come to love the Earth so much. But it was known, that your time of flowering was coming and the stage of the Earth must be clear, so that the Great Play that you have mentioned could begin in earnest. There were many who left at this time, who had been helpers and some who had been hinderers. And in the clearing, there was allowed space for Humanity to grow and to come into its own. To grow up and out and down and, in the growing, others who observed from far off could learn about themselves. For the Earth has always been a place of wonder for many civilizations and cultures gathered through space. We are endlessly intrigued by your actions and adventures and from them we learn both about you and ourselves. We feel for you as brothers and sisters in your conflicts when so much pain pours onto the Earth. And we sometimes wish that we could intervene to help, but we know that this would not be appropriate. So we stand back and send our love and our prayers and we wish you a speedy recovery from the spilling out of the pain. For there is growth in this too.

Each conflict is a lesson and allows a new growth as each conflict also clears a space in the most drastic and dramatic way. Yet in the space after, in the peace after, there are new opportunities for healing, once the mourning has flowed through. For Earth has known so many wars, great and small, so many cycles of conflict, so many patterns of pain and release.

In the flow of pain, journeys are made, through the flow into new spaces, like swimming through a dark river to find the light blinking up ahead. So many millions have had to swim through the dark rivers until they have seemed like an ocean, deep, dark and impenetrable. Yet we honor your bravery, for Humanity has swum hard through the centuries and has battled bravely in its own way, against what it could not see or understand. And we honor this in its intent, however mistaken it sometimes was.

For there is great Heart amongst the Humans. And many races envy this depth of feeling and passion for they and we sometimes cannot muster such feelings. For we are differently made and we honor the difference. And even in the ugliness of the conflicts, there's a beauty there of intent and passion, belief, trust, hope and faith. And in this great drama, the players that emerge, find themselves taking on unexpected roles and growing more quickly than they would in other circumstances.

This is when the heroes and heroines are made, those working away, healing in forgotten corners, quietly working to heal the wounded heart and body. Those quietly weaving the spirit back together again. So many heroes and heroines, and they too are a tribute to Humanity; they shine like candles amidst the darkness when it descends. We see them at work and learn new ways of loving and caring, for they show that it is possible to love even when one does not know why, even when one does not know what will happen in the next hour –or whether one will be alive in an hour's time. They show the power and strength of love, in its simplicity and strength, in its beauty and endurance. They show that the faith of love cannot be conquered by even the greatest empire, the strongest leader, the largest army.

A single woman or man with love in their heart, burning brightly, can defeat these forces through the simple power of Love. Such is your gift to the Universe. One of the many you have given, and we have tried to learn your lesson, for you have in your own way, prevented conflicts in other places. For sometimes you have acted out conflicts, which would have happened in other places. Yet the participants have been able to observe your actions and their outcomes and moved away from the course of war or conflict, so you have indeed saved lives and spirits elsewhere without being aware of it. It is perhaps a small consolation for those who have lost loved ones, but in that favorite Human phrase, "Their sacrifice was not in vain." For the learning and the lesson went out into the Universe and the family; the family of light and darkness, the family of the spectrum, has been of learning the lesson.

We will return soon, with a story or two perhaps, to explain the influence of Humanity on other cultures, scattered through time and space. In the meantime, we wish you to know that when you are observed, it is with they eyes of Love and that there will be no interference. For the drama that Humanity is playing out will have its ripples in the universes. And the threads of its stories will stretch to the ends of Time. We honor your work, your gifts, your play, and withdraw so that another may have their say.

Falling through time and space with a bump – it is a journey to be experienced! But we bring a cushion, to soften our landing... We are adjusting to the new space, and to this new body. [Long pause]

No, we have not forgotten what we were going to say. We are taking our time in fitting in, observing the wonders of Earth, the little marvels... For we, too, come from far away, spinning down the thread of light into this...little place. And we are glad of your welcome – your fiery welcome. The fire is beautiful, is it not? We do not see such things often. We are perhaps too advanced for our own good! Sometimes in so-called advancement, the simple pleasures get forgotten. Amidst all the serious civilization, simple things get left behind, until only the children and the open ones notice them.

So we are glad to be here. It is not our first visit to this world, for some of our ancestors came here long ago, when you were forming and growing in the womb of the Earth. When, in the mists of your world, other almost-forgotten creatures were forming and growing. Many, many changes were taking place, evolvement was accelerating beyond any that was foreseen, and the new humans were soon standing up for themselves, wanting their own space, and the right to direct their own affairs. And this was all to the good, for all of us. Those of us who were the watchers, the safe-guarders, the keepers, stood back more and more and allowed events to take their course. Though, in later times, our hearts bled for what was happening, more often than not we were overjoyed with the discoveries and expansion that we saw happening amongst the humans. You were learning very quickly, how to live and play, how to create and discover, how to worship and wonder.

We saw the cave temples, we saw the new leaders emerge, we saw the sacred groves appear, the sacred spaces being made, the connections between places being mapped out. We saw you working with the Earth, seeing in her, your own image and finding images in her that allowed you to grow. We saw you grow in wonder at her marvels, great and small. From the power of the elemental realms, to the beauty of the deep places and the mountaintops, nowhere was beyond your reach then. You flew where you wished in spirit, and returned with tales of what you had seen, for that was when the first humans learnt how to fly with the wings of the spirit.

They were the shamans, the bird people, the healers, those women and men who looked into the mysteries and interpreted them for their tribe. They made sense of the incomprehensible, but they also accepted the unexplainable. They held the mystery, and they revealed its facets, or they simply accepted the beauty of the mystery, with wonder. There were many times, later, when they would single-handedly hold the tribe together. They wove the people's hearts back together when they had been shattered and they wove together broken hearts around the world. And they wove the hearts into the world, into the heart of the Earth. They braided the souls of the Earth together through the dance, through their spiritual work, through play and creation. They are the source to which you are now returning, for it is time again when such women and men will be needed on the Earth. These will be the new weavers, and they will work and play to weave this world together as one again.

Across time and culture, across space and separation, they will pull the threads together, with the help of their guides and helpers, their invisible friends and with the co-operation and participation of humanity. For they will have no wish to conquer or dominate, they know that they are here simply to help, they can take no one's freedom, and they have no wish to do so. The freer and more playful they are, the more they will manifest the growth that is possible for all. For it is their joy that will show the way, not their learning or wisdom; not the beauty of their words, but their simple joy and love that will shine out, brighter than the clearest crystal.

These Crystal People are seeded throughout the Earth, and they have been waking up, and will continue to do so, to polish their hearts to let them shine more. And ,as they sparkle in the love, others will see other worlds in their eyes, and the future of this old world shining there. They will show the way, by simply being themselves and doing the simplest of things, but doing them with love. In the Circles of play and pleasure, wonder and simple worship, they will weave the new world, then others will take up the threads and keep weaving into the next generations.

Many old threads will be found, many ancient threads, the stories and wisdoms forgotten, tales of the Tribes, stories of individuals or forgotten deeds. These threads will be taken up again, sometimes found within their own hearts and sometimes found in mysterious places, forgotten, in half-forgotten corners of the Earth. Those who are now held low, whose hearts are heavy, who feel cast aside or left behind, those who are lonely, who feel the emptiness, the absence of joy, will gather in the new spaces and wake up to their own true beauty, their own deep wonder, their own living heart, in all its splendor. They will need no great leader, no masterful guru, for they will know where their heart will lead them. If we are all lead by our hearts, we can never truly be lost.

For once we are *Heart-led*, our own light will guide us in the weaving to this Tribe of Light again on the Earth. This Heart Tribe will cross all boundaries and bring many surprises to those "great leaders" who now stride the Earth, who will find they do not have the power they believed they had. For this new tribe will seem to be emerging everywhere and they will call themselves by many names, have many faces and wear different symbols, but the Oneness will shine through. The One Tribe will be there behind the masks and the superficial differences. The Tribe of the Heart will lead the Earth into the new millennium, into this new era that is forming. And you are the shamans of the new tribe, which is the old tribe, which is the first tribe – the One Tribe.

The Heart of the One will sing in infinite voices and the Harmony of One will ring through the Universe. And all will be revealed in their Oneness, beyond time.

Tangled threads! Oh, I spend so much time untangling threads. You Humans are so good at tangling things–so good at weaving things, too, when you try. But so seldom now do people weave...too busy tangling! Making work for me and all the other Weavers; you keep us very busy. Our legs and arms get tired, weaving away in the dark of the night, while you sleep. When you awake, you admire our perfect weave, then you trip up and tangle it all again! So we help you untangle yourself and off you go with the threads tangled round your ankles, undoing our work as we weave away behind you...

Yet we know you are unaware of the work you make for others, so we merrily weave away, as you weave your way through the world, for we know the time will soon come when you will weave with us consciously again–and then the fun will start. Your fingers still know how to weave, and your heart still knows the ways, so we, who hold the old weaving wisdom, wait patiently for you to remember what you know, deep inside. What patterns are hidden there? Wonderful patterns that we haven't seen for centuries, the weaves of the ancient tribes, which you can now weave with the new wisdom and learning, with fresh colors, to make the new tribal patterns of the future. This is the open weave of the open tribe, weaving between heart and heart, soul to soul. You will weave as you go, weaving across the Earth in the spiral spider dance. Of course, you will get in a tangle now and then, tripping each other up and finding yourselves in a knot, but that can be the fun sometimes, once you know how to unravel things. A lot of people walk around knotted up, these days. Of course, knots can help you remember things – so you'll be remembering lots of things in the future!

Maybe the many knots will remind everyone what you need to remember to feel whole again, to know your role in the life of the tribe, to recall the connections between us all. Each tangle holds a different meaning, and each can be unthreaded and unraveled in different ways, so this will be a learning, too. While you are unraveling the knots, who knows what you will remember? But, there are some old tangles even we could not unravel, so they will have to wait until Humanity remembers how to weave and unweave, to ravel and unravel.

Of course, we have been playing this game much longer than you, so we will be patient while you catch us up and show us what wonderful weavers you are. We know you will surprise us–you always do! Oh, what a joy it is to weave, when you let yourself believe. When you believe in your own heart and weave from your own love, you will surprise yourself every day and amaze yourself with the threads that you spin out. Yes, you will be showing off to friends how colorful you can be until they are green with envy. Then they will try out their own colors, because even green can be boring after a while. So, you will find rainbows being made in the most unexpected places.

Some tribes who have kept the weaving-wisdom will again emerge, and they will gently lead the others in the ways of weaving, for we are glad to say that there are many who have not forgotten. And you all have the potential to remember your origins, your true depths, all the beauties hidden within. You need only spin the threads out and begin to weave them, then the tangles will come out into the Light, too. There, in the Light, we can work on the tangled masses together, the light and dark threads and those of every hue. In these bright spaces of gentle healing, we can safely weave our hearts together as One and know that none is bound or trapped or tangled in any web which is not of their making and their participation. For we will all keep the freedom that Humanity so desires and needs.

We spiders have been free for a long time and we never feel trapped in our webs, and when we drop on your heads, we only come to wake you up! To remind you to look up at the beauty of a single thread, because that single thread leads back to the beginning. That fragile creature swaying in the wind, hanging from a thread woven from deep within, that spider weaves from the same source as you. That slender thread reaches back to the source, for at the heart of every web is the Creator, Who is you and me, too.

Oh, we'll weave some wonders… And the clumsy ones will learn, too, and we will not mind the extra work, for maybe those with the thick fingers will have the greatest joy, seeing the webs they can spin and the beauty of their weaving. And we will be ready to help all who tangle themselves up. For we are going to weave a whole world, and that's quite a weave!

So all hands, feet and hearts will be needed, and the graceful ones will work with the more graceless in weaving the one work, for we all need each other. Meanwhile, watch out for the spider-dancers –please don't step on them when you are tangled in your web, because they can help untangle you, if you only ask… Happy weaving!

I have traveled far. I am new to you, and you to me – yet do not be alarmed, for I come as a friend, a distant friend, perhaps. I come from a quiet place, a distant place, a place where much is remembered and little forgotten. We hold the knowing of the old times, when Earth and the stars were more closely woven. The peoples of the stars were frequent visitors, who trod the Earth in their different forms. This was when Humanity was in its infancy. These visitors were mostly discreet, for the Guardians of the Earth kept a close eye on those who might have taken advantage of the innocence of the new Humans, of their openness of heart. Some visitors saw them as children, without noticing the potential for growth and maturity that was evident to others.

Some came who seized on the child-like aspect of the Human nature and bent it for their own purposes, for ends that were not good for Humanity. They introduced new concepts of slavery and domination onto the Earth. They introduced many ideas that were unknown on the planet, and Humans, as you know, are quick learners. Soon, the original innocence was shattered. Some of them did not understand what they, themselves, were doing, while others did not care, since they thought only in the short-term. It pained us greatly to watch these developments, yet we were constrained, as others were, from intervening. But we did what little we could to heal the worst of these transgressions. In time, these interlopers left or were made to leave, but the damage had been done.

Some of the seeds sowed then are still sprouting on the Earth, and they spring up in shadowy places and sometimes in bright places, to the dismay of all. But these seeds can be found and they can be isolated. They can even be found in your own hearts, but if you do not allow them to root there, they can be brought out into the light, where their energies can be changed and transmuted. These dark seeds, if gathered, can make many a basketful of shadows, but, in examining their contents, you will learn much about humanity's history.

Of course, humanity has since scattered many dark seeds of its own making, and still the harvest of these is being reaped. Some are scattered in innocence, some in ignorance and some with malice, but they all give their lessons in their sprouting and fruiting. They have spread many poisons into the body of humanity, and this was part of the learning. Yet, now that you know these seeds exist, they can be gathered in the fields and the battlefields and taken to the sacred places, the places of healing, there to be transmuted. For all energy can be changed and transformed through the power of love, and there is no greater power.

So you will be as seed-gatherers, finding these seeds in your own hearts and bringing them forth in these safe places, then working together to transform them into the golden seeds of the future. You will be doing the vital work that will lead Humanity on, until there will be no more dark harvests. The times of shadow and bloodshed need not continue, for the lessons have been learnt long ago, and now only the empty roles remain. These roles are still being played out, over and over, so that they seem to have purpose, yet the play is hollow now and has lost its meaning. It is but a re-enactment of an old, old story that we no longer need. All know the lesson in their hearts, and the play need not detain us any longer. We can now move on.

In those parts of the Earth where these seeds have collected over the centuries, that is where the work will be concentrated. The gleaners will go out into the battlefields with their backs bent, gathering the seeds of fear from the soil. They will fill the baskets of their hearts with these dark seeds and take them to the sacred place of change and transmutation, and there, the glowing seeds of the golden harvest will be created. This hallowed harvest awaits Humanity and it will soon come. So let the gathering continue, and when the battlefields are clean, the new seeds of Light will open, and new shoots will rise up from the Earth to stand in the sunlight and shine golden. They will shine *their* light to the Sun, so each will reflect the others' glory, and the Sun will shine brighter for the reflection of its love.

There *will* be a golden harvest, and *you* will sow its seeds.

The Sisters

We weave a new tale for you, a tale of two sisters, one light and one dark.

One was as light and blonde as the other was dark and raven. Some wondered how they could even be sisters, when they seemed so different from each other in every way, but they loved each other as only sisters can. The ways of the light one and the dark one, their looks and mannerisms, were such a stark contrast that some asked themselves if the girls had different fathers, but they had only the one. Their mother loved them each uniquely and equally and they were allowed to be as different as could be. Their parents watched them in the garden in springtime, two young girls holding hands and spinning round each other, orbiting one another's worlds, their eyes locked in mutual delight, and they knew these two would have a special bond all their days.

Each had different ways of playing, so, sometimes, they would play apart, each going deep into her own world. At other times, when they found a game that they both enjoyed, they would play together, creating a little bubble of a world, right then and there. These shared times were golden for them, magic moments that they opened up, the light sister and the dark sister, laughing, playing, exploring as one. When they went out into the world, they would each lead the other to different places, often places that the other would not have thought of exploring. They trusted one another, so each would follow where the other led, though at times they wondered where on earth they would end up. Though they did not really understand one another's ways, they knew their sister would not lead them too far astray, and it was safe to trust. They sensed each other's pain and joy, and they usually knew how the other was feeling, even if they did not understand why.

The children would go deep into the woods, exploring together, playing in the shadowy places and the open spaces amongst the trees, finding new beauties each time and little corners they had missed before. One would part the undergrowth to reveal hidden places, while one craned her swan-like neck to peek into secret spots, ones that human eyes had never looked into. They found special, magical spaces that they ventured into together, each holding the other's hand for support. For some of these places were dark and mysterious, and it felt good that the other was there, to help her sister walk through fear and beyond doubt.

The sister who was drawn to dark places would lead her sibling into these, and the sister attracted to light-filled ones did likewise, so they would both find themselves in unexpected surroundings. So, together, they discovered the dark behind the light and the light behind the dark. Sometimes the dark sister would seem to come into her own, becoming her sisters' guide through the shady places. At other times, the light one led her sister, who might be lost in the shadows, through to a clear, bright space, making her way through the tangles as if she could scent the light on the air. How they laughed at their revelations, how they reveled in their discoveries! And the golden laughter of the one and the silver laughter of the other would echo through the woods and delight the listening trees. Between them, as they played, they created a world that only they could truly enter and share. And this world seemed to move and grow with them. Between their open hearts was a special space, invisible to the world. Through the woods, they wandered on long, rambling walks and their conversations wandered a long way, too, through territories explored by few, into places only brave souls go. One, with her ravenous hunger for knowledge and experience, often leading the way. When night came, they would share a blanket to lie on the grass and watch the stars circling them.

They learned by seeing through the other's eyes, they noticed what was invisible otherwise, they found a shared vision, which they could then share with others. Yet, between themselves, there was an intensity they felt with no one else. Between them, there was a special language flowing that was their own, one that needed no words, no explanations. It felt like a language that had always been there. It was put to the test, this intangible connection, its invisible threads were stretched to breaking, their tolerance was tested. In a world with little tolerance of what cannot be known or controlled, they would come to find themselves surrounded by apparent chaos. But that time was still in the future.

As years went by, they brought each other to new places, they stumbled into fresh experiences. They learnt new dances together, they explored the ways of growing up. They observed the games of the adults and played them in their own way. They were outgrowing childhood, so now they played with clothes and makeup, and they played at being the women they would someday become. They played with styles and identities, opinions and ideas, and each often lamented the other's terrible taste and ill-informed views. There were also their fights, so fiery and impassioned, then their distance and coolness, and finally their melting and making-up. There were the boys that they argued about, the ones who broke their hearts, and the sisters' shared tears and tenderness that mended them again. So they cried, at times, together, but they shared much more laughter, and they had grownup subjects to laugh about now. And how each loved to hear the other laugh, to see the spark of light in the other sister's eye.

They were dancing on the threshold for they were soon to step into the world as women and they were excited, looking forward to the mysteries that would be unveiled. They dreamed of the places they would go, the people they would encounter, the stories they would have to tell in later years. They watched one other change and blossom, growing through the phases of girlhood into growing maturity. Their bodies were changing fast, and at times, they felt like a stranger in their own skin. They were glad when they could face the world together, when the world seemed mysterious and dark, or full of secrets they couldn't understand. Then the dark sister seemed to come into her own, burrowing deep into the subjects and unearthing all manner of motives and meanings. But her taste for the obscure, and the riddles of life, sometimes took her on long trips through the corridors of the mind. When the dark sister was spending too much time alone, or had been hidden away indoors, buried in her books for days, her sister would come to open the shades and remind her there was still a world out there. She would take her by the hand and lead her out into the sunshine she had not noticed, and they would walk a while, side by side.

In their teenage years, they found a new closeness and a new distance, as each felt the need for more time and space to find her own way. They felt more confident by then, more ready to face the world alone, more able to understand things for themselves, able to express their own thoughts with their own voice. They still cherished their time together and they still delighted in each other's company, but each was becoming a woman who would have to make her own place in the world, a place where sometimes another could not enter, for it was hers alone. They found that what delighted one sister, could enrage the other. One wanted so much to change the world, one wanted, above all, to understand it; one raged at its senseless ways, one wanted to bring peace to them; one quested for truth, one wished to find it inside her. As each grew they had more to share, more stories to tell, experiences to swap, more places to go together. And they still found joy in the other's joy, and each loved to see the light of surprise in her sister's face.

So they stepped out into the world and each changed and grew as they learnt the ways of the women that they were becoming, each different, each unique. They delved into the mysteries of womanhood and embraced their own transformations along the way. They danced their different dances and they attracted new friends, and they found lovers. And they danced the dances of love and made new discoveries. They seemed to love in different ways; one sister's love was golden and hot, the other's was more silver and cool. Like the Sun and Moon, they loved equally, but in different ways. Each had their share of pain and heartbreak, their share of laughter and joy. There were painful days and nights, when each was grateful the other was there, one with a golden smile, the other a silver one.

The dark sister was drawn to wilder friends, who led her into wild experiments and adventures, and frenzied weekends. The light sister's friends, and her life, often seemed safe and tame by comparison, but she enjoyed her time just as much. When one went crazy for the night, the other would stay sane and watch out for her sister. Or, if they were both taking the crazy way, they would make sure they stuck together, to hold each other up when the night was over. The men they drew to them were as different as men can be, and the lessons they learned were usually worth the trouble. The lessons they learnt separately, they shared when they came together in their special Heart Space. Through their heart-to-heart exchanges, they shared their hard-won wisdoms, and each enriched the experiences of the other with their insights. After days and nights spent apart, they would meet again to swap stories of their exploits and experiences, or simply be quiet, side by side. If one sister's dream had been shattered, the other would hold her soul together. And when there was nothing else to be done, they simply held each other and waited for the pain to pass. They would hold each other closest in those moments of the deepest pain, holding hope for a wounded heart, until it was strong enough to face the world once more.

Each became a mother in her own time, to their mutual joy. They were each a different kind of mother, and each loved in their own way. They discovered that when a child began to grow within their womb, a new space opened up inside their heart. As their children grew, they found their shared Heart Space grew to fit everyone in. And new spaces appeared within it, growing and opening, as each child made their own space there. These grew, like circles connected one to the other, the circles of parent and child, mother and father, sister and sister, brother and brother, all connected yet unique and independent. All the spaces flowered in their season, and the mothers tended this family garden carefully, year by year.

Then the days of their greatest test came. As the chaos gathered around them, it seemed the world had gone way past crazy and was racing itself to its own end. Everything they had known was falling apart, all they believed in was fading away. Everyone was being divided from those they had loved and becoming divided within their own soul. The sisters felt themselves wrenched apart by events, caught up in the maelstrom raging around them. They were taken to places they never thought they would be, they lived through the destruction of all that had been familiar. In the midst of it, the women found themselves drawn into this madness. One of them became a flame of anger, and in the face of her rage, her sister placed icy armor around herself. But, behind the cold façade, the embers of her own anger smoldered, choking her throat and blinding her eyes. They moved away from each other then, they put an empty space between them, a dead place where communication seemed impossible. And time passed and their world seemed set and frozen in its ways. The two women had walked so far from each other now that neither knew the way back. They thought they had lost each other forever. And without one another, they became sisters of sorrow.

Yet something slender still connected them. Though their bond seemed to have been stretched past breaking-point, it did not break. There were still the threads that the madness of the world could not break, that nothing could put asunder. Somehow, the invisible threads bridged the rift, and held the living bond that was beyond breaking. And there came a day when they embraced again, heart to heart, and held one another as sisters once more. And something shone out from them into the gloom surrounding them that made those days more bearable for those near to them.

And the world around them changed, and the space between them became a garden again, where they could lighten their hearts and heal. When their children came into it, they could even feel playful again. Their differences did not go away, but dimmed in importance, as they grew to accept their differing ways once more and find new meaning in all that been.

Over the years, the paths of the sisters diverged and returned to each other, running parallel or crossing, and their shared space became richer and more complex. The threads between them stretched further across space and time, and though their meetings now were fewer, they found a word or a touch could say even more than it could before. For they had woven a web so wonderful, so full of finely woven threads of love, that it was a web of incredible beauty and complexity. Between these two sisters, the light and the dark, in their great Heart Space, this heart web shone out and shimmered in its delicacy and strength. Yet even they could not imagine its full beauty.

As they grew older, and had less time to spend with each other, this web became not weaker, but stronger, for its threads were tested and stretched in and they were found to endure, to have resilience and strength. It was a web of unity that was unbreakable and it remained a web of comfort and support for them, as they grew and changed and moved through the world. When they came together again as sisters, like the children they once were, they would find themselves deep within this loving web they had woven from their first moments together, from their days of play, their joyful experiences, their arguments, their times of struggle, their times of shared pleasure.

Now, as they move through the years, they find the living web grows ever stronger, it seems only to deepen its roots into the earth. When their children become parents themselves, the fresh, exciting colors of their grandchildren are added. The proud grandmothers braid together the bonds of child and parent, parent and grandparent. They strengthen the generations through their web of love and weave love between them. They weave a tribe of the heart together.

When they move on, out of physical form, beyond time, they will find the web of love waiting there. They will find themselves moving through a shimmering tapestry of incredible beauty and complexity, woven of their heartthreads. A creation of such astonishing beauty, that they could never have imagined they had woven it through their living and their loving. Its magnificent patterns will fill them with pure joy and true wonder at their own beauty, at their own specialness as creators. Its perfect details will be magnified in their new vision. All the invisible relationships will be revealed in their new awareness. And they will spend a long time out of time wandering through this web of their own making, laughing together at the forgotten moments. They will explore its special weavings, its secret spaces, the places they had long forgotten, the shadowy corners and the bright clearings.

Within this web of peace, they will comprehend the strength and depth of their own hearts. They will enjoy the weaving-in of the people they had loved and the creatures who had woven their lives with theirs. All that had entered their orbit, all those they have loved will have their pattern woven through, and their web of love will be a source of astonishment for all. The grand pageant of all their days will be there, yet not as a tapestry of the past for, here, every thread of the stories is alive. And, together, they create one story that flows through all. It grows now like a living garden through which they walk, and the seeds of each moment they plant will have its flowering in this living tapestry. It stretches into the heart of the Earth, and it stretches far away to the stars. It bridges times and worlds, and it is unique in all the Universe. And the Creator will rejoice that such beauty poured forth from the hearts of two women, the hearts of two sisters, who are One in the heart of All.

And that web hangs in sacred space for all the worlds to wonder at...

The bowl of the open heart fills with light, and the light spills over the edges of the bowl like milk, as liquid love nourishing the Earth. The Earth drinks in the light, taking in the love and the Earth heals. The very dirt of the Earth drinks in the love and the love flows through her veins, down deep through the rocks, through the sediments, down through the levels of Earth, trickling down, down towards her Heart. And the light flows together, the trickles become a stream and the stream, an underground river of liquid flowing love, of light pouring into the heart of the Earth, healing her scars, healing the wounds made by the actions of mankind and others. For the Earth has been wounded – though her heart is intact, bright and blinding. She drinks in the Light and the dirt of the Earth awakens in the Light, each grain, each crystal, each molecule remembers itself. It feels its power flow, feels its light increase, it feels the pulse of the Earth more strongly. The Earth calls to the stars, the stars reply and their echoes ring.

The songs intertwine, they mingle in harmonies, they twine together in the One Love. And Earth and stars unite as they were once united and the threads thicken, they grow more light, they strengthen and the Web is strengthened. The universes pull together a little, the threads grow more taut, and the Web repairs the rents and tears. And the Web is made One again as it was One and is One. All that was torn is healed and what was separate is threaded together.

So the Web feels new life, feels new pulses, new rhythms and shimmers, new patterns move through it and the planets and stars in their movement through and with the Web, weave new patterns as they move, weaving new worlds, creating new spaces. And in the closing of the tears, gaps and holes, there is an opening too. For now there is more room to move and grow. The new open spaces are created in an *open weave,* so the light floods through, expanding new spaces and, within the universes, more spaces are made to explore. For the weaving of Unity can create new universes within the universes – new worlds appear as if by magic, like rooms suddenly appearing and multiplying in an old house. Until what was a small cottage becomes a vast mansion and, within the once tiny space, room after room appears, peopled with beings and creatures, new life in half-forgotten corners. In the new spaces never explored, there is new life, new creation evolving before our very eyes, this new life coming to a sense of itself, evolving quickly and growing.

Other beings and creatures return to life from the long sleep of hibernation, to find themselves in wonderful new playgrounds. And the tombs that they thought they were trapped in open out – to become multicolored playgrounds of the spirit and the body.   They begin to play again, and be as children and they feel the   joy running through their old bones, their skin filled with light; their faces shine once more, they are reborn. They are the children of the New Age, they join the others who have been waiting in the wings and on the stage, holding the space for their brothers and   sisters to join them. For none will be forgotten, none will be left out of the Great Play. For there is room for all, and each have a   role to play, a song to sing, lines to speak and a dance to be danced on the great stage of life.

The curtains are now opening all over the universes, the veils are opening and light is flooding in to the forgotten places. As the players wake up and remember their roles, the Great Play finds new depth. The meanings are revealed, the stories and patterns open out like flowers into the light, to spill their inner wisdom and flood their perfume out into the world.

And in the opening, in the flowering, in the blossoming forth of the new life, the gardens fill again with new blooms. Flowers and fruit of the heart, the rich, intoxicating perfumes of love and joy, the dancing leaves, the rainbow spectrum of floral hues, the birds in their multicolored feathers weaving between, and all dancing, all interweaving.

And the garden comes to new life. The gardeners are busy, remembering their skills, and the Gardener who taught them looks on with joy, for the world has come back to life. We breathe in the new perfume and our hearts fill with its deep sense of Love.

From each heart flows forth a new garden and the gardens grow together, each weaving together at the edges to make a living tapestry. The tapestry weaves itself together into one great Garden, full of life, with living love in every thread, filled with creatures of the spirit, dancing and rejoicing, flying, crawling, dancing through the planet, spreading their seeds, planting the new blooms.

The gardeners weave the one work, the one joy and the Garden of the One Heart is woven from the open gardens of simply open hearts. The infinite heart gardens weave into one great Garden of the Heart, which is the Garden of Creation, as it was in the beginning and is Now.

So let it be… And so it is.

In the beginning, there was Creation and it never ends. For Creation is truly the Heart of Life, the Heart of All. In the act of creation, the moment of creation, something is called forth and brought into being which had not yet existed in that moment, so to speak. So Creation is always a surprise to the Creator. In the act of making the new, the old is gone beyond and the universe is added to and expanded, new spaces made and all expands.

And the heart expands a little more and, in a sense, we move further from the original act of Creation but also closer to it. For each act of creation unites "then and now," so the space between is made new; yet it also somehow grows, for now there is a new space, yet it is connected to the old space and still connected to the Source. And so while the space between has shrunk, the space created has grown. For the Creator allows infinite space to be created, there are no limits, there are no boundaries. All is permitted in the Great Game.

Only the lessons to be learnt need to be chosen or discovered. For free will is the gift given, and Humans have been given the gift in abundance. Though, of course, often the gift has not been cherished or used as it was intended. At times it has seemed like a burden or a curse, yet within it is hidden the greatest gift of all from the Creator, directly from the Creator, so that if we embrace this gift, use it and explore it, we are manifesting our love for ourselves and for our Creator.

For the gift was given to expand to expand the heart, the mind, the spirit, to allow exploration of the physical and the body, the physical vessel. And for Humans there are fallen to them many difficult tasks of learning. For the gift of free will creates endless possibilities for tough lessons, as well as easy and enjoyable ones. So it has been from the beginning on the Earth; those first Humans, who explored the gift of free will, often found it disorientating and confusing as they discovered their own boundary-less-ness.

As they found that their play had no borders, their free will to move, to gather and to explore sometimes led them into difficult situations. Into dark corners, over the cliffs, into the rapids, sometimes tumbling headlong into places they had no wish to go; but once there, they certainly learned quickly. Others watched with wonder at this lesson – learning, for the new Humans had been given a gift that others did not have access to in the same way. They had been differently gifted. There was jealousy amongst some of those that observed the Humans at play and in their exploration. They too, wished to be part of this new learning but they did not realize that they would come to interfere with the growth of the Humans. For in the intermeshing of free wills there is great scope for both conflict as well as joyful interaction.

Some of those that came into the places of free will, did not respect the free will of others, but only chose to express their own and to test it to its limits without care or regard for others. The Humans sometimes found themselves facing adversaries they could not understand, beings that they had no comprehension of, but whose powers seemed greater than theirs. For the Humans were not as they are now; they had not learnt the ways of conflict, the ways of war and aggression. In many ways their lives were simple and joyful expressions of creativity and exploration. And to these other beings they seemed like simple children, to be dominated, to be used in different ways. The Humans found it difficult to resist, for they did not know the ways of protection; they had had no need of such. Until then, fear had been more of a distant stranger to them, a seldom visitor. One that could be made to leave with the help of a sharing, a story or time around the fire, the hand of another or the gift of laughter.

During this time, Humans had been exploring the Earth and all of its wonders and possibilities. They had found themselves in a sacred place and they set out to make it even more sacred, to express their inner sense of the Divine. All around them was the magic of Creation. All was growing and evolving, all a breathtaking display of color and of light, of life in every possible expression and dimension. They knew themselves to be part of life and part of the Creation. They knew the world to be alive, as they were alive; their wonder and sense of play was what others envied.

Then other beings came into these new spaces and they sought to make them their own. They sought to remake themselves as objects of divinity, as if they are more sacred or important than the Humans. They used their accumulated knowledge to bamboozle and fool some of the Humans, and others, who they could not trick or dominate, they used violence against.

This brought great sorrow to all of Creation. For this was a new experience on the Earth. And the hearts of so many bled as they learnt of these events. And, with our eyes wet, we watched the events unfold. Yet we knew that something must be played out. We held the Humans in our hearts and wove them into our prayers, for we knew the times ahead would be difficult. And into the sacred spaces, woven by the women and by the men, there came new figures. New objects of devotion, new cults of worship, which did not honor the Human spirit, which did not honor the Earth. They caused separation and pain, they created cliques and elites who gathered mystery around them, like a mist of incense, and then who sought to convince others that they were more sacred than others. Of greater light than they, that they were chosen to lead, that they must be followed, that their word was law and that their deeds were divine. They convinced many, for they had learnt the ways from those who had placed this power in their hands and in whose name they wielded it.

The sorrow that was felt through the universes rang like a lament among the worlds, calling out its cry of anguish through the stars. And on the Earth things changed as the simple, sacred spaces of play and creation, of celebration and unity, became divided from each other more and more. The new priests and leaders gathered their flocks, their followers and gave forth their new teachings which they sought to justify by convincing them they came directly from the Creator, in the form of the new gods. The beings that set these events in train watched and worked behind the scenes – and manipulated when necessary.

The temples grew in wealth and power, as the cities grew. Clans and families expanded into towns, villages and the beginnings of the great cities. New elements came into the equation of power and now the plundering of the Earth became a pattern, feeding the great machine that had been created. For the institutions needed their wealth and prestige, they became places of opulence and magnificence gathered from the Earth but used to glorify power and domination – and the Earth Herself wept. For She knew her children were in pain, She knew their hearts were heavy and that their burdens would grow in time. Each time Her heart opened she felt more of their pain.

As the cities grew, the states grew and soon the empires began to emerge. The leaders brought together great armies to protect them and their belongings. Now the body of the Earth herself was carved up amongst the warring cities and states, her bounty was fought over. Her riches that were meant for all were plundered by the few. And again Her sorrow was great. Her very body and face were defiled in the years that followed as the empires warred, as the leaders claimed their spaces and fought off the claims of others. Their armies marched back and forth, tramping across the face of the Earth – leaving a trail of destruction and blood, spilt in the name of power. And on and on it went, like a great wave coursing over the Earth.

Until it seemed, over the centuries, every corner of her was claimed, every part of her body was fought over and every beautiful inch was made a place of conflict. Much blood was spilt onto the Earth, and she was desecrated in these acts, as her children died in great numbers.

All this for the pleasure and power of the few; but those who profited by these acts did not themselves enjoy such power for long. For it seemed endlessly that these states and empires rose and fell, waxed and waned, the borders moved here and there, forward and backward, and the sanctity of the Earth was forgotten in the heat of conflict and war.

Yet after it all, there came a remembering and as the battlefields grew more silent, many came to realize that something had been forgotten in the centuries that had passed, for they knew there was more to the Earth than this, more than the struggle for place and power, for wealth and the hidden riches of the Earth. They knew there was something even richer, hidden within her, which had been missed by all the scrambling hands, by the eyes of greed. For She was alive, they could feel Her heart pumping through them in the quiet places, they could still feel her heart beating, still hear her song rising up through their feet, through their bodies, filling them with the memory of Her love. And soon the times changed, and these new awakenings increased in number. They multiplied and those who were awakening found each other, stumbled across each other; they found they had shared awareness, a shared love of the Earth, of Her living nature, of Her own expression within them.

They found that there was a unity that was unforced, one that was simply there, as if it had always existed, for of course it had. They were simply waking up from the long dream or the long nightmare, to discover that the original dream was still alive was still being dreamt somewhere. And now they are coming together, they are claiming new spaces, not for themselves, or for the power of a few, but claiming the spaces of the Earth for the Earth Herself and for Her children living in harmony with Her. And they will find that the old power game will lose its meaning very quickly. Millions will awaken to the new possibilities. They will feel the dream again, inside them, and they will awaken from one old dark dream, into another more ancient, brighter dream; a dream of a world reborn, and yet to their surprise it will seem more real than anything that they have ever experienced.

For they will feel the very Earth come alive, under their feet, around them. They will witness with their eyes, the Earth Herself coming to new life. See Her myriad mirrored faces everywhere. Experience Her creatures again, making friends with them, coming closer to the creatures of the Earth, know too that the old ways of conflict are being laid aside. Know that the older ways of unity and harmony are being remembered. We will see the weaving together of the Children of the Earth.

And the Heart of the Earth Herself will open anew. The Earth Herself will sing forth new songs; new hymns and chants of celebration will pour forth from the people and the creatures, the beings of the worlds and dimensions when they see that the dream is truly alive. That the patterns, those old patterns of struggle, war and conflict will become a history, and a lesson of history. And the book can be closed, to be opened again only as a warning. For now is the time of rebirth, for all and for each. The weaving of the ways will be joyous and wondrous. And what rejoicing there will be!

You will all hear the Angels sing and know that you are part of it, All.

The Dancer in the Garden

There once was a little girl who loved to dance.
From the moment she woke up, it seemed that she danced all day. She would leap out of bed, skip her way downstairs to begin the morning, and then dance her way through the day in every possible way she could imagine. She would dance out the door and skip her way down the street, dancing with her own feet, lacing them around each other. She would dance around the feet of the adults, prancing and skipping past them. Dancing with and through their shadows, playing with them, weaving her way amongst them. And how the grown-ups loved to watch her, smiling at her joy and her endless energy. She skipped out to the park and danced amongst the trees, dancing round and around them. Lifting up her arms and dancing as if she, herself, was a bird. Landing lightly on the grass, then flitting lightly from blade to blade, barely touching the ground and only tickling the Earth when she did. So the Earth smiled too.

So she would dance with the birds and even with the fairies she could see and feel around her. And when she danced with them, her legs seemed even lighter. She felt they knew how to dance best of all on the Earth. Like her, they skipped and danced their way through life. They danced the dance of how they felt – whether it was sad or happy, whether it was glum or joyful, bright or heavy laden. They danced the dances of all the moods and emotions. They danced through the flowers and they danced through the gardens and the parks with her, wending their way through the flowerbeds, yet never crushing a leaf. And the little girl would follow them, laughing to herself, knowing that even if she was caught by the park-keeper, she could honestly say that she hadn't damaged a single flower.

Sometimes she even led the fairies on a merry dance and they danced happily behind her as she taught them new steps. They laughed with delight at her discoveries, her little inventions, as they tried out her steps and added new ones of their own. Through the gardens in the parks she danced, sometimes in the sunshine when all the flowers were at their brightest. Then, the colors would dazzle her, as all the flowers wore their brightest dresses and they competed with each other in their brilliance and extravagance. So she would put on her brightest dress and dance amongst them. How the flowers laughed at this dancing flower in their midst! They swayed all the more and their glossy leaves waved like her arms as she taught them new steps, too. From them, she learnt how to dance with your roots in the earth, for they could dance in the one spot, while the world danced around them. And, she found, so could she.

So from the flowers and the fairies, she had magical dance lessons and when she was beneath the trees, she danced with these great dancers too. Although they are so deeply rooted, trees dance all the time. Their branches wave and their leaves dance in the air while, inside, their heart pumps strongly, dancing away inside them, pumping life into every cell of their being, rejoicing in their life and strength and their deep roots in the Earth.

Of all the trees she loved, she had a favorite one. And as she circled the tree, round and around, she loved to feel its skin, its rough and smooth places, its ridges and little hollows where the insects lived – they would come out and dance sometimes, circling and wriggling and crawling around. She would try to imitate them, learning some of the insect dances and their funny wriggling ways. She danced with the long-legged spiders in their elegant dances and she watched them dance in the air, or gracefully dancing their way across the faces of their webs. She danced across the face of the Earth as if it were her web, she made her own spider-dance while the spiders watched, and they too were pleased. So she brought great joy to all the creatures, to all the flowers and plants, the trees and the grass, the birds in the air above too, all rejoiced in her. All found her a joy to be with and a wonder to behold.

Then, one day, she came to the park and she did not dance.

She walked through the gardens as if in a distant dream. Slowly she moved, one step at a time, her legs heavy now, her arms swinging lifeless by her side, her face set and frozen. She stopped on the path and stood still for a long time. But it was not like the stillness of the tree when the wind is quiet, or the stillness of a flower when it rests in quiet moments. Hers was a stillness, a quietness, a heaviness that was new in the garden.

The creatures felt a chill run through them and the flowers felt their colors fade, somehow, their leaves droop just a little. The birds stopped flying and landed in the branches of the trees. The trees seemed to be frozen, too, as if watching and wondering what had happened to the little dancer that they loved so much. Every creature and every living thing felt something strange in its heart. Instead of the joy they felt whenever she entered the garden, they felt a kind of coldness now, a kind of pain. Even her favorite tree, so strong and so old felt something inside it that it did not understand.

She seemed to have brought the garden to a stop, to have halted its very growth. It seemed all Creation held its breath as it watched its child, this child that it loved, stand there without dancing, without moving a single muscle. A silence descended on the garden. Even the bees stopped buzzing, they clung to a leaf and waited, for they too felt the pain, they too, felt their little hearts slow, as if almost stopping. In this frozen moment, all were held, for what seemed a long, long time. In the child's face nothing stirred, not a single finger of hers moved, he feet seemed stuck to the spot. Even her hair, which used to bounce and dance with her, seemed frozen now, and clung, lifeless, to her head. All was still.

Then, she moved. She turned to leave. She took a step, to go out of the garden, never to return. For whatever held her seemed to have her locked in its cold grip, forever. She took another step and then another and her eyes saw the gates of the garden ahead of her. She took another step and around her the creatures and the plants, the flowers and the trees wished they could take the step with her, to come with her, to be with her, to comfort her somehow. But they did not know how. The gate was nearer now, but, for a moment, she turned back, and looked around her at the garden she had danced in so many times. Yet it looked so different to her now, it seemed so still, so flat, like a photograph. Nothing moved in it, nothing seemed alive. She turned away and took another step. And with one more, she stepped slowly through the gate. She turned the corner and was gone.

The garden waited for her to return the next day – and the day after that and the day after that, until the weeks passed. And weeks became months, and the months passed, until the months became years. Then the years passed as the garden changed, the plants and the flowers lived and died in their turn. The grass grew and was cut and grew again. The trees grew new rings, more branches and leaves; all the insects lived and died and multiplied. The birds nested, had their families, left and came back, and the cycle of life went on in the garden. But not as it was before, because something was missing now. It seemed that all life in the garden knew that something had been lost, and the memory of this was passed on through the years, somehow, in some mysterious way. The years increased in number and the gate grew rusty as the paint flaked, and the garden now was more overgrown, as it was not tended as much as it had once been. Now, few visited it, for many felt a coldness there, and they did not stay long if they ventured in. The garden seemed to close itself more, year by year. And, year by year, it seemed to forget the joy it once felt. Joy seemed, now, like a distant dream.

Then one day, after the Sun had risen and the rusty gate was opened, while a cool breeze blew through the garden, someone came and stood at the gate to look inside. A woman stood there, with hair that clung close to her head and rested neatly on her shoulders. She stood there for a time, dressed neatly in a coat against the coolness of the day. Then, she moved, she took a step forward into the garden. She stepped off the path into the soft grass that seemed to cushion her feet, to respond to her. She walked through its green weaving, sliding her shoes through it, so that the dew swept across them and they glistened. With her head down, looking at the crystal dew on the grass, she walked on, and she knew she was the first to disturb it that day, to shake it off the blades on which it had settled.

Then she stopped and looked up to realize that she was at the edge of a flower-bed, one that was a little overgrown, a little untidy, it seemed. Some litter had blown in and become tangled in the leaves, even the thorns of some of the roses had pieces of paper and litter stuck amongst them. Without thinking, she lent forward and began to pull away the litter. At once the flowers and the roses seemed to brighten up. They looked a little different, their colors seemed clearer and sharper.

As she moved through the flowerbed, pulling away at the twisted pieces of paper and rubbish, the colors of the flowers seemed to glow more. She found herself going from bed to bed, kneeling down in the damp grass and working away, scarcely realizing that her knees now were wet. When she had finished, the beds of flowers seemed to shine out more strongly in their colors and she felt a kind of warmth inside her. Something in her responded to the display of beauty she saw around her. Then, over her head, she heard a rustling and a swishing, and up she looked, to see the great branches of a tree overhanging her, swaying gently in the cool breeze. She walked to the foot of the tree, put out her hand and touched its bark and something seemed to tingle in her hand. Something in the tree seemed to move, and it seemed that the leaves suddenly danced their rustling dance more strongly and the branches waved about a little more than they had. She placed both her hands on the tree, looked up at its great height and felt something inside, a kind of greeting that seemed to be echoed in the music of the leaves.

She looked around, and now the garden seemed to sound different too. She could hear the buzzing of the bees and the bugs, she could hear the birds sing more clearly around her. They were landing in the branches above, as if to welcome her. Across her hands were crawling little insects who seemed to have appeared out of nowhere. She looked into her hand and saw a spider walk across her palm, across the web of lines in the heart of her hand. There, it stayed a long moment, before it walked back to the tree.

She felt something stirring inside her, a shudder of something unwinding. Something inside her was unspooling like a tape, unraveling itself slowly. She began taking deep breaths of the sweet air in the garden. She felt an excitement running through her, a sense of something she had not felt for a long, long time. And now she felt warm, so she unbuttoned her coat.

She began to walk through the flowerbeds and around the tree, looking up and down and around in every direction, noticing things she hadn't seen earlier. Little details and tiny beauties she had not noticed when she had first come into the garden. It seemed they were everywhere, wherever she looked. She found a smile on her face and something deep in her chest slowly opening, like a deep sigh. Then she took off her coat and hung it on a low branch. She wrapped her arms around herself and rubbed her arms, as if to convince herself that it was not just a dream. She was really here in the flesh, and she was alive in this garden. She took off her shoes, to feel the damp grass under her feet. And this coolness she liked, for it woke up her feet and made them feel alive again. She found herself walking more quickly around noticing everything, trying to take it all in. Walking more and more quickly, then running from spot to spot as she noticed things, as if she was greeting old friends and they were greeting her.

Then her run became a skip, and she began to skip from place to place. Sniffing this and touching that, holding something a moment, then skipping onto something else. Suddenly she stopped and looked back at the gate. She was checking if anyone was watching her, but to her relief she was alone and no one had entered the garden. She regained herself, and again began to skip around, raising her face now to the sky, to feel the light upon it, for the sun was higher now, pouring in over the overgrown hedges. Without realizing it, she found that she had started to dance. She was dancing with her face to the sky, her feet on the Earth, holding out her arms, as if to sweep everything into her heart. She began to dance through the flowers without hurting them, without damaging even a leaf.

Now that her legs were long, she found she could leap across the flowerbeds in great balletic leaps. Around and around she danced, through the trees and the shadows of their leaves, through the dancing flowers, and the waving leaves of the plants. Around her, the trees danced and the birds wove amongst the branches, singing. The insects wriggled and crawled around on the body of the trees, and the flies and the bees buzzed around her.

Something burst open inside her, like a flower long closed. And as the bud opened, the flower burst forth its life and light. Now the dancer was reborn, and the little girl and the woman danced together through the garden. She found there were tears on her face, but this time she welcomed them. These were the tears of joy and of release and of the end of pain. The tears ran down her cheeks, but the air dried them while she danced on.

The garden danced as her heart danced. And, on and on, they danced as one.

We fall into density of our own accord, none are pushed.

Though some fly down more gracefully than others, none are compelled to come to the Earth. Those who come, come out of love, and come from love. They come here to learn the lessons of love, understand it from a new angle, to approach it from new perspectives, and see the possibilities that love opens up in the world of matter.

For here can be learnt lessons that cannot be learnt anywhere else in the Universe. For Earth is so unique, it holds so special a place in the hearts of so many, and in the heart of the Creator, that it has been given a role no other planet has been given. This is said, not to inflate the ego of the people of the Earth, but to open them up to the importance of their lives here, to the importance of their lives in their smallest details, the tiniest events. They are given an opportunity to grow more quickly than it would be possible anywhere else. For there are places in the universes where such growth would take many thousands of years – that same growth can be accomplished on Earth in a week, or a day. Such is the vital nature of this planet, this living planet, this vital web, with its interpenetration of dimensions, its interweaving of complex intelligent energies.

Earth is made in such a way, that those that live on and within and throughout her, can interact in ways not possible elsewhere. For the lives of those who inhabit the surface create ripples, which affect the lives of those who live within the inner levels of the Earth, and far above it – and far away from it, through the Universal Web.

Each Human being is a cosmic crossroads, a meeting point that the Universal threads weave through. These living threads are moving through all the points of their body – their many *interwoven* bodies – so that each Human is a meeting point of energies from all corners of the cosmos, which pass through without their being aware of them, them most of the time. These energetic threads pass through and weave out of each Human being and are concentrated mainly in their heart center.

Here their connection to the web is densest, and most complex in its inter-weaving. Here, within the heart, the threads are woven in a way that is unique to each individual, sometimes a very dense mesh, sometimes a very open weave. These threads connect them to all their aspects, which go beyond the Human, to their other-dimensional selves, to their other aspects and to lives elsewhere, in so-called past, present and future, all those lives, aspects, or dimensional selves, to which they are still connected.

Through the heart, all passes. Here in this Heart Space, the universes are connected. That is why it is through the heart you can have your greatest influence on the Universe. Here are the threads held, and here you feel the ripples that pass through this universe, the shivers of energy you send out, the thoughts and emotions and sensations. While those of the universes pass through you, "filtered," of course, so as not to overload you. For you are usu-ally protected from those energies, those ripples that would, as it were, "knock you off your feet" – or knock you into the middle of next week, or last week or somewhere you would be very surprised to wake up in...

So you are protected, yet even these subtle effects are important to you, as you also have subtle effects on the universes around you. It can be discon-certing to realize that your thoughts and actions, the tiniest deed, can have effects that you have not foreseen. Though it is not necessary for you to take on guilt at having caused a hurricane somewhere by stirring your tea the wrong way!

Such exaggerated analogies do indeed worry people, and Humans take on shame or guilt for things and events, which are not of their making. Much breast-beating and many tears have been caused by this misplaced guilt, and we are here to remind you, that you are responsible only for your own actions. You need not take on the mantle of guilt for the actions of others or for the larger events around you. You can indeed seek to intervene in or interact with these events, or for the larger events, if you feel so compelled to do so. But, of course, it is important that you seek to interact across the Heart Space, that if you are going to weave some of your own threads into these events con-sciously, they are woven from the heart. In this way you will be linking heart to heart. In this way you will be linking heart to heart, you will be making these connections of love, which can indeed influence positively the events around you.

This can be achieved by a simple heart-felt ritual of your own devising, a placing of clear intent, or simply being still for a moment and allowing love to flow through you out into the wider world beyond. You need not take up the cudgel or the sword to try and right wrong. There are many, many ways in which you can bring your love to the world and help to influence events. For of course you have free will; you have the right to try and influence events if you so wish, if you feel that is your role.

We only advise that you are clear on your motivations and intent, then you need not worry about the outcome of your actions. For if your motivation and intent is rooted in the heart and flowing from the heart then the outcome will be positive. Love will reach out into the world, its threads will stretch out from heart to heart, from place to place. You will bring forth your inner love, which is also flowing from the heart of the Creator.

Then you will be truly playing your role. A single thread of your love can be sent out into the world, entwined around a wounded finger or a hurt heart, a damaged tree or a broken flower. A single thread can be entwined around the heart of another being to give them solace, to let them know they are connected to another who loves them. This simple act of twining threads can do so much to heal and connect, to re-weave the web in clear and simple ways. And it can be done simply, without words or grandiose actions, without elaborate ritual. It can be done in a moment, yet its effects can last for years or centuries – or forever.

For an act of love lives beyond time and stretches to the ends of time; it truly never dies and the thread is never broken. The connections made, stretch from heart to heart, from creator to creator, from love to love, in the great circle that connects us all. We are all spun from a circle and we all move within the circle. And at the center of the circle there is only love.

So spin out your threads from the spinning wheel of your heart; spin them out and when you know they are strong and well made, spool them out into the world and weave them as your heart guides you. And you will have given a gift to the world beyond price or measure, for you will have strengthened the web, and the web of love will be stronger for your actions, your intent, for the love you have given freely. There is no end to love, and the threads have no ends, so spin them out freely from the great spinning wheel of your heart. And we will weave the web between us that will last to the end as it flows from the beginning, flowing from the Rainbow Heart.

We take our place in the circle. We also come from a distant place. We may seem strangers to you, now, but we know you more than a little. We know something of your ways from long ago, though since, of course, much has changed. You have grown in ways we never imagined. You have scattered yourselves in great cities, peopled the quiet places, the hills and mountains, the forests, the deserts. Places that were virgin and quiet when first we came are now busy with people, teeming with Human life and all the activities and affairs that take up your time.

For you are busy beings, always so busy! But it was not always so; once you gave more time to other things. We remember the early days, when spaces were seen as sacred and great care was taken preparing spaces for all kinds of purposes. If a clearing was being made in meadow or forest, it was done with great reverence, great respect for the plants and creatures that may be displaced. The tiniest insect was given reverence and given a new place of dwelling, so that all would have their place, inside and outside the new space. For none were truly outside, all were seen as part of the One Sacred Space, all seen as part of the One Earth, children of the One Earth Mother, and children of the Creator.

Those places as they were prepared were not places of exclusion or places to be defended from others less holy. They were places for special events, for particular purposes – usually temporary. In time, the Earth would claim them back, use them for her own purposes; other places were prepared for longer use.

As the knowledge and wisdom of the first peoples grew, they prepared spaces for divining the movements of the stars and the planets in relation to the Earth, and in relation to their own lives. These spaces were prepared with stone and wood, prepared with painstaking care and precision. For the first peoples found they had within them great inner wisdom which seemed boundless. They found that they knew things without knowing, at first, how they knew them, then they danced and sang their joy when they remembered from where the wisdom came.

In these events, in the moments of knowing from where flowed the wisdom, they would realize that the Source dwelt within them. Of course this brought them great joy and they danced their pleasure in these special places. They learnt about the balances between creatures, between living things and the environments in which they lived; the balances between the stars and planets and the Earth; the balances between their actions and the actions of others, about the outcomes and effects of their actions on others, and theirs on them. They were remembering that all is connected; they were feeling out the threads of the web. They felt these living lines around them as they passed through them and they knew they stretched out far, far away out into the stars, and down into the Earth. They could look around and actually see them stretch in every direction and know that they were connected to All. This in itself was a source of great happiness, for to know that you are connected to All in such a way, means that you do not experience the loneliness of separation or the loss of place, the isolation that comes with the sensation of separation – that great illusion.

They were indeed open, sensitive creatures and found that they had to be gentle with each other and with all the creatures around them. They were to learn that a thoughtless action – or more accurately a heartless action – could cause great pain. They could damage and inflict pain on others quite easily. So there was gentleness and reverence between beings that still has not been quite forgotten. For though you may be surrounded by the busy-ness and bustle of life, the frenzied activities of the cities – even now the bustling activity of the villages. Yet, when a quiet space is created, a place remembered as sacred, a space in which people can remember themselves and open their hearts, you will find that, within moments, the gentleness is remembered, the reverence is recalled, the joy and fun of creativity is rekindled.

Once this peaceful place has been created, we remember ourselves, we remember the Creator within us. The noise and bustle seems to fade away into the distance and we feel the peace within us that was there at the beginning, the sacred space within expanding out. We remember that we can each create a sacred space from our creative powers, the Creator within. We can also invite others to share our space and they can invite us to share theirs, and in the shared space we will have created between us, is a circle of peace that encompasses us all, a gentle place of love. Or, if we are in the mood for celebration and wilder fun, we can stoke up the fire of love in the center and dance around it and through it, weave our laughter and clapping with its crackling, sing and dance with its lively dancing flames.

There is, now, a remembering taking place. We each remember ourselves a little more each day. Not just the beings of the Earth, but those in other places too, far off places, those you may have forgotten about or which may have forgotten about you. But, somewhere deep within, you remember each other, for you are still as connected as you once were, the living threads are still unbroken. So there is hope for the future, great hope – for something that has never happened before, is taking place. The great weaving of which you have heard, is weaving wider and wider still, and many more circles are being formed, in places which would seem very distant in time or space, which would seem to exist in incredible dimensions. Yet you are connected to them, and the Circles that are forming. All this weaving that is going on is bringing us back together.

We will remember some of the old tales, the old threads of the stories, spun out again around the fire. And we will spin and weave our tales around the fire, as we once did so long ago. For sometimes in the night we would come to your firesides, and we would be welcomed. We would talk and laugh with you – around you and above you – and you knew us as friends. We who were your brothers and sisters, and we are still kin within our hearts. We have kept a special place in our hearts for you since then and we have waited a long time for you to remember us. But we knew that we were not truly forgotten, for love is never truly forgotten. The help we gave each other then and the love we shared, is still as real as it was then. And the spaces of love we created then still exist today, though a little difficult to see perhaps, and harder to find.

But some day, you may be walking through a forest and find an outline of an old clearing and feel something stirring as you enter it. A bright feeling of something unusual moving within you. A sense of deja-vu, a memory stirring. Perhaps you will have walked into one of these ancient clearings which may since have been overgrown. In the space made, where a Circle was opened, the love shared there still hangs in the air. Like a gold and silver cloud, it still weaves through the trees and their leaves.

You will feel, perhaps, something sparkle in the grass beneath your feet, something that scattered onto the Earth in those times of long ago, scattered on the grass like stardust as we danced together on those long nights, and the creatures watched from the trees in a circle of curious eyes around us, watching us as we danced.

So we wish you happy hunting, for you might find such a space sooner than you think. And we will hear the echo of your laughter; the laughter of recognition, and remembering, will ring from space to space. For all these spaces are connected to the web, across and through the Earth, through the Universal Web. And the joyful laughter of one can be heard by many who seem far away. So we will listen out. And we ask you to watch where you put your feet!

We take a golden thread and stretch it still further. Spinning from our heart into an unfamiliar place, which may seem distant and strange. This golden thread snakes its way, spiraling out to the seeming darkness of space, as if searching for something.

Seeming to circle and search for a particular star, on it spirals, the end of the thread like the head of a golden snake searching for something in the great open space between the stars. Then, at last, it seems to have found it, the spiral becomes tighter, coiling like a spring, drawing its energy in tighter and tighter, until the thread is coiled as tightly as it can be, so it seems a thicker, stronger, rope-like thread, still spinning through infinities.

Then, just in front of it, it meets a point of light and it connects – there is a flash of light as the thread connects to this point, as if a tiny star has been born. For the meeting point shines like a star, glittering brilliantly, the thread is still spiraling, entering through this new star space, reaching into the light beyond. It spirals through, apparently entering a new space and so we hold on to the thread to see where it will lead us.

It pulls us through a point of light – we enter it in a blaze of bright colors – into this new space in which we are disorientated, in which we feel new. We drink in the light, it floods through us, we seem to be floating in infinite light, to our surprise, here in what seemed the blackness of space.

We adjust our senses quickly to where we are, to find forms amongst the colors, to find shapes amongst the shimmers of light. We discern patterns in the movement, as is our nature, we work out patterns and shapes as our senses put a meaning on that which we see. We realize quickly that all is flowing around us. Nothing seems fixed. The colors and shapes flow like liquid, they flow around and through each other, and the patterns we thought we saw have soon shifted to others. The forms we believed were there have transformed into new ones. So again we have a moment of disorientation and we find we must accept that there are no easily discernable forms or patterns around us.

We know, somehow, there is meaning to it all. We bring our attention back to ourselves, and see that in entering through this tiny star portal we have transformed into a brilliant light being, of iridescent colors, a creature of scintillating brightness. We are amazed at how we look so different from our everyday image of ourselves. Yet we know this form and we wonder what we can do with it. So we begin to swim out into the new space, to swim and kick our way, and to flow out in this space. Sometimes flowing with it, other times making our own currents, wheeling and spinning, passing our fingers of light through the thousands and millions of threads, through which we are swimming, without effort but simple intent. We breathe freely here, for it seems a place of infinite expansion, a place in which anything could happen. For a moment we feel the fear that sometimes shadows freedom, if we doubt ourselves, and we think we might not know how to use this freedom wisely; that our fears will create monsters that devour us, that our imagination will bring to life creatures, who will haunt us, terrify us. Then comes the knowing, the peace we feel inside, the flow of loving peace within us, for it is creating the flow around us.

Our fingers stretch out, and from them stretch out threads of light, as far as we can see. We can play with these, admire their beauty, astonish ourselves at how, by a simple action of moving and flowing, our fingers can create such beauty. We realize the light flowing from our body is sending these threads in all directions too, and in turn threads from all directions are passing through our body. We admire these for their magnificence. What a spectacular display they make, what a wonder we are! We believe now that we have swum quite far from the portal from which we entered, and for a moment we wonder how we will return there when we wish to leave – if we wish to leave. For it seems at the moment that this would be a perfect place to spend eternity! Here, surrounded by beauty and knowing our own true beauty.

But something impels us on, so we go exploring, following the flow of threads, for now we are learning a little about their patterns, how they flow and move. How the light threads shimmer and ripple in response to our thoughts and feelings. How we can ride waves of energy, sometimes surfing or floating along, other times becoming like a dolphin, swimming through this sea of light. We are learning our own connectedness, our own sense of ourselves in our extended nature. We are realizing how intimately we are part of the web. Something now tells us that we must return through the portal with this learning, for we still have work to do on the other plane.

We still have time to play and co-create, and now we can play and co-create with this new wisdom we have gained, this insight into, and vision of our true selves. As we feel this intent to return within us, to our surprise we see the point of light in front of us, the star portal glittering like a tiny crystal. It grows in brightness, expanding, increasing in brilliance until we effortlessly flow into it and the light surround us and envelops us. For a moment we are blinded by the brightness of the light, but then suddenly we are out on the other side. And we can remember the wisdom within.

We look at our physical body and surroundings now in a new way. We know more about what the eye does not see but the heart knows. We steady ourselves, we feel our feet on the Earth. We step back into our lives knowing that the gift is within us.

That knowing and that world is there all the time, we are always moving through it; though our physical body and clothing conceal its existence, now we know it is there. We can ask ourselves how we would use and explore this wisdom, how it will change our lives. For we are all web makers, the web we make by day and night determines much of our experiences and the stories we weave with the threads of our life will contain the colors we choose to weave into them.

So we hold the threads tight in our heart and the threads hold us tightly with love. We each flow through each other and are connected through each other. The Web is One, but the colors and threads are infinite.

The Seven-Legged Spider

There once was a spider with seven legs. Yes, she might seem like an unfortunate creature, but she was far from that, as we will see.
I won't tell you how she lost her leg – that is a story in itself and we could be here all night. For everything has a story attached, even a spider's leg that is not attached to its owner. But I'm losing my thread now…so back I go to the beginning, and the spider with seven legs.

She wasn't the happiest of spiders, it must be said, because she felt rather inadequate and clumsy. She would watch the other spiders in their webs near-by, prancing proudly along on their eight legs, scuttling here and there, quickly and gracefully. She would look on, feeling uncomfortable. Sometimes she felt so clumsy she was afraid to move at all. She knew she limped a little, and she felt the other spiders were watching her, looking down from their silver webs thinking, "What an ungainly spider she is. Spiders should have eight legs, that's that. Why a spider with seven legs is hardly a spider at all!" She imagined them looking at her web and making nasty comments. "Just look at her web!" she thought they would say, "Look how badly its threads are woven – those angles are all wrong. Why, some of those threads are crooked all the way along. They curve where they should be straight and they're straight where they should curve. She's a disgrace to spiderhood!" She never actually heard them say these things, but that didn't stop her imagining them.

So the spider with seven legs spun her web in the darkest corner she could find, where she felt that she would not be so visible. For she knew that her web could not be as beautiful as those of the others. Still, she made it as carefully as she could, and she wove its threads with as much grace as she could muster. She wove the web with her own kind of precision, making her own pattern; maybe not the most beautiful web in the cosmos, but it was her own pattern and she loved it in her own way. Her web did not shine like the others, since her corner was so dark, and the light found it hard to catch. But sometimes she found it quite beautiful in its slightly crooked way and she would move around it, examining its pattern and carefully repairing it, if the wind tore it or a careless bee buzzed through. She would pull the threads in and knit them back together as best she could.

So, day after day, she stuck to her dark corner, peeking out occasionally to admire the other webs. How magnificent they seemed to her, so perfect, so intricately patterned and symmetrically exact. How they shimmered and shone in the light. She knew those spiders were very proud of their creations; they made sure to hang them where the sunlight and moonlight would catch them to best effect.

Then, one day, she was sitting in the center of her web, daydreaming, not thinking of anything in particular, when a fly flew into her web with a flutter of wings and tangle of threads. It buzzed and buzzed, tangling itself ever deeper in the web, waking her abruptly from her daydream. For a moment, she circled around in her own clumsy way, thrown into confusion by this sudden arrival. When she had gathered her wits, the fly was well and truly caught, having wrapped itself in a tangle of threads from which it could not escape. As she circled it once, then twice, then three times, she looked at it as it buzzed, hanging helplessly there, caught, confused and dazed.

After her third circuit, she stopped and felt something inside of her that she had not felt before, a kind of pity and compassion for the fly. Though she was hungry – it must be said she was not very good at catching flies in her web – she did not look on the fly as a meal, but as something else…but what? While she was considering this, the fly buzzed a low moan, a drone of sorrow. He felt so stupid for having flown into the web and entangled himself in its threads. Then the fly noticed the spider looking at him. She was not the most frightening spider he had seen, but a spider is a spider after all, and he wondered why she was not rushing to tie him up even more tightly and finish the job. He was quite a well-fed fly and he knew he would make a tasty meal for a hungry spider. He was quite plump, having eaten well recently, though that was not much use to him now; it only made him a better feast. So the fly waited glumly for his end.

The spider, meanwhile, wondered why she felt these feelings. Why was she looking at the spider in this strange way? Then, to her own surprise, she went forward and began to bite through the threads, to pick them carefully away from the fly, releasing his legs, his dizzy head and then freeing one wing, which began to flap and catch the light. She looked at his wing for a moment and realized that she had never really looked at a fly's wing before. She had usually been too concerned about being sure the fly was being woven into a tight bundle, to appreciate its wings. She looked now at the light coming through this thin wing and admired the patterns she could see. The wing was a shimmering veil of thin silver, with golden light pouring through the lace-work of veins, like silver threads.

The fly for his part was more confused than any fly has ever been, because the spider was making no attempt to eat or tie him up. She seemed to be gazing with some kind of amazement at his wing – or maybe she was looking at something beyond it, since his wing was no more special than any other. It could scarcely be that fascinating! But he felt something new inside him too; his fear was ebbing away and he didn't feel the same horror as when he had first found himself trapped in the web with the spider advancing towards him. Then, she had been an object of terror and revulsion, for he had often thought how terrible it would be to be caught and eaten by a spider. For he was a proud fly who liked to fly high, eat as much as he wanted and enjoy life to the full. He had been told often that flies did not live long, so he had done his best to enjoy living. Now when he thought it had come to a sudden sticky end, he had been given a reprieve.

The spider was still looking, mesmerized, though his wings. She had even unraveled the other one and was peering through that too, admiring the lacy patterns. And he looked at the spider truly for the first time, in the light coming through his wings. It cast delicate patterns on her, of soft gold crossed by silver filigree over her face and body. Now she did not seem as horrible as she had at first. He noticed, to his surprise that she had five, six, seven legs, when he thought all spiders had eight. He wondered at this, and thought he might have been misinformed.

Then the spider noticed him looking at her. It was hard not to, since a fly has so many eyes! And, as they say, their eyes met – her eight eyes looked deep into his hundreds of eyes. They each truly saw each other for the first time. They both found something unexpected there. He did not look so much like a meal, and she didn't look so much like a hungry predator. In this moment they shared, something moved inside them and something moved between them.

The spider realized he was not staring at her missing leg, he seemed to be really looking at her in this light falling on her, the light he was reflecting on to her. She was looking at her own reflection in his many eyes – and she saw beauty there, multiplied many times. Now he did not look at her with fear like a fly would, or with disdain like the silly spiders might. And she felt herself suddenly grow a little. Meanwhile, the fly found himself admiring the spider. Although she was a strange creature, she had a kind of beauty, like that you sometimes see in the edge of a leaf you land on, or in a droplet of glistening honey when you look through it, or in fruit as you suck its juices. After a while though, they both became a bit uncomfortable, neither knowing what to do next. What exactly does a fly say to a spider, or a spider to a fly?! Yet something was passing between them, that was for sure.

He was just hanging on lightly to the web and he knew he could leave now, since his wings were free. He could easily pull himself from the web and be gone, never to return and the sky would be his again. But something held him there a little longer than he expected. And the spider also found herself standing there as if she was stuck fast, instead of returning to the center of her web and going about her business, as she somehow thought she should. But, in the silence between them, something was flowing and they both enjoyed the feeling. It was new and unusual, especially when you are a fly and a spider meeting face to face; it was a sense of connection and a kind of appreciation of one another. So after a while, the spider took a few steps backwards, just to reassure the fly that she had no intention of eating him. The fly, for his part seemed to know this already, so he flapped his wings a little to show her that he knew he was free to go, but had chosen to wait awhile.

She watched again the display of light gleaming through his wings, admired him a little more and took another look at herself in his eyes. Because she was stepping back, she could see her whole form now, and she realized that she was not as ugly as she thought she was. It struck her also that her web mustn't be as bad as others made out – hadn't she caught a nice plump fly in its threads? It had held him as well as any of theirs could. Granted, she was doing something very un-spiderly by releasing him, but she was a free spider, she could do what she wanted in her own home.

By now, she was back in the center of her web. She arranged her legs as gracefully as possible, and tried to look casual as she could. The fly wondered what to do next. Part of him wished to thank the spider for her kindness, especially since she seemed a bit thin and spindly – even for a spider. Though it rather suited her, he thought… Meanwhile, she felt a sadness come upon her, for she knew he would soon have to leave and go on with his life. And he could not really return or he would get himself in another tangle. So she resigned herself to the fact, raised one of her legs as slowly as she could and waved to the fly. The fly flapped his wings, and the two looked into each other's eyes one last time. Then, with a buzz and flash of gold, he was gone.

The spider was still for a moment, pondering the broken web and the space he had created by his arrival. She did not feel dismay or believe the web had been ruined, instead she felt that he had opened something inside her, a space inside she had not known was there. This made her feel good, for she knew the next time the spiders made fun of her, she could remember that moment with a fly, when they each, to their surprise, realized the other's beauty. She would not feel the sting of their words as much as she had.

Perhaps, she thought, she should move somewhere a bit more open, some place where the air and light could flow through. She would make a new web there, with a new pattern, one of her own making. In this new web, she would leave an open space. Some of the spiders might make rude remarks about how incomplete her web was, but she would know that space was the most important part of her whole web. She was going to leave a small opening, a doorway just big enough for a fly to fly through, just large enough for love to enter.

Someday, she might see a familiar face appear there. But, in the meantime, she was content, sitting patiently in the center of her web, a glint in every eye, wearing a little spidery smile.

There was a time when all the tribes of the Earth were One Tribe.
A time, which might seem misty and distant, an age, which may seem mythical. Surely, some will say, there could never have been such unity; surely the differences and divisions must always have been there, somewhere? Could it be, that there ever was true unity? We look at the warring groups and factions that go under so many names, fighting under so many flags, acting so alike, wearing uniforms that are so similar, yet seem to be fighting for different things. We look at the wounded Earth, so scarred by warfare, and we wonder, could there ever have been peace? We look at the broken families and scattered tribes, and ask can there ever be peace again?

Yet humanity was conceived in peace and born in unity. There was a time on the Earth, when the realms worked closely together. When the Earth was a great weaving-point, which drew out threads from her center and drew them in from all over the Universe then wove them together in her creative core. Then was created the most complex web of life so far seen in all Creation. These living, Rainbow Threads, now known as DNA, were drawn in from all over the Created Universe, and, within the womb of the Earth, they were braided together in new ways.

The great weaving took place with those of the Angelic realms and the Earth's Devic realms working closely together. Around the heart of the Earth, representatives of every realm were drawn together to help weave this wonder, for humanity was in formation. Within her creative heart, these diverse ingredients were being blended. New genetic threads were formed, as the basis of a diversity of life never seen before.

This preparation was of a complexity impossible for any mortal mind to comprehend, but within the Heart of the Earth the blending and the weaving took place, between many great hearts working with the great heart of the Earth. The love generated at such a weaving point was of a brightness that shone like a star to the ends of the universe, and her threads of light, spinning out from the Earth, extended to every realm. Many traveled to the Earth along these threads to be a part of the weaving. Earth was surrounded by a circle of many circles, working in co-operation, weaving a world together.

It was a time when great discoveries were made, a phase of great experimentation, of trial and what might be called error, of testing and stretching the limits of life, of exploring its possibilities. So the life that emerged on this new Earth was seeded from many realms and worlds, so you could say that Earth had a thread linking it to every realm – as it still does. The links are still alive, most of the threads are still bright with life, and these connections can still be felt, within the Heart of the Earth, and by those who work with her. So Earth became a world with many worlds within it. It became a microcosm of the cosmos, and yet, within itself, a new creative cosmos came about.

The Earth became a world with an unparalleled breadth of life in all its forms. The Earth too, became a meeting place of the dimensions, a world of shared dimensions, where many dimensional threads wove together a shared space. So you could say that Earth's different dimensions were overlaid. The Earth's webs and grids, its inner template held these levels of dimensional life in balance. The Earth's magnetic heart and the heart-flows of energetic life, began to flow more and more strongly, as the poles were placed and re-placed over the process. The whole weaving took a great deal of time, which allowed an enormous amount of learning. The world-weavers of all realms accumulated a vast living library of knowledge and wisdom which is still being drawn from and added to, and is still available to those who walk the Earth now. The creating, the weaving, still continues, life is still evolving, the Earth is still revolving through her phases of change.

Though the time between then and now seems vast, to those of us who were involved, it seems but a long moment. We saw a world come into being, more marvelous than any those involved could have wished for. It was a dream coming true on the greatest scale; we wove the dream and made it real. Earth took on a life of her own, exploding in the brilliance of life, in forms never seen before, in interwoven habitats, of hitherto unknown complexity. Of course, the process was not linear but cyclical. Within the great cycle were smaller cycles of life, death and re-birth, of degeneration, transformation and renewal. The light of life transmuted, and passed on into new forms, which

214 EARTH WILL BE REBORN

mutated and multiplied into many more. And the Earth, whose weaving had begun with what would have seemed like a few points of light around a central light, became – through an endless succession of miracles – the shining miracle that she was, and still is.

The many faces of life on the Earth reflect the diversity of origins of life here. Here, life of other dimensions and realms, meet face to face, to learn and explore, to mingle, mate and multiply. In the Heart of the Earth, the threads of all realms come together, in a heart of Love. The great experiment continues, the magnificent miracle still manifests itself in new life. The Earth is ancient but ever-new, and she is in a state of constant renewal, of re-formulation. Now, she is in a time of truly great renewal. Once again she moves into a phase of re-birth, once again the future is yet to be decided, the potentials of life, the new possibilities are yet to be opened. Many of those who worked in the first weaving, are here again, some in new forms and playing new roles. Some are coming to the Earth for the first time, but the old souls and the new souls will work as one.

Once again, a New Earth is in formation, and the busy weavers are at work beneath your feet and around you, they weave the air above. The dimensions are threaded together in new ways, new connections are being made and new openings are being revealed. Old doors that have been closed for a long time are opening once more, old corridors and pathways are being cleared. Along them, run ancient threads still bright with life under the dust; just shake the threads and you will know they are still connected, you will sense a wave flowing to you in reply from somewhere unseen. You may send music along these living strings and begin simple and direct communication. You can awaken ancient connections that are far from dead or forgotten. Who knows which old friends you will shake awake! At the end of each thread is an old friend, you can be sure of that.

Home is where the heart is, so some old friends will be coming home to the Earth they still feel so at home with. For they helped make a heavenly home of it in the first place. They did their great work and then withdrew, to allow life and learning to evolve. They helped make a new space for life to play in and they allowed the games of life to begin. They supplied the seeds that were planted in the virgin Earth, which then were blended in her great creative womb, in the belly of the Earth. From the seemingly simple seeds, with the help of a lot of love, magnetic magic, elemental weaving and simple patience, a miraculous array of forms arose.

The human race, also, was a weaving between many realms, a melding and a blending, a loving creation within which diversity became unity, in which the many threads of the realms and dimensions were woven into a new oneness. Your ancestors came into being and stood on the Earth, holding within them the wisdom of many worlds, and the wisdom of the Earth as an open library, a living web of reference and connection. And they walked the Earth with great reverence, with profound joy, and they knew within that they were a very new creation, a manifestation of love in a new form. They lived as one Tribe of Love, surrounded by abundance, with deep, high wisdom within, in a world of abundant love and life. They lived the ways of peace and, you could say, they knew no other way. They were exploring love in its new forms and exploring the Earth, who was already ancient.

They knew the Earth as their loving Mother and they were in constant communication with her, in all her many manifestations. They sang to her, heart to heart, just as she sang to them in myriad ways. They heard the song of love within them and they responded freely. They lived in love with the abundant Earth and held themselves in balance. They held the balance on the Earth too, for they had been given the great task of balancing the living energies of the Earth, and through them flowed the threads of connection.

They had been entrusted with a sacred trust, as guardians of a sacred place. How well they acted the role of guardian would determine the fate of the Earth, as well as determining their own development, their own growth as a race. The wisdom with which they lived would decide the fates of the other creatures who shared the Earth with them.

The sacred threads were placed within their hands and it was the sensitivity and gentleness with which they held them that would decide the quality of life. its balance, by the equality of esteem in which all creatures were held. Free will had been their gift and they would create the future with the Earth herself, they would shape the days of the future and they would mould the ages to come. Through it all, they would hold the wisdom within them, but, in times to come, only some would remember it was there. Forgetting and remembering, losing and re-learning would be the experience. Learning to remember would be the lesson; remembering to listen to the wisdom within. The wisdom would not be lost, but the way would not be easy, and many would become lost along the way.

Yet we remember the Rainbow Race when you faced your first day upon the Earth. You were ready and eager to face the new day. And, today, you are readying yourselves once more. So that when the new day comes, you will be more than ready.

We were there at the dawn of that new day, when the Rainbow Tribe rose from the Earth. We helped them rise into their new life. We are the deep weavers within the Earth, those that dwell within Earth's inner worlds and hidden dimensions. Though we may not be visible to most now, once we were not so invisible.

We worked within the Earth, weaving the energies in the living threads that went into the weaving of this new creation, this new race who were created and created themselves in a process of co-creation. They came forth from the body of the Earth in Rainbow glory. We watched them rise to their full height with pride, we saw them walk tall. We knew the great weaving had resulted in perfection, which then had to evolve to greater perfection through the wisdom of experience. They would be wardens of a new world, they would walk as guardians through the garden of the Earth. They would hold her wisdom whole.

Within them, were woven many threads into one, the threads of many realms and dimensions braided in new ways to create a new race of beings. The Human race was one that expressed its diversity in a multitude of hues, which was multi-dimensional in its nature, which had inborn wisdom and innate potential, wide enough to comprehend the wholeness of the Earth, her sacred nature and the interweaving of her patterns of life. Human beings carried within them the knowledge of these patterns and they could express them in many forms. These were creative beings, who sang, who danced, who created great art, who created new sacred spaces, who wove through the living stories of the Earth, stories of their own. From the ways of the creatures, they wove stories of wisdom; from the wisdom of the creatures, they wove ways of being, in wholeness and in harmony. They knew how to gather the threads and weave them as one, they knew how to gather in peace and come together as one around a fire of peace, and braid the sacred flames into One Flame, as they themselves in their diversity were braided into unity.

We sat with them in the Circle, we of the Inner Earth, we who weave our ways close to her heart. Our wisdom was listened to. We were part of the circle of honor, as we honored the Rainbow People in their walk upon the Earth, in their chosen role. In their walk upon the Earth, they did, in time, stray from the ways of wisdom, but we loved them none the less. We simply sang to them all the more and raised our songs higher. We reminded them that the threads of their very bodies were spun from the heart of the Earth. That their living spirit and their heart were one with the heart of the Earth, and that their walk, with its zigzags, its turnings, its wandering ways, was but a moment in the circle walk.

We reminded them that their Earth walk went in a circle, back into the heart of the Earth, to rise again from her in a cycle of renewal and re-birth. It was their gift, their role, their task, to honor the ways of the Earth, and seek not to break the circles from which the Earth was spun. For if the ways of the circles were forgotten, then the wisdom would be lost for a long time and the wandering would go on, until the circle of wisdom returned to those who walk on the Earth. No walk of life is a straight line, as no Earth walk is. The walk of the Rainbow Race has wandered and meandered, but the circles were never broken, the cycles still flow complete. Though the circles were tested to breaking point, though the wisdoms were stretched to what seemed a point of no return, they are returning now in the flow of time and in the flow of life.

The wisdom is awakening in the Rainbow Race once again. The great remembering sends ripples through the world, which awaken and remind the ones whose minds are hazy, the ones whose hearts are veiled. They will walk again in the ways of wisdom; they will walk in their own wisdom once more. They will leave behind the crazy ways of the killing cities; they will remember the reverence they held for all life, for the Earth herself, for all others of their race with Rainbow faces. They will walk in unity again and gather the scattered threads. Within themselves, they will braid the Rainbow flames of passion for living, of the love of all life. They will rise to their true height and stand tall once more, and we who have waited for this day will rejoice in its coming. A new day will be dawning in Rainbow Light. As the light rises from the Earth, we will rise in new light too, and share again the Earth with you in the open circle, face to face, heart to heart. From the Earth, we will rise as one and stand together in the sacred circle, still unbroken. In a circle of sacred light, we will circle the Earth with all the circles of her life. They will rise high from the Earth and dive deep into her core. Between us all, a new light will rise, and weave a new world whole.

We flow out from the heart of the Earth in the Rainbow Circle, as all the Rainbow Circles flow out endlessly. And, in time, the light will rise, as around the Earth is woven a robe of new light, woven with the heart-threads of billions of beings, weaving through her heart in the Circles of Love, until these Rainbow Circles have woven a great Rainbow Globe about the body of the Earth, filled with the light of renewal.

Within this sacred space, the Earth will be reborn, as we will be reborn with her. The light of this new world is rising now. With us now, you are on your Rainbow journey of return into the heart of the Earth, to rise again in new light. Journeying in the circles of return, again and again, in brighter light each time, in brighter wisdom each time, until all the Circles of rebirth are woven whole. Then the Earth will weave from their spinning Circles of Love, a new Earth, a new world of greater Oneness, of higher light and deeper wisdom. We see that world forming now before our ancient eyes, soon to be renewed with new inner light, and we will return to sit with you again, as we do now, in a new Oneness.

We hold our old hearts with yours in the Circle of renewal, and soon our hearts will feel new and young again, as they were in that morning of the world, as children of a new Earth long ago, in a moment that we both know, and shared but a moment ago. Between us, we hold the circle of that moment now, whole and complete. Within it we are ever-new, we are reborn.

The Cormorant and the Clam

There was a cormorant who swore he would, one day, reach the ocean floor.

For this bird of the air was a deep diver, too. And, though he loved the lightness of the air and the freedom with which he could fly, he also loved to dive into the deep flows of the ocean. He seemed compelled from within to dive as deep as he could go, and he loved the challenge of cutting through the resistance of the water, making himself as sleek and smooth as could be, so he could dive like a dark arrow into the depths.

This cormorant would sit on the great rocks that rose out of the waves and stare down into the ocean for hours, his black feathers shining in the sunlight, as he wondered what was truly waiting in the depths, so far below. He would look below the waves, beyond the surface of the ocean, watching the patterns of the shoals as they swam, the flashing displays they made in the water as they moved. He would watch the dark silhouettes of sharks moving through the ocean, the playful ways of the dolphins and the spiraling ways of the seals. He would catch glimpses of mysterious creatures from the deep and wonder how many more were down there, unseen. Beyond and deeper than all these, something drew him, something called him, and he knew he would answer the call of the deep.

He knew, also, that the other cormorants thought him a little crazy. The ocean, thereabouts, was extremely deep and no cormorant had ever reached the bed of it – in fact, no cormorant had ever thought of trying to do such a thing. It seemed an impossible task, even for a diver like one of his tribe. The other cormorants were quite happy to dive down for a few fish then come back up for air. They saw no reason to dive too deeply when there were fish to be had closer to the surface. It seemed a waste of time and energy to dive deeper when they could find all that they wanted to eat in the shallows. But this curious cormorant wanted to know more; he wanted to learn the secrets of the deep.

So he practiced diving for many hours, over many days and months. At first, he tried leaping from the highest cliff he could find, but even that was not high enough to allow him to reach the depths he wanted. He learnt, over time, how to fly higher, in order to dive deeper into the mystery of the ocean. He would fly higher and dive deeper each time, learning a little more and seeing a little more each time; yet always striving to fly even higher, in order to dive still deeper. Over time, he perfected his timing, learning how to breathe deeply and hold his breath long enough to reach the depths. Early on, there had been moments when he thought he would pass out and get into trouble, but he discovered it was only when he became panicky and fearful that he had any problems. He found that, if he remained calm, he could cope with the stress and the pressures acting on him. As the months passed, he perfected his technique of breathing and was able to truly relax and enjoy the experience.

After much effort and many, sometimes lonely, hours, he began to reach the depths where he believed he would find what he was seeking. He had become a great diver, and he made many discoveries on his dives, encountering many creatures that were new to him, many strange and wonderful creatures of the deep. He had learnt how to avoid the sharks and the other creatures that might like to try and give him a bite, though usually they were too shocked to see a cormorant swimming by to react with anything but surprise.

He even invited some of the other cormorants to come with him, offering to show them how to reach deeper, but they seemed reluctant, as if unconvinced by his tales. A new world had opened up for him and he longed to share it with his friends, but though some found the stories of his discoveries intriguing, they didn't seem inclined to follow his example. But at least they would listen to his breathless accounts, though most found them very hard to believe. If they hadn't seen him disappear into the deep each day, they might not have listened at all. When he made his dives, some of them still feared they would never see him again, but he always reappeared eventually, albeit exhausted sometimes.

Yet still he had not reached the floor of the ocean. So, every day, he traveled in great circles between the worlds of air and water, circles that opened wider with each dive. His dark silhouette reached deeper each time, until, one day, he glimpsed the bottom of the ocean. Then, on his deepest dive yet, he finally struck mud. For him, it was a cause for celebration, and never had mud seemed so beautiful. There in the murky depths, where only the brightest light could reach, he began to explore what lay on the floor of the ocean. In a series of dives, he swam over its surface, noting the shapes of the shells, the odd forms of the fish and its other half-hidden inhabitants. The ocean floor was certainly vibrant with life of many kinds, and he met strange creatures with many moving arms, and others who inhabited fabulous shells. On his many fleeting visits, he shared a moment with many dwellers of the deep, most of whom seemed to enjoy the experience – once they had overcome their surprise.

They realized over time that he was not there to take a bite. He had come to discover, to meet new friends, see new faces, discover new forms and uncover some of the mystery of the deep ocean. He became, in time, a friend of these deep dwellers and they were not surprised by his flying, swimming visits. These creatures had never seen the sky, so he told them what life was like above the surface, where the sky was open. The creatures of the deep sea became used to seeing his graceful, black form pass by with a trail of silver and gold bubbles, heading into the depths. He discovered that there were ships down there, like those that passed by on the horizon, but these ones in the deep did not move and were covered in all sorts of shells and were homes to creatures of great variety. He would fly over their decks like he had seen the seagulls do. Unlike the gulls, though, he could fly through openings into the hulls of the ships to explore them. He even swam down long corridors and through doorways into rooms full of strange objects – surprising some strange creatures there, too – before popping out of a porthole.

Over many dives, he explored more and more of the ocean floor. He began to know it so well that it was as if he had made a map of it within him. But, on one of his visits, as he swam along, suddenly the bottom of the ocean dropped from under him, and he found himself falling into an abyss. The sound of a low rumble shuddered through the ocean as he was tugged down into the churning, dark water. He tried to fight the pull, but his efforts seemed to make no difference and his senses could not tell him anything. Then there was silence and a moment of stillness, before he felt himself being released. He let himself rise up towards the sunlight. He was floating over a great abyss that he could not see the other side of. And, when he looked down, he could not tell where it ended, or if it had an end at all. So, he thought, there is still deeper to go… He surfaced to breath, and as he bobbed on top of the waves, he resolved to make a fresh dive, to find out what had opened up down there.

Far below, on the very bed of the ocean, lay a creature, dreaming. Within her shell, she dreamt of the wonderful world that awaited her above, beyond her reach. She lived, with thousands of other shellfish, at the bottom of a deep trench. It was a gloomy place, where little light reached, and even less sense of the splendors she knew existed, somewhere. She had always been fascinated by what life might be like up there in the light and the air. And could there really be dry land? She had heard hints and whispers of what existed there, but she knew that these conflicting accounts were just based on rumors overheard from the other trenches. None of the shellfish had ever left the trench in their whole lives. Most had not even moved an inch in years and had no intention of doing so in the future. Overhead, they heard the mysterious rumbles and booms of distant explosions, while, beneath them, the floor of the ocean shook and shifted

She would dream within her shell of life above and what might be, someday, but to others it seemed like idle dreaming. She was warned many times by her shellfish family and friends that the world beyond the trench was a dangerous place. They repeated, with great authority, an old shellfish saying, "A curious crustacean never lives long". If she ever even showed her face out there, they told her, she would most likely be eaten alive in an instant and that would be the end of her. Over and over, she was told the old proverb: "A hard shell, shut tight, will keep you safe, both day and night". All this had frightened her a little when she was younger, but now she had heard all the sayings a hundred times and was tired of them. She longed for another life so much that the longing became an aching pain within her. This pain became part of her life and, at times, hopelessness overwhelmed her. She would sink into her shell and burrow down into the sand, as deep as she could go. But, still, she hoped.

She loved to peek out at the ocean above, so she was always being told, firmly, to shut her shell. But she enjoyed watching the distant sparkle of sunlight on the surface, so far away, and she would dream of reaching it, though it seemed she might as well be trying to reach the stars. Sometimes, she would look up when the Sun was high above and watch the bright beams streaming through the ocean, though most could not quite reach the end of the shadowy trench. Yet there were moments when a sunbeam would pierce through the gloom and seem to stroke her, and she would feel a little tingle inside. Then her pain and frustration would fade away for a while.

Yet her restless spirit did not feel at home there, and the day came when she knew she would have to make a move. Maybe it wasn't so great to be safe all the time, she thought. Maybe she didn't want to be an ancient crustacean with nothing to look back on and no tales to tell. Maybe she wanted to live a little… So she made up her mind to make a move right now, before she had to listen to any more old shellfish sayings. She opened her shell a crack, and a little light shone in. Something inside her urged her on. She opened her shell wider and took a gulp of water then, shutting her shell, she squirted it out in a jet that propelled her forward. She did this again and again, until she had traveled a few inches. She got into a rhythm of gulping and squirting so that soon she had moved a few feet and she began to get quite excited. The other shellfish began to notice what was happening in their midst and a few opened their shells a sliver to catch a glimpse. When they saw she was leaving the safe space of her family and friends and heading off on her own, a shocked whisper rippled around the seabed.

Every time she opened her shell, she could tell that the edge of the trench was a little nearer. There was a slope to the sides of the trench, but the walls were very steep and she didn't know if any mollusk could ever make it out. When she reached the trench's edge and looked up, it seemed dauntingly high, but she knew she had come too far to turn back. She swallowed her doubts and, with a gulp and a squirt, she began to ascend the slope. The progress was slow, since she often slid backward in the shifting sand, finding herself back where she had started. Behind her, she could hear shells snapping open and shut with an odd bubbling, and a babble of voices calling her back, complaining about this unshellfish behavior. She was trying to ignore the bubbling hubbub behind her, though she did notice a few voices were being raised in her support. She redoubled her efforts and, soon, the top of the slope was near and the voices seemed far away. With a last great effort, she shot up over the edge of the trench and landed on the open sand.

She had made it! Her heart leapt and she opened her shell to drink in the light that was all around and take in her surroundings. The ocean was so huge and the shining sands stretched so far way. She suddenly felt very exposed and, for a moment, her fear came back and she felt tempted to start digging into the sand to hide. But the beauty all around her was starting to have its effects. There were waving plants and bright flowers, beautiful fish and strange shells; so much to enjoy. She didn't know if she had drunk too much water or was simply intoxicated by the sights, but she couldn't do anything but stare, open-shelled, for a long time. When she finally set off on her way, it seemed that with every jet, she met more wonderful creatures than before.

With one of her spurts, she arrived at the edge of something. When she looked over the edge, she was glad she had stopped, rather than hopped, because she could see only a sheer drop going down into the deepest darkness. This was no trench – this was an abyss deeper than anything she could have imagined. It felt so frustrating to have come all this way, only to find a chasm, beyond crossing. She could not even make out the other side of it. Her hopes dimmed and her enthusiasm began to fade. It seemed as impossible to cross that gap as it was to reach the sky above. But, as she looked up, she noticed that something dark was spiraling down towards her. The cormorant came down as fast as a black arrow, spinning to dislodge the air bubbles that kept him buoyant. When he started to circle her, the shellfish thought the worst. Maybe the others had been right after all. She braced herself, ready to be eaten. But the creature greeted and asked her if she was waiting to cross the chasm. She answered a "yes" from within her shell, just in case it was a trick question.

With that, he picked her shell gently up and they shot off across the expanse. On the way, they spoke from heart to heart, and when she discovered that he was actually a bird and came from the world above, she began to open up to him. How she would love to see the sky, she told him, and she longed to know what land looked like. He promised to bring her to the upper world and the happy clam thanked him in advance. In buoyant spirits now, she opened her shell a little and looked forward to the experience. Suddenly, they heard a low rumble from far below them, and when the cormorant looked down, he saw the glow of fire far below them. There were booming sounds, too, and deep in the abyss, more glowing fires appeared, like fiery flowers. The curious clam looked out of her shell and realized these were what made the distant noises that the shellfish were so afraid of. How beautiful they were! Both noticed that the ocean around them was growing warmer, and they rose up on a spiral of warm water. Below them, a river of fire was growing within the abyss until it became like a bright valley.

The cormorant swam back up towards the surface, up through the levels of the ocean, while the clam sensed the light rise around them. Then he burst out into the air in an explosion of water, and soared up into the sky. The clam looked out from her shell, excited by the strange sensation of rising through the air. She felt the exhilaration of a new freedom, as the bird flew higher and higher into the sky. She felt the joy of this new experience, of being so far from home, yet safe in the company of her new friend. The cormorant took her on a tour of the upper world, flying in a wide circle, while she enjoyed a survey of the whole domain. She   the clouds within the bowl of the sky, and the patterns of the dry land. They flew along the coast, where the earth and sky met, and, for the first time, she saw the horizon, where the ocean met the sky.

After a time, she felt quite overwhelmed by it all, and she closed her shell to rest a while. At that moment, a knowing burst open inside her. She saw the circle of fire beneath the ocean growing brighter and wider. Then she saw the fiery flowers rising up in the ocean and opening, and islands emerging from the sea. The rivers of fire rose up and became ridges, and some became bridges between the islands. In time, green life appeared on these new lands and, soon, the abundant life became more multicolored, until this circle of new life glowed like a great coral reef. But this new world was emerging above the waves, with creatures and plants that she had never seen before on these bright and shining islands. The cormorant flew to the great cliff on which he liked to sit, put the clam down on the rock and sat with her while she told him of the vision she had seen in her heart. Then she felt that she should return to the trench for a time, to share it with those who were still there. On the high cliff, where earth and sky and ocean meet, the clam had a last look at this wide world around her. Then the cormorant picked up his friend and dived off the cliff, plummeting down, back into the ocean with a silver splash, diving right down to the deep bottom of the ocean floor, to lay his friend gently on the bed of the ocean. Those who were in the trench were rather startled by the scene.

The clam thanked the cormorant for the experience they had shared and then told him she had a gift for him. She opened up her shell, to reveal within something the bird had never seen before – a shining pearl! It seemed as luminous as the Moon, here in the deep of the ocean. The cormorant did not want to take such a precious gift, but his friend told him it came from her heart. So he reached in gently with his beak and took the pearl from within the shell. The iridescent light of the perfect sphere enveloped them both, and they stayed within its peaceful glow for a long moment.

Then they bade each other goodbye for that day, and the cormorant returned to the surface of the ocean. Rising out of the water, he flew once more to the great rock to dry his wings. The Sun was setting, so he stretched his wide black wings in the sunlight. In the fiery light, they glistened as they dried, while the bird wondered what to do with this gift from his friend. Then he turned to face the setting Sun with the pearl held carefully in his beak and as he did, it was as if a great light opened within the pearl, a bright point of light, as bright as the Sun.

He opened out his wings to the Sun and it was as if they shone with golden light and his breast feathers shone with a golden glow, as in his beak he held this perfect gift, given with love, from the heart of another. Something new was shining from him, something new was flowing within him. After his endless circles and circles between the realms of the air and ocean, the high and the deep, now something had burst within him, and this gift of love illuminated all.

In the light of it, now, all is golden.

Let the Inner Sun of your heart rise. Feel the love rise within you.
Allow your Inner Sky to open to the glowing colors of the light. Feel the blazing sunburst in your heart, and its nova-glow of love stretching its arms of light around the Earth, out into the vastness beyond, shooting its light out to reach the furthest corners of the Universe, on into infinity, reaching out and embracing All. For, from your heart, you can truly embrace All.

You can hug the Cosmic Tree of Life, and your wings of light will embrace its body, will circle its girth, and stretch as far as its furthest branches can reach. You are ever-expansive, you know no limits, but the false ones you create, the illusions you devise. This is a kind of magic too – how you manage to create the illusion, day by day, of restrictions, of narrowness, of being small. It is a wonderful trick you have mastered! It was a trick you learned for a purpose, but now the purpose has been served. Now there is true magic to learn and to teach. Now there is new expansion coming…

There is a Wave coming, a Sacred Wave heading towards you, towards all humanity. A rolling Wave of Love, a cleansing flow of liquid compassion, a Rainbow Wave of iridescent Light.

When you see it tumbling towards you, you may, at first, be shocked or surprised. You may have the reflex reaction of wanting to run the other way, to try to outrun it and escape. Something of that size, you would think, could do you no good. You might fear it would wash you away, and you would disappear forever. So your mind may think it best to scamper away as fast as you can to look for higher ground, a tree to climb or a handy ladder. Then you will be safe, the wave will pass and the waters recede. The streets and the earth will dry out, and all will be as it was before. You will descend from your perch and get on with life as normal. This will be the reaction of many, at least their first reaction.

When you face the Wave, simply remember that you are deeply loved by the Earth, and you will not feel frightened by this Wave of Love, of Living Light. Remember that you are of the Earth, part of her body, and this is your living space, then relax and stand your ground. Ground yourself, and feel those roots growing from your toes, from the soles of your feet into the Earth. Know your heart is always connected to her heart. This will be a Heart Wave rising from her core, so you can safely open your heart to it. All in the way of the Wave will be safe. In the face of the Sacred Wave, hold out your arms as it nears you, so as to embrace it. You will feel the Wave hit you full in the chest, deep in the heart, then it will flow through you and flow on.

As this love flows through you, you will feel overwhelming joy, so you will only be drowning in bliss. You will find you are still connected to the Earth, still holding your ground, strong and unharmed. In fact, as this Wave flows through you, you will find something unexpected happening. You will not feel yourself disappear or dissolve into nothingness, or be swept off your feet, God knows where. You will find the Wave is rooting you even deeper and strengthening your connection to the Earth beneath your feet. And the Wave will be renewing you, every cell will be cleansed and detoxified, every cell given a burst of new life. You will feel every particle and wave of your body and being renewed and reborn.

You will feel your heart open wider than it ever has before and this liquid wave of energy will flow through you at an astonishing rate. You will feel your heart widen and open, stretching beyond anything you could have thought possible, for it will seem like the whole of the Wave is passing through your heart, which in a sense, it is. You will want this sensation never to end, the experience is so exhilarating, so exciting and renewing. Then the Wave will seem to come towards its end, as all waves rise and fall, and you will feel the last of the energy pass through you and move on. You will take a moment to steady your senses, to check if you are still truly alive, but you will find yourself more alive than you ever have before, more alive than you ever thought you could be.

You will feel, see and sense the Light flowing from you, as if you have been given a new Light Body. Your Light Body will have been renewed, and you will feel you have been clothed in a garment made of threads of love, to go with your glowing body. This new robe of compassion will stay with you and be part of you, just as your body will glow and continue to grow in its Light, day by day. Though the Wave will seem to have passed, its effects will stay with you. Your heart will be transformed forever, for it will have experienced a cleansing unlike any you have felt so far in your life. And you will not be the only one to experience this.

All those who stand their ground on the Earth, who cling to and stay with her, all those who sing with her, who welcome love with love, will feel this Wave. And it will roll around the Earth, like the lesser waves of energy that bathe her by day and night, even now. Some will experience much and some less, but there will be few who will feel untouched. Yet those who wish to keep themselves "dry" will have their choice respected. Those who wish to hide from the Light will have made their choice too. For them, there is always the consolation that a later wave may arrive and they again will have the freedom to choose. In the meantime, the Earth bathes you all in her love every day, as she is bathed in the Love of the Creator every moment, and we can always choose to enjoy the experience and soak in this warm bath, or we can keep our feet dry.

So we say to you to be aware of the Wave, for it may arrive at a moment you least expect it. But you will know of its coming when it comes. And, for those who like to surf waves, this is one time we advise you to leave your boards in the shade. Simply stand in its path and let the Wave surf over you. Face the Wave and embrace it from your heart. We wish you good wave-watching. But there is no need to become obsessed with the coming of the Wave, for when it arrives, you will know, and you will rejoice at its arrival as a glorious dawn.

We fall into density, but are not harmed, and our arrival is a pleasant experience, though unfamiliar. We have no need of a body such as this, though we know they have many uses, many pleasures and gifts.

We come with a word of warning. For some will choose to use some of what is said for purposes for which it is not intended. This is, of course, to be expected, but still it is good to know in advance of this possibility. For we know that those with sincere hearts can sometimes be misled by others who are, perhaps, somewhat more devious. We simply mention the possibility and leave it at that for now. For we have much to tell, as so many others have, and we are all excited and joyful at this Gathering. To have so many working as one is, in itself, an occasion for joy. The work as it is woven is a wonder to behold, even for those who lead exciting lives! And for those of us whose lives are quieter, it is even more wonderful to observe and be part of. We are indeed glad to be part of the process.

We come from a planet near Sirius. We are not visible to you yet – in any sense – but we know you from long ago. Indeed, we taught each other something in those years, and we were teachers as you were teachers. And we were all pupils of Creation. We did forge a friendship in those times, a meeting of equals. Though, of course, we were different in many ways, some superficial, some less so. But we made an understanding and bridged our differences. And in the meeting on the Rainbow Bridge was the point of light, the light of unity.

We did not find each other by accident; we were guided together. For we had some experience and skills that would be of use to you, the new people. And we were, indeed, part of the growth of the Earth over a long time. We watched you grow so quickly, and we were extremely pleased and honored to be part of this growth. For we saw you rapidly develop, from simple structures to complex ones, from simple ideas to difficult and abstract concepts. You used the intelligence and the inner love you had been given wisely in those years, and you produced marvels, which would astonish you now, when many have a very distorted view of "human nature'.

They are amazed by the remains of structures left by the early peoples, because they have a caricatured view of what these peoples were like. But we know they were wonderful creators and teachers, gifted dancers and poets, builders of impressive dwellings, sacred places and lodges, which were as beautiful as any palace, and made with more love. We saw the tribes find ways of working and living together, learning how to communicate across distances, how to govern themselves, how to resolve any disputes. Also, finding how to live wisely and love the Earth in practical ways, how to love life and enjoy physical experiences while honoring the Great Creator that made all this possible. It was truly a wonderful experience to visit the Earth in those times, when so much was being constructed and laid out in ways that did not damage to the Earth, that did not harm her or scar her body, using methods that left her surface vital and alive.

As we neared the surface of the Earth, we would see their dwelling places, their places of cultivation, the tribal lands, with their beautifully decorated dwellings. By night, we would see their fires burning, these points of light and unity, and, around them, the even brighter points of light – the humans, the true Light-Bringers, those who were learning to work with the Earth, to dance with her and experience her love, day by day.

Above them, they could see great constellations, and they observed them with more understanding than the greatest astronomers living today. This may surprise you, but it is, indeed, true. For they still felt the connection to the stars very strongly in their very bodies and hearts. They knew themselves to be of the stars as well as Earth, and they knew that they were here for a particular purpose. They knew that their life here was a sacred one, and they knew their living was a joyful exploration of the possibilities of life.

How I wish I could help you feel the joy that they felt, the connection, the sense of being at one with all! If the peoples of the Earth now could feel this feeling inside them, even for one moment, this planet would be transformed within a day. The people would suddenly wake up to their true purpose here, to the true wonder of their own being, to the great joyful task that is theirs, and the great liberation that awaits.

Those early times can seem very distant and unreachable, while the present can seem quite dark, with so many lost people, so many wanderers in the shadows. The Earth can seem so hurt and damaged, the world can seem so full of conflict and division. How, you might ask, did we get from there to here? How could such a magical world, with such wonderful people, have become this world, with these people...? And we would say; much has changed, but much has stayed the same. Within, you are the same being then as now. Within your heart, you are the same being now as you were then.

For it was *you* who walked the Earth then, *you* who drank her waters, *you* who gathered her fruits, *you* who ground her corn. Yes, *you* who measured the heavens, *you* who arranged the stones on the Earth to mirror the stars. It was *you* who lit your magical light on the Earth, *you* who lived that miraculous life, and here you are again. Have you changed? The answer is both yes and no. Within, you are the same child the Creator made, and your true face is unchanged. In the intervening period, you have learned much and experienced much. You have faced the fears and the terrors, lived through the joys and the sorrows, drunk deep of the pleasure and the pain, and you are still as beautiful as you were then. You still shine the same way, and your true face has the same stunning beauty it has always had.

So within you is the answer to any questions you may have, for you are the beloved Child of the Stars and of the Earth, and you are still fulfilling the purpose for which you came here, for which you were created. The Creator loves you as deeply as always. And you *are* Love, before all. Your presence will transform the Earth, and your Ancestors will sing a song of unity for the victory of peace, and you will sing with them in flawless harmony. And time will have lost its meaning in that moment of bliss. You will hear the Earth's song and know you are in tune with her. The Divine Mother of the Universe will sing through you. Her song of One Love will be heard to the ends of the Universe.

You are not forgotten; we are all with you in the unbreakable Circle, and we always watch over you. Remember your true heart is pure, always pure, and know you will be renewed. When we return the next time, we will laugh with you, even through the tears. For we cry with you and laugh with you, and we love you truly.

The Light increases. Its brightness reminds us of what awaits within us: a never-ending abundance of Light flowing from within. In the pouring forth of the Light we give our gift to the world, we give our heart-gift, and freely we give it. The more we pour love out into the world, the more the world is transformed. The more we empty ourselves of love, the more we are fulfilled. As we seem to empty ourselves of our compassion and love, we are refilled even more with an abundance that never runs dry.

We are each a vast reservoir of love and learning, of insights gathered, of pieces of wisdom, which are part of the greater whole. And we have access to the whole as well as its pieces. For that vast reservoir we are is, in its wider sense, a universal Ocean of Love from which flows all, and it is broader and deeper than any ocean that can be summoned by the imagination. It contains all life, conceivable and inconceivable. This ocean, we are a part of, and we flow through it as it flows through us. Its waves and ripples we feel, and as we feel and react, we ourselves make waves and ripples.

So the Ocean knows where we are, and we can know where we are in the Ocean. Though we are not of those shoals that seem to follow blindly an unseen leader, and change direction, we know not how or why. They are, indeed, enchanting to watch, as they change direction all as one, as they shimmer in the sunlight of the warm ocean. But our nature is different, as yours is different. The human does not react to the shoal in this way. As you know, it takes a great deal of difficult training, of learning and forgetting, a great narrowing of the spirit, to make human beings move in regimented shoals. And when they do, we all know, to our cost, that the results produced can have terrible effects or harm the individuals of the human shoal itself, and those who come into the path of this earth-shaking shoal as it moves. Uniformity and regimentation have nothing to do with the Oneness of which we speak; it is not blindness we are encouraging, but an opening of the inner-sight.

We are not calling forth leaders for others to blindly follow, we ask you simply to look within, to the leader that you are, and to follow your own lead, your deepest instincts and inner guidance. Then you will know the direction in which you should move and flow. You will understand then the ripples and waves that you feel passing around you or through you. When others follow their inner guidance, you will find it easier to flow with them, even though you are all so different from one other. Though you would seem to be going in opposite directions and doing different work, playing different games, somehow you will know there is a unity there. In spite of all your attempts to be different, once you let yourself be true to yourself, you will find you are more in unity with others – especially, if they are also being their true selves.

So, in the growth of your individuality and specialness, you will find you have made a bridge and a link between others who are also forging themselves in the image that they know to be theirs. You will have stumbled across true unity, and found togetherness. You will have found that now there is an apparently haphazard shoal gathering, made up of happily diverse, multicolored beings, who are differently formed and clothed, who all seem so unique and different, individual and diverse. No two faces seem the same, they are startling in the spectrum of their differences, yet they are one Tribe, one shimmering shoal who are moving as one, unerringly towards the Light of the Creator. Each in their own way, as they are guided, swimming and flowing, yet somehow they are all moving in the one direction. And not blindly, but all with perfect clarity and clear inner vision. This is a shoal to see!

When this One Heart Tribe fully gathers its wits and its senses, and remembers itself, it will already be flowing effortlessly back to the Creator from which it flowed in the first instance. Those who realize they are within it will feel the joy of returning to awareness; they will feel the Light in the Circle coming full-circle. They will feel an inner starburst of happiness and Oneness, knowing that they are flowing Home.

The Foal with the Golden Mane

There was once a foal with a mane of gold.
Her legs were graceful and long, and her coat was a golden-brown, the color of light and earth. Her lively eyes were an even brighter golden-brown. Her mane shone in the sunlight like fine-spun gold, and, when the wind blew through it, it would scatter light in all directions. When she stood on a high place or a hilltop, those far off would see it glinting, surrounding her head in light, and they would stand still, dumbstruck by her beauty, for they had never seen a foal as beautiful as she was. Some even thought she could not be real,

that they must have simply imagined her, since such a beautiful animal could hardly exist. But there she stood, and she was real, and she was free and happy. She was one of a band of wild horses who lived out in the dry scrublands, and, as well as her mane, she had a wild streak that shone out.

She loved to gallop on her long legs up ridges and hills, right to the very top, leaping over bushes in her way, whinnying to herself with joy. When she made it to the top, she would make a little dance of exultation; she would circle around and leap and kick her heels, leaping as high as she could in celebration and pleasure. Her mother would watch her with almost equal pleasure and her father felt great pride in this foal they had brought into the world together. She was a splendor to behold, and they enjoyed watching her explore her surroundings, her galloping and jumping. For she loved to test her legs by leaping every stream she could find and flying over every obstacle in her path.

She truly seemed to be able to fly when she wanted to. She had endless energy and her poor parents often felt tired simply watching her. She would gallop and dance on until dusk, and only when it was too dark to see where she was, would she return to her mother's side and sleep a happy sleep. But at first light, the very first glimmer of dawn, she would be back up on her feet, galloping off again to the highest hill she could find to watch the sunrise, to enjoy its spectacular display. She never tired of watching the dawn. The birds certainly celebrated the event, and she could not understand why every hilltop was not crowded with people and creatures of every kind, gathering to watch it. To her, it was the great beginning of that morning's joy, that day's adventure.

One morning, she awoke, as always, as the sky was lightening. As she opened her eyelids, she saw the clouds coloring and their shapes forming to greet the Sun. She came quickly to her feet, shook herself and galloped off to find her favorite hill, the highest one for miles around. She galloped through the countryside, bowing her head under the trees, leaping over the bushes, jumping over the little streams, until she came to the foot of the hill, the one that stood forth proudest from the plain. She cantered up it, as fast as she could, to its very top, and stood there, breathless and excited, breathing fresh, clean air through her nostrils.

The Sun was just rising on the horizon, and she felt the light flooding onto her skin and filling her bright eyes. She breathed deeply of the new light of that day, which always smelt and tasted different to her, for each day was unique and held new adventures and discoveries. Sometimes, in her first breath of the light, she might get a hint of what was to come that day. When the Sun was risen fully above the distant hills, she looked out over all the land around; over the wide open space with its scattered bushes and trees, the sparkling streams, all the hollows and high places and, in the distance, a few small houses of the people. She felt how special it was to be alive, how lucky she was to be here on this hilltop, greeting the Sun as it opened the sky for her and for everyone. Her heart was filled now with enough love to last the day and on beyond it. She turned and trotted down the hill, skipping and leaping as she went on her joyful way.

Yet this morning, as she played and grazed, she felt something different was in the air. When she sniffed the air, she found an unusual scent, one that gave her a mysterious sensation inside, a sense of something opening. Yet she could not place it or find a meaning for it. After a while, she would let herself forget about it and go on playing. But, sooner or later, she would catch it on the air, and she would raise her head and wonder what this new scent was. She decided to ask her mother and father what this special smell was and what this unusual feeling she felt inside could be. But, when she asked them, at first, they could not even smell the scent. They suspected she might have imagined it, until they suddenly caught the subtle aroma on the breeze. They had to admit they had no idea what it was, and the foal went away, even more curious. She asked the oldest mare she could find what it was, and then one of the young colts, but they could not help her with an answer.

So she did her best to ignore the scent and the sensation, and tried to carry on as before. As the morning went on, however, she found that she seemed to be searching for something. She was playing less than normal; she found herself looking behind vegetation, even picking up branches with her teeth to look under them, much to the surprise of the startled insects underneath. With her hooves, she nudged stones around and she peered into the shadows inside bushes and between trees. She even went to one of the hills, which had huge stones around it, and deep caves and openings in its face. She sniffed around there, hoping to catch the scent again and trace it to its source. But the stones looked much the same as they had when she had admired them before. They did not seem to know anything about what she was looking for; they seemed to ignore her, and after a while, she ignored them. She peered inside the caves and openings, looking for...she knew not what. But the mouths of the caves and openings were silent also. Even when she whinnied into the spaces, all that came back were echoes of her own voice, which faded away to silence.

So she looked around to see what else she could look into. She scanned the surrounding landscape, right to the horizon, until she saw, away in the distance, a great tree growing in a very green place. It stood further off than she would normally go, but it somehow seemed to be calling her, drawing her somehow to it. So she decided to set off towards the tree. She soon broke into a gallop as she came into the wide flats, enjoying the open space. While she galloped along in the sunshine, she was looking all around her, as she was passing through places she had never been before. She could see interesting places she knew she would like to explore at another time and some unusual trees and stones that were well worth a look some other day. On she went, though, after a time, she began to grow a little tired, so she slowed to a canter.

But now she was coming near to the tree, and she could see it up ahead, very large and grand, with a profusion of leaves in many colors, in a glowing spectrum of greens, reds, oranges and yellows, with so many tones in between, she could not count them all. For this was the time of Fall and the tones of the leaves were turning, and the trees were transforming themselves, putting on their autumn robes and dresses. They were gathered around a large watering hole, and the pool sparkled through the leaves. When she came near the tree, she slowed down to a respectful trot, since this tree felt very different from any she had encountered before. As she came near it, she stopped and looked up, admiring this marvelous tree. She felt its specialness and magnificence even among the other beautiful trees. It stood higher than all the rest, so maybe it would know more, too. She hoped it was a very wise tree, indeed.

She was lost in admiration for quite a long time until she remembered the scent and her feelings of that morning. She was sure the tree would know what they were. So she stepped forward and walked under its branches, into the cool shade, where her skin was scattered with hundreds of colors and shadows. It felt so wonderful, here in this cool place on this hot, hot day. She looked about her, and up at the whispering leaves, wondering if they would have the answer to her question. They seemed to be busily whispering about something, so she asked the leaves her question and waited for an answer. And they did whisper busily, but it only seemed to be amongst themselves. They seemed to be ignoring her, too.

After a time, she turned to the broad trunk of the old tree, with its marvelous bark. And in the gnarled bark, carved by time, she could see faces of many ancient beings, some of which looked very wise. Others, though, looked a little mischievous, some seemed silly and a few just looked peculiar. She knew she would be wise to ask her question of the wiser ones. So this she did, and she could tell they were thinking very deeply about it, as they were silent for a long time. But then she recalled they had been quite silent when she arrived, so she could not be sure whether they were thinking about her questions at all, or something else entirely. Still, she thought she had better wait and see what the result was of their deep deliberations. The mischievous ones still stared at her cheekily and most of them seemed to staring at her unusual mane. Sometimes, she almost wished she did not have such a mane, since it made others stare at her. For the moment, she felt she had better put up with it or she may never get an answer to her question.

So she waited, but no answer seemed to come. The wise ones looked as wise as ever – some looked even wiser – but still they did not answer her questions. She breathed a sigh of disappointment, and looked up at the fine tree with its whispering leaves and many wise faces. She wondered why she had come here, if they would not tell her what she wanted to know. But then she remembered she had only seen one side of the tree and only asked some of its many faces. She had not asked the tree itself. After all, they were only part of the tree and the tree itself was greater than all of them. Surely, she thought, it must be wiser than all of them put together.

So she would ask the heart of the tree her question and its heart was sure to know the answer. She stepped out of the cool, dark space, back out into the sunshine, then turned and looked up at the tall, broad tree. It was the hottest time of the day, and the Sun was overhead, blazing down, right above the tree. She could feel her golden mane glowing on her forehead and down the curve of her neck. Golden threads were falling over her eyes, filling her eyes with light that dazzled her, so bright it was. The Sun shone into her eyes through the glowing threads and she could feel the warmth of the Sun flowing down her golden mane, down her spine and down to her earth-brown tail.

Then she remembered her questions and opened her eyes. She gazed at the great tree and, respectfully, asked her questions about the special scent that so intrigued her and the feeling of opening she had felt inside. As she waited, patiently, for the tree to consider its reply, she closed her eyelids and enjoyed the heat and light of the Sun, such a contrast to the cool space under the tree. And she was feeling a little sleepy and dreamy now.

Then, in the darkness behind her eyelids, light began to flow and something moved within the light, something strange and yet familiar. She could see the flowing manes of many horses catching the light. Manes of every shade and color, rising and falling as these horses cantered on together in a vast herd, more horses than she knew were in the world! Thousands and thousands of horses, the herd stretching into the distance, to the far horizon, and beyond for all she knew. All cantering along together, traveling in patterns that reminded her of something. All of these countless horses were flowing the one way, yet each had its own unique life and joy. She could see no leader; each seemed to be moving uniquely, expressing their own joyful desire. So many horses, with the Sun glinting on their manes all the way to the edge of the world! As she watched, she suddenly felt the opening she had experienced earlier, and, soon, something even greater was bursting out from inside her.

It was a wave, like one of the little waves she would see in the streams when the wind shivered the waters. And she saw the horses moving now like these waves, but in higher waves and more complicated patterns than she had ever seen before. Some had golden manes like hers, and others were silver or white. And she was aware of something filling her nostrils: the special scent, with a sense of freshness and openness that opened her heart still wider. Now, she knew herself to be part of that great herd. When she finally opened her eyes, she could see waves rolling through the leaves of the great tree, and now the leaves were like horses of brown and orange, yellow and red. She gave thanks to the tree, for now she understood why the answers had not been given to her. Everyone she had asked knew that the answers were within her and would, in time, be found. She drank from the water of the pool, then turned and headed back to find the others of her band, waving farewell to the tree with her tail. But now the Rainbow herd was traveling with her, and she was galloping with them, and they moved as one. She felt all their colors flowing within her. She knew that they would always be with her now, and, when next she stood on the hilltop to greet the dawn, she would not be alone.

Time flowed on, and in the days that followed, she kept the sense of connection and felt the presence of her brothers and sisters of the Rainbow herd. She felt real joy that she was not just part of a little, isolated band who lived on the edge of the wilderness. When she had told them of her vision, her parents and the other horses had listened, though they were not really sure what it meant. They were resourceful and hardy horses, and simple survival was their main concern; most did not have much time for visions.

She, herself, sensed there were other meanings to her vision that she could not fathom them yet. And, at certain moments, the scent returned on the wind to intrigue and tantalize her. Something deep in her yearned to find its source. Others had begun to notice the scent now, but still had no idea what it was. Their band had wandered the dry lands for so many generations that its memory of the ocean had long gone. None of the horses had never even seen a lake, so they could not imagine that the wild waves of the foal's vision could really exist. She could not cool her burning curiosity, so, one day, the foal told her parents that she was setting out to find the source of the scent. Her parents sensed this was something important for her, and perhaps for all of them, so they wished her well on her quest.

As she set out on her trail, the foal knew that their hearts, and those of the whole band, would be with her. She set off swiftly, burning up the scrub beneath her hooves, until they watched her disappear into a cloud of dust in the distance. She settled down to a steady traveling speed, moving through the scrubland, with its spiky tufts of grass and sparse vegetation. It was not long before the land became even drier, and, at the end of the first day, she reached the edge of the territory that the band wandered in its search for food and water. Beyond this invisible boundary, was true desert, but the foal knew she must cross it, somehow. She felt doubts creeping in as she looked out over the sandy void ahead of her. She found a little waterhole and drank deeply, while, in the water, she saw herself reflected. Around her face, her mane created a golden aura, and it seemed to give her hope for the journey ahead.

She set out across the expanse, but, in the unrelenting heat, her progress became slow. She felt lonely, until, when she stopped to rest, she had a sense of her clan and the whole of the Rainbow herd around her, as if they were catching up with her, and they traveled on together. But she soon realized it was not wise to travel in the heat of the day. From then on, she traveled though the desert by night, during its cool hours, making use of the moonlight to see her way. Now, after the Sun had risen and the heat began to rise, she would find a shady place to sleep. One morning, when the time of sunrise came, she stood on a sand dune to welcome the event. She had traveled through the night and was weary. To her surprise, when the Sun appeared, she could hear a rushing sound like a great wind approaching. As the fiery orb rose, she heard more great waves flowing from the Sun, which went rolling through the world. She could feel the light flow around her, lapping at her ankles and wrapping around her body. And she could hear the light! As the waves of light embraced her, she closed her eyes to listen to the song of the Sun, and felt herself floating in an ocean of love.

That night, as she traveled on, she noted that the landscape was changing around her, becoming greener and more abundant with life, and there were streams now that she had to jump across. From then on, she traveled by day, and soon she was cantering through green meadows where the grass reached to her knees. She came to a land where the soil was black, rich and fertile. The grasses and plants tasted so sweet, and she happily roamed through the meadows, tasting the delights. She had never known such lushness before! If only she could bring her band here, she thought, they would never want to leave. She, herself, did not want to move on in a hurry.

But then the scent suddenly came, more strongly than ever before, and she closed her eyes as her body filled with a delicious sense of lightness. Something wrapped around her and held her, and she felt weightless, as if she was floating. When the sensation had passed, she knew it was time to continue on her way.

It was easy, now, to travel through this greenery, and people watched, open-mouthed, as the foal with the golden mane galloped past. More than one tried to catch her, thinking she had escaped some enclosure and must belong to someone. But she knew she was free, even if they did not, and no one came near to catching her. She crossed that land, with the scent growing stronger in her nostrils every day. One afternoon, as she stopped to drink from a stream, she looked up to see a handsome colt, as black as the earth, watching her. When their eyes met, both looked away, a little shyly. But the young colt found he could not take his eyes off her for long, and when she turned to go, his heart went with her. As she went on her way, he followed her with his eyes, until her flowing mane disappeared into the distance.

Later that day, she first heard the song of the ocean. It had come to her on a wind that was heavy with the special scent, and she stood still, as the music of the waves washed over her. She felt, inside, an opening, like the first time, so many days ago. And the song was like the sound she had heard by the tree; the sound of the leaves when the wind flows through them with its rushing waves. From above, she heard a cry unlike any she had heard before. She glanced up, and, soaring overhead was a kind of white eagle. Then more appeared in the sky until a whole flock of white eagles with pointed wings were circling. Their calls cut through the air, and the foal called out in response, before she set off in great joy, knowing her goal was near. She galloped at great speed through the countryside, soon coming to a ridge that she made her way up with ease. At the top, she almost flew over it and found herself hurtling down the other side. But at the foot of it she suddenly stopped, unable to believe her eyes.

Before her was a gray wall that she could not see through, barring her way. She looked into this thick mist, but could see nothing but mysterious shapes and eerie forms. This was not what she hoped for, at all. And it was moving towards her, crawling across the ground, as if to swallow her up. She took a couple of steps back, and, for a moment, part of her wanted to turn back the way she came, but she could hear the song of the ocean calling her, louder than ever before. She stood her ground and let the mist envelop her, then she began to take one step at a time, moving slowly through the mist. Step by step, she carefully makes her way forward through the cloud and her own confusion, letting the song carry her on, reminding herself that the mist is thick with the salty scent that has led her on.

Then she sees the glow of the Sun burning through the mist, and it begins to thin around her. The light increases around her, until suddenly she bursts through the other side of the cloud in elation. To her surprise, she finds herself back in a desert, with fine sand under her hooves like the driest of dry land. The foal looks about her with fresh confusion, yet the song of the ocean is calling her even louder now. She looks up to see undulating dunes, like those she knew from the desert, and she makes her way towards them, following the music. Then she stops, startled by what has appeared before her. Between the peaks of the dunes, are sparkling blue veils, that stretch across the horizon and seem to hang from the sky. She canters up the dunes with her heart beating wildly, until she reaches the top and looks out at the glorious vista. The ocean stretches out below her, from where the ocean and the sands dance at the edge the worlds, to the hazy place, far-off, where the vivid blues of sky and sea merge. The broad body of the ocean glows in tones of turquoise and azure, to deep blue-greens, while through her move millions of joyful waves, their manes bright in the sunshine. The foal stands in wonder before an unknown realm, filled with wonders, yet something in her knows of it... How could this magical realm ever have been forgotten?

Raising herself on two legs, she salutes the beauty of the sea, calling out from her heart in exultation. This narrow desert was just the edge of an ocean of abundance. Down the powdery dune, she makes her way to the broad sands below that run along by the ocean like a golden road. She gallops and canters along this road, which stretches further than she can know, rejoicing in her arrival and her freedom. Along the golden sands, she wanders, dipping her hooves into the little pools, testing the water, until she knows she will have to take the plunge. Yet how can she brave the waves? The foal puts a hoof into the water, and then takes a step into it and another, going a little deeper each time. But the she turns and walks back onto the dry sand. Perhaps the sea is not for creatures like her, at all.

Then from the water, a creature leaps with a cry of joy. The foal watches her, amazed, while this foal of the ocean jumps over the waves in her path and seems to fly, like she would do. The foal calls out to the dolphin in sheer delight, following her along the beach, their paths running parallel, as they call out to each other, from one realm to another. The dolphin leaps over some waves and dives beneath others, and the foal longs to join her in her world.

She feels inspired to dive in, and so she does. The warm water rises beneath her and lifts her up, and she relaxes until the water is holding her, strongly but gently. Her feet leave contact with the sand, and, somehow, her body knows what to do. She finds herself afloat, moving through the water, welcoming the embrace of the waves. And, somehow, the vastness of the ocean knew of her presence, and she felt herself in the presence of love, which held her precious. The dolphin appeared beside her and began to circle her, and together, they played in the waves. She became a happy sea-horse, and spent the day in the embrace of a great mystery, moving between sea and beach, exploring the shore and navigating the waves. Though she only touched the edge of its mystery, somehow she touched the whole of it, for it touched the whole of her.

There comes a moment when she is floating, calm and peaceful, and a new vision arises in her. Amongst all the other waves, she sees a special wave, a wave of love approaching. It flows through her with great lightness, filling her with delight and bliss like she has never known, and flows on to touch others, and flow through the world. She can feel it so deeply, yet, when she opens her eyes, she knows it has not yet come. She will have so much to tell, when she returns to her clan!

By the time she comes out of the water, the Sun is sliding towards the edge of the ocean, soon to sink beneath it. The fiery tones of the sunset are washing over the waves and the sandy landscape. There, standing proud on the red dune is the black colt. In his eyes, the fire of the Sun is flickering, and, on his forehead, is a single star. He has been drawn to her, her beauty enflames him, and he waits to see how the foal will take to him. She looks shyly at him, and he at her, while the Sun sets and the land and sea are transformed. The ocean seems to have become deeper as it has become darker, and, when the Moon rises, her gentle light kisses every lapping wave.

By the time the Moon has risen high, the filly and the colt know each other well enough to step into the ocean together for a moonlit swim. And, by the time the Sun rose next morning, she knew they would cross the lands together and make some waves of their own on the way. There was so much new love within her, now, that it would carry her through any desert on a wave. And nothing that it touched would ever be the same.

The unfolding of the heart is like the opening of a beautiful lotus flower, unfolding in many dimensions at once.

In the unfolding of the petals, the inner dimensions open to be entered. In this opening, new openings are made into other worlds, for the heart truly opens all. The heart is the great key to all that is closed or locked, to all that is hidden or forgotten. And the unfolding heart opens the Universe within. The Light, which spills out, sends its waves and rays beaming out through the cosmos, carrying its message of love, shining like a lighthouse through the darkness and the seeming shadow. The heart illuminates all, for nothing can remain hidden from the heart; it sees all and knows all. It is God and Goddess within.

Our opening holds open a portal through which we can enter ourselves and, through entering ourselves, by going into the heart of the flower, we have begun a journey directly into the Heart of the Creator who made us. So we pass now through the petalled portal....

As we dive down into our deepest heart, we swim through the many levels and currents, we pass through all our pasts, all our future possibilities, all of our unexpressed love, all that still waits to be revealed. We dive down and down into this Ocean of Love, into the limitless ocean that we are… And this ocean is alive, it teems with life; all the forms that exist in the Universe are here, present and living in microcosm, represented within realities we have not even touched upon. This ocean may well have cold layers and chilly currents, which, as we reach them, make us want to turn and swim back up. But, if we go on, there is much to discover beneath the coldness. If we move on beyond, we soon discover the warmer layers.

There, we can relax and bathe in the warmth, rolling and spinning in the form of a sleek seal. We are spinning our fins, turning ourselves in a spiral, flicking our tail to send ourselves down deeper, for we know that our seal body is designed to dive deep. And we are curious, we seek out that which we do not know or understand within ourselves, and this inner curiosity can open us up to the deep currents of wisdom, which move through us. Once we dive in, some feeling or force within will seem to guide us down deeper and deeper into ourselves, and we will go into the deeper layers. Sometimes passing through dark zones, inky, cloudy places we may feel we need to avoid, but if we swim on and head straight to the heart of them, we will find ourselves penetrating our greatest mystery. For here in the inky blackness, even the tiniest spark of light can be seen – a spark we would have missed in the lighter zones. In these tiny sparks, floating here in the deep dark, there is hidden wisdom, for these sparks rise from the deepest depths.

We go down deep, following them to their source... We see they are rising from a source of fire, our own resource of Inner Fire, a volcano deep down on the floor of this Ocean of Love. And we follow the sparks down; now they are like glowing red and orange stars in the darkness around us, and we are swimming through them. How bright they glow, here in the deepest depths! So we follow them down towards the place of fire. Flames rise up, bursting out into the ocean and being instantly extinguished, yet they create in their little death, these sparks, these star-sparks which live on, rising up into the darkness above. Below is an unending fire, which cannot be quenched. It pours out molten fire, to cool in the waters, through an opening like a mouth from which the stars pour, being blown out through its reddened lips into this Ocean of the Heart. And we wonder how far we can venture down into the fire, for will we not be consumed by it? Yet we are curious, and something seems to draw us on... Something tells us that this fire will not harm us, because it is our own Inner Fire.

We realize now that something is changing within us, and our form is becoming fierier. We are flowing into this new experience as a new being... So, with a final spiral, we dive deep, down into the heart of the fire – with a splash and a hiss and a flash of flame. For a moment, we see nothing but fire, nothing but the blinding flames and we wonder if we have done the right thing, but we know we are still here and whole and have not been consumed. Though we feel we are still changing as we are flowing into this new reality. While we flow down into these volcanic flames, we see forms within the fire, living shapes in the flames. Some of which seem familiar as they flash past us – there are faces there of creatures dwelling within the fire....

Now we know we have become fire, alive – for this is the Realm of Inner Fire and here, we too are fire. Here, we swim again, bathing in the flames, which are cleansing and purifying us in the Fire of the Heart. Because we are fire, we are not uncomfortable or hot; we are at home here, we are as comfortable as on the coolest day. So we go on to explore this Realm of Fire, for it has its own hidden, living wonders. Around us, we see the beings and creatures who are formed of living fire. Their faces and forms are all around us, greeting us, swimming with us, laughing with us and dancing around us. They are pleased to greet us, welcoming us here into one of the realms in which we, too, have our place. For we are a being of fire in one of our deepest selves – we are elemental, also, and we know this place as a home. We look around us, with our fiery eyes, at this wide ocean of flame, this ocean of living fire. The flame-waves ripple through it, and the shoals of fire-fish pass through us and swim around us. Below, we notice the cooler fire-coral glowing, forming and re-forming. We swim on, to explore further...

We discover deep fire caves from which the flames flow out into this ocean. Above us passes a huge creature, a dweller in the fire ocean, larger than a great whale; a being of living flame passing through its habitat, at peace. For there is Peace here, and all have their place here. All know where they are flowing and that, here, they belong, for they are of the One Fire and, within, they burn as one. Love is burning within them, and they are love made flame. In this ocean of fiery love, all its denizens are creatures made by the Creator of fire, as we are, and we flow with them.

Then one of the caves catches our attention, one of the fire caves from which flows the liquid flame. We decide to explore it, so we swim towards it, flicking our fiery fins and spinning into its mouth, into the liquid flow. Here, we are in the stream of fire issuing forth, and we follow it down to its source, deep in the fire cave. We are turning and spiraling down, wondering where we are going. Through the flow of fire we go, until we feel something cool against our fiery face, a kind of coolness rippling against us, which feels strange, but not unpleasant. We sense this pleasing coolness wash over us and we feel ourselves changing within. We feel our fieriness dying down as this sweet coolness enters us. We know we are flowing from one form to another, and so we flow on. Now, we can see no flames, but we hear their roar behind us – a roar we had not noticed before – but now that we are entering a silent zone, we hear it behind us, the sound fading away. And we bid Fire farewell.

Now we are in an icy place, and we become, once more, like a seal swimming beneath the ice, with the light flowing through from above. We swim our way through water, which is thick, icy and crowded with crystals. The crystallized water will not freeze solid, for fire warms it and keeps it flowing, holding the balance between fire and ice, so that both have their place and both flow in perfect balance. We are swimming on through these crystal waters, which sparkle as they catch the light. We notice, around us, are thin walls of ice through which the light flows – we are moving now up a wide, icy tunnel. Our seal form knows well how to swim through these icy waters, so we are enjoying the cold now; how sweet it seems, a new pleasure after bathing in the flames. We playfully flip our fins and we flick our tail, moving faster now. We are warmer than the ice through which we swim, so we cut our way through the ice like a warm knife.

Ahead of us, we sense a soft brightness shining through the icy water, glowing through the crystals; it guides us on, and we follow the light. The walls of the tunnel have widened and lightened, and now we see reflections in the glowing crystal. In the mirrors are glimpses of your Aquatic Ancestors, and they are you, too. Their ancient faces and forms have graced this planet through the epochs of her evolution, including those Ancestors of humanity who rose from her oceans. They are swimming with you, and their wisdom swims within you. Your form changes to an ancestral form of silvery-blue, smooth and beautiful, a strong body you know. With it, you swam through the ocean of knowing, long ago. The space around us has opened up into a great crystal chamber, filled with ancestral memories and the treasures of the deep, the lore of our shared history. We circle here, moving through beams of crystalline light, as long as we wish, bathing in the deep love from the sea of living memory.

When we swim on, the tunnel soon turns a corner, and we swim around it – ahead of us, we see the light growing as bright as a sunny day, and warm.

So warm, we feel it on our soft skin, on our nose and eyelids; it feels good and we want to reach it, to experience it, after the lovely coolness through which we have been swimming. We feel the water warm around us, and the tunnel opens up, wider and wider, for the ice has melted here. It opens out as we swim into warmer water, enjoying the pleasure of its warmth on our skin, and we roll our heads, flick our whiskers and spiral our tails, joyfully.

Then, something changes within us and, again, we feel our shape change, our form flow into something else, something familiar... When our eyes open, we can just make out our soft blue beak in front of us and we sense our strong fins at our side – we are a dolphin, swimming in our home waters. Now we are in the shimmering light of a warm ocean that opens out all around us. The blue-green tropical waters embrace us warmly, while the rainbow colors of the fish and the coral shimmer around us. We swim up in a spiral, enjoying the sights and sensations...

Upwards in a wide spiral, we climb, moving through the fish in their millions, the teeming life of all kinds, the plankton and the tiny creatures. Up and up, and the water is warmer now, warmed by the Sun above, a bright glowing orb above us. We swim on up, until we see the surface just above us; we can see its waves, its rippling surface, and we know we want to reach it. So we swim faster now, moving up faster and faster, until, suddenly, our beak reaches out into the air and, with a flip of our fins and a flick of our tail, we are up into the clear air. We breathe in this air, clear and clean around us, as we rise above the waves, slowing down to pause mid-air a moment, then we dive down into the warm ocean again. We feel the water rushing over our smooth skin, and listen to the whispers of the bubbles.

Amongst the bright bubbles, we hear whistling and singing tones, and we see familiar forms flowing through the blue. A school of dolphins has come to accompany us on our way, and their delightful faces appear around us. Along the way, they play with us and celebrate our presence. Then we raise our head and flip our strong tail, lifting our body clear out of the water with a joyful shriek. Around us, our sister and brother dolphins leap high, then dive into the blue. Once more, we leap from the water, to feel ourselves flowing up through the air. But, as our form reaches higher, this time we are not falling. We are rising higher and higher through this crystal-clear air, which is holding us up and lifting us higher, on and on upwards into the blue of the sky... We reach higher and higher until, once again, we feel the changing of our shape, our form flowing into a new one. The air is passing over us, caressing us, and we feel our form so new, yet, somehow, familiar....

And we open our eyes, to see the wind rippling through our feathers! Our wings are glowing in the sunlight, and we are flying upwards, our wings stretching wide, carrying us higher. As our wings spread wide, we feel something expand within us – in our bird breast, our heart opens. We reach out wider, flying higher, towards the Sun above, which seems to draw us up and beckon us on, like a golden beacon.

Our wings are strong, they carry us almost effortlessly towards it, and our heart feels warm and open. Reaching on upwards towards the Sun, so well we fly, so high we soar, that now we are in the clouds. We flap our wings through them and part the clouds, dividing them to make a path for ourselves, with the light of our heart lighting a clear way. Through this tunnel of air we have created, we can see the Sun shining through the clouds, and we fly on through the clouds until, with one strong flap of our wings, we are out into the open air again. The air is warm as it moves through our feathers, and the Sun beats warm on our heart.

We are flying on higher and higher until we feel the air cooling now; the air takes on a cool, crystal quality. We feel ice hanging in the air, and as we fly through it, we scatter the crystal droplets with our wings. For our wings now are hot and fiery, warmed by the Sun and the love within us. We clear a path through the crystal droplets and the fire burning within our heart carries us on, the love burning there melts the ice through which we fly. Our flight is effortless, for we know that we are flying home. And the journey home is a light one. On we fly, until the ice is at its thickest, but our heart melts a way and our wings clear a path.

Above us, then, we see the last skin of ice, which divides the air from what lies beyond. With one great beat of our wings, we break through the icy skin to find ourselves in a warmer world, a layer of familiar fire. We fly on into the fire, which is our friend, now as it has always been, and our fiery wings are at home here. Through the fire we fly, enjoying its heat, like that of the Sun we are heading towards. With our wings of flame, we fly on, and ahead of us we see the velvet darkness beckon; the darkness beyond the fire, where the fire ends and the great open space begins.

Above us is the Veil of Fire, which divides fire from that which lies beyond it, and with one great beat of our heart and our wings we burst through it, out into the deep darkness beyond. Here, we are surrounded by the stars blazing through the dark in all their glory; all the shining, burning lights of many home fires....

But one of them draws us on, and as we head towards this one Sun, which shines brighter than the rest, our wings become lighter and lighter – and they shine now as brightly as the Sun. We know ourselves now to be one with the Sun, as we shine through the darkness towards this shining Parent who is calling us home. On we fly, on our wings of light, and our heart of light shines within and we feel great peace, a peace brighter than any we have felt before. Before us, the Sun flames forth its glory, shining and burning so brightly that our eyes cannot bear the brightness – so we close our eyes and know that we will be guided into the Heart of the Sun. For we need no eyes to find our way Home.

The Light flows through us as we flow through the Light. We feel the light welcome us, gather us into its Heart and our heart opens further and further, we can sense our heart uniting with the Great Heart into which we fly. Heart and Heart are melting together now, and we are flying through Living Light, through Living Love into this Great Heart. Into the Heart, from which we flew in the first moment, into the Light of the Heart which gave us life. Into the Heart of the One who gave us form, into the Heart of the Sun, which is no sun, but the Source of all suns – the great Central Source of Light that gave birth to the infinite suns, that created all light, all darkness, all fire, all ice, every element and being.

Now we are Home and we are One and we are at Peace.

A celebration begins, an opening of a new Heart Space, which we all can share. We who are of the many, the many within one, the many making One. We weave our unity around the Central Source of Light, like the tribes in ancient times gathered around the fire to weave their unity, sing their songs and dance their dances.

We are the many tribes gathering, and we are from every tribe. From all corners of the Cosmos we have drawn our threads, drawn them forth into the Center, and in the Center they are woven into One. In the Central Light of the Creator, these many, many threads are knotted together, tied in an unbreakable knot, fused together in unbreakable love. From this Center-Point, the threads reach out to all the corners of all the worlds and in every direction around us, above and below us. The threads stretch from this single Center-Point out into infinities, like a vast stringed instrument that waits for the Great Player to come and pluck it into life, to sing Its great Heart into it, so the strings will vibrate, sending the song out to all the stars. And they will send back more threads to be gathered into the Center, into the new unity.

The gathering of the threads will continue, and we who are connected through the threads will know our hearts to be connected to the One at the Center, from where all the threads were spun. There, in the great spinning wheel of the One Heart, that Great Heart of Life, from which we drew our thread in the first instance and which always connects us back to our origins. We have woven our divine life-thread through many realms, through many lives, through many strange places, and worlds beyond imagining. Yet we know our thread began somewhere, and along this thread flows the love from the One who spun it out of Their Own Heart, and back along it flows our love. And this singing Heart-thread, this Heartstring vibrates with the music of the stars....

From there we came, in the distant days. We were gathered from the stars to come here to this world, which dazzled us with its beauty. How our hearts burst with joy and wonder as we approached it! As we came closer and could see its wonders more clearly, we cried with joy and delight at its breathtaking beauty, its abundant wonders. Never had such a world been created!

How privileged we felt to be able to set our feet upon it, to walk through this sacred place, to bend down and drink its waters, to feel its soft earth beneath us, to know its special stones, to enjoy around us all the plant-life and flowers. The air was singing, buzzing with sounds and songs, life was fluttering and flying in every direction, and the great trees stood tall above all else, sharing their splendor with everyone. We had never seen such a world. We could never have dreamt such a world into existence. But we knew the One who had, and we were here with a mission, a task. For these numberless sacred places in this great sacred place, this sacred world, were fragile in their way, for they were all finely balanced. Balanced so minutely that we could not truly comprehend how they were held together, and only dimly could we glimpse the greater patterns in living form around us. These balances would need to be maintained and the sacredness of this place guarded, for there were special beings here who had come with a special task.

They were the people, the new people of Human flesh who were learning to live among the people of Stone and Wood, of Plant flesh, and the peoples who were furred or scaled or feathered. These new people knew themselves to be part of the One Life, they knew they held a balance in this world and they had been given the task of holding this balance in their lives and in their hearts. They understood that, as they grew, they would be custodians of this balance, for we were here merely as helpers, to ensure that the new people had everything they needed in their new life, a solid grounding for the years and centuries ahead. So we stayed only as long as was necessary to complete this task, and we gave that knowledge that was asked for and that wisdom that was asked for, and no more. For we knew these people were here to learn these things for themselves, as they had been given great brightness and intelligence, along with other skills with which to make their lives as pleasant and comfortable as they could, while maintaining their balance and the balance of the world around them.

We watched them grow in knowledge and in wisdom and, though these were not always in perfect balance, we were very pleased with how these people found their way in the world, and the great respect and reverence they had for all life. We witnessed their love and their inner-knowing increase, too, as they learnt to trust themselves more, to trust their inner-instincts to lead them to what they wanted to find. The other creatures and beings of all kinds co-operated with them and knew them as friends, for they all collaborated in this great task because all life had knowledge and wisdom which was being shared. All knew themselves to be part of the One Wisdom, all knew that they depended on each other and could rely on each other in this great task. We saw trust flower and grow amongst all creatures, since the setbacks were very few and they were always outnumbered by the flowerings of new insights and discoveries.

We, too, were welcome at the firesides, for we came as friends and we made no great claims and gave ourselves no great graces – we were there simply to help and it was understood and accepted that we would leave when our part of the task was complete. In a way, this gave a kind of gentle urgency to our work, though it was a very stress-less kind of urgency, because each day was filled with laughter and with deep, loving joy. For we, also, discovered new things each day, new relationships and patterns. We had been given a deep knowledge of the workings of this world before we came, but its subtleties, its intricacies amazed us every single day, and we grew in appreciation and love of the One who had brought into being. We also grew in respect and reverence for the Earth herself, who maintained the overall balance and brought forth the life from her own heart. Her moods and seasons, her intricate lacings of life, her threading together of that which seemed different and disparate, also filled us with wonder.

So we were disappointed and dismayed when things began to change. For there came times when the balances were disrupted, when the delicate fabric of life was torn, when the Web itself was torn and ripped apart in places. Though in those times, it was much easier to repair these tears in the Web, we felt sorrow and we hoped that the balances could be restored in future, for we did not wish to see a world of such incredible beauty damaged or imbalanced in any way.

The forces that unbalanced things came initially from without. There came onto the Earth those who were, in their way, explorers but who had a very limited understanding of the world in which they found themselves. They looked at this world through the eyes of fear and the eyes of greed and were quite blind to its deeper beauty and the delicate balances that held it together. In their ignorance, they crashed through the Web and tore openings that created damage, which rippled across the face of the Earth.

Something harmful entered the body of the Earth and the bodies of the beings of the Earth. This was a subtle vibration at first, an energy which rippled through the Web, which could even be ignored in the beginning, as it seemed a temporary effect – like a wave that passes through space and hits the Earth, then passes on, whose effects die quickly away.

Unfortunately, the effects of this wave did not die out as quickly as we hoped. The vibrations of fear transmitted from creature to creature, though most were able to withstand their effects and most creatures were, in a sense, immune to these vibrations. However, the new people were affected most of all. They had obviously not been expecting any such arrival and they had no apparent defenses against such an intrusion into their system.

So there was confusion amongst these early peoples. Many were disorientated, as if they had been hit by a strange virus that had entered their system, unbalancing them from within. And this, in effect, is what happened, for a kind of virus did spread across the Earth in those days and those who had contracted this virus of fear expressed it in different ways;. In some, it died out quickly, becoming a very, very subtle vibration, which had little effect on them, but others found their systems were taken over by this viral vibration and they expressed its effects more directly, in forms of anxiety and panic, aggression and greed. These unbalanced ones upset the harmony of the tribes and the balance of the Web of Life, though many were barely aware of what they were doing. Most simply acted on impulses they could not comprehend and found difficult to resist. For a few, it seemed as if they were merely experimenting with or exploring these impulses and sensations, but no one knew what the effects would be in the long term. This new element that had entered the living system was to have results that we could not have foreseen.

We knew that our task and our time on Earth would be ending soon, and we wondered what we could do to help the balance be restored, before we had to leave. So we followed our inner guidance and our highest guidance, and went to meet with those who were closest to the original vibrations, the old ways; those who could raise their voices in the councils, at the firesides and in the dwelling-places. They would make their sisters and brothers aware of the dangers they were facing. This we did, and we passed on our message, gave what guidance we could, then stood back to see what the effect would be, what decisions would be taken.

To our dismay, our efforts had little effect at that time, because the ripples of this new vibration were growing, and becoming heavy waves, and those voices which were raised to explain the dangers were drowned out. Some of the tribes survived quite well, and re-balanced themselves, but others, unfortunately, became unbalanced and began to fight amongst themselves – and then fight with other tribes. Our tears were many in those long nights, as we saw our brothers and sisters in conflict with each other, for the new vibration of fear seemed to pulsate through the Web of the Earth until it seemed to drive some mad.

In time, a new balance was created as the Earth and the guides and helpers worked with the peoples to try to minimize the effects of this new arrival. There came, then, a period of greater stability. For if this vibration could not be removed, it was obvious that it would have to be incorporated into the frequencies of the Earth until a way could be found to integrate it into the greater Web. Then, perhaps by balancing it with other frequencies, its effects could be transmuted into something more healthy. This was a difficult and delicate task, because these heavy vibrations were very unsettling to the sensitive natures of these peoples and of the beings of all kinds. Trust was damaged by the actions of some of the tribes who broke the ancient contracts of trust that had existed. The creatures of the Earth and Air, Fire and Water found it difficult now to trust the people, for their promises were often broken, and the people seemed to be forgetting the great and simple wisdom that had guided them so long.

But, over time, there came new leaders who tried to show a way to balance life on the Earth and the greater scheme of life. Individuals appeared in the tribes who seemed to have a wisdom beyond their years – and they were, indeed, the Elders returned. These young people held the wisdom of their Ancestors and, to the surprise of their parents and friends, they reminded them of what their Ancestors had known so well; that there was a delicate balance of life, and it was their task to maintain it in all its complexity and simplicity.

In this period, there was a recovery, and life did regain a balance of a new kind. In this time of re-balancing, much of the damage was repaired and relations between the people and all beings improved. This was a time when a wave of new sacred spaces was created across the Earth, as people rediscovered and remembered their original links, their deeper nature, and beautiful were the creations of this age. They even tried to surpass each other in the beauty of their spaces and temples, for there was indeed a new competitive vibration amongst the people on the Earth. This could at times be expressed in healthy ways, as the people competed against each other in many different manners and most of these were quite healthy ones.

By now, the tribes were growing in size and new tribes were being created. The Humans were moving across the face of the Earth in greater numbers and they were sometimes displacing other creatures as they went. So the Earth constantly needed to re-balance herself to cope with these changes, but still the Earth maintained much of its original balance, for she had learnt ways of counteracting the earlier imbalances.

At this point, we leave the story of this Age, in a time of new balance, when the fear vibration had been understood and brought into a kind of balance with those multitudes of vibrations, which hold the Web of the Earth together. We will continue the story at another time.

The Rainbow Fish and the Shoal

There once was a fish of shimmering colors who swam away from home.

It happened one bright day, when the sunbeams were stroking through the ocean, passing through the shoals like golden fingers. All the shoals of fish shimmered even brighter than usual, and one particular fish looked around at those who were swimming with him in his school and thought how beautiful they all looked, how their scales shone, how they glowed in their wonderful skins. They were each a rainbow in themselves! He hadn't appreciated it recently, as he had not been a happy member of the shoal. It had not always been that way. When he was younger, he had followed the shoal without question and, at first, it had been a simple life. The shoal moved through the ocean to where the life was abundant, and you only had to open your mouth for it to be filled until your belly was full. He just had to go with the flow and move as one with the shoal. Things seemed simple and clear and he enjoyed each moment as it came and passed.

But there came a day when he felt something different inside; a peculiar, unsettled feeling. He thought, at first, it might be something he had eaten, since the shoal had just passed through a very abundant zone of the ocean and all had gulped down as much as possible, gorging themselves a little. So he wondered if he was just ill after over-feeding, but no one else showed any ill-effects and the feeling stayed with him as they swam on. To the left and the right of him, above and below him, all were flapping their tails and moving their fins in unison, all moving along as one in perfect rhythm, and he was in the middle of it all. But, for some reason, he felt out of place. He looked about him and wondered, were any of the other fish feeling this way? But all seemed to have their eyes fixed straight ahead, on the lookout for warmer water and juicier food, and none seemed troubled like he was. He was disturbed by this peculiar sensation, yet he swam on with the rest and kept his mouth shut. He thought it best not to tell any of the others about this feeling and, anyway, it was sure to go away. But, as the days and weeks passed, it only became more intense and he felt less and less at home with the shoal.

He would be the one at the back of the school, trying to catch up, or staring out of the school at a fascinating coral tree. He tended to get distracted by the beauty all around him and find himself falling behind or drifting off at a tangent. But the other fish made it all look so easy… These days, he couldn't seem to get the hang of their synchronized swimming and he found their line of thinking rather boring. Whenever they settled into a steady, swimming rhythm, he would get the urge to syncopate it a bit; when they were all executing a smooth turn, he couldn't help doing a loop or two, just for fun. Some of the others thought of him as an odd fish, and he knew it, so he did try to fit in. Recently, he had tried hard to show he was just one of the shoal, but he still didn't feel right inside.

Often, he was just being pulled along in the wake of the shoal while he was half asleep or daydreaming. Over and over, he was almost left behind. At first, he would feel a moment of panic, but then he began to wonder... He asked himself, would it be so bad if he didn't follow the shoal? If he was left behind, could he survive? Maybe it was time to drop out of the school for a while and look at the world through his own eyes!

That very day, he finally decided he must do something, as he did not want to go on feeling strange. There came a moment when the shoal was about to turn a sharp corner. It was a place they had come to before and they would always turn left there, at the edge of the coral reef, and head off to where there was great feeding. But, at the moment the shoal turned, our friend, the little fish, decided that no, he wouldn't go with them. He would stop right where he was and let the shoal go on, until he had figured out what these strange sensations meant. He watched the shoal swim on, regardless. No one seemed to have noticed that he had stayed behind.

After a moment, he felt a wonderful feeling rise within him, a kind of release, a feeling of freedom. He had never felt this sense of liberation before, and he felt a little intoxicated by it. He began to swim freely around, making patterns and shapes in the water, flapping his fins and tail as wildly as he could. Oh, if the shoal could see him now! They would say he was a crazy fish. Look at him, dancing in the water like something wild! They would think he did not belong in their shoal, because one fish like him could send the shoal off-course and then were would they end up? What if they all started dancing in this crazy way? What would the other shoals think of them? So he was very glad that no one had seen him stay behind for, now, he was free to dance and explore his new freedom. He felt lighter already, and those unhappy feelings were gone.

He turned and swam in the opposite direction to the shoal, venturing into the unknown quite happily, feeling his freedom flowing within him. Some in the shoal might think this a stupid thing to do, but he knew he was quite bright in his own way, though he had never had the chance to truly shine. On he swam, looking around him at all the sights of the ocean. All of the flowing forms of life seemed new to him now, everything looked so different from this vantage point of being on his own. Up until now, he had only seen things through the eyes of the shoal, and the members of the shoal often blocked his view, so he only got a glimpse of wonderful visions while they swam past.

Now he could see things in their true beauty…it was as if the scales had dropped from his eyes, and all the colors shone more brightly than he ever remembered. Now that his view was not obscured any more, the ocean seemed so much bigger. He felt so excited, so happy, he felt truly at peace inside. And he noticed, to his surprise, that those old feelings had been replaced by all sorts of new sensations that were shooting through him at an amazing rate. He felt like an adventurer. He thought he must be the bravest little fish that had ever lived, for to set off into the unknown takes a lot of bravery, and he had shown he had the courage to set out on his own. His senses were so filled with new sights and pleasures that he felt he could swim on and on forever.

And he did swim on and on, exploring new places deep on the floor of the ocean, weaving in and out of beautiful coral formations, dipping his nose into shells and surprising some of their inhabitants. He flew through the green fronds of the plants, which grew on the seabed and he swam up as high as he could go, to the very surface of the ocean. And he could feel the sunlight on his scales even more strongly than ever before, as he had never been up this high. He even poked his nose out of the water for a moment, opening his mouth to breathe in some of the air from above the surface. All these new experiences made him a little dizzy, so after a while he let himself spiral down for a rest. Down he drifted, and on the way down he took a few mouthfuls to feed himself for his energy was waning a little. He had swum all day without a break, so full of his experiences that he had never thought of food. He deserved a rest…

He must have slept for a little while, as he drifted along, for when he opened his eyes it was quite dark. The Sun must have gone down shortly before, as the ocean was growing very dark, indeed, and when he looked up, he could only see the faintest glow of light above in the sky. He knew even that would soon be gone and there would then be total darkness. He would be alone in the dark for the first time, in a part of the ocean he did not know. He felt something rise inside which he did not like – it was the feeling of fear, which gradually gripped him. He felt cold inside, suddenly, and now the sense of being alone and free changed into the sense of being lonely and fearful. Below him, he could see just a few distant shapes disappearing into the depths to sleep. Soon, they would be gone, and how would he feel then? As he looked around, he could see no others of his kind. And he felt himself shivering with cold, as well as fear, for the ocean was growing colder, as the warmth of the Sun receded.

He tried to see something in the darkness that might guide him or give him a clue about which way to swim, but there were so many directions and he was so afraid, he just found himself swimming in a tight circle, going nowhere. He was flapping his fins and his tail frantically, as if he could somehow get rid of his fear that way, but it only seemed to make things worse. So, finally, he stopped, as he was tiring himself out. He was not even sure now which way was up and which was down, which was left and which was right. It was so dark that he could see nothing, absolutely nothing. He could just hear the gentle murmur of the ocean as it moved around him, and the sound of the water sliding over his scales. Beyond that, his senses told him nothing.

This felt like the most terrible moment of his life. Alone here, in total darkness, not knowing if he would survive the night. Then something within him told him to stop his panicking, to simply let go and drift, to trust that he would find his way. He couldn't think of another option that was any wiser, so he decided to take the advice of this inner wisdom. For what else could he do, but drift? So he rested his fins and his tail and relaxed all his muscles, sensing the water ripple over his scales, as he moved with the subtle currents. He felt the ocean take hold of him in her gentle grip, and a kind of peace grew within him. And he felt it was not so bad here, drifting in the dark, now that he had let go of the fear. Even if he did not know where he was heading or what his fate would be, something in him told him to trust the wisdom of the ocean. He asked the ocean, as kindly as he could, to look after him. He had spent the day exploring her as he never had before, and he realized he loved her more deeply now than when he had been just one of the shoal, swimming along, feeling nothing in particular and experiencing little. So he made his little prayer of love and gave himself to the ocean. On he drifted, and he closed his eyes, for it was the same to have his eyes open or closed, so dark was it.

He did not know how long he drifted for, but after a time, he opened his eyes, and to his surprise, saw a great light around him. He shook himself, blinked a few times and looked more deeply into the light, and he could see there were brightly glowing beings around him. He wondered if he was dreaming – or dead! Perhaps, this was where you go after you die... He looked around at these shining beings and asked them where he was. They were rather surprised at his question, but they answered that he was on the floor of the ocean and this was their home. The little fish was rather relieved, for he was not sure if he was ready to die yet, when there was still so much to see. These fish gave out such a bright light that he thought they would be wonderful guides for him to find his way through the ocean. So he asked them if they would guide his way for a while, as he wanted to explore this new realm. They were only too happy to oblige, as they had never been asked this before, and it seemed like a very noble task to be given. So the Light-Fish formed a glowing circle around him and set off to show him the wonders of the deep. The little fish was in the middle of them all, looking out at the world from a new vantage point, illuminated by these beautifully glowing creatures. His own shoal had never ventured down this far into the unknown, and he had always rather feared going down so deep, to the bed of the ocean, for it seemed so dark there, so muddy and murky.

They had not swum far, when the fish felt a cold shiver run through him. It was as if something invisible had touched him, and he shuddered at the touch. It was like the strange feeling he had experienced in the shoal, but much more intense. The Light-Fish sensed his feelings and realized what had happened. They gathered more closely around him, holding him in their light, and the sensation slowly faded away. As they swam along, he understood from them that he had passed through a place that emanated rays, like those of sunlight, but these rays did not warm or bring life. The waves that came from that place could make you ill, so they were well to move on to a safer place, deeper in the ocean. Meanwhile, their light would keep the strange waves at bay.

On they went, that swimming circle of light and, soon, the little fish was opening up to a huge, new world, as these luminous fish guided him through their realm. With their light all around him, he could make things out quite clearly. They showed him all the unseen sights, the spectacular coral-covered palaces, the stone temples decorated with beautiful shells, and they wended their way through places hidden in the deep that were dazzling in their beauty. They swam through the hours of the night, while the Light-Fish showed him all the secrets of their world, and they truly glowed with pride. After a very enlightening few hours, the little fish looked up to see a faint glimmer in the sky.

Now that day was coming, he thought that maybe it was time to return to the shoal and tell them of all the wonders he has seen. As much as he enjoyed being with these Light-fish, maybe he should rejoin his brothers and sisters that he had left, since now he could open their eyes to beauties around them they had never noticed before. He could lead them toward experiences that he knew they would enjoy, and all these new wonders would open up for them. So, while the sky grew brighter overhead, he thanked the Light-Fish for their guidance and he bade farewell to them. He promised them he would return with his shoal and show them all the wonders they had been missing, deep in the ocean.

As he swam upwards, he could see his way by the light rising in the sky. Above him and around him, he could see glimmering fish waking up, and he began to search for his own shoal. He searched and he searched, spotting shoals of many different kinds of fish, but not his own. So on he swam, and now that the Sun had risen, it was shining out above in its magnificence, with its brightest rays piercing into the ocean. He followed the paths of these rays, swimming along them, enjoying the sensation of following these threads of light, until, up ahead, he saw something familiar shimmering in the distance, something which moved in a way he knew well.

There was his own shoal, swimming along, and he swam up behind it, quite discreetly. as they swam on, winding their way through the ocean. Without anyone noticing, he joined along behind, sliding into place beside one of the other fish, who blinked and turned to look at him, then looked back as if nothing had happened. Inside, he felt the feeling of homecoming, of being happy to be part of the shoal again, yet also happy that he was bringing something special back with him. For there would be a time when he would find himself at the front of the shoal and, in the moment when the shoal has to decide which way to turn, he could lead them somewhere new, and the shoal would follow that way for a while. What special places he knew now, what new friends he had made in the depths! And what wonders were still to be revealed...

As he quietly rejoined his brothers and sisters in the school and swam alongside them, he looked forward to all the surprises that were in store for them all. Off they moved into the ocean, swimming as one, their scales and tails flashing in the sunlight, before disappearing into the deep turquoise water. On into the ocean, which holds many shoals, they go. And the deep, which holds many secrets, waits patiently for them to arrive.

Oh, do you remember us? We are the Weavers, and we are the Mothers.

Fire holds many secrets, for the Fire-folk have seen and heard much. When they rise in the midst of us we should welcome their arrival, for they sometimes bring a message as well as a warming. In their crackling language, you can hear whispers of yesterday and tomorrow. In the hissing and the whistling, whispers of old things and memories not forgotten. For Fire was there at the beginning and will be there at the end, and Fire is still here, reborn again and again.

Fire has traveled through the Earth, from Her heart to our heart, and Fire has come from the stars and traveled to the Earth on its wings of fire, and landed in our midst with a message from the stars, our original homes. And they helped us make a home of our new home, the Earth. For the Great Mother of the Earth held us all and welcomed us into her Heart. Within Her body, we all dwelled and she warmed us and fed us, nourished and nurtured us, gave to us the finest fruits to share and enjoy. When the messengers from the stars came on their wings of fiery light, they were welcome, for there was no fear then on the Earth. Love met love, and love recognized love, for this was a meeting of hearts.

And every heart has wings, no matter how heavy and large the being, or how tiny. These are the wings that bore this heart from the Core of Creation, and will carry it back into the deepest Heart of the Creator when that journey is to be made. We flew here on them and, with them, we will return Home into the One Heart. We are all Winged Ones, though we take different forms, but behind the endless differences, we all share the one face and the one body and being, and we all share the One Heart. The space between us is an illusion, and the differences between us an illusion too. A necessary illusion for the purposes of the journey, but a temporary one, all the same.

Now we are all being called to remember our true face behind the illusion. We feel the call within and all of Creation is hearing this call. This is a moment of great importance for, although all will hear the call, not all will heed it and some will deafen themselves to its cry of love. But those who hear the call and answer it with a simple song of Love, with a simple Heart Song; those who open their hearts will know a great peace opening within them and bursting forth in liquid light. And they will hear a song rise within them, a Heart Song that will be sung by an infinity of voices singing as one.

The Heart of Mother Earth will soon blaze forth brighter, and in this opening, a Great Wave of Love will roll across the face of the Earth, rolling from pole to pole. Every form of life and every being will feel it roll through them in an unstoppable, cleansing wave of rebirth, as the Earth is washed clean of those frequencies that are negative to her. These vibrations are shuddering through her very body, and must be cleansed for life to renew itself. This Wave of Love will roll like a wave of fiery Light across the Earth, through the hearts of all. But some beings will seek to escape the Love which is coming, for they have rejected the Love within their own hearts and they have closed themselves to Love, so their hearts are cold now. We will need to be very gentle in helping them to unravel their knots of fear and of pain.

After the Wave passes, all will look and feel different, even what you eat will seem different – the taste will be clearer and more delicious. For every cell of the Earth will have received its share of Light, its little seed of Light within. So all will seem to glow from within, while from our own fingertips, we will feel the energy flow. We will feel our bodies more alive than they have ever been before. For the Earth will be coming alive in a way she has not been for a long, long time.

In her lifetime, of course, it has been but a day since Humans came into being, but it has been a long day for her, a day of great changes. She has brought forth many generations to walk the Earth and she has hoped in her Heart that each one would find happiness. For within her, burns all the Love she had always had for her wandering children. But, to her sorrow, it seemed that each succeeding generation remembered less and less than the one before. It seemed that they became more and more forgetful, more foolish and they made the same mistakes over and over and over again. So, for the Humans too, this long day has been a long journey.

There have been times when most people seemed to have forgotten her. But there have always been some of her children who remembered her, who gladdened her Heart, who honored and loved her. And though she loved all her children, foolish or no, these were her special children – these were her seeds of hope. She hoped from them would grow a new generation who would remember from whence they came. Who would again remember the old ways, and know that those ways were the wisest ways, the ways which flowed from those days when the Earth was first made a home for its creatures, when life burst forth from within her body.

This wisdom of life once flowed through all, and this wisdom still flows through you at this very moment – it flows through every cell of your body, through every particle of Lightened Earth that makes you up, every wave of energy of which you are woven. Through all of you flows the wisdom and you need simply open up to it. As we open up our heart, our true colors shine out and we honor ourselves as the miraculous creatures we are. As we step forth into the world in our new selves, all will seem new.

The Song of the Earth is flowing still. We will know ourselves to be a part of her great choir and we will sing with all the creatures and the beings, singing a song in praise of Love and Oneness and the beauty of Creation. All will be singing their own Heart Song, and the Earth will sing with us, and within us, singing her song all the sweeter through us, in the great Circle of song. And we will all hold hands in the circle, linked heart to heart, all the creatures and beings, all life. Then all will know beyond any shadow of a doubt that the change has come and the change is real – that love is alive and peace is realized and lives amongst us. This will be the great Coming, the great Advent that so many await. Love will be reborn on the Earth to burn and dance again, to flow through all things, to fly higher than before. And we all will fly, every of us, for all have wings, the wings of Love.

Humanity has lived through many times in a short time and many lives in a short life. And, though humans have been on the Earth but a short time, they would seem to have wandered far away from their original knowing. They have run away from the great wisdom that was gifted them, deserted the places which they themselves made sacred and special, as if they had become empty, when it was they who had come to feel empty. They had forgotten that they were full to begin with, full to the brim with wisdom and love, and all they lacked was experience and knowledge, and these could be found in time.

In the time of which we spoke earlier, the people had reached a new balance. Each day, of course, this was tested, for it was not static or unchanging. This living equilibrium had to be maintained, for the delicacy of this balance is fine beyond description, yet also strong beyond understanding. But when the new energies burst onto the Earth, the shock of them immediately sent waves of change across the Earth's body. The shock waves of fear rolled across the Earth like the wind rolling through fields of wheat. The shock was enough to knock many off their feet and many clung to the Earth in fear, hiding from the invaders, from these beings who seemed so strong and powerful, who seemed to have little mercy or compassion.

They would walk through the most peaceful groves, step into the most finely decorated lodge and see nothing there of value or beauty unless it was of some use to them. For these beings were truly short-sighted and they had stumbled into a paradise. They were intoxicated by the possibilities it presented them. They had long forgotten their own inner nature, their own true beauty within, and they had masked themselves in false power and robes of stolen glory. They had armed themselves with weapons of great destructive force, and they strode across the Earth, seemingly proud and vain and powerful.

However, they lacked the sensitivity to know what it was they were destroying by their very presence. And there were those who tried to reach them with words of advice and wisdom, who tried to teach them the error of their actions, who tried to speak to their hearts. But their hearts were so armored, so defended and closed that they could not be reached.

These were dark times in the Garden of the Earth, for into this Garden of the Heart came a long shadow. These beings who marched through her sacred places, who strode across her body, thought only of plunder and hollow treasure. They defiled the Earth in a way that could have never been imagined by her... Her pain was terrible enough to crack the heart of any – any but the most armored and closed.

They took from her that which would have been freely given, if only they had asked, and if they had been worthy. And the stars shivered in horror, as fear went shuddering through the Earth in waves. The fear frequency interfered with the song of Creation, with the weaving of Life itself. For deep fear fills the body with an alien frequency that was not part of the original design. So the beings of the Earth found themselves in great pain, for all felt each others' pain, and there was disorder and chaos, because within them were rising feelings they could not recognize, impulses they did not know how to control.

They were faced with strange Beings who demanded their obedience and who did not seem to feel the Love they knew to be the gift of All. It is to the credit of the Humans that they responded, not with violence, but by trying to meet with these Beings and explain to them the effects of their actions. But these Beings were deaf to wisdom. They had grown too hardened in their pursuit of power, in their aggression and acquisitiveness.

So this was the end of the First Age. And the Earth would have seemed a sorry place, for hard as they tried, the Humans and their helpers found they could not maintain the balance while the strange energies disrupted their work and wrecked their weaving. However, the helpers could not intervene directly or confront these beings in an aggressive or violent way. That too would have destroyed the peaceful balance, would itself have given a wrong lesson and torn the Web even wider. It would have sent a message through the centuries, which would have clouded the wisdom even more. Meeting the violence with greater violence would only have perpetuated the horror and brought the victory of aggression and ignorance.

So it would seem the invaders were allowed an easy victory, for they took their plunder and seemed to have their way, meeting little opposition. But after a time, when they had taken all they wanted, they withdrew from the Earth. And, slowly, the balance began to recover; the Web of Life was re-woven. There was a breathing space where the Earth could recover herself and re-cover herself in new life and new growth. Some of the scars could be grown over and some of the memories could fade and the peoples came together again and recovered themselves as best they could. Though of course, life was different now, for there were new energies and frequencies on the Earth and those that could not be removed had to be woven into life in this Second Age.

It was a time of rebuilding and reweaving, as the sacred places, the lodges and temples were rebuilt. The peoples of the Tribes wove themselves back together and told the stories around the fire, they cried with each other and dried each other's tears. Wrapped in their blankets, they told the old stories and the stories of what had occurred, the stories of the coming and the dark times and then their release and the leaving.

It seemed so much had been lost, but, of course, something is always gained, even from painful experience and difficult learning. So new stories developed and grew, and the stories had these recent events woven into them. Threaded through the new tales, were the lessons they had learned. Once again, the Shamans and storytellers came into their own. These women and men, the Medicine teachers, explained to the Tribes the truth of what had happened. They helped them to understand and to grieve, to learn and to remember. Around the fires, the tales were told, and all those of the tribes, young and old, wise and not so wise, listened to them and wove themselves into the tales. And they helped themselves heal, as the Earth herself was healing.

Around the fires, they warmed themselves and held each other and into their blankets they wove the new threads, so they would not forget. Again they began to dance, for they had not danced often in those years; their hearts were too heavy, fearful and confused. They danced now around the fires, their hearts warming and opening. The dance and the chants brought them back to themselves, so that they remembered who they were, and again could be joyful. They could safely open their hearts, once more. The helpers returned, the Winged Beings of fiery Light. And they too helped them to heal, helped them understand what had happened. They danced with them and chanted, until the magic they had felt was felt once again. And as the sparks of the fires rose up to the stars, they gave thanks that they had been spared and that the Creator had granted them this life to enjoy and share.

So began the Second Age, an age of new learning, because now the Humans had to learn how to live with the new feelings and frequencies within them and around them. And it was the children who showed them how to live now. For the children knew both old and new, yet they still played and were joyous. They still felt the amazement of discovery, since to them the Earth was new, as it is to each generation of children, and some were souls coming to the planet for the first time. From among these children came the new Shamans, those who showed the others how to integrate old and new, and balance light and dark, fear and love. As they grew, they reminded their parents that this damaged world was still beautiful, that it was still possible to be deeply happy here. They warmed and gladdened the hearts of their parents and grandparents and of all the tribe.

And there were some children who had been born of the union of the Beings who had come and the women of the Earth. These looked different from the rest, and sometimes they were rejected and feared, because they looked so strange, and so different from their mother's tribe. Yet Love won out and these children too became part of the Tribes. They, too, had children in their time and, though few in number, they also brought something new into the bodies of the peoples of the Tribes. They too were teachers in their own way, though sometimes they were tough teachers. For they had a sense of the Earth as being strange to them, and they sometimes had less sensitivity than their brothers and sisters. They held within them some of the energies of the strangers and it was sometimes difficult to integrate their nature into the Tribe without difficulty. But in time, the weaving was complete and, over the generations, an integration took place which was a long healing.

Over time, as the Tribes strengthened and increased, they again began to expand. But they developed in a new way now, for there was now more of a warrior-nature on the Earth. Men, in particular, had changed from the natures of their Ancestors. For they more felt themselves to be protectors now, more ready to be aggressive. They felt within them impulses that they had to learn to master and navigate. For some had learnt "lessons" which would prove to be damaging to the wisdom of the Humans. For some, just a few, had taught themselves that aggression could secure one dominance, that the channeling of anger and aggression would allow one to increase one's power, wealth and status.

This was one of the dark seeds that had been planted in the time when the Earth howled in pain. Some emerged as leaders, and tried to lead their clan or tribe on to new paths, believing that if they could take the lead and school it in the ways of war and aggression, they could win greater space and bounty for it and, for themselves, a greater reputation. For their egos were being expanded, rather than their hearts. The aim of control and power can hypnotize and dazzle he who seeks it, so that the actions that are taken on this path seem less important than reaching the goal of dominance. So the warriors emerged, they girded and armored themselves – like the invaders whose ways they were imitating – and some of them strode across the Earth in search of plunder and treasure. The way of the warrior, in some tribes, became a narrow one, a way of individual glory, of increasing the power of the tribe, rather than being the way of the protector, the noble son or father of the tribe, the keeper and guardian of the weak.

So, again, life began to fall out of balance, as tribes jostled for space and some competed with each other for control of the creatures who had once been their friends and trusted companions. It was, it must be said, a different story in different places and only in a few were great crimes committed against the nature of Love and the nature of Life. But it was enough to, once again, damage the delicate Web of Life on the Earth. For people were increasing in numbers now and increasing their influence upon the Earth, and their actions had greater effect than before.

Yet the Tribes and their leaders still held much of the earlier knowledge and the original wisdom. They would still come together and gather at the fireside to share the wisdom with each other. The Shamans were still honored; those Medicine women and men who held the sacred trust, who revealed the hidden wisdom, who bared their hearts so that the Tribe might know what love truly is. They wove the stories and danced the dances; they sang the songs, which held the Tribes together. Those special ones who could fly, while others had forgotten. Those who could still reach the stars, speak to them and return with their wisdom. They were still honored, though now the balance was being tested between Shaman and warrior, between leader and led, between wisdom and war, between peace and conquest, between conflict and balance.

This was the Second Age, when a difficult balance was found, and the Earth was able to recover her equilibrium. For the damage she received was, usually, slight enough to be repaired, and the wounds could be woven together quite quickly, though the scars remained. The helpers came less frequently now, yet they were still remembered and revered. The magic and the wisdom still had a wholeness that had not yet been shattered, though it was tested severely at times.

So we leave the story at this Age and will continue with it later.

The Fawn and the Stars

This is the story of a young deer, a fawn born in the heart of a forest.

She was born in the shade of the highest tree, deep in the forest's heart, and she was the firstborn of a new generation. When her mother had carried her young one to full term, she had gone far into the forest to give birth. She had left the Deer Tribe and gone alone to seek out the safest place, but all of their hearts went with her. For this would be the first time she had brought new life into the forest, and hers would be the first to be born after their time of trial and sorrow. Many of the Deer Tribe had been lost, and the scattered Clans had been hiding in deep, shadowy places of the forest to be safe from harm. Now the Tribe was gathering itself once more in a secret place in the forest, to heal their hearts and their sensitive natures. There, they waited for the news that would lift their spirits again.

As the mother walked between the trees, she made not a sound, and there was a hush in the still and heavy air, as if the creatures were holding their breath. She could hear her own heart beating and, beyond her nervousness, there was a beat of deep joy and high anticipation. She could sense a second heart beating that sounded out a note of hope into the forest. She could feel a new life kicking within her, bright and excited, eager to enter the world. Soon it would be time for her fawn to step onto the earth, and the mother made her way towards the tree that called to her. When she found it, she stepped through its curtain of leaves, which almost reached the ground. There, in the shade of the ancient tree, she made a place for herself and her fawn, like a nest amongst the soft grass and ferns.

She laid down to rest, feeling herself held in the love of Mother Earth, and a warm feeling wrapped around her. She looked about her at the veil of leaves, through which points of light sparkled, like the stars glittering in the sky of night. Each was an eye of light beaming love to her, and she felt less alone. She remembered her sisters and brothers of the Deer Tribe, and felt their invisible presence in her heart. She knew to trust her body to know what to do, and she opened to the flow of intense sensations. She felt waves and pulsations move through her, the waves becoming deeper and the pulsations more profound, until she felt her body opening to the mystery of what was taking place. When the moment came for her to give birth, she rose and then began the birth itself, this new and powerful experience for her, and she felt wonder and love rushing through her heart in a flood greater than the breaking of the waters. Soon she felt her young slide from her and fall to the earth. But the young one sees only dimness around her for a thin, cloudy membrane separates her from the world outside. She knows she has to break her way out, and she kicks and kicks until the membrane breaks. She senses space open around her and a gentle light surrounds her now.

Her mother turned to see the beautiful creature who laid there in the soft grass and, at the sight of her, she felt a new rush of love and joy burst from inside. She rushed to lick her young one, to kiss her with her lips and bring her fully awake into this new world. Around them, the forest seemed to celebrate, and the trees were full of birds singing, while even the squirrels chirruped in tune. All seemed to sense there was something new and unusual about this one, and her mother could see the signs before her own eyes. Instinctively, she knew that fawns had patterns of dappled light and shadows to camouflage them, but her young one had a coat of warm, pale gold that, even in the shade, seemed to glow a little. Across her back, bright dots and splashes were scattered in delicate patterns.

This newborn child of the forest had a whole choir to welcome her and some curious forest dwellers came to catch a glimpse of the new arrival. They looked down at her from the branches and peeked from between the leaves, or poked their snouts between the tall grasses to catch an eyeful of this new wonder in their midst for she was, indeed, beautiful and strange to see. As she tried to rise from the earth, her mother licked her and nudged her with her nose to help her come to her feet. Her mother licked so hard, the fawn thought her wet colors might come right off. As the fawn raised her head, she looked into her mother's eyes for the first time and she felt the love shining there. She knew this was going to be a good place to live, if it had even one creature in it who could look at her with such love.

So she began to try to come to her feet, clumsily at first, though her mother helped her all she could with a nudge here, a sound of encouragement there, a lick in the right place. But she knew the task of standing herself up could not be done for her. The fawn rose with great difficulty, for her legs were long and felt very new to her. And, though she admired their length, she thought that they were not the easiest thing to stand on, when one was but a moment old. However, she knew she must stand and was eager to try out her legs. With a great effort, the fawn straightened her back legs, then after a moment's rest, one of her front legs. She placed the hoof firmly on the earth and now she knew she was nearly there. With one great push, she straightened her other leg and planted a fourth hoof on the earth. She felt very unsteady and almost fell over, but quickly righted herself. She wobbled a little and it felt as if the Earth was swaying in sympathy with her. Each seemed to be trying to steady the other, before she could, finally, stand still and catch her breath.

He looked about and was fascinated by the waving leaves hanging before her in a shimmering curtain of many colors. Meanwhile her mother was circling around her, proudly admiring her beauty and newness. And, noticing her motion, she decided she would step forward and walk just like she had seen her mother do. So she took one unsteady step, then another and another, until she found she was walking in a wavering circle around the trunk of the ancient tree. After a few steps, she lost sight of her mother and thought maybe she was gone, so she walked more quickly until, to her relief, she found her on the other side. So she had discovered what a circle was.

She walked around and around the trunk of the tree with its ancient patterns, enjoying this sensation of walking tall, of being free, of breathing in the clean air with its many distinct scents. After a while she paused, pondering what to do next. As if on cue, her mother poked her nose through the rippling leaves and a beam of light poured into the little space. The fawn was surprised – she had not realized there was so much light out there, beyond the curtain. She peeked through the gap her mother had made and she could see even more light and, within it, more of everything. Springtime was still celebrating its own arrival with a colorful celebration of life. Growing from the ground, were more of these wonderful trees and, between them, these beautiful slender-stemmed things of different shapes and colors, which waved themselves at her. And amongst them were moving creatures who came through the greenery or who flew through the air or jumped from branch to branch. They all seemed pleased to see her, as she poked her nose through the little opening. She decided she would venture outside and see what other wonders were there. She hesitated for she was, in truth, a little nervous. She had been so long in the small space inside her mother, and now the world seemed so big!

She had been quite happy in the circle under the tree for a time, but now the world seemed to be a very big circle, indeed. Her mother understood her feelings so she parted the living curtain with her body and stepped out into the world first. The fawn did not want to be left behind, so she followed her out into the world, where she stopped after a single step. Stunned by the beauty around her, she tried in vain to take in all the sensations, the breath-taking variety of life. So many creatures were there, as if they had all come to welcome her; the frogs and snakes, the spiders and insects, the birds and furry animals. She greeted them all as best she could.

Her eyes were quite dazzled by the light flowing down from above, after the darkness of the womb and the shade of the tree. Within moments though, she was exploring her new surroundings and trying out her long legs, proud-ly stepping over tall flowers, showing how steady she was becoming. Her mother looked on with pride as her child examined everything in the small clearing minutely, going from flower to flower, following paths of fallen leaves, chasing a butterfly who flew by, to get a closer look. Nothing escaped her attention and she wanted to drink it all in, but after a time her mother began to tire, for she needed rest after the birth. So she led her fawn through the forest to the gathering-place where they could rest. The fawn followed her, moving through the path her mother made, her eyes blinking at each new apparition around her, all the glorious creatures she was meeting and who were greeting her. Her sensitive ears delighted in all their sounds, she breathed in the sweet and subtle scents of the forest, and she experienced a whole range of novel sensations. No matter which direction she looked, this wonderful world seemed to go on and on forever, as if there was no end to its beauty. They walked on through the shade of the trees to arrive at the sunlit, open space where the Deer Tribe was gathered. And now the mother was eager to show off her new arrival.

They arrived at the clearing and as they entered, a tall, strong stag, the father of the fawn, gave a great bellow of welcome. All of the Tribe gathered there began to bleat or bellow in celebration, joining in the song that sang of the gift of birth, of being an honored child of the Tribe, of the joy of belonging. The fawn was surprised, but happy to be welcomed in such a way. She had been keen to meet them all and enjoy their company, though she did feel rather shy and overwhelmed now that all the eyes of the Tribe were upon her and the deer seemed so big and so many in number. She was glad there were some other young deer there, though even they were much bigger than she was. Her father, the stag, who was the tallest of all the deer, gave her a loud sniff and nuzzled her with his lips; he seemed very pleased with his child. Her father, whose scars were still healing, felt a new lightness inside him at the sight of this bright one who looked up at him with such love in her eyes.

One by one, the other adults came over to greet the fawn, inspecting and sniffing her as they towered over her. Though they were friendly, some were rather intimidating in scale and, more than once, she wanted to run and hide behind her mother's legs. After all the Tribe had made her welcome, her mother laid down to rest in the late afternoon sunshine and the fawn curled up beside her as close as she could. Her father went around reminding all to be quiet, to end their excited bellowing and chattering, in order to let them sleep. And so they slept a while in the light of the slowly sinking Sun and they soaked in its warmth.

The fawn drifted quickly into a dream, her first dream on the Earth. She dreamed of all of the wonders she had enjoyed that day; the face of her mother and the creatures she had met; the birds and furry creatures, spiders and insects, frogs and snakes; the face of her father and the warm welcome of the Tribe. When she awoke later, it was growing dark and the deer had gathered closer to settle down for the night. Around them, the air was becoming a little colder and the shadows were lengthening as the Sun slid down behind the horizon. The fawn felt a strange feeling as she watched the shadows cover all the glory that she had witnessed over the few hours of her life. As the shadows grew long and shrouded the trees, it seemed as if a dark blanket was rolled over the Earth and all its beauty was hidden as the sky darkened.

Then she noticed lights twinkling between the branches of the trees and, when she looked up, they were appearing overhead, scattered across the sky in delicate patterns. The very sight of the stars excited her heart and she felt love running through her, reaching out to touch them as they had touched her. She was just about to sing out in pure delight when she remembered the deer were asleep all around her. She could just make out her sleeping mother's form beside her, as a silhouette against the sky. She turned and saw another silhouette, one that stood out against the sky, that of a great stag, and she knew it was her father watching over them as they slept. He stood sentinel over the tribe, his antlers outlined sharply against the stars that had been revealed. The fawn felt safe and at peace here, curled up beside her mother, with her father standing proud under the stars.

She listened to the sounds of the night; to the night birds screeching in the trees, the hooting calls of the owls. But, above all, the stars fascinated her, though she could not tell why. Her eyes told her the stars were further away than the treetops, yet they seemed almost close enough to touch. What were they? Why were they there? Questions appeared within her, one by one, and then connected to form intriguing patterns.

As she watched, a falling star suddenly flashed across the sky in a streak of light. She was so surprised that she cried out and her father, hearing her, made his way through the sleeping bodies of the deer to see if she was safe.

When the fawn told him she had cried out because a star had blazed across the sky, her father laughed softly to himself, saying that he would have done the same when he was that size. While the stag towered over her with his magnificent antlers, the fawn found it hard to imagine her father ever being her size. As if sensing her feelings, her father bent down, lowering his head until he and the fawn were eye-to-eye. He told her that, from then on, he would call her, "Fallen Star", and the fawn felt happy with her new name. Then she asked her father the question that was singing out loudest of all: Why did she feel so much love for the stars?

Her father was silent for a while. Then he answered that those who asked this question, like her, were the very ones who best knew the answer. So he would give her no answer for, by asking this, the very first question she had spoken on the Earth, she had shown that the answer was within her. Her father raised his great head again and moved quietly away. As he did, the fawn saw his antlers spread out like dark branches amongst the stars.

The young one was rather disappointed, at first, since she had hoped her father would know all and so give her an easy answer to set her mind and heart at rest. But then she realized that her father had given her a great gift by believing her, a tiny creature, wise enough to answer this question herself. So she gazed up at the stars for a long time, asking herself these questions to see if an answer would come. She admired the arrangements and patterns the stars made in the sky and wondered if there was a meaning to their different shapes and relationships. At certain, special moments, it was as if creatures appeared, like the ones she had seen on this, the first day of her life. She pondered this for a long time, but eventually she fell into sleep, still asking the questions to herself.

She dreamt then of herself, out among the stars, running through them on her long legs, just as she had run through the bright flowers of the meadow. She skipped and leapt, weaving her way through the star-flowers, while she admired the patterns in which they were arranged. These patterns seemed to take on a life of their own, until suddenly they came alive as creatures. She saw, coming to life, the frogs and snakes, the spiders and insects, the birds and furry animals. All the creatures that she had got to know that day were here in starry form, along with others that were new to her, and they were all greeting her. How happy she felt among her new star friends! And they began to celebrate and play together until the great vastness seemed a small and friendly space.

Then she noticed another starry form approaching her. It was a familiar one; her mother with her body made of stars, looking even more beautiful than she thought possible. Beside her, walking proudly to greet his beloved daughter, was her father with his body of shining stars. Their radiant faces shone with love as they both came and kissed her face, warmly. Their starry bodies were warm to the touch, and the fawn looked down to realize, for the first time, that her body, also, was made of stars! She gave a little bleat of delight and laughed at herself for not noticing something so obvious. She danced around the legs of her parents, then danced amongst all the other starry creatures around her while they hopped and scampered, wriggled and skipped. Here with all the starry tribes, she felt delighted to be alive.

Then she noticed her parents were gazing down, into the distance. She followed their gaze until she saw something far below, something the like of which she had never seen before, as bright as a whole garden of star-flowers, glowing in incredible colors. It was a world that looked so mysterious and magical, slowly spinning there, among the stars. The sight of it filled her heart with a happy kind of longing. So she asked her mother and father, why she felt such love for that world. They both looked at her with deep love, and then her mother said, "If you have asked that question, then you know the answer is within yourself." So the little deer looked back at this magical orb below her and, as she did, it seemed to grow bigger and bigger. It appeared to be coming nearer to them and she realized that all three were moving towards this place. As they neared it, she could see that on its surface there were broad oceans and islands of all sizes, forests and great plains with wide rivers between, and huge mountains that were growing larger as they came closer. Then the Sun appeared from behind this world and illuminated it in its full glory. They came so close then that she could make out the little streams, the trees and the patterns of grasses and plants. Soon they would be amongst it all and part of it all.

Then their hooves landed in the soft grass and they found themselves in the heart of the Deer Tribe. All around them were deer, sleeping. And the three stood there, watching with joy, as the Tribe woke up and roused itself. One by one, the sleepers shook themselves, and their drowsy eyes opened wide to the light of dawn. They felt the Sun warm them as they came to their feet and stood in the rising light, while the birds sang their choruses for this, the first dawn that the little fawn had witnessed. She watched this golden dawn turn into a blaze of many rainbow colors painted on the clouds, and she saw her parents silhouetted against the fiery sky. She noticed their starry bodies seemed solid, like the earth on which they stood. She looked down to see that she too appeared solid and she marveled at the magic that made it seem so. And now they and all the Tribe were being bathed in the colors of this magical dawn. Their coats glowed now in a rainbow of colors, with many that were new to her and a delight to the eye and heart.

And the young fawn found that her own eyes were open now, and her dream was real. She leapt to her feet with a joyful bleat, to celebrate the new day. She understood that she had, indeed, answered her own questions, that the answers had been hidden within her all the time. She felt quite wise for one so small, standing here in the heart of the Tribe. She pondered that if those answers were inside her all the time, how many more answers must be inside her? Perhaps she could find the answer to her every question hidden within! And, now that the Sun had risen, off she went to play.

The fawn grew quickly, and when she was a year old, there came the Moon when the bucks and stags begin to grow their antlers. To everyone's surprise, two bright buds appeared on her forehead. They soon grew into two golden spirals, which branched out like strong saplings. Along her spine, ran a starry path, from her bright tail to her branching antlers. Every year after that, she would wear her crown of golden branches.

Her gentle presence became the peaceful heart of the forest. Amongst the trees, she would walk majestically, and some saw her as a golden hart, others knew her as the golden hind. All who saw her, recognized her as the sign that peace would someday reign in the forest, and the harmony would be whole once more.

Fire dances tonight! It hisses and whispers, and Fire knows many secrets, for what fire holds closely, it consumes and swallows up. So the Heart of Fire knows many secrets that others have forgotten. Fire is wise; wiser than you know. It dances with a bellyful of fire and it burns away what is no longer needed, and what it needs to keep, it remembers.

So, sometimes, you can ask the fire to share its secrets and whisper a few stories to you. You will find it hides many surprises! Fire flows, as love flows and the waters flow. Fire and water stay in balance, and they love each other too, for they dance around each other all the time. But they are subtle lovers; they seldom touch, for when they do, things get steamy… And in the steam, secrets are revealed. Fire and water talk or whisper, sharing their secrets. Those glowing rocks, whose hearts the fire has warmed, transform the water. The water-beads dance happily on the hot rocks. Steam is created and, in the spiraling steam, dreams and images emerge in the living mist. We open within the white steam that we breathe in, which flows into our lungs, moves through the pores of our skin, filling our bodies, opening us deeply. For it opens up more than pores – it opens up memories.

Here, in the Lodge of Memories, we dream in the sacred steam and remember ourselves. The dreams that come back are ours, the dreams of other times and other faces, the stories that we made with our minds and bodies, with our hearts and our intentions. These are the living stories we reveal. And the stories dream us, and the dreams seem more real than the day we left outside. For, here in the place of steam and dreams, we sweat out the stories and our pores release our Heart-Stories, like ancient tears. We remember then from where we came, we see our own faces, and the faces of those we loved.

And we drift through the steam, which is a great white cloud. We drift through it as a bird, our wings cutting through the steam, through the white veils of cloud. Our eyes peer ahead, to see something beyond the whiteness.

Our sharp beak cuts through the cloud, our eyes strain to see beyond it, while on through the veils we fly, parting them with our wings. We know we are going deeper, we know we are heading in the right direction, though we see nothing but the white cloud. Then in front of us appears a golden glow, and our wings beat faster and our heart lightens, for now we know we have not much further to go through the clouds.

The glow brightens as we near it and we cut through the last of the cloud and there before us is suddenly a great orb, blindingly bright. It bathes us in golden light and warmth and our wings become golden. Our eyes narrow in the glare as we head closer to the bright orb. As we near it, and the light increases in strength, we bank gently and, as we turn, the Sun reveals a rainbow-hued planet behind it. We make towards it, our wings beating faster and our hearts beating faster and stronger. And the Sun seems to pull us around it in a wide arc, sending us towards this beautiful planet, for we are quickly coming towards it, faster than we thought we could fly.

As we near it, we are surprised by its magnificence of color and scale. We have truly never seen anything like this planet before, for we come from a long, long way off. Our heart lightens more, and faster, we fly. We are very near this shining world, and as we get closer to it, our golden wings become ever more fiery. Now they are glowing deep red, in crimson fire. We open and close our great wings of fire, and this world comes nearer...

Now we enter the atmosphere of this planet for the first time. Down and down we fly towards the surface in a wide, wide spiral. Ahead of us, we see expanses of white clouds and we fly through them, our wings of flame cooling a little as we fly through this cold, cold air and these mountainous clouds of fine-woven water, woven finer than lace. As we come out of these fine white clouds, we see below us the most breathtaking sight we have ever seen. For a whole world stretches out beneath us, a world of glowing, incandescent beauty. We breathe in this sight, for it fills us with love and wonder. We fly down further seeing, as we do, glittering seas stretching over its horizons, the land rising up as we fly down over the snow-capped mountains, covered with trees of countless hues. Between them, we glimpse rivers of silver, glinting, and beyond them, forests stretch further than even an eagle's eye could see.

As we fly in lower, we see the animals in vast herds covering huge areas of its surface, moving as one across its face, like moving forests. They move across the wide, open plains, weaving around and through each other. We look for a place to land, for we know in our hearts there is a place we should be. So we fly low over the treetops, close to their topmost branches, searching for something we know we will recognize. Then, ahead of us, we see a large clearing, circular in shape in the center of a great forest. Through it, a trail has been made, a narrow trail through the trees.

And there in a clearing, we see a gathering of creatures, of two-legged beings dressed brightly in many colors. They sit in the sunlight around a great pyre, a high pile of wood, which has just been lit, and smoke is rising from its center, slowly drifting on the wind. More two-legged beings are entering the clearing and being greeted, welcomes are being spoken and sung, and their songs float upwards through the trees. And the two-legged ones are taking their places in the great circle around the fire and they are carrying with them bags, pouches and bundles. They wear blankets and fabrics of many colors and patterns, they wear the skins of the other creatures I have seen earlier, and they wear the feathers of the birds through which I flew. They arrange themselves around the fire, which is burning brighter now, as the wood catches and the flames begin to rise in smoky spirals upwards.

And I begin to circle on the edge of the clearing, and, as I look out over the treetops, I see the Sun is touching the edge of the horizon; soon it will have set for the day. The clearing is growing a little darker, and the figures below are seating themselves, making themselves comfortable for the night around the fire. Each group seems to wear a different pattern or a group of patterns, and they talk amongst themselves and there is a little space between each group. I land and rest my wings, landing in the topmost branch of a great tree that overlooks the clearing. When I look up, the Sun has disappeared behind the distant mountains, and the clouds display their finest colors to bid farewell.

Below in the clearing, some are standing up and speaking while the others listen intently, amidst the sounds of the birds in the trees making themselves ready for sleep Except for those few around the clearing who watch the proceedings. For there is a ring of eyes, high above those seated below. There is a circle of winged ones around the clearing, guarding the opening, and they all listen, as I do, to the words that are spoken. And we watch the faces of those listening. We watch how some nod in agreement and others murmur in dissent, their faces scowling. Others shake their heads and make signs and their hands and faces are busy. Their minds are busy too, concentrating on the affairs being spoken of, for those gathered are speaking of peace and war. Each one that rises to speak carries the discussion on or in a different direction. Around the circle travels the discussion, as the voices, one by one, speak the heart of their owner.

The clearing fills with thoughts and words, and the feelings of hearts that are at peace or hearts that are troubled. The trees hear every murmur in this open space, and the leaves shiver at some of the words spoken. For some down below are angry, and some raise their voices or make great gestures with their arms, sweeping them open as if they were birds. But these ones are not as wise as the birds, for their faces show the colors of hate. The faces with which they entered the clearing now wear a mask of anger, and others try to calm them, trying to pour water on the heated words, thrown like hot stones into the center of the clearing. But the steam that rises here reveals nothing; it only obscures those in the circle from each other like a fog. Much smoke and steam is generated in this great discussion until, finally, others rise with wiser counsel.

One rises and speaks words, which create a great silence over the clearing. And there is silence now, but for the one voice. Even the restless birds are quiet and the leaves listen. For these are the words that come from afar. And they clear the smoke and the steam and the fire again brightens, sending its flames higher into the night sky, shooting sparks off to the stars. These words travel around the circle, and some whisper to make the words clear to those who do not know the tongue of he who speaks. But it seems that all hearts understand his words perfectly, even if their ears do not recognize them. For these words have come from a great heart, an open and wise heart that speaks the words of the Great Spirit.

These words are known in the hearts of those in the circle, for they were written there in the beginning in letters of light that cannot be forgotten. In the silence, the faces of anger are smoothed out and calmed, the words of bitterness disappear, sinking down into the earth, and the harsh words of anger cool in the night air. And I wonder if some see, glowing behind him, the shadow of a woman; a white shadow.

Some, as they listen, let their eyes drift off to the dark canopy of the sky and the stars above them, for he who speaks reminds them from where they came. And when he opens his arms wide, as if they were wings, they know his heart is open and his words are true. And the feathers that he wears of the great eagle glow in the darkness, as if they are feathers of light. I watch from my perch, and wrap my feathers around me a little closer, for now I feel warmer and happier that these words have been welcomed and that he who speaks with an open heart has been acknowledged. I look around me at the circle of winged ones and know that they too are pleased, for he who wears eagle feathers has now become a leader and he will be listened to. His words, which are more than words, have revealed great truth.

And he holds his arms open like wings, as he takes those who listen on a journey upwards, carrying them with him, as he lifts all their hearts up. So wide are his wings, it is as if they made a great circle round all the Tribes gathered. All find themselves raised up and their hearts are high and light, and they know the feeling of peace within their souls. They remember this gift they were given by the Great Creator, for it was there all the time, waiting to be revealed. After a long time, he slowly lowers his arms, as if closing his wings, but leaving his heart open. And he sits on a stone in front of the high fire, and a great cry goes up from those seated around him, which is taken up by each of the Tribes in turn, until all sing a great Song of the Heart, a chant to the Great Spirit, a cry from their souls to the Great Soul who gives all life. And the clearing is filled with ringing voices.

Some there rise to their feet and drum with them a rhythm on the earth. Their feet rise and fall, and through the clearing, a soft sound is heard of their feet dancing on the grass and rich earth. And they sing now a song of the Great Mother, a song of the Earth herself, their Mother who gave them birth. And these who are warriors, who are the chosen ones, the chiefs, the bravest of the brave, dance in a great circle around the fire, each singing in their own tongue. From all their tongues comes a song of Unity, and between the words is heard one word, crying out louder than all the rest, a word which is more than a mere word – and the word is "Peace."

As they dance on, their faces look to the Earth, then to the stars above, to the Earth again and then to the shining stars. A few notice the winged ones, overhead there in the top branches, forming a circle of light above the clearing. We watch the celebration and our hearts celebrate, too, and we sing out our song. We open our golden beaks wide and sing our song, so that all creatures of Creation may know that it is time to celebrate, for the way of Peace has been chosen. On through the night, they will dance and we will watch with them. And, when their time comes to sleep, we will open our wings wide and fly up and out over the treetops, looking back one last time at the clearing, the open circle in the forest, before we turn our faces to the rising Sun, towards the clouds stretched like rainbow wings across the sky.

We will look to our left and to our right, and see our brothers and sisters with their wings glowing golden, all heading home to roost. And, together, we will cross the face of the Earth and make our way home.

In the years when peace was woven among the tribes of the Earth, life became easier and more fruitful. The spirits of the people could grow and learn and the children could be raised in the ways of peace. But, in the years of war, great damage was done to the human spirit. For what is suffered by one group of people affects others, far away.

All are subtly connected, invisibly, so conflict between tribes in one part of the Earth would have its effects elsewhere, often far away, in a place which did not even know that the tribes were at war. This new warrior energy was creating much difficulty for the humans for it was hard to contain or balance;

it was expansive, yet it had a narrow vision, wanting victory, conquest and domination, whether in small ways or large. This was a major change from the earlier days, for then the women had often been the leaders, spiritually and in other matters.

There were not such sharp distinctions in life then, between the roles of men and women. People would follow the wisdom, and the wisdom often flowed through the women first, for they were still more connected to the Heart of the Earth Mother. They heard her murmurings more clearly now than most men. They knew her rhythms and her needs, and they sensed her subtle changes through the year. Their instincts were usually sharper and more reliable, and they would know ahead of time where the tribes should go and dwell in those times when it was necessary to move. Though some men could still hear the Mother clearly within, and there were times when they took the lead.

The time had come when spiritual teachers were needed on this Earth, to remind the tribes of the truths they had forgotten. The first such teachers were mostly women, for they held the deepest wisdom, still unbroken, in their hearts and bodies, and, through them, the wisdom flowed out into the tribe. They were honored and revered as daughters of Mother Earth, who embodied the living Goddess. These were the first shamans, teachers and Medicine Women, and they are the ancestors of all those today who follow this path, men and women alike.

But in these times of which we speak, the balance had been tilted in favor of the way of the warrior. Each tribe was tilting one way, then the other, swinging between war and peace, as if it had been placed on a weighing scales, where its heart was weighed, and whether it measured heavy or light determined the way the tribe would go. Often, in these times, the voices of the wise women were drowned out, for there were those who spoke of quick victory, of easy pickings, of new lands just over the hills, which could be theirs if they dared to claim them as their own. So the brittle peace was tested often across the continents as the clans and tribes moved. They were evolving in different directions and exploring different paths and ways of life. Some of the tribes flourished and prospered, becoming rich in material things,

while others stayed close to their original roots and listened often to the murmurings of Mother Earth and the songs of Great Spirit singing through them.

Some set off to claim a piece of the Earth as their own, as their permanent
home, a place where they would be masters, where they would hold more
power, from where they would not have to move with the seasons. There, they
could make large villages, broad lodges and high dwellings; there, they could
command the land itself to do their bidding. The tribe would settle in one
place and its strength could increase and be more concentrated; its riches, too,
could be accumulated. And, now that they had gathered more material things,
they would not move easily. Their homes would be fixed and planted in the
earth for generations to come. So the first of the tribes claimed their spaces,
and new villages emerged, some of which grew into towns and, between
towns, trading began that was different from the earlier forms of barter and
exchange. Now, things were given the greatest value that could be established
and demanded. Payment could be asked for in definite measurements, and,
soon, all things acquired a price and a measure of value that they had not had
before. The people began to judge things according to these values, and relations between people changed forever.

Now, it was not wisdom which was valued, but wealth. It was not the riches of the heart which were desired, those that are shared freely with all, but
the material riches which were gathered and hoarded – and guarded against
those who coveted them. So, very quickly, the tribes who still followed the
old ways found themselves in a strange landscape, where each creature
seemed to have a new value different to that which was given them by the
Creator. Even the trees and the land itself had taken on different meanings and
values, and, in time, people looked at the Earth through different eyes, with
narrower vision, and they saw less and less of her True Beauty and her true
worth.

The world found itself in a Third Age. The Earth was now divided into
very clear demarcations in parts, though most of the Earth was still untouched
by the humans. For the two-leggeds did not wander too far from their places
of habitation now, for they feared the wilds and the forests more than they had
before, since now they understood her less, and she was becoming a strange

place to them, filled with creatures who now had, also, changed in nature. For many creatures did not trust the two-leggeds anymore, since they had come and plundered them and stolen their homes. They had taken their children and killed them for their skins; taken their lives without respect or reverence. Now, the animals knew, all had changed. After their period of grieving, they, too, had accustomed themselves to the changed ways. It was only in rare places of the Earth that her creatures retained their original character and nature, and even then, this did not survive very long into this Age that had begun.

Those who came to the Earth, who spread their wings and flew over her face, saw beginnings of towns and cities on the edges of the forest and by great rivers, where dwellings were increasing in numbers until they came together in great conglomerations. Now the Humans had increased in such numbers that it was difficult for them to avoid conflict with each other when their lines of demarcation and their competing claims crossed.

This, however, was a time of much learning for the humans, because although they narrowed and shrank in some ways, they expanded in others. Their knowledge and skills increased in many areas as they competed in their learning and they accumulated the fruits of their learning, which they guarded jealously. They created many beautiful works of art and architecture, and developed new inventions; they brought forth onto the Earth much that was new and inventive and showed the brilliance of the minds with which they had been endowed.

We, who looked on, were often impressed by the innovation and creativity displayed. Ruling groups tried to outdo each other in achievement and, in the competition between the cities, they did, indeed, surpass the efforts of their ancestors. The goals often promoted now were to be richest, the best, the most powerful. We say these things as generalities of course, for it was only a few who truly lived this way of life to its maximum. Most tried to carry on their lives in this fast-changing environment, to find a way to raise families and be as happy as they could in this world that had sprung up, seemingly from nowhere. Yet all were being influenced subtly, most without their knowing. Around the world, as development increased, the threads of the tribes were slowly being unraveled. The old bonds and ties were untied, and many lost their way entirely when they were sucked into the new towns and cities, where they lost sight of themselves and all that had once had meaning for them.

This was the Third World, when the tribes were dying, their hearts being eaten away, while the world of the merchant expanded until it seemed everything on the Earth and everyone on it had a price and a value which was not of the Creator's making. A civilization was forming, based on the rapid advance of technology, one that would achieve unprecedented levels of technical complexity. But its growth was not founded on wisdom or grounded in the love of the Earth. Its cities became the model of development for the human future, even to this day. To hold the complexity of these cities in form, new modes of control were developed that were not healthy for the human spirit. Disunity deepened as hierarchies rose to dominate life.

The more the sense of wholeness was lost, the more elaborate methods of repair were devised, but their effects were temporary. Healing techniques became increasingly sophisticated, while the simplicity of the solution was forgotten. The more complicated the problems seemed, the more the simple solutions eluded them. The more conflict replaced harmony, the more impossible communication from the heart seemed, and even communication from a clear mind became difficult, as forms of mental control were put in place. The distances between humans grew, even as they were crowded together in greater numbers, in closer proximity to each other. Indeed, numbers were becoming almost as important as people.

Crystal-based technologies were developed that could produce apparently miraculous results, but the main result of their use was to endanger their users own way of life. The technologies came to be revered and feared, and because competition between cities and rulers was intensifying, warfare became a sophisticated game. Powerful systems and weapons were developed in an attempt to dominate and control life on the planet, trying to manipulate natural forces and prevent natural events occurring. Cooperation with the realms of the Earth was devalued in favor of imposing the will of the few. Life was falling further and further out of balance, and the precious crystal lattice of the planet was being damaged. Those who tried to rule had undermined the foundations of their own world, and its collapse became inevitable. Mother Earth, and her messengers from within and beyond her body, tried to awaken these humans to the dangers they were creating for themselves and others, but only a few could hear.

There came then a time of great pain, when the Earth shook and her waters rose and fell. The mountains rumbled and roared and the forests shuddered with great waves, which flowed through the Earth itself. A destructive energy had entered into the Earth with terrible force, causing her great shock and pain and her body reacted to cast out this virus that had entered. Her body shook and convulsed like the body of a great bear who was ill and in agony. On her surface, the dwellings, the villages, the towns and cities shook. Her water spilled over onto the land in great waves. It washed away the dwelling-places and many ran and tried to escape. The god of technology had failed them, and many were drowned, including those who hid in the great temples and called on their carved gods, asking for protection, for they did not understand what was happening.

For when the pain in the Earth increases beyond bearing, her body itself convulses, shaking and pulsating, making waves to shake herself free. Much sank without trace and much was swept away, and we who watched from above, saw the landscapes change. The seas now covered the cities. Slowly, the forests reclaimed back that which had been human habitation. After the mourning and the silence, came a great peace. For many doubted that they had been following the right path, now that they had seen the foundations of their world collapse and the fine cities turned to rubble, and that which they had thought would last a thousand more years was gone in an instant. Some believed these events to be a kind of judgment, but there was no punishment involved, just the consequences of actions taken in the past.

Mother Earth was in deep pain, also, over those of her children who perished, and it was a long time before her pain and her grieving eventually subsided. Then there came a time when some of the tribes repaired themselves and re-wove a new unity within them and between the tribes. Some abandoned the ways of the Third Age and set out either to return to the old ways or, more often, to blend the old and the new in a way that would ensure the longevity and survival of the tribe. Hard lessons had been learnt, and in these years there was space for some of the original wisdom to be remembered. Many of the tribes on the Earth did indeed weave peace again amongst themselves. Some hearts that had grown acquisitive and shallow and materialistic again opened to the light of Spirit. Again the love of the Earth was rediscovered, for they treasured her beauty more now, since they had seen her face change into one of pain, and they were glad that she had returned to her face of peace. The days of plenty seemed assured as this Fourth Age began.

But life could not return to the ancient ways for humanity had learned too much and remembered too little. There was a coldness now in many human hearts that had not been there before. Coldness was slowly moving over the Earth, also, and places that had been green and lush acquired a coat of ice and snow. The tribes found themselves facing a changed landscape, one which seemed cold and sharp and unwelcoming. Though in time many adapted to this new world, others moved further and further away from the ice and found themselves in places that humans had scarcely touched in the preceding years. Some kept the ways of the tribes and others who had forgotten the lessons again began to build towns and cities like those their ancestors had built. Again, new forms of civilization slowly emerged, though they began very small now for much of the learning had been lost, and those who knew the skills of city-building had been mostly swept away.

But there came those who tried to help Humans to find a way between the extremes, those who tried to show Humans how to live again in balance. They came to try and teach the people how to live in harmony with their Mother, the Earth, while still following these paths they felt compelled to follow. For history was now taking courses that seemed to have settled into definite patterns, and rather than trying to turn back history, it was felt that it was better to mitigate the worst effects of these developments by teaching humans how best to integrate their desires with their needs and those of the Earth.

A Fourth World emerged, in a slow journey from tribal beginnings, through scatterings and migrations, to the small pockets of civilization that appeared, once again, across the Earth. When the ice finally stopped its flow and slowly began to recede, like every great wave does, the villages and the tribes had a different energy and attitude within them, for they had, in many ways, grown harder. Many would not trust the Earth as they had earlier, for they did not understand her moods and seasons now, and the changes that had taken place. They felt they had a right to take from the Earth what they wanted, in any way that was necessary, as if the Earth was a stern mother from whom they had to steal.

Yet there were others who kept the original vision and knowing of the Earth Mother. In the tribes, the Shamans still tried to keep the tribes on the spiritual path of harmony and happiness. Now they faced the warriors, the merchants and other forces that they could not fully comprehend, for they did not see the world in a materialistic way. So their power waned as this Age found its feet and planted itself into the Earth and carved its spaces from the forests. Now trade seemed to be a dominant language on the Earth, and the wisdom was often drowned out by the language of trade and exchange, and talk of wealth and acquisition. These new desires and wants were difficult to balance within the tribes and even more difficult in the villages and towns. Increasingly, authority was placed over the people by those who had chosen themselves as being more able to lead, for they knew the ways of this new world and they knew how to profit and prosper from trade.

So in this Fourth Age, the Shamans became distant voices for many; quiet whispers in the background, trying to remind the people of where they came from, of who gave them birth, of who created them. Now even some of the Shamans were forgetting, for the world was quickly moving on, and Humanity was marching somewhere in a hurry, without knowing where it was going or what its destination would be.

The Flight of the Golden Eagle

There was once a golden eagle who flew higher and saw further than other birds.

Yet her wings were no longer and her eyes no sharper than those of others. Though, when she flew, her grace made it seem that her wings stretched further and her feathers shone brighter than any other eagle's. How she loved to fly! It was her bliss to leap off a cliff, spread her wings and then soar over the canyon, climbing higher and higher, riding every tiny breeze, shifting her body and tilting her wings to find the warm currents of air that would lift her up a little higher. Her instinct led her to the invisible currents, to any helpful gust that would carry her up, and she would soar beyond any height ever been reached by an eagle.

She still remembered her first flight over the canyon as a young eagle and the warm welcome she received when she flew past the ancient cliff-faces. As she circled the great stone bowl, the great stone faces blew their hot breath beneath her wings to lift her higher, so she could float effortlessly. Those who looked up and saw this shining one were gladdened in their hearts. Every day after that, at sunrise, she would fly in a great circle above the canyon, and all who saw her shining form would fly with her in those moments. The rabbit and the raccoon would look up and feel themselves flying with her; the deer and the bear could peek out through the trees, see her high above and their spirits would soar. Even the smallest insect crawling on the ground would notice her and, for a few moments, feel themselves moving, not on the earth, but across the face of a soft, high cloud.

All who saw her felt light as air and, though some envied her, most took pleasure in her freedom and her flying skills, and were happy to watch her climb the sky and enjoy her soaring. She would begin her slow, spiral climb upwards, gliding on the warm updrafts, her wings glinting in the sun, yet barely moving. On and up, she would fly, tilting herself to best advantage, until she would reach the clouds above. Those below saw her as a radiant, golden bird against the blue of the sky and the white of the clouds, floating as if she were weightless. Still higher she would rise, until she became a point of light, high above the circle of the canyon.

So this had been her life. Yet life in the canyon had been changing quickly while she grew for, over the years, a strange transformation had been taking place. Long before she was born, the great river that fed all life in the canyon was broad and deep, and those who lived there expected it to always be so. The valley that the river had carved over millennia was a favorite place for hunting and feeding, and an abundant provider for all. But month by month, year by year, the flow of water had diminished and the river had narrowed to become no more than a stream. And the rain, which had once run down the sides of the valley in deep channels, became a rare visitor. In recent years, the rains had not come at all. As the land around had dried out and life had become harder, more creatures came to the valley in the hope of finding a way to survive. Hunger and scarcity became their daily experience, in place of the abundance all had once known. As the valley became more crowded with hungry mouths, it seemed to grow narrower, even as the river narrowed to a trickling stream. In the air above the parched earth, many birds now competed for kills and swooped down on each other from out of the glare of the Sun or from out of the deep shadows. So now the eagle would have to fly high over the valley, above the squabbling, when she wanted to find peace for a while.

While others searched for food to fill their bellies, she went on flying to see how high she could go, how much of the open sky she could explore. But, most of all, she moments when something special would happen as she soared. Sudden bursts of insight, like flashes of lightning, sometimes lit her up inside, and she would suddenly glimpse and know things. These moments fed her and sustained her through the trials of life in the valley of shadows.

One day, the golden eagle was circling above the canyon, while the other birds were scanning the ground below for prey and others were engaged in intense, aerial combat. She felt a strong urge to lighten her heart, so she spread her wings as wide as she could and spiraled up to where the air was thin and even the highest peak was far beneath. Soon the other birds were like specks below her, and she floated there, blissful and calm, while the air held her in its open palm. And now she entered the state she loved next-best to flight, that heightened state where visions came to her like a vivid daydream.

In her flying dream, she was circling a nest of golden twigs in which were two white eggs. She wondered whose they were, and if they might even be hers, and so she placed her breast against them, but pulled back sharply for they were cold, shockingly so. She flew out of the nest, and she noticed the nest was in a tree that was also of shiny gold; its every branch, its every twig was solid gold and even its leaves were of fine gold leaf. She had never seen this metal before and she wondered how the tree came to be. No birds nested in this lifeless tree, and she could not see a single insect. The tree was not growing or even moving, even its leaves did not bend in the wind. But as she looked down its trunk, she had another surprise; she saw its roots disappear into soil that was white.

As far as even her eagle eye could see, the earth was white and blinding and bare, and all the other trees also seemed to be covered in this white substance. High above now, she flew over this strange, white earth, unlike any landscape she had ever known. All around her, pieces of the sky were falling; so many that they began to make veils around her. She felt cold here, so cold she began to shiver, so she began to beat her wings faster to try to warm herself. Through the white veils, she could just make out cliffs on each side of her, and she realized she was flying through a valley. And, when she looked down, she could distinguish the outline of a river, so she swooped down to land beside it.

To her surprise, it was not flowing; it seemed to be stopped in time. When she bent and pecked it, the surface was hard and impenetrable. She could sense water somewhere under it – her senses told her so – but no one could drink it. Confused, she flew off, back up into the cold air, to see if she could find anything recognizable. She tried to beat her wings even faster now, as the cold was increasing, but her muscles seemed to be seizing up. The whiteness around her was getting thicker, and she tried to open the veils with her wings. But her wings were growing stiffer and her feathers were gaining a coating of crystals as the cold substance gathered on her golden wings. Soon, she thought, she might turn white, and then what would become of her?

Her heavy wings were growing more tired and stiff as this white substance built up and weighed her down. She knew that, here, there would be no hope of warm up-draughts of air to lift her higher. She was dropping ever closer to the ground, and as her face and beak became covered with this crystal ice, she could scarcely make out anything ahead of her. Somehow she knew she must find shelter and something to warm her, for she was so cold now, her muscles were freezing up and she could feel the cold chilling her bones. Now she was barely above the treetops and her wings were moving slow. The sky was darkening above her and, with her heavy wings, she knew she could not fly much further. So finally she chose a tree and flew into its branches, to land on a snow-laden bough. There, she gathered her wings as tight to her as she could, huddling close to the body of the tree, and shivered and shivered. She became encased in ice

For the first time she wondered if her death was near, for as she looked around her at this white landscape, she could see no shelter, nothing that would feed her, nothing alive but the trees, and even they seemed in a deep sleep. She felt herself drifting into a state of unconsciousness, so cold she was. Her eyes began to dim, but, with her last strength, she cried out from her heart for someone to help her, for she did not want to leave life. As her eyes faded, she saw the whiteness in front of her begin to move and swirl and take on a new shape. Something grew in her field of vision and she heard a sound a familiar sound, a sound she loved – a sound of wings. Through her fading eyes, she saw a great white owl appear in front of her. It spread out its wings and landed on the branch in front of her. This Snowy Owl looked at the stranger who had arrived. She looked her up and down and realized she was cold and shivering.

Owl asked from her heart, why she come to this snowy place for she had never seen a bird like her before, there in the land of ice and snow. With difficulty, Eagle replied that she had somehow come to this world from the hot lands, but she did not know how… She explained that her kind flew in the canyons and high mountains and that this was the first time she had found herself in such a place. Owl listened and knew that unless she could eat soon, all the warmth from her body would be gone and, unless she found a place of shelter quickly, she would die. Owl told her the tree that she had chosen was a wise choice, for it was a hollow tree, an old tree, a tree nearly dead now. It was one that held many hollows within it, and in its trunk was a certain hollow space, which was always warm and would be very welcoming to her. In there, she could rest and warm herself. The helpful owl told Eagle that she would go and hunt for her and bring her things to eat, for the owl knew the ways of the snowy lands. Owl's eyes were used to the snow and were even used to seeing in the darkness. The night was falling deep around them, but Owl told Eagle that this was the time when she was the mistress of the woods, since she could see what others could not see.

So, with her last shred of strength, the eagle opened her wings, dropped from the branch and saw below her an opening like a mouth in the tree and a hollow space. She landed on the edge of the opening and stepped inside. In here, the tree seemed to warm her from its heart, which was still living, though the tree was mostly now hollow. She shook the ice from her feathers and felt her warmth return. Sure enough, within a very short time, the owl returned with tasty morsels for the eagle, which she swallowed hungrily. Soon she felt her strength return, and she felt her blood flow again. The owl stood on the branch outside the opening in the hollow tree to shelter her even more from the cold wind. Owl told her that, though this land seems like a desert of ice to those blinded by its whiteness, she sees it with different eyes. After a time, Eagle felt strong again; she felt like the strong, golden eagle she was. The owl admired her great wings and golden feathers, though the eagle thought to herself they were not the most practical things for such a place as this.

That night, Eagle slept a sound sleep until, at one point, she began to dream with the heart of the tree. Through the memories stored in the tree's heart, she saw the story of a river unfolding. She felt the desire to follow the river to its source and she knew immediately this was the same river that flowed through the valley of shadows. She also knew, at once, that its source was in a distant mountain. Once, the river had poured out of the heart of the mountain and roared down its side in full spate. But then a great change came over the landscape and snow fell day after day, to be shaped by biting winds, and ice and snow began to coat the mountain. The dreaming eagle could see, in the distance, a snow-covered mountain, and the spring that fed the river emerging from its side. But the opening was mostly choked with ice, so the flow was constricted. Over the generations, the river had narrowed and its flow had become weaker. Life had become harsher for those who relied on it.

At that time, the dwellings of the two-legged ones, the humans, were plentiful here. But now their crops withered and the fruits died on the vine.

Their world seemed to have become harsh and cruel and, in desperation, they tried to find favor with the gods who seemed to have turned their backs on them. They gathered all the gold that they had accumulated and began to make the solid gold tree as an offering to their gods. The finest craftspeople were brought together to work on it and their creation was a work of great artistry, but their labors were in vain. It seemed their pleas fell on deaf ears, for the snow and ice piled even higher and they began to leave these lands with what they could carry, never to return. And the tree still stands, a silent witness to the end of their world.

At dawn, the golden eagle was awakened by a beam of sunlight that found her through the opening and it warmed her heart and body. At her feet, she discovered more tasty morsels for her to have as her breakfast, for Owl had been busy in the night. Now that the Sun was up, she could look around with her sharp eagle vision and, in the distance, she noticed mountains that looked quite inviting. The mountains themselves were of a great height and, between them, she could see deep valleys of green, broad lakes and bright rivers. The more she saw, the more the golden eagle became excited. If she could fly to them, they would make a fitting home for her, she who loved the great heights, who loved to dance in the clouds.

Then Owl came to tell her that it was time for the owls to take their rest and she was going to sleep nearby in her own hollow tree. Eagle told her that she would leave now, that her strength had returned and she would fly to the violet and blue mountains that she could see far off on the horizon. She would dwell there, for they seemed like a good home for a golden eagle. Owl wished her well and bade her goodbye and Eagle positioned herself on the branch, then said goodbye to the kindly Snowy Owl. Then, pushing off, she opened her wings out into the cold air. Stretching her golden wings, she headed towards the blue and violet mountains, towards her new home.

Suddenly, the golden eagle snapped out of her daydream. For she had been riding a high, high current of air, so warm and light that it had carried her higher than she had ever gone before. She looked below, and at this height, even the greatest forests were like moss by a stream, even the widest lakes and tallest mountains seemed small. She felt cold here, for up this high, she now learnt, was where the cold began. She looked to see that her wings had a coating of crystal ice. She was cold and growing colder, because at this height even the Sun could not warm her; this was a place where birds did not go. So why was she here?

Far below, she saw the bowl of the canyon surrounded by the thirsty lands, and she saw the deserts stretching into the distance. But, beyond them, she could clearly survey the fertile mountains and valleys, rivers and lakes that she had seen in her dreaming. They were real! The flame of her vision flickered into new life inside her and, in a moment, she felt herself aflame with hope. She knew in her heart that was where she was to go, yet she knew she would have to rest before the long journey. She knew, also, that she was to share her discovery with all in the valley and then the news would spread beyond. So she put down her beak and tucked in her wings and let herself fall. She fell steeply, hurtling downwards at a speed that she had never reached before. The wind rushed past her, icy cold, and she was hurtling fast towards the surface of the Earth, straight as an arrow. She was a golden arrowhead, and down and down she fell. So fast was she traveling that, in a few moments, she could see the bowl of the canyon open underneath. No eagle had ever moved so fast before, for none had ever reached such a height. As she came closer to the surface of the Earth, she felt it pull her closer to it, to bring her back. At the last moment, she opened her wings and opened her heart to the Earth. Suddenly she slowed and soared down into the bowl of the canyon, feeling lighter and wiser for her flight.

She flew to the mouth of the valley and she opened her beak and her hopeful heart and let flow a song of her vision. Though her voice might not be as sweet as those of other birds, the truth in her telling echoes from the cliffs, until the ancient, stone faces awaken to its beauty. And they dream it with her, as they breathe their love around her and carry her through the valley on a wave of hope. The birds and other creatures stop to listen and some cry out their joy, and the message echoes out beyond, that, for those who will cross the desert, abundance awaits.

Having reached its end, the golden eagle leaves the valley and circles above the open bowl of stone. When she has fed and rested, she will cross the desert, whether alone or with others, and the new life will there begin. As she joined the other birds soaring above the floor of the canyon, she knew that though they were all flying at the same height now, something inside her had risen higher and opened wider than before, and it was a great peace she felt within.

Make a single thread. Take the fibers of light from your heart and spin them until they make one strong, single thread.

Then stretch it out, twisting the fibers together, to make the thread longer and longer, spinning out in front of you. Follow it with your eyes, see it stretch far away, and still the fibers are binding together, the spinning just goes on. If you look down, you will see the thread spinning from the center of your own heart. The thread spinning out, like a line of light, stretching out further than you can see.

You wonder where it is heading, and you realize it is aiming straight to the heart of a star. This thread travels many times faster than the speed of light or the speed of thought – it travels at the speed of Love, which connects beyond and outside time. So it does not even take a moment to connect to the heart of the star. Your thread has already connected, while you were wondering how long it would take. The star itself seems brighter now, and it sends bright light back along the thread. You can see the thread glowing brighter; the starlight is coming towards you, coming quickly along the thread. Now it hits you full in your chest, it enters your heart, the energy pours in from this not-so-distant star. You feel it speaking to your heart, and something opens up within, a space is made and the space fills with starlight.

Your heart fills with starlight and you are beginning to shine now like a star. Your Star Heart shines out of you into the Universe and you feel connected to the star and all the other stars. You are a star, too, and they are your sisters and brothers; you have rejoined the family of stars. When you look, you notice other threads now, connecting your heart to the stars. You feel them all filling you with starlight, and you shine even brighter, your heart opens wider to take in all the starry love coming along the star threads. These widen into star streams, and your love returns to them as the star streams sing with the music of the stars, the songs of connection.

Your feet are firmly on the Earth. You reach out your arms and, from the ends of your fingers, threads of light are pouring. From the top of your head, more brilliant threads stretch up, connecting to all the stars. From your feet, more star strings, and all pass through the heart. You are a five-pointed star.

Your light stretches out, your love spreads out in every direction, your heart is open. Now the light is pouring in from all the stars and your love is returning to them all in a flow that is constant and will stay with you always. For it was always there, though you may not have been aware of it in your conscious mind. These star connections are unbreakable, so that when you walk or run or leap or dance on the Earth, the threads will vibrate as you move. As you think, feel and communicate, laugh, cry and sing, the threads will vibrate and the stars will hear you – and you will hear the stars reply.

You are a Star Child. And the stars hold you in their hearts, for the hearts of them all shine from the One Heart. And their light is of the One Light as you are, Star Sister, Star Brother. The Family remembers its children and its children remember the Family. And Mother Father God – the One Parent – rejoices as the One Family we are celebrates.

The Fourth World had become a time of division and distinction. Fences and defenses sprang up; trenches were dug, hedges grown, walls built to divide the Earth, and to divide her people from each other. For it was now believed that people needed to be protected from others, even the others of their own tribe. For the tribes too had divided, and from the many scattered fragments of the tribes, a patchwork world was being made, frayed and tattered in parts. Unity was being torn apart, and something new was being stitched together quickly in its place, often without the golden threads of love that had held people together in community.

The torn pieces were being stitched into this vast quilt, which covered the Earth. The quilt was now held together by threads of gold for it came to be that gold was what held these communities together, rather than love or tribal ties or common unity. Year by year, generation by generation, this crazy quilt held together by golden thread, covered more and more of the Earth. Sometimes, the patterns in it were hard to discern, but there are patterns in all things, and as we observed, we could see the patterns repeated. For in different parts of the world, the same patterns were being woven, then cut and shaped and stitched together with the gold thread of trade and commerce. In some places, the Earth was smothered with this quilt, built up in heavy layers piled on top of each other, just as the new towns were made, of people piled on top of each other. These towns were built up in layers, with those at the top getting more of the light, and being more visible than those down below. They it was whose lives were richly stitched and decorated, while, for those below, life could be dark and drab, sometimes with scarcely any color at all. They dwelt in the dark, while those in the layers above, shimmered and shone in the light.

But there were other parts of the world where the tribes were still held together by ancient loyalties and heart weaving, for in some places peace had been woven within and between the tribes, and the tribes lived on, and sometimes even thrived. In the Americas, though, the tribes would become deeply damaged by the effects of the dark seeds planted in their midst. They would come into contact with forces that sought to crush their spirits and push them into zones of control and conformity. While much of the wisdom would become hidden and lost, many still tried to live in tune with the old ways and in the rhythms of the Earth. Many clans and tribes were still weaving from the heart. Though, as time went on, they found themselves having to weave in the new threads of gold and silver, and, sometimes, the new cloth produced lost the original patterns. Some only noticed the surface now and the familiar patterns that had been there, and their meanings, were obscured.

The warriors had increased in confidence and numbers, and they had now tipped the balance in their favor. In the tribes of the Americas, they became the dominant force and their voices were the loudest. Now the stories that were woven around the fireside between parent and child told their stories first, for their stories were most glorious and some of the threads of wisdom became buried under layers of tales, layers of threads, tales of battles won and lost and great deeds. While neglecting the gentler threads of life, the story-weaving became twisted and distorted by placing too much importance on the deeds of the warriors.

The wisdom of the Wise Ones was sometimes buried under the threads of their tales. The threads of the Wise Women and Men and the Elders were over-woven with the fiery threads of tales of war and hunting and tribal honor. So, over the centuries, the patterns of the tribes, their living, their weaving changed. The simple and open weaves became more elaborate and overlaid, richer and more decorated, as the tales were. Now it was easy to lose the threads of wisdom in the great panoramic patterns, with their fine details and expensive threads. Some still carried the stories, some still held the wisdom, but now there were fewer who would listen and it was not the story-tellers' way to raise their voices above those of others, to be loud and aggressive, as the warriors could be at times. So the quiet, wise voices drifted into the background.

And the female Shamans now were dying out. The Wise Women were not honored as they once had been and they were pushed further away from the central fire and the heart of the tribe. They sat further back, in the shadows of the men; the braves and warriors, the chiefs and the Medicine Men. The Wise Women held their wisdom still, but, as their bones grew old and brittle and their frames became more frail, even they began to loosen their grip and lose the threads. For who was there who wished to know the wisdom of old in this new world, where all was change and the surface seemed dazzling, where victory seemed easy and defeat a passing day?

And there came an apparent silence. But, behind it, some of the women still held their wisdom and, within circles, they would still tell the stories, and weave the threads again. Around a small fire or a little lamp of oil, they would gather and weave between them the stories of Creation. The threads of time, and the threads that held them in the hidden heart of the tribe, they wove again into the light. From their hearts, they wove out the rainbow colors, they re-spun tattered threads with frayed ends, and repaired their fibers with their love.

Between their hearts, they wove a Rainbow Web, with the Light at the center. Their hearts were united there and, within the small circles, the world could be re-created. Great light would shine around these women in these moments, as amidst the laughter and the tears, they retold the sacred tales and re-created the world between them. They it was who kept the threads from breaking completely for they spun their threads from the Source of All, and they remembered the Source within their own hearts. So the wisdom did not leave the Earth, but was held behind the great silence, behind an invisible wall that was their only protection against a world that did not honor their Truth and Wisdom.

In the patterns of their blankets, they stitched their secret threads and, deep inside their blankets, more secret threads still. Each thread was a connection to the heart of Mother Earth, Father Sky, the Sun or Moon, or to the Great Spirit, who they remembered and who they knew as a loving parent. Although their numbers became fewer, the few who remained grew stronger; the threads did not break. Those of the women who had left the Earth in body, stayed here in spirit to guide those who remained and remind them, to guide their thoughts and hearts through this new and ever-changing world.

So the Mothers and the Grandmothers did not leave and they continued to weave, though now their work was invisible for the most part, for the world would not welcome their weaving. Their stories would now bring ridicule and opposition in this new world, where things had greater value than people, people had greater value than the creatures and the creatures only had value as things. Yet, around the world, circles still were formed, appearing as circles of light across a world that seemed darker and more chaotic, its people less peaceful and more troubled. From these circles, invisible threads spun out, connecting one to the other. Their threads, spinning out, were weaving a cloth across the Earth. Above the chaotic crazy-quilts which had been stretched over the Earth, they wove fine fabric in rainbow colors, a fabric of light in which it was still possible to see the patterns clearly.

As they looked up, they would see this shining cloth woven across the sky, spun from the colors of the clouds, woven together with the colors pulled from their own hearts. For these women were the Rainbow Weavers who did the quiet work, spinning light over the Tribe, over the land, connecting Mother Earth and Father Sky. They were weaving the Great Web together, keeping the Web open and connected, repairing any breaks, weaving love between Earth and Sky, heart and heart, between the people of the Tribes and those of all Tribes. They wove on through the dark times, through the times of plenty and little, and they wove the families of the Tribe together by holding them in their hearts, and connecting their hearts to the Earth and Sky and the Source of All.

They were the weavers then, and they are the weavers now, still spinning out the great Rainbow Domes from their hearts, connecting across each continent, from continent to continent, connecting across the world. The work they have always done continues, whether they are visible or invisible, for it is the work of Love and Creation and they do it with a willing heart and an open one. Though the threads are sometimes wet with their own tears, they spin them still and know they will dry in the light of the Sun. From their hearts, they spin a thread to every tree and every tipi, every rock and every mountaintop, to every house and every cloud, to the face of the Moon and to every star arrayed above, as they sit on the Earth.

They are the Mothers and the Grandmothers of Love, they are the Sisters of the Heart. They are the Spinners of living threads, which they weave into living patterns, into the story of Life, which is woven of countless stories of the Heart, for only these can reveal life's meaning. And still, they spin the colors of the rainbow into golden light, still they spin the rainbow threads to weave the rainbow over you, and it starts in their own heart. Like busy spiders, quietly spinning, they may be in the dark corners, forgotten, but they hold Love in the world together and they will hold the world itself together in the future, when their wisdom will be needed and their stories will be remembered. Once again, their weaving will be truly valued.

The Goose and the Golden Egg

There was once a goose who laid a golden egg.

She was very surprised, since until then all the eggs she had laid were white, but this one was an egg of gold. Despite this, she was still happy to see it and wondered if her gosling would even have a golden feather or two. She had been looking forward to having a playful gosling to cheer and warm her heart, but when she pecked the egg with her beak, it sounded hollow. She pecked it again to check, but still all she heard was a hollow sound, and when she touched it with her wing, she noticed it was not warm the way an egg should be, but cold. Her longed-for egg was cold and hollow and her heart grew sorrowful as she realized there was nothing living inside it, and no new life would ever come from it.

After a time, through her sorrow, she wondered what she would do with this empty egg in her nest. She did not want to look at it, for it only reminded her of her sadness, so she put her beak under the egg and, with great difficulty, she rolled it out of her nest. The heavy egg landed with a dull thud on the earth, with a sound like a dead bell. Though it was lifeless, thought the goose, there must be someone who would appreciate its cold beauty. Perhaps it would gladden their hearts, though it had not gladdened hers.

So she began to slowly roll the golden egg out of the little hut where she nested and down the gentle slope to the road nearby. Perhaps she would meet someone who would have a use for a useless egg and they would take it from her. Soon, she heard footsteps approaching and along the road she saw, walking, a man who carried on his shoulder, a pitchfork. He seemed tired, and he was dirty and sweaty. He scarcely seemed to notice the goose as he approached, so she gave a loud honk, but he barely glanced at her. She honked loudly again, still louder, but she realized he was just going to walk past her, so she stepped out in front of him, flapping her white wings. The man stopped suddenly and she beckoned him with her wings to the golden egg standing at the side of the road.

The man's eyes widened and he blinked in amazement, but he could not move. He seemed frozen to the spot for a long while. Finally he wiped the sweat and the surprise from his eyes with one arm, but still the egg was staring at him, bright and gold in the sunshine. He looked around to see who it had belonged to, but saw no one for miles, then he looked at the goose who was still honking and beckoning to him, as she tried to tell him her story. Perhaps she had laid the egg after all, he thought. The farmer stepped forward and laid his pitchfork in a ditch and bent down to the egg. He inspected it for a moment then picked it up, with difficulty, for it was heavier than he expected. He raised it up and rested it on his chest to examine it more closely. It looked real, but he shook it, tapped it and tried to scratch it to make sure and yes, it seemed real. It was an egg of pure gold, and his face lit up in its glow.

He turned to the goose and thanked her, then turned to hurry home with his special egg to his wife and child. The goose watched him go as he disappeared down the road and her heart was lightened a little since he seemed so overjoyed by this cold egg. Somehow it seemed to have brought a happiness into his life and as she walked back to her home she hoped some good may have come out of her sorrow. As she settled down on her nest to rest herself she wondered what it was about the yellow metal that made the man react to it that way. For she loved to see gold in the fields of wheat and in the clouds around the Sun, but she did not wish to hold on to it and hurry back to her nest with it, the way the man had.

Meanwhile, at the door of his little cottage, the man took off his hat, quickly wiped his feet on the well-worn doormat and clutching the egg carefully to his chest, he opened the door as carefully as he could, though his heart was beating wildly. He composed himself as much as he could since he did not want to alarm his wife or make her think something bad had happened. His wife was there at the kitchen table with her back to him, chopping vegetables for their supper.

She heard him enter and greeted him, but did not turn around. She kept on chopping as he crept up behind her and he smiled to himself, anticipating her surprise. He stood behind her with the egg in both hands and said "Put down the knife a moment dear and turn around – I've got a surprise for you!"

Wearily, she did as she was asked; she knew he liked to do this sort of thing now and then, and his gifts had warmed her heart before when she was worn and tired. She knew they were meant well, even though they were not always quite what she needed. So she turned and prepared to smile, but she saw a look on his face that she had not seen before. A strange look in his eyes that held her longer than usual and she realized that his face was lit up by a golden glow from underneath. She looked down to see what was held between his earth-browned hands – and now it was her turn to open her eyes wide in amazement. Her mouth fell open, but after that she didn't move for a long time. She could not move or speak and the man was staring at her like a statue, with a kind of crazy look in his eyes and a frozen wide smile. They both seemed hypnotized by the sight of the egg, so much so that even when their child came home they could not move. The boy had been playing in the open fields and had come home dusty and tired, hankering for a drink and something for his empty stomach.

He walked in to see his parents frozen in this peculiar pose and he stopped in his tracks. He could not see what was hidden in his father's hands, only the golden glow on their faces and the strange look they shared. He wondered had they been caught by some strange spell; whether a magician had practiced some bad magic on them. Would they be stuck like that forever? Forever, he knew, is a long time to be held in a spell or frozen in time, so he began to cry, since it hurt his heart to see his parents this way.

And it was as if the spell was broken, because they both looked around to see why their son was crying. "Look!" his father said, "look what I've found – it's a real golden egg!" And he explained how he came by it.

"But what will you do with it?" the boy asked.

"I'm going to sell it. It's worth a lot of money," said his father. "Then we will be rich and we'll have everything we ever wanted! We can get a bigger house and buy as many animals as we need," said her husband. "We can even buy as much land as we want."

His wife realized that their lives were about to change forever, and she felt confused feelings within her, as if this gift was a mixed blessing. Tears came to her, and the man kissed his wife, hugged her and dried her tears. Then he kissed and hugged his boy. He told them he was off to the town to sell the egg, then he was going to come back with a lot of money and everything would change from then on. He hurried out with the egg under his arm and waved goodbye to his wife and child. He set off in such a hurry he left his hat behind and they watched him disappear down the road, trailing a little cloud of dust in the afternoon sun. On the way, he dreamt of all the things he could buy with the money and he thought of gifts he could buy for his family, friends and relations and by the time he neared the town he had spent quite a piece of the money already. He was very hot now, and a little dizzy too from the excitement and the heat; but he hugged the egg even closer to his chest and it seemed warmer now too and he loved it even more. But, with every step, it seemed to get heavier. On the outskirts of the town, he thought it best to stop and rest, maybe clean himself up a little, since he did not want to reach town looking like a scarecrow. He was covered in dust by then and his hair was wild and tangled by the wind.

He spotted a trickling stream near the road, and the water looked cool and inviting. He laid down the egg with relief, but he felt anxious about how exposed it was on the roadside. Seeing an old, broken tree trunk by the side of the road, he put the golden egg in amongst its dead roots and pulled up some grass to put around it, hiding it out of sight of strangers. Then he bent and drank. He washed his face and hands and tried to flatten down his hair; he dusted himself off as best he could. He felt he looked as respectable as he was going to get, so he went back, picked up the egg from its hiding place and set off into town.

He made straight for the office that the miners took their finds to. He placed the golden egg on the counter and the assistant behind it glanced up at him briefly – then caught sight of the egg and it was his turn to gape, amazed at it. An older man beside him, busy counting tiny grains of gold, noticed the glow of the egg and turned. And he, in turn, froze in amazement.

By now the man waiting at the counter was growing a little impatient, so he reached forward and tweaked the frozen older man by his neat tie. Startled, he snapped out of the spell and started muttering figures to himself, then he weighed the egg and made some more calculations on paper. Finally he wrote a long, long figure on a piece of paper and presented it to the waiting man whose eyes became wide again and soon grew tired of trying to count all the zeros. The two men behind the counter took the egg, and it disappeared into a deep vault.

Luckily, the dazed farmer only had to walk to the bank next door, where he handed in the piece of paper. When the man told them he wanted to make a large withdrawal, the rather gray-faced bank-manager went down to the main safe and staggered back with the sum he asked for in a cloth sack. He swung the sack over his shoulder, bade everyone goodbye and left the bank, stepping back into the light of day. He sang happily to himself as he headed straight home to show his wife and child his fortune. When he arrived home, dusty and wild looking, he burst straight in with the big sack of money and placed it in the center of the table. As his wife and child gathered round he opened it and the notes spilled out all over and all three gasped in shock. For a long time the three stood looking at the pile of money, their minds racing at the possibilities. Then the man shook himself out of the spell and began to stack up bundles of notes in a mound in the middle of the table. He continued stacking the notes until they formed a thick layer of green covering the table from end to end.

After admiring his handiwork a while, he began to divide the money into high piles, thinking aloud about what they could buy. Then his wife began to make piles too and added in her suggestions of what could be bought with it. The dark of evening was falling now, so the father lit the lamp and placed it on the table beside him, while he and his wife sat on either side of the table to look over their fortune. The boy, who had been looking on, sat too and now he could hardly see his parents over the great piles of green. Only their heads were visible on either side of the table but the boy thought that, in the lamplight, the faces of his father and his mother looked liked the faces of the Sun and the Moon on those evenings when they shared the sky between them, one on either side.

He found himself imagining all the things that he could buy, all the wishes that could come true and all the things that might happen now that everything was possible. The evening was falling now and the room grew darker still and the shadows cast by the mountains on the table seemed longer. His parents were still talking and discussing and the boy heard little, for he noticed their faces now had become more serious as they discussed and changed their plans and their earlier smiles seemed to have faded. Then his parents stood up and started to divide the mountains again and form new ones and their voices were raised louder now. Sometimes they were both trying to divide the same mountain, but in different ways, and valleys and chasms appeared between them. Over the hours, as the night grew darker, the boy watched the dark landscape change again and again, as mountains rose and fell and valleys and dry rivers appeared. His parents had changed now too, for now they were like two angry giants struggling with each other, their voices loud and booming as they cut deep gulfs between themselves. They each made a high mountain in front of them with a wide rift between and as the rift grew wider, the boy knew great sorrow in his heart.

And when one of the giants turned to him and shouted fiery words of anger, he ran to his small room and curled up on the bed. As he cried himself to sleep, he heard words he had not heard before echo through the thin walls. He remembered the egg then and saw an image of it in his mind's eye, still gold and shiny – but he noticed something that no one else seemed to have seen. As he looked closely, he saw a crack down through the center of the egg, a jagged crack through its heart, dividing one side from the other. Somehow the egg still held together, but he knew that some day the crack would widen and the egg would split apart. And then he saw this moment when the egg cracked open to reveal nothing but its hollowness inside. The two halves of the egg with their jagged edges fell apart to lay side by side, divided forever. As he fell asleep, he sobbed quietly to himself, but his last wish was for a dream that would lighten his feelings, for now tomorrow seemed hollow, too, and he wished for a dream that would heal his broken heart.

It seemed only moments later he was woken by the urgent voice of his father. "Wake up, son! We have to get out!" He opened his eyes to see his father's face with a look in it he had never seen before. Then he heard a terrible sound and a wall of fire appeared behind his father so the boy could only see his dark silhouette. He felt himself being scooped up in his father's arms to shield him from the heat and he was carried to the door – but they were met there by a barrier of flames and the heat seared their faces. The door itself was now aflame and the boy could feel his father's heart pounding in wild panic. Then they heard the sound of a small window behind them open and they felt the cool breeze on their backs. The man turned to see his wife standing outside, calling to them and beckoning. The boy's father kicked the door closed and ran to the open window. He passed the boy into the arms of his mother and then he squeezed himself through the small frame. No sooner had his feet touched the earth than the door that was aflame burst open – a fountain of fire flew through the room and tongues of flame licked at them through the window. His parents each grabbed one arm of the little boy and they ran with him into the night, as fast as they could, through the line of trees illuminated by the flames, into an open field. Now they could no longer feel the heat of the fire and the grass was cool and damp under their bare feet, so they stopped running and turned to watch what was left of their home disappear into the flames.

Over the inferno rose a cloud of gray smoke, high into the night sky, as if it was mingling with the white clouds that were flowing gently towards the Moon. They all felt a great tiredness and sadness now as they watched the scene and all three felt tears cool on their faces. Then the father spoke. "When you had both gone to bed, I fell asleep at the table – I must have knocked over the lamp right into the middle of all the money. And the more I tried to beat out the fire, the more the notes flew everywhere… Before I knew it the room was ablaze." He held his wife and son closely to him. "Now it's all gone, everything we had… I'm so sorry."

His wife spoke as calmly as she could. "We've still got each other and we're not even burnt or hurt – that's a miracle in itself." She lifted up her son, who was crying and shivering in the cool night air. "I don't know how, but somehow we'll make a home together again." Her husband embraced her and their son and the three held each other as close as they could. The flames were dying down now, for the little wooden house was almost consumed. The father was looking out into the darkness, wondering what the future held when he realized that he could see, in the fields around, torches approaching them. He soon realized they were carried by their neighbors, coming to see how they could help. They were soon surrounded by a ring of torches carried by their friends who had come hurrying with blankets and solace and words of comfort.

Amid all the offers of help and support, they felt their tears come again, but now they were tears of relief and togetherness. They felt safe, here in the ring of fire made by the torches of their many friends. And they knew that, together, they would make a better home in the future.

The One Heart is always open to you.

Draw forth a thread from the One Heart into your heart. Spinning it between your fingers, twisting it into the fibers of your own heart, where it will instantly entwine and you will feel the sense of reconnection. You will feel the light flowing along the thread, deep into your own heart and you can thicken this thread or draw forth more threads, braiding them together, until they thicken and thicken and you will feel the connection stronger and stronger, the threads spinning deeper into your heart. The light is flowing down the thread that is an unbreakable cable, down which flows the power of Love, straight into the heart of your heart.

As we watch the light flowing down this thick thread, we follow the light pouring into us – and now we are on this wide thread of light, riding this thread of light into our own hearts. The fibers are still gathering and thickening, like fibers of lightning being gathered together, twisted into one solid thread, one strong beam of flowing light. We are traveling on this thread, so wide our arms hug around it and our legs wrap around it – we hold tight as if we are clinging to the body of a white horse. Down the thread we go, feeling the fibers of the thread, like the mane, the glowing mane of a great white horse. Our hands run through the fibers and our body clings tight, and now we close our eyes and all we feel is the warmth, the heat, the light and the sense of love.

When we open our eyes, we are on the back of a glowing white horse, on an open plain, deep within us. For within us there are plains and great spaces without end. We raise our head and with our fingers comb the mane of this magnificent horse. We feel the horse beneath us, its body warm, its skin smooth and soft; its body is strong. It is vibrant and alive and we realize that we know well how to ride this horse. This horse has no saddle, no bridle, no stirrups – it is a free and wild horse, but she has allowed us to sit on her back, for she is our good friend and guide, an ancient guide.

She knows these plains well. We hear her thoughts. She tells us to tuck our knees tighter to her flanks; to sit upright then bend forward a little, grasp her mane between our fingers and hold tight. Then her front hooves leave the ground for a moment; she rears up a little before she launches herself out into the great plain. Galloping, galloping; she travels faster than we believed any animal could travel – she truly hurtles along.

Around us, the plains become a blur of speed; only the mountains in the distance seem not to move, as if they are fixed and everything else is a blur. For now she gallops so fast, her hooves barely touch the grass beneath her. You feel her joy and excitement rising and you both feel the freedom and exhilaration. Her mane blows in the wind like white water flowing. You yell with delight and scream for joy and she whinnies in response.

For now you are traveling even faster; even the mountains begin to shimmer. These ancient, proud mountains, blue and violet, seem to become a shimmering veil – as the plain has become a veil through which you now pass.

Then, as you move still faster, the great white horse also becomes pure speed, pure freedom; she becomes white light. And you are holding on to this living braiding of white light with your fingers. For now you are moving faster than you thought possible and your form is dissolving; you too are becoming a glowing light being. You and the horse, this great white horse that was, are becoming a blend of pure light. Your light and her light – for you and her are one. She is your freedom and you are her joy. You both hold and guide the other.

Now you have become pure Light. You are the thread too, for you have braided yourself into the thread, which is pure Light, pure Love. On it flows and now even the speed has lost its meaning. Around you, all has become color, moving, softly shimmering, flowing past. You look ahead of you and you see your thread stretching into infinite space, through the infinite sea of color. As you look back, you see the thread stretches infinitely behind you too. You notice, as you adjust to this speed, that these soft colors that you are flowing through are themselves twined into thread. As you look closer, you notice all the colors composed of fine threads; everything is an infinite weaving of threads, and your thread passes through the weave.

Although there are an infinite number of threads, *your* thread is clear and distinct to you and you see it clearly stretching ahead of you. And you see, as you move through the threads, that it touches all the threads through which you move; it links to them and they connect to all the other threads , which stretch out to infinity in every direction. So you are connected to All and you feel your Light expand and your thread glow even brighter as its sends it Love out into this infinite weaving of threads.

You see your light pulsing out into these threads, pulsing in every direction. You see your thread thicken and fill with light, for you remember that your thread is connected to the One Heart and from it, it draws its Love, its Light. Through it flows the One Love. The more you draw it into your thread, the more it glows; the thicker it grows, the more light it sends out into the Great Web of threads around you.

It feels as if your Light can keep growing and growing and growing without end. You feel your Love growing and growing and growing. As your thread grows, it connects, flows its love out to all the threads, in the Great Web of All That Is. You know you are Love and, to All, you are connected. The Love of the One Heart flows through your heart into All. And All is the One Love.

And the Fourth World continued to separate and grow apart from itself. The world fragmented and separated from itself, like the pieces of a giant jig-saw puzzle, breaking the original image even further. The original vision was shattered again and again, its pieces becoming smaller, and even these were shattered, until they were smaller still. Though each tiny fragment could still hold the original image, like a tiny crystal hologram containing the image of its original parent.

The original vision of the Creator was being lost, for within the villages and towns, and the growing cities, there were deities of gold and precious metals, encrusted with jewels. There were gods emerging, being fashioned and carved from the richest materials, and hoarded away in great temples that were guarded like the storehouses of treasure they had become. Some rulers and leaders of the people had laid claim to the image and face of the Great Creator, and each claimed to have found the true face. They would fall before it and ask for greater wealth and riches and power. Each town and village and city now had its gods and goddesses who they hoped held the promise of greater abundance and growth. The faces of these many deities seemed numberless, and they multiplied across the Earth.

The tribes began to dissolve in the new cities and towns, and their vision of the Creator fragmented further. In the fractured images, scattered across the world, they searched for something they could not find, and they lost the whole vision of themselves too. And their gods were often angry, these gods threatened and exacted revenge, they gods demanded tributes of riches. The people had strayed a long way from the wisdom that had been theirs in the beginning. The vision was still there in their hearts, but clouded now, and they had lost sight of their original face, which was also still there, but masked now in faces of fear and greed and doubt.

Those individuals who could still carry the original, living vision were themselves scattered. All around the Earth was the dimming of the Light. The great Web of Life shook and shuddered, great waves of shock passing through the Web, rippling through the Earth and out into the cosmos. For the fragmentation was breaking up something that had once been whole, that was unique in the Universe. Yet, out of the shattering, something new would eventually be created. In the separation, new spaces were created and these allowed new energies to flow in. New possibilities opened up, terrible and traumatic though they often were in the short term, for the weaving never ends. While the Earth had now become this patchwork-quilt of jagged pieces, roughly sewn together, there were those who still worked on with the weaving, who tried as best they could to weave the world back together from their hearts, through the One Heart.

These were the shamans and Elders, the healers of hearts and spirits, of all the tribes across the Earth. Tribes of many names, colors and traditions, of many tongues, which grew in number as the people divided further. As some tribes became smaller, others grew. The patchwork-tribes of the towns and cities grew also, woven together by the golden threads. Their communities were more hastily woven than the old ones, but many would last, for the gold and silver threads of trade can stick a community together in a design that serves the needs of commerce. Although it may not have the beauty of the old designs, it can have longevity, because these threads also bind, though often they bind like chains – the chains of gold and silver, the chains of steel and fear.

Across the world, slavery grew, and chains were made that stretched across the planet, crisscrossing in many directions. It seemed as if a divided world was being pulled together, by binding people hand and foot, one to another. Not by bonds and ties of family or loyalty, love or respect, but cold chains, that enchained bodies and hearts to the service of the new gods of commerce and control. For this was, as we said, the time when the gods seemed as infinite in number as the stars in the sky.

The temples flourished and the priesthoods grew, and into them flowed the people and their wealth. Into these, often cold, temples flowed the love and energy of the people, but often Mother Earth was forgotten, for these gods seemed to drink the love of their followers and share none with the Earth. These priesthoods were not like the holy men and women of earlier years, for they served not the tribe, nor the Earth, but the images and the temples – and the rulers who owned them. Much love was poured into dark pools that did not feed the Earth. These places grew cold and dark, and those who came to them were not comforted or renewed, for they felt the coldness grow within them too, as if cold chains had been placed on their bodies and on their hearts. They did not often dance, for joy did not dance in their hearts. In these times, the sacred dances were for the few and for the "special" ones, chosen by some mysterious means. There were still some who kept their heart-flame burning in the temples, even through these dark times.

In the cities, many forgot how to dance the ancient dances, and the ancient songs faded away, and in the silence came the chants of the priesthoods. These did not feed the Earth and they seldom gladdened her heart, for the Earth yearned for simple love and simple gifts. A simple dance, a simple song from a pure heart; one, which gave with love and loved itself. She did not demand these gifts of gold and silver, of diamonds and crystals, of great temples and palaces, and nor did the Creator call for these gifts. For they were theirs all along, and what is not given with love, with simple love and gratitude, is not a gift at all.

So the temples did not last and, in time, they fell into disuse and ruin. They became hollow shells and what magic remained there was only the love given by those who came with simplicity of intent and gave from their hearts. All the chants of power faded away to nothing. The gilt and riches returned to the Earth, and the fine orations and ornate prayers were blown away on the wind. All that remained was the love given – for that was all that was needed in the first place. All else is but dust. To the Earth returns her own, and what is gone is forgotten, and the love lives on.

Around the world, then, the tribes were dwindling; for those who knew the ways of gold and silver, the ways of chains, the ways of power were spreading across the Earth. Their influence grew and widened, and their empires spread. They sought always to quell the spirit of the tribes, for this they knew they could not comprehend or control. To them, the people of the tribes were wild, and they knew their spirit would be difficult to tame and contain. They spared scarcely a moment to consider their wisdom, for they were blinded by the lies they had been told. They came from lands where the tribes had died or dwindled, where many had been tamed and others had been reduced to scattered circles. If the original wisdom had still been strong in their homelands, they could not have committed these crimes against their brothers and sisters in different skins, and their ignorance would not have been possible.

They came to these new worlds as adventurers and explorers, and they arrived hungry and thirsty, with mixed intentions. Like those in ancient times who stumbled across a new world on Earth, they had little understanding of what they were about to destroy. In the first meetings, there was often time and space for mutual recognition and peaceful exchanges. In these meetings of worlds, there was the possibility of a real meeting of hearts and a bridging between differences.

But those who came were heavily-armed and armored, and they carried the burdens of their old world with them. The hunger of their states and empires, the needs of these machines, had to be fed. And when they finally planted their flags of conquest, the Earth bled.

But, through the days and decades of pain, the weaving went on. And though few in number, those who held the wisdom still worked on in the light of dawn or in the dark of night. Some still gathered to share the wisdom, to keep the memory alive. For they knew their sacred task was to make sure the dream was dancing, like the fire round which they sat, to keep the flames of joy flickering in their hearts.

What they carried within their hearts, within their sometimes heavy-burdened breasts, were gifts of wisdom for their children and grandchildren. They knew that though they must dance and talk in secret, that this knowledge, these stories, these weavings of wisdom must not be broken or lost. That when they passed through the veil, into the world of clear spirit, even then they would continue the work. They would return, to stay at the shoulders of those who wove by night or day, who kept the threads of the traditions clear between their fingers; those who still lived the songs, whose hearts still danced, even if it was a limping dance now.

There would come a time when their children or their children's children or the children of their grandchildren would dance these dances with young legs; and the songs would again flow from young throats; and they would be watching and dancing with them, though they were solely spirit. For they would not leave the Earth; they would stay and watch the healing of the hearts, the weaving of the Web together again. They would see the sorrows trickle away, they would feel the darkness of fear fade. In the spaces created, they would join the circles to sit with the children and the old ones and those journeying between youth and old age, to guide their fingers, to whisper the stories in their ears, to sing the songs loud enough for them to hear and remember.

They would dance amongst the young and the old, weaving between them, they would cry for joy and their old hearts would be warmed again. They would feel again the fire rise in them, as all their hearts would dance as one around the Sacred Fire. And their joy would fan it and expand its light.

They would feed the great weaving with their threads of love and happiness. They would make the dance of the Rainbow Heart. They would see the children of their children's children dancing with them as they had once danced, as girls around the fires, between the legs of their parents; skipping and weaving. They would know that what is important had not been lost, for the love had not been lost, and that love has returned to the Earth.

The heart-fires would again be lit across the lands of the divided worlds, so that, from above you would see the stars of the Earth again come to life; the fires of Love would make their pattern across the face of the Earth. When the fiery hearts of Love burst into life, the flames leap from one to the other, until the Earth is scattered with the lights of divine fires burning in the hearts of her people and all her creatures. Every plant and tree will feel its heart rekindled too. These stars will cover the Earth from pole to pole, and the light will increase and the stars will unite into One Light on the land and in the ocean; countless stars glowing brighter and brighter, and uniting to make One Star of the Earth.

Her Love will rise from deep within her heart, and will burst forth to unite all in Love. Her heart will overflow with liquid Love, flowing again through all life. And all who open to the Love will bathe in its bliss, or they will drown in its blissful agony; for if they close their hearts to it, it will flow over their closed hearts like stones. The Love will not enter their hearts and they will remain cold. They will be left behind in the wave of Love, as cold as they were, and they will feel themselves wither as others around them grow and are renewed in life. All those who open their hearts will be reborn, will feel their love expanding beyond their comprehension, as they feel the love of the One Star Heart flowing through them, filling them from within and without. And each one will shine like a star.

Every living thing will shine forth from its heart its true colors in flowing phosphorescent love, bursting out of its own heart. This will be the bright day of revival when true Love is renewed; the shining day when Earth is reborn. The great starburst of rebirth will fill the Earth with Light, overflowing and abundant.

The Earth will know her children are reborn, and those who wish to go

will go, and those who wish to stay will stay. Those who go will not be forgotten, for they too will stay in the One Love, whether they reject it or not.
Those who stay, will find themselves in a new world, for all will look different in their eyes and seem different in their hearts. Their own bodies and spirits will seem new to them, as if they have woken into a new dream. But this
is a dream dreamed by you and the Creator, together united in love. This
great, shared dream will *be* the world, as the Earth dreams and we dream with
her, and the Creator dreams it into existence.

In the new spaces created, we will weave a deeper Unity and live again in
Oneness, not to recreate something that existed before, but to weave a new,
fresh weave. One that entwines all the threads of the learning, all the threads
of experience into the One Wisdom, which we will share with each other. So
that we will understand each other again, and know that the wisdoms of our
hearts are acting as one, acting with the Creator, who creates the One Heart,
from which we all flow.

So we come closer to our conclusion, as we draw the threads together. And
those threads that seem loose will be gathered and woven in. For the weaving
has been busy, has it not? We have all been busy weavers!

We commend your work and your patience of vision, for it takes time to
spin and weave, but we hope that now you can see the greater image emerging in the threads, within the patterns there. The little glimpses are now forming together into one image, a bright one, full of color and life. It may not all
be understood, for it is a complex image of many layers. The threads are
woven tightly together and others are stitched through them finely, so the
detail is very fine and will repay much close attention – as when we examine
an ancient tapestry, marveling at how fine the work is and wonder how patient
the maker was. Yes, weavers are patient beings and they have been weaving
since before the beginning of time, so they know that there is always time to
weave. For more time can be woven as needed; one must only weave the
threads more finely, and weave threads between the threads. And the finer the

threads and the deeper the weave, the more time will seem to be woven. So time spent weaving is never wasted!

You know not what a wonderful web you weave when you finely take the time to weave… But you will truly believe when you see the weave come to life and realize you were weaving all the time. And now you are aware of it, you will find less tangles and fewer messy corners. The weave will be clearer, and, now that you know you are weaving your own life, you will be aware and careful of what you weave into it. You will weave plenty of freedom in, plenty of light and joy, lots of breathing space where you need it, so you can weave other things in later. There will be other places where you will weave time finely and these might be the quiet times, when you do the finest, most detailed work. Other times, you will weave more freely, in dancey, playful, open weaves. And you will lead your threads through the world with grace and fun and ease. For you can dance as you create, and sing as you play – and you can talk to the other weavers from your heart. And tweak their threads or weave amongst theirs when you wish, and when they are open to it.

We will create great weavings together, and you will feel the Tribe of Weavers around you. We will be weaving the spaces in between, for weavers always fill the empty spaces, just like a spider does, that is our love and our joy. When the web appears, the spider stands back, proud, for it has created something where there seemed only nothing before. Humans, too, can be happy weavers, and you will weave circles between people and creatures across the Earth, and across the cosmos. Big weavings! We will help you of course, for it takes a little time to navigate the threads and keep them clear. When your fingers get tangled, do call on us and we will whisper some advice. When you seem all thumbs, and are judging your fumbling fingers harshly, we will remind you that you have always been a weaver, and you had just forgotten for a time.

You will remember the ways. Your ancient skills, they will return. Your ten thumbs will transform into fingers that seem to know how to place the threads. For even those who have no fingers, no limbs like yours, can weave, since all weaving truly comes from the heart, and all creatures can weave from the heart. All weave their own lives and patterns into the great weave that is the Web of Life, of Creation. So simply keep your heart free to weave, and we will help, as others do. And you will find the weaving light, as you weave the Light. And a vision will emerge, the vision of love woven into everything, and you will reveal the weaving of the Light through your life-story and the life-story of humanity. This is the Way of the Web, the way of heart-weaving, the way we weave life between us all. These heart threads, through which we are now communicating, are truly unbreakable. So never fear you will break any as you weave, for those that break are not true, living threads and are meant to be broken, while those you make anew are meant to be woven in. And your guidance will come from within.

The weaver that you are – that weaves through you, weaves through your hands, your heart and your life – the great weaver that you truly are has woven many, many lives, has woven its threads through the universes, explored its stories through the worlds. Stretched its threads as far as they will go and come back into the heart, where all threads begin, then stretched them out into the darkness, to explore and enlighten, see where the heart will lead. To find out where the threads of the stories will go.

You have followed threads, your own and those of others flowing through, and you have followed mysterious threads – threads that led you into strange places – and you have proved your courage for you followed them, though you did not know where they would lead you.

You tested your own heart and proved it true, for the threads you followed, were the threads pulled out of the heart of Mother-Father God. And though they led you through places of difficulty and pain, you followed them on and did not think of cutting them. Although sometimes your body grew weary, and fear tried to make you turn back, your heart went on and your spirit moved on; you followed your thread through the darkness. Although your heart could not see where this thread of light was leading, you knew you were following it for a reason. Sometimes it seemed wide, and at other times so thin that it seemed near to breaking, yet still you followed it, as it disappeared around blind corners that led you into dark places.

But now you know that *you* were the Light there, illuminating the thread from within. Your Light within revealed this thread, like a great torch shining into the darkness; you chose to follow this thread and you defeated the fear and proved your heart strong. For you had faith in this thread of light when it was all you could rely upon; and when it seemed thinnest, your faith was strongest and it was your hope that got you through. You sensed that you were being led to something greater and so you followed on, though your body was heavy and tired and your spirit seemed to be losing its strength. You went on until your strength returned and you felt the Light filling you within again. You were seeing with the eyes of the Creator within. For the Creator sees through your eyes and they are truly the eyes of Love; you must simply open them, these eyes of the Creator within you.

And you will see with love as the Creator sees, and see yourself as the Creator sees you, and see the beauty of things as the Creator sees them. You will know that the Creator looks out through all of us and in the eyes of all you meet you can see the eyes of the Creator looking out at you; and through the eyes of every creature. And even through those without eyes the Creator shines out, sometimes even more strongly, for these are truly the eyes of the heart, shining out from within. This is the Vision of the Heart we all share, and it is our deepest vision. This is the truest vision, for this allows us all to see through the same eyes and see ourselves as One.

We are, all of us, One Heart Tribe, created equally. None are greater or lesser than any other. For the greatest of us is loved no more than the least. And this Love is the truest reality, the truest vision, the truest and brightest illumination. For when we see through these eyes of Light and Love we can see all the threads clearly, all the connections sharply. We see the threads that unite all things, the living threads of which all things are spun; of which the universes are spun into life. We, ourselves are spinning, too, from moment to moment, and being spun, being woven from moment to moment, and ourselves weaving all the while...

For the weaving never ends, until One Thread is woven of all the threads again and then the Weaver of the One Thread, the One who wove us all, will spool the thread back into their Great Heart and we will return into the Heart of the One Weaver. Spiraling home, all the threads becoming one thread, spiraling into the center of the One Heart...

The Bears and the Ancient Cave

Our story begins with two bears, a mother and cub, asleep in a deep cave.

The bears had slept through the long winter in the ancient cave, way up on the side of a mountain, close to the clouds, and were just about to come out of hibernation. The bear cub opened his eyes first, but could not see anything in he dimness, and wondered why he had woken up. Beside him, his mother seemed restless in her sleep. Slowly, the first light in the sky came outside and a faint glow filled the cave, revealing its little glimmers of quartz. When he realized what time it was, the cub shook himself and dug his paws, a little impatiently, into his mother's brown fur to rouse her. But she grunted and rolled over, slipping back into slumber, so the cub padded his way to the mouth of the cave, which had many ancient markings around it. On this frosty morning, the carvings sparkled with fine crystals of ice. He looked out and breathed in a deep breath of fresh air. The mountain was surrounded by deep forest of tall pines, so the mountain grew out of the trees, just as the trees grew out of the mountain. And in the forest below, morning mists were drifting through the trees. It was just a few moments before dawn.

The bear cub sat, framed in the doorway of the cave, while he waited for the magic moment. Around the cave opening, were great rocks on which were many markings, and they all glittered with crystal clarity in the rising light. The cub loved to explore them, and they held special meanings for him, because he could find stories there. The symbols seemed to be pieces of a big story, and the way they were arranged, told tales. But he could not sit still for long, especially on a morning like this, and the cub came out of the cave to find there was still a coat of snow on the mountain, and everything was glistening around him. When he saw the crystal mountain, he laughed with delight, for, though he was of the Brown Bear Clan, his own coat was white as snow. He looked up to the snow-capped peak of the mountain and saw it suddenly light up. The hopeful cub turned to the horizon, and there was the Sun he had not seen for so long, appearing through the unfolding clouds. He felt a burst of joy inside, and began to clamber up the mountainside for a better view.

He watched the Sun rise, and felt himself wake up and warm up a little more. He seemed to have woken up early this year, and he could see no other bears about, but there were plenty of birds singing up the Sun. It was time for a game, so he started to roll down the mountainside, tumbling in the snow and laughing. Every time he clambered back up the slope, he felt heavier, and he was building up quite a coating of snow. He was rolling down the slope again, when a bleary-eyed bear put her head out of the mouth of the cave. The world seemed very bright and loud to her just then, and she was a little surprised to see a large, laughing snowball rolling towards her, but she knew that laugh, and was glad to hear it again after so long. When the snowball rolled to a stop, four paws popped out of it, followed by two ears and two eyes, blinking ice out of them. When the mother caught sight of her crystal-coated cub, she laughed too. He ran to her, and they hugged in a big bear hug, their laughter ringing out across the mountain. She licked off some of the snow, while he chattered about everything he had seen and everything he planned to do right away. He wanted her to come and explore with him, but she was still trying to remember a dream that had been with her just before she opened her eyes. She was also wondering why they had woken up just then, when the other bears in the mountain seemed to be still asleep. Maybe the mountain had moved and shaken her and her cub awake, or the mountain's belly had growled and the sound had roused them. After all, it *was* called Bear Mountain.

She told the cub to go ahead and she would catch up with him later, so off he ran, down the mountainside. He was a curious and playful young bear, and his furry ears were always open to the sounds around him, listening out for new ones, and his deep, earth-brown eyes were always looking for something new to explore. He would watch the river for the tiniest glimmer, which might mean a fish hidden in its depths, but more often than not it was just the glint of an insect's wings. The bear cub quickly learnt the difference between illusion and reality, for there was a big difference between the glint of wings and the glimmer of a fish, and his belly knew that well!

On his playful way, he greeted all the ancient ones, the rocks and stones with their wise faces, and he looked along the symbols on their bodies. He could see shapes of creatures there, strange faces, too, ones that he had never seen anywhere else. But most of the creatures he saw there, he knew well, and, of course, he always liked to find bears. There were so many different bears there – running bears, dancing bears, bears walking and standing, even cubs playing. Between them, there were bright points that looked like they had been pecked into the stone by some tribe of birds, and these reminded him of the lights he saw at night, way up on the roof of the world. Maybe these stories could tell him something about what it was to be a bear; useful things about life, which might be helpful to him as he grew up. Or maybe some day, he might be able to see what the big story is that all these signs combine to tell.

He greeted all the trees he passed, and he stopped at the foot of a few of these giants of the Tree Tribe. They had patterns and markings in them, too. He recalled the moment when his mother told him that their Clan called the trees, "Standing Bears," and how pleased he had been to know they were all his relations. She told him they held a lot of stories in their bodies and their hearts, for trees were the keepers of the lore of the forest. Over their lives, which were longer than he could know, the bears carved stories with their claws into the trunks of the trees. And the Standing Bears kept their stories in the storehouses of their hearts for the following generations. He would spend hours enjoying their stories – or trying to decipher their signs, and, when he could not, he would make up stories of his own. He felt he was becoming quite a good storyteller, and his stories not only interested him, but, at times, even intrigued others. Sometimes, when a spider happened along, he would tell them one of his stories, and they would listen intently while spinning their web. When he looked into the web later, the tale would be there, written into it! So spiders were good listeners who enjoyed his stories, he decided. At times, in the cave, a spider would even tell him one in return. They were always spinning threads between the symbols, so they could use their invisible threads to move easily from one symbol to the next. The cub would follow the sequence and try to make sense of it, while the spider went between the circles and dots and diamonds, or the triangles that he believed stood for the mountain itself. But it wasn't always easy to follow the thread of the story...

That morning, when his mother caught up with him, they went wandering through the forest, sniffing out interesting things and grabbing a bite to eat along the way. By late afternoon, she felt like a nap in the sunshine, so, while she settled down on a warm rock, the cub went off to explore some more. That evening, he arrived back at the cave first, and, while the cub waited for his mother to return, he gazed up and could just make out the shapes and figures on the walls and roof of the cave. He had to squint at them as the daylight was fading. He knew they were best seen at dawn on certain days, when the light shone up into the roof. They had been painted long before and were fading a little, but, to the cub, they were a mystery he wanted to shed light on. Who made them all, and what did they mean? Most mornings, he would look up to see the symbols and images on the roof of the cave. He was especially fascinated by the strange creatures he had never laid eyes on; these thin, stick-like two-legged ones. He had often wondered who they were. He had never seen one and was not sure if they had ever really existed. He thought they looked like they could not survive a winter; how weak and scrawny they seem, not an ounce of fat on any of them! No wonder there are none to be found. If they were ever on the good Earth, surely when the first winter came, they would have died of cold. Perhaps they were not wise enough to survive. Or maybe, he thought, the other creatures had simply dreamed them up out of nothing, and then made these stories up about them in the long nights.

He decided to ask his mother about these markings when she came back, so he lined up all his questions, ready for his mother's return. But when she came back, she was tired and sleepy after a long day and was truly not in the mood for such questions. Of course, she was a mother, so she listened to her child's questions and tried to think of good answers for them, ones that might satisfy him. She had not thought about such things for a long time, as it was quite a while since she had been a cub. She dug deep for a moment...and a distant memory seemed to stir. She told him that, when she was a cub, she had, also, wondered what the signs in the trees and the rocks were saying to her. She had even sometimes found herself dreaming up stories to fit the images she saw. At other times, the markings made up stories all by themselves. Sometimes, they would speak very clearly to her, especially when the light was fading, and the shadows in the trees and rocks were deeper. She could then see the figures more clearly and they would seem to move in the fading light of the sun; most of all when the clouds made the light of the Sun flicker. Then they would come to life in the most surprising way, seeming to move and flit across the faces of the trees and rocks.

She remembered all this, and then she recalled something she had been told by her mother, back when she was a cub, and her heart was warmed by the memory. She had been told that some of these markings told the history of the Bear Tribe and of the other tribes of creatures. If only you could read the signs, there were the stories of how the tribes had lived since the time when the trees were young and the rocks were new and smooth. For in the lifetimes of the generations in between, those stories had been woven into the faces of the rocks and trees. Then the cub asked her if the bears had carved the signs in the stones. He was amazed when she told him they were not made by bears, but by two-legged relations of theirs who had gone from the mountain long ago. She told him there was a time when the bears and their two-legged cousins lived in peace on the mountain. These ones were not as strong as them and had not much fur, but they were like bears in many ways, and they loved the bears in their hearts. Then another kind of the two-leggeds came here, ones who were more like rabbits, because they kept digging into the mountain to find things, and they could not seem to stop. They chased away the bears and the two-legged clan who were like bears, because they wanted the mountain for themselves, so no one would disturb their digging. Soon they had made holes and tunnels all over Bear Mountain, and they took all the shiny metal and sparkling stones out of her belly. Then they had gone away and the mountain had become quiet again.

The eyes of her cub were wide with wonder and curiosity for he had not guessed that these markings were so important, fascinating though they were to him. The light was falling fast now, and it was too dark to see the figures in the cave, so he asked his mother to come with him as he wanted one last look at the tales of the trees and rocks before the light of the day faded into night. She was a mother, so she came, wearily, with him since she did not want to disappoint his young heart. They went a little way into the forest until they came to a group of very ancient trees, with even more ancient rocks between. The Stone Folk were going to sleep for the night – as she should have been, she thought – but the bears could still see some of the stories in their wise faces. Together, they watched as the glimmering twilight played across the faces, revealing the forms and figures of many creatures, carved there in the bark and deep in the grooves and markings of the rocks.

They were both held in a spell like curious young cubs – at least, the mother felt like a young cub again as she sat there, fascinated by these old stories. Whereas the young cub suddenly felt very, very ancient, like an old grizzled Elder, looking at the story of his tribe and the other tribes. He felt himself to be very old and proud, indeed. His mother, meanwhile, felt the spirit of a young cub within her again, of her young heart listening to the ancient stories of her mother, long before. They both watched until the very last glimmer of light was gone from the sky. Then, slowly, starlight appeared. Still they stayed, for now the Earth was warm beneath them while the air around was a little chilly, so it was better to stay put and enjoy one's own warmth, rather than walk off into the cold night air. A new display of tales was beginning in the flickering starlight; they could see new faces appear, new forms transformed out of the old forms. Even more ancient stories appeared by the glimmer of star-shine, and both gazed at these tales coming to life before them.

Among all the stories told, one shone out above the rest. It was a story from the time when the Bear Tribe was very young and they were still finding their way in the forest. There was a time when Winter came, but never went away, and the trees went to sleep to wait for Spring, but Spring never arrived. The land had frozen over, the trees had no berries on them and there was nothing green to be seen anywhere. The bears could not fish, because every river and stream was frozen over so thickly that even the strongest bears could not break through the shell of ice. There came ferocious snowstorms that raged for many days and in the thick of them, the clans of bears wandered, lost and confused. They began to argue about which way to go, and they became separated from each other. It happened that one clan of bears wandered off and became lost in a forest that was strange to them. They were not yet wise enough to make their own way and they soon became fearful and hopeless. They could find no shelter from the cold, or the blizzards that blinded them, so they wandered aimlessly, unable to find their way to a warm cave. One night, they rested in the bowl of a valley, where they huddled together for warmth, while the cubs cried with hunger and the older ones feared the worst. All they had was the light of a New Moon above them, but, at least, they could see each other by her light.

Suddenly, they all looked up, their faces opening with amazement. Crowned with the crescent moon, the giant figure of the Great Bear Mother from the stars had appeared on the ridge above them. Surrounded by scintillating stars, she was standing tall on two legs, with her arms raised to the heavens. Starry light shone from her and her furry coat was covered with stardust, so, as the Great Bear Mother walked down the ridge, she left a trail of stardust behind her. She walked right into the midst of the bears huddled there together, her form towering over them. She was so tall, so full of strength that their fear and fatigue disappeared in an instant. She sat in their midst and they gathered around her like cubs. Young and old gathered in her loving presence, and all felt the warmth of the light come from her, this light of the stars. They no longer felt lost or forgotten. In her eyes, they could see the twinkling light of many stars, and as they gazed into her kind eyes they could find no end to them. It was like staring into the vastness of space, and yet there was nothing cold there, only warmth and love. For a long time they were silent, for all so enjoyed her presence and the love flowing from her that no one wanted to move or make a sound to disturb this blissful silence. It was she who finally spoke, in a voice that was clear and strong, gentle and loving.

She spoke to them as the Mother of their Tribe, and she told them that she had come to raise their hearts, to warm and gladden them, for they had begun to feel that they were lost forever. They had been forgetting the ways they had lived before; the sacred ways of bears that they once knew, but that now seemed distant, as if their memories were fading and something else was taking over. The forest, which once they knew and loved, now seemed to be full of dark shadows, and they filled these shadows with their own fears. This she knew, for she knew everything that was in their hearts. She had heard their hearts crying out for love and she had come to tell them that they had not been forgotten. They were not truly lost – for still they had the wisdom they were born with within them. They listened closely to the words of the Great Bear Mother while her eyes shone with starlight and her fur glistened with stardust. She told them that their future would not be as they feared. "Remember this hope that you now feel in your heart; remember this warming, this gladness. Your fears now are far away. Here, within our circle, there is no fear." Indeed, the bears knew that she was right, for at that moment, they felt hopeful and fearless.

She said, "You look at me and see that I have no fear and so you feel your own fade away. But I am here simply to show you that this fear is not real, that the forest is still your friend, that Mother Earth still loves you and the stars will guide you. I am of the Earth and of the stars, of the Sun and of the Moon, I am of the forest and the rivers, as you are. The great Bear Tribe will again be united, and they are looking for you, as you are looking for them. You will soon be one with the tribe, and my strength is the strength of you all when you are one. The Bear Tribe will be united with the Tribe of Wolf and the Deer Tribe and all the other tribes of the forest and the plains, the sky and the oceans. You will know you are one – one Great Tribe. So remember this moment of love, this moment without fear, this moment of hope, for this is what will bring you back to your Tribe. The Tribe will strengthen and increase again and you will know that you are never alone or forgotten. Soon you will be back in its warm heart, and you will enjoy times of plenty and happiness once more." She rose to her feet and sang out her Heart Song, and all the bears danced around in a great circle of joy, singing and celebrating, for their hearts were high and happy now. The bears began to sing and growl with joy, some crying tears of happiness and the young ones began to dance on their two legs with delight. The Great Bear Mother smiled, for she knew they would soon be back again in the bosom of their Tribe.

They celebrated until near dawn, and she danced in the middle of them, like a high dancing tree. Then, stooping down, she scooped up the cubs in her giant arms, holding them to her loving breast. She sat down on the snow while the hungry cubs began to suckle. She told the older bears to climb up onto her broad shoulders, so they did, and then the great Bear Mother rose up on two legs and walked up out of the valley, carrying that bear clan with her. With giant strides, she made her way across the land, leaving a sparkling trail of stardust behind her. Soon, those elders sitting on her shoulders could see a mountain rising up in the distance, its snowy coat tinted by the warm morning light. And, when they looked back on the way she had come, they could see that the ice on that sacred trail was melting!

The Bear Mother's ears filled with their laughter and joyful songs as the happy clan watched the mountain come nearer. When they reached the foot of the sleeping mountain, she placed everyone gently on the snow-covered earth. She walked up the mountain in a spiral path until she reached the biggest cave there, high up on its slopes. She entered it and disappeared into the heart of the mountain. There, she sang and she danced, and the mountain rang like a great bell. It is said the Great Bear Mother of the Earth came up from her deep cave to chant and dance with her beloved sister from the stars, and their songs and the rhythms of their feet echoed through the land. Suddenly, the mountain shook, like a giant bear awakening, shaking the ice off its trees and casting off its coat of snow, revealing the rich, red earth beneath. The very earth had a warm glow to it, and soft light began to come from the crystal caves, while the springs began to flow again.

When they looked up, there was the Great Bear Mother of the stars on the mountaintop, shining so bright, they could scarcely look at her. She became even brighter, until she was as bright as a Sun, standing on the peak, showering light like a beacon over the icy landscape. Her light was seen far off, and creatures from all over started to make their way towards it. Hour after hour, the path on the land widened as the snow melted, until it became so broad that it reached around the mountain, and finally became a red circle of earth surrounding it. The warmth and light from the Sun of her Heart warmed and dried the land, awakening the sleeping seeds. By then, creatures of all tribes had come from every direction to witness the miracle and celebrate the return of the Great Bear Mother. Her Heart Songs rang around the circle with theirs through the day, and when night came, she was a star on the mountaintop and her brilliance lit up the land. Then came a moment of silence, when every creature held their breath. They watched as the Sun of the Bear Mother rose into the night sky. They heard her voice in their hearts, and she told them, "It seems that I am leaving now, but I will always be near you, because I will be with you in your hearts. And you will look up at the stars and see me there, too, looking down over you, protecting you, just as Mother Earth looks after you and protects you. I point always to the North Star, so you need never lose your way again."

From then on, all the creatures knew that sacred place as Bear Mountain. The night the Great Bear Mother returned lives on in the hearts of the Bear Tribe, and somehow it found its way into the stories written in the faces of the trees and rocks, just as it was carved into their hearts, carved there with love and remembrance. As the mother bear and the bear cub watched the story come alive in the starlight, they found their hearts raised too. And, as one, they both looked up to see the Great Bear in the stars above their heads – for she it was who was illuminating the story in the faces of the Stone Folk and the Standing Bears. Then they felt the tears of joy rise from their eyes and they hugged each other and felt the love of the Great Bear Mother within them, blended with their own love for each other. They stayed there a long time in warm embrace, and they did not notice the cold air around them.

When they finally rose, they made their way home through the darkness, guided by starlight and the light of the Moon. Back inside the cave, the mother lay down on the ground and her cub curled up on her belly where it was warmest. They wrapped their bodies together and drifted into sleep. On their faces was a look of pure bear-faced joy. I need not tell you of what they dreamed, for I'm sure you can guess....

Through that night, the mother bear and her cub slept a deep sleep, and they dreamed much. They enjoyed their slumber so well, that when the first fingers of dawn light entered the cave, they did not stir. But, in the light of dawn, the stories painted in the ancient cave come to life!

The creatures begin to move, the little ones skip and run amongst each other, weaving through the trees, while the herds move through the plains. The four-legged creatures and their feathered friends spring into life, and even the skinny two-legged ones wake up. Soon, a whole world has come to life on the walls of the cave, while the bears sleep and dream beneath. Who knows how many times this has happened before – the stories coming out of darkness into light, being dreamed awake… All around the mother and cub, the stories are alive, they whirl and weave amongst each other, they play in the golden light of dawn pouring in. There is fire in the dawn light, too, and the painted fires above them spring to life and warm the two-legged creatures there, so now the darkness of the cave fills with light and the sounds of life. The silent cave has begun to echo with voices, and the bears stir. When the bear cub finally prizes open his eyes and looks around, he is amazed at the sight he sees! He watches the scene in great excitement, and he shakes his mother, whispering in her ear, and slowly she wakes up. She pulls her eyelids open reluctantly, since she thinks the cub is still dreaming. But she follows his eyes upwards, and she sees the painted images have come to vivid life.

She watches them, as wide-eyed as her cub, laughing to herself, as the creatures dance and gambol, scampering about the roof of the cave. Then she notices that one of the two-legged stick people is walking amongst the other creatures, watching them and talking to them, but listening to them most of all. She observes this two-legged one, and she realizes that it is learning from them. This two-legged learns the wisdom of the other creatures, and then returns to its little stick tribe to tell them what it has learnt. They begin to dance in happiness and she realizes that they must have been hungry. But now they are learning the wise ways of the other creatures, so they will soon fatten up!

Then, to the surprise of the two bears, they see all the creatures are gathering together and coming along in a great procession through the forest. The feathered ones are leading in front, for they can fly high and fast, and see furthest. And the little two-legged who came to listen to the creatures is leading the tribe of stick-people along. They are following the other creatures in the great procession, going through the painted forest, through the high pine trees waving in the whispering breeze, and into a clearing. In the clearing, the mother bear sees that a fire of red, orange and gold is already burning in the center. She is no great admirer of fire, but this fire rising from the Earth seems warm and inviting. All the creatures are going into the clearing in a great circle, with the two-leggeds following them. Around the clearing, they move in a great circle, the ones with the long necks and the short necks, the long legs and the short legs, each in their own way, at their own speed, dancing their own dance, while above them the feathered ones weave the wind. She is glad to see many bears there, and the bears are proudly marching along to show the two-leggeds the way. Some of the bears are dancing on their two strong legs to show the two-leggeds how to be proud of who they are. Although they seem skinny and weak, they are beautiful too, for the Great Creator has made them as they are. And when they stand together, are they not strong? Just as each of the tribes are strong when they stand together and love each other and dance as one.

Round and round the clearing they go, and the mother bear and the cub watch them with great smiles on their faces, the bear cub sitting wrapped in his mother's arms, enjoying the great spectacle, this shining vision. Now she sees that these creatures of all kinds have come to a halt, and are excitedly chatting and singing, talking and laughing, in their own tongues. Each of the tribes is there, and the two-footed ones take their place in this circle around the great fire. She can feel the great joy and happiness in this circle in the clearing, with the fire in the center. In their vision, they can see it from above, too, and they see all the creatures assembled in a perfect circle. Then it seems as if a silence descends, and all the creatures settle down comfortably onto the earth, as if to wait. There is a great hush in the air, not a sound in the forest, even the leaves cease whispering and they listen too. And all the creatures are held in a great silence, a happy silence, a peaceful silence. She knows their hearts are full and bursting with love, as hers is. She hugs her cub closer, for she can feel the fire warming her, and the heat of that fire of love within her. She sees bright rays of love coming from out of the fire, to warm the hearts of all the creatures there. All watch the flickering flames dance in the center of the clearing. They watch the sparks rising above this fire that she knows is a deeply sacred fire.

Then the sparks begin to come together above the fire. The mother bear watches the sparks gathering; they seem to flow into many shapes, faces and forms, and she sees in the points of light, the shapes and faces of all the creatures of the Earth. She sees in these sparks of love, the forms of all the tribes created, including those of the two-legged ones. When all these shapes have flowed through the sparks, she sees the fire burn even brighter. Above the circle, the sparks from the fire are mingling with the stars... Now the starry sparks of love extend out into two great wings of fire, which grow and stretch out over the clearing, above the heads of all assembled there....

Above them, blindingly bright, a great Bird of Rainbow Fire appears! So bright is its body that they can scarcely look at it. Its wings cover them all, extending over them like a giant rainbow arch, as it hovers above – the Firebird of Rebirth. This Winged One of fiery Love has risen from the loving heart of Mother Earth, bursting forth from her body, and everyone looks up with awe. Through the heart of this great Fire Bird is pouring Love, abundant and everlasting, into all their hearts, into all their bodies, even of the tiniest creature there. The Light is shared with all and the Love is for all to share. The love is pouring from the Heart of the Earth, and from the source of All, from the One who made them with love in the first moment, when the great story began, long before this world was made...

They bask in the Lovelight of the One who created all the creatures here represented, all the tribes assembled – who created All. Now the Firebird rises higher, its wings spread further, opening out and out and out, until above the clearing is a great dome of Light and they are all bathed in the Creator's Love. Then the Bird of fiery light rises still higher to the heavens, and the dome of light grows out further and further, extending out wider and wider, spreading the Light and the Love. The mother bear sees the light extend over all the Earth, this Fire of Love, which has risen from her core, stretching up into the heavens and surrounded her and all her children. A bright fire, bathing all the creatures with the love of Creation in love with Itself. All are united then. In that moment, all the tribes are One Tribe, and they all share the One Love.

The Light extends to the end of the Earth and the Love never ends. And this vision will never die, for now it will live on in the hearts of all who have seen it.

The bear mother knows in her heart that this is a vision of the future and that this vision will soon come true. She feels great hope and joy arise within her and she hugs her cub still closer, for she knows that before he has grown much older, this vision will become real. Then they will share a new life together, one of greater love, and all will be changed forever. For here, in this sometimes dark and lonely cave, they have seen something of the great future that awaits all the tribes of the Earth. Now the brightness of the vision increases so much that all they can see is the light and the two bathe within it as the cave is filled to overflowing. So bright is it, that they close their eyes and they feel the light pouring into their hearts, filling them, opening their hearts wider than they ever thought possible, so that they can be filled deeper than ever they thought possible. They feel light flowing from them, also, and their bodies glow brightly.

When they finally open their eyes, they realize that now it is *their* bodies that are glowing brighter than fire. The Light that was shining in the cave is now living within them. And when the mother bear looks at the roof of the cave, the vision has disappeared, for now it lives within her and the story is within her. Above her is only bare rock – all the images and symbols have danced their way into her heart, to stay there forever in a living vision. A vision she now wants to share, because she realizes that the other creatures have not seen this vision yet. For this cave is a small cave, with only room for two, and few come there. But now she and her cub have this light burning within them, and she sees that he is glowing as brightly as she is. She knows what they must do. And when her young cub looks into her face, she knows that he does too, for he is already coming to his feet to go to the opening of the cave. The mother rises to her feet, and they both stand at the doorway of the cave, looking out at the beauty of the Earth below them, illuminated by all the rays of dawn.

How new and wonderful it looks to them, for they look now with brighter eyes, eyes with new love shining within them. They can see further now, in every direction, it seems, and they love all more deeply than they ever thought they could. They love every rock and tree as their brother and sister. They see, with their hearts, all the tribes stretching out across the Earth; the feathered and the four-legged, the two-legged and the tiny crawlers, the Stone Folk and the Standing Bears. They see the great insect nations buzzing through the air, crossing the sky, they know every little pool is filled with life, and those tribes, also, they love as they love the biggest of the creatures.

Both know that it is time for them to share their vision with those of the other tribes. So they come out of the cave, stepping out into the bright sunlight and they feel themselves glow as brightly as the Sun above, who smiles on them more brightly than ever before. They make their way down the mountain, already looking forward to the journey ahead, to telling the other tribes of what they have seen. They know that all who hear of this vision will see it within them; they will know it is true and that it will soon come to pass.

The mother and the cub make their way down the mountain and, once more, the mother feels herself become a young cub on a bright morning, as if it were again her first day of life. She lightly skips down the mountain, like the most happy and playful cub there has ever been. Her cub meanwhile, makes his way down the mountain with his new vision and he sees through the eyes of an elder now, so he looks about with great understanding and wisdom. He comes down a little more slowly, for his bones are old, but he is happy nonetheless. He, too, is young in his heart, ancient though he may be. They make their way down the mountain; the cub and the mother, the elder and the youngster, and when they come to the foot of the mountain, they see the forest stretch out ahead of them, filled with life of all kinds, and they look at each other and smile. Again they hug each other, a big bear hug, and they feel the love flow between them. Each of them has the same thought as they wonder if, within the forest or beyond it, they will really meet some of these two-leggeds they have seen.

They know they must find those of the two-footed tribe who will listen to other creatures. Now they are eager to meet them, and curious about how they will respond when they tell them of their vision. These will tell the others of their kind, then they will share in the great vision. For they know it already within them and will remember it, as if they had once dreamed it in a great dream. So the two bears set off into the forest, and the Sun shines down upon them, the light dances on their furry backs. And the birds sing around them as they disappear amongst the leaves and the trunks of the trees. They go to share their song with all and share their dream. Soon, they know, the forest will sing a new song that is an ancient song, and the creatures will share one song together, a song of loving unity.

Each will sing this song in their own way and each will be heard by the Creator. And they will know and remember the Creator's Love within them, feel its fire again inside, so that when the great day of fiery light comes, they would be united in Love with their Creator. Then the Earth would be one Living Light, as she once was, and as she will be again.

The Flame of Hope will rise in the tired heart of humanity.
The promise of Rebirth will bring a hopeful flicker out of a darkened, weary heart, and its true flame will rise.

This world can seem heavy-burdened, a place of many cares and worries, where it is easier for bad things to happen than good, where disaster seems to lurk somewhere just out of sight. Our inner dreams, our secret hopes can seem too brittle and fragile to bring out into the light of day, for we are afraid they may dissolve before our eyes and be revealed as nothing but hollow dreams or vain hopes. But this view of the world is false, it has been fabricated through time, and kept in place over many centuries. It has been carefully woven in its way, created as a veil, which now hangs thinly over the Earth – and is thickly draped in places.

Some are wrapped in this veil so tightly they feel they will never escape, but they have played their own part in the creation of this veil. The weight of this veil is shared and spread across the world, yet each individual who has created it, who has woven their part of it, can also unweave their part of it. Or they can take a sharp Sword of Light and cut a hole in this veil and keep on cutting until every tattered strand of it is cut, and they can tear the shreds of this shroud away, cast the rags into the fire and watch them disappear. They will feel the light and warmth flood in. They can vow to themselves never to remake this veil, which had wrapped them so tightly. If they do this, they will breathe freer, for they will not feel the strangling of the veil around their throats, they will dream more easily, as their inner vision unveils. They will speak more freely, they will sing out more often, for their bodies, minds and spirits will feel lighter for having cast off this veil.

The more holes that are made in this net, the more it is weakened across the world. For the thread you have unraveled or cut is connected to all the other threads, as you are. So many others be helped to escape this veil of illusion, for thought it can seem thick and strong, it is in fact extremely flimsy. It is only held in place because people have been trained to live in fear and they have made fear a kind of cold friend since they feel they can never be rid of it. So they feel they must make it into their ally and at that point, it often becomes their master.

The fear of which we speak is not natural caution or instinct, it is fear that has been woven as part of this veil, woven like a gray mist across the face of the Earth and it can dim the hearts and the eyes of many. It even makes it difficult for people to see each other clearly, since their eyes are partially blinded by this veil of fear and illusion and their hearts are veiled from each other. This can happen in all kinds of relationships, from those of the social kind, to those of the family and relationships of two people. If they are each wrapped in a veil and between them hang other levels of the veil, they may be looking at each other through many screens of illusion and fear. When they face each other, they will see only a tiny glimmer of the real being behind the veil. Yet if each, with clear intent, were to start to unravel the veil around them or to cut through it, they would make greater and greater space for communication.

But they can reach out to each other through the veils and keep widening the opening. Between them, they would feel an open space, a clear Heart Space, for crystal-clear communication from heart to heart. If they are vigilant, if the veils did not reappear between them, they would find their lives and their relationships transformed. Now they would be revealing each other as the true beings they are; they would be seeing the true face and faces behind the false veils.

This of course can be a surprise, even a shock, but it is always to the good in the end, for to live behind the veils of illusion is truly not to live at all. One's life is so circumscribed and narrowed by this kind of living that it leads into much regret later on, if one has allowed illusions to rule one's life. The importance of this process holds true for all relationships and all interaction between people, between creatures and beings of nature, and all life. For the veils can constrict vision in all directions, and create barriers between life and life, heart and heart, light and light.

So if each one strives to remove the veils from your lives, you are doing yourselves, the world and the Earth a great service. For each one who succeeds in this task, has made an opening in the vital energy of the Earth.

Through this opening, can again flow love and clear sight; whoever opens this space will feel new energies flow through to them. They will find themselves making contact with all life more directly. They will witness and notice more and they will begin to sense the connections between all life. They will sense the weaving happening around them, through them. They will comprehend the connections between events and sense the synchronicities occurring and notice the patterns of them. They will then be able to sense events that may be about to occur more clearly, for they will feel what is passing along the threads of the Web and know the possibilities. They will become more sensitive to the vibrations of the Web and learn to recognize their nature, because their system will now be open to receive these sensations more directly, without them being muffled and distorted.

They will be able to sense themselves more clearly as a weaver of the Web, know that their actions and thoughts, their love and intentions send out messages, vibrations and energies through the Web every single moment. They will know that from their fingertips flows the future that they are creating, that they are weaving the future as they move through the now, that they are choosing which frequencies they wish to tune into. They can discover which ones give them pleasure and a sense of connectedness to all life. They will then be able to generate these energies for themselves and send them back out to the vital Web. They will be able to send their love to the Earth in every moment, drawing it in from the One Heart within them, and pulsing it out from their heart.

They will feel life flowing around them, people healing around them, relationships growing around them; other creatures will look different, and seem to act differently. They will attract those who they wish to attract to them and these that come to them will see them more clearly, for they will somehow notice that the veils have been torn. This is the beginning of true interaction, of true being on the Earth, without the encumbrance of these heavy veils that now mask the people and creatures of the Earth, and hinder their development. At the moment, many are like fish caught in a heavy net; they struggle and struggle within it, often entangling themselves more strongly. They do not realize that the power to create and un-create, to weave and to re-weave, to mend or cut this net is within their power.

So it is time to choose whether we wish to be one of the shoal of fish caught in this dense mesh, or whether we wish to free ourselves, to burst out of this dark net and swim freely again through the Ocean of Life. For the Ocean is wide and ever-growing, and freedom awaits.

The spacing and timing of every event is finer than you might think. Every event is finely woven together with every other event, rather like beads on a thread, and these beads are carried on the Web. Each event is an intersection of threads, and each is connected to every other, nearby or far off, for space has little meaning in these matters. For all events are connected in the Great Web of Existence, and the beads would seem to shimmer in the waves that flow down the Web, to influence events, making them shimmer and rattle. In the music they make, is a clue to the nature of the event and its connections.

It may be the soft whispering of quiet events, gentle gatherings of subtle energies; or there may instead be major waves, dramatic pulses that shoot and flow along the Web. Now the beads will rise and fall in great shuddering movements that may pulsate wildly as waves flow across each other or meet and crash together. These waves will ripple out, making more waves across the Web. These events are hard to ignore, for if we are near to the center of these events, we may be influenced by, and influencing, them. If we keep our sense of connection to the wider web, we will not be as affected by localized events. We can still find our point of stillness in the midst of it all. We can remember we are held gently in the Web of Love and allow events to flow around us, so we will not be hit by the impact of these ripples as they flow around this point of stillness.

Alternatively, we can flow with the events, moving with them, as a fish moves with the currents passing through the ocean. Like the seal and the dolphin, we can learn how to flow with the waves when the waves are working with us, and when it is better for us to swim our own course, for our lives to follow a different current. These are a couple of the alternatives that face us at each moment; to be in the point of stillness, unmoved by events, or to flow with them as far as possible. In both instances, it is necessary for the heart to be open and for the being involved to be centered in their own way – or the one who wishes to be still may be swept away by the waves, perhaps into confusion and disorientation. Or the one who wishes to flow with events will find themselves unable to follow the flow, as they may, without realizing it, be trying to anticipate the way it is moving or control the current, instead of moving with it. So this will be part of learning – or remembering – how to move, with awareness, through the Web of Life, and will be a vital part of the future. Each of you will be growing into your awareness as co-creators of the Universe, and your responsibilities will seem greater once you know that you are creating the reality in which you live, while influencing the realities of others – and sending waves of influence into the Earth and out into the Cosmos.

This can seem a heavy responsibility if one wishes simply to curl up with a cup of tea and a book, and we do not wish to burden you with these thoughts and spoil your moments of peace and solitude. These moments are also important, since they send out waves of peace into your life and surroundings, to influence all that you are connected to most closely, and they send peace into the heart of the Earth and into the wider Universe. So you have full permission to curl up with a coffee and a novel, to forget the grander scheme of things for a while and enjoy something simple! Moments of simple pleasure – that may even seem infantile or silly – can send healing through the web. They can even allow something very complicated to be untangled.

You may recognize these moments when knots in the web are untangled and illusions are unraveled. Your vision will lighten, as if a light has been switched on in the room, or an invisible sun has come out of the clouds. What will have happened is that the veil will suddenly have thinned and hope rises in the heart as the illusion fades. Therefore, we need not burden ourselves with heavy tasks, for the lighter we are, the more joy we have within us. And the more lightly we take the work, the more we play, the more we can truly tear the veils. By embracing the simple truths, we sense the single threads more clearly, even among the connections in their countless billions, which make up the web of realities. By following that single thread through the Universe, we are seeing the strength of simplicity, the connection to All That Is, and how all is connected to our heart and flows from there. If we simply follow that thread into our heart, we will be back at the beginning, for Love is where it all begins and from where it all flows. And all Life flows from Love.

Fear-weaving has become quite a craft all over the planet, a craft that has been kept alive for many generations. Unlike other practitioners of crafts, fear-weavers do not get much satisfaction from their work, nor do they find it relaxing or fulfilling. In fact, they truly suffer for their art and exhibit all the tell-tale signs of stress and anxiety. Some spend countless hours weaving their worries together, stringing them with worry beads, and lacing them with a little hate. Even when their creations go on display, unfortunately, they bring little real pleasure. Despite this, fear-weaving is still very much in fashion. Unlike most traditional crafts, it gets a lot of support from many sources. In fact, fear-weaving itself has become a very widespread industry. Some have made it big, and their creations are projected as moving tapestries of terror, to be watched with an appropriate sense of anxiety, including screams and nervous laughter on cue.

Most fear-weaving, though, is on a smaller scale, with home-made creations. Blindfolds are the most popular item, with gags a close second. Sometimes, they are made to old family patterns that have been in use for centuries, inherited and worn with pride. Of course, rather than going to the trouble of making them yourself, these products of fear are readily available. Some come with guarantees to last a lifetime, but most are flimsy affairs that, all too easily, can tear and let in light. Yet, instead of worrying over the latest pattern for our blindfold, we can loosen it a little and let it drop. Breathe a little light and color into it, and it might become a fetching scarf....

In fact, why not let your whole robe of Light shine in the true colors of your heart? If you have wrapped yourself in gray veils, or allowed your colors to become clouded, then breathe Light into the weave of your being. Let the Rainbow Robe that surrounds you be constantly refreshed and renewed, whether you are awake or asleep. Let any holes be repaired and its colors refreshed, if they have become muddy. The well-worn stories of your past are woven into the threads of your being, and these tales may be jaded and frayed, no longer reflecting who you are now and who you are becoming.

You can let go of any outdated images of who you are and breathe free. Rather than clinging on to old robes, perhaps you need to let go of them, or give your old robes away if they are outgrown. You can go out into the world wearing a new set of threads, shining in your true colors. When we let go of old sorrows or hatreds, we breathe new life into the living weave of our being. We allow hope to open up our Rainbow aura, so it can become truly a golden robe, woven of all the colors of love. And if you ever feel some shadowy moth has nibbled a hole in your robe of Light, you can weave it whole again in a moment. Remember within you is the source of Light, and the best protection is connection – connection to the sacred Source, with its limitless abundance of love that is ever-expanding.

If your threads seem tangled and your mind a fog of confusion, reach deep into your heart to the Source, sense the guidance that sings down the heart-threads connecting you to the Creator. Joy and peace are there, waiting behind and beyond all that anxiety. Let laughter crack the mask of fear, allowing a truer face to shine through, let joy break the spell of fear, and love dispels its lingering fog, to clear a space for something new. And now that we are opening up spaces, we can check if we have surrounded ourselves with a wall or two. All this light will reveal how solid or flimsy they are. Yet, instead of agonizing over the choice of paint for our crumbling walls and worrying if the cracks will show, we can let them fall.

There are truly no walls within Oneness, no barriers at all. Oneness and openness are synonymous. Yet boundaries founded on love and respect are different in nature. These allow one to develop and learn, while still interacting with the wider universe, without feeling overwhelmed. They allow discovery and new learning, rather than shutting one off from new experiences, as barriers can. Boundaries that honor personal space, respecting the health and sensitivities of natures are to be respected and upheld, without being held up as barriers against growth and new experience. Barriers based on fear and hatred diminish the ones trapped within them, denying them a view of the potentials that surround them on all sides.

Living without borders and barriers may not seem a comfortable concept, when such divisions define this current world. Yet the only thing more definite than they are, is the fact that they will, some day, fade away. What begins as a small opening can expand so fast that, before long, the walls fall down and borders bend beyond any recognition. The screens will lift and the curtains will pull back to reveal a bigger story, then open wider to show the bigger story beyond that. Artificial grids and nets of control have been thrown around the Earth, and dark waves emanate from artificial sources, creating frequency fields in which many become trapped. But these, like the web of wires, the metallic matrix that entangles the planet, have a limited lifespan. These filaments of fear, while entangling many, do not form a living web, so they fade when their artificial source of power dies away.

Love will outlive them and the tide of Light will rise to break their hold and erase their traces. Can such a world as this one be transformed by love? Is love strong enough for such a task? It is as well to ask if one person can be changed by the awakening of love. And you know the answer within yourself.

So now let us flow out of the confines of the net, beyond the tangles of the past, as the veils fall away and the Ocean of Living Love opens up before us. This is an Ocean of countless currents, of living streams, crisscrossing and connecting. Within this Ocean, flow the Rainbow Rivers of life, and where they meet, their living waters mingle. And at the meeting of the waters, a spiral is seen, where they blend and meld, in lively threads connecting through space and time. These river-stories all connect to each other, all tributaries are threads of the One River flowing from the Source. And this Rainbow River flows into itself in a great circle, returning into its own ocean, the Ocean of Love from which it created itself, from which it flows and to which it returns.

So a stream may flow through an ocean and know the story of the ocean, and tell its own story as it goes. For an ocean holds many stories, especially in its depths. And the deeper you go, the more you see of what has sunk down to the bed of the ocean where sleep so many secrets, so many souls, so many stories told and untold...

We dive down to the depths and, there, at the bottom of the ocean, we find what we have forgotten, or think that we have never known. We find the true treasures, the riches of the sea. Now we see a glow there, we see in the dimness the oranges and reds of a deep glowing fire. As we move towards it, we discover a deep cave of fire with molten rock flowing slowly from it, so hot that the waters bubble and boil. We know it is incandescent heat, the heat of the deep Earth...yet we go closer for it seems to call us in.

Now we are looking into the cave, and we see it leads down, down into the fire of the Earth, though we know that its heat will not harm us, for now we are not in our physical form. We feel ourselves becoming more fiery; we are transforming. Now we feel the cave mouth open wider for us and we slide down to enter this cave of fire. We feel only a glow of warmth and welcome, for we are at home with Fire and Fire is at home with us. We are pouring down this tunnel as living fire; we are coming home to the Heart of the Earth. We flow quickly down on liquid fire and the walls around us are molten and glowing. We reach out and touch them with our fingers of flame, and they are soft. Our fingers ripple through them as we flow down even more quickly now for we are keen to be closer to Earth's radiant heart. Our form of living fire flows through this tube of red-hot rock, and the tunnel is opening wider now, so we open our fiery arms wide. Beneath us, fire is moving too; we are flowing on a stream of cleansing fire. Now the tunnel is very broad and we see glimpses of crystal appearing around us, which glow and flash in the widening tunnel. We flow fast down the fire stream and we see all around us a kaleidoscope of colors and forms.

But now the stream is slowing and we enter through an opening into a vast cave, taller and wider than anything we have ever seen before. We look down to see that the fire stream has entered a pool of fire, which spirals slowly as we flow into it. Slowly, we come to a stop and, there, we rest and center ourselves. Then we step out of the pool of fire onto the rock that surrounds it. We feel around us a sweet coolness, which seems to still and calm us. We look around, to admire the beauty of the breathtaking spectacle for which we were not prepared, yet which seems somehow familiar. We notice first the ceiling, so high above; a great canopy of rock encrusted with countless crystals, glistening like stars. On every side are high walls of rock and crystal patterned through each other. Huge crystal trees reach up to the ceiling and from their branches hang giant chandeliers of hanging crystalline forms. All around us are these enormous columns of pure crystal of different patterns and hues. With our feet of fire, we walk down a row of steps and at the bottom of the steps, we see there is a broad pillar of crystal in front of us, the trunk of a familiar crystal tree.

We step towards it, and as we do, we see our fiery reflection, as if in a mirror. Our reflection creates brilliant colors in this giant crystal and our light seems to move inside it. We step forward to touch this crystal…it feels cool to our hot fingers, which enjoy the sensation. We embrace this pure crystal column and feel its coolness move through us. And suddenly we feel that we are melding inside of it – we feel our form flowing and entering it. Soon we realize we are within the crystal column. We feel its energies flowing through us strongly as beautiful sound and light surround us. And now we feel our form changing; our fiery form is beginning to transform into something else….

We change slowly into transparent, flowing, living crystal. We marvel at ourselves in our new form. Surprising patterns pour through our form and illumine us from within. We look up this pillar of crystal, and notice a point of light above. Light is pouring down to us from above, filling us with even more light, so that we feel our form glow and pulsate. Light is flowing upwards too, up through our feet, the trunks of our legs, filling our crystal body. We feel very at home in this form, we feel clear and vividly alive. We know that we can move as freely as we want to in this form of living crystal energy. We step out of the column, and look at the cave through our new crystal eyes. It seems even more wonderful. We see all in a new perspective, now that we are crystal also. We know this realm to be the home of our crystal form. For we each have a crystalline form, waiting to be remembered and reborn.

As we stand there, we notice a glowing Light-Being entering the cave through an opening in the walls. Following behind is another brilliant being. Another opening appears and another Shining One enters, until approaching us are a number of brightly-glowing forms. We feel our pure crystal heart open wide. As they come near, it takes a little while for our new crystal eyes to focus on these tall beings who are approaching, glowing with deep love and welcoming us into their home. They are living crystal beings, as we are, alive and shining, luminous with love. Their arms open wide to us, as their hearts are open wide to us. So bright are they, that we find it hard to discern faces and forms, but we know these are beings of living light, ancient and wise Devas of the crystal realms. We know we are privileged to be in their presence.

The Shining One who is nearest to us reaches out her arms, coming forward to embrace us. We feel our hearts opening to each other, like crystal melting into crystal, love meeting love. We are enveloped in her light, too bright even for our crystal eyes. We feel the flow of love between us both, and the love fills and revives us until our crystal body rings with a note of purity and renewal. After what seems a long time, we begin to see forms and patterns in the light, as we seem to adjust to its brightness. We can see faces and patterns, shapes and colors, moving as in a kaleidoscope. We can reach out into this world of light, color and form, for now we have melded with this being who has allowed us to enter into her depths and heights. And we see the infinity within, the patterns, the forms, stretching all around us in every direction. This inner world is alive, filled with liquid light and the flow of love. We are swimming in crystal waters, through which light and patterns flow. In the cool crystal waters we can move freely, we can spin and dance as we wish, we can shimmy and swim. Our crystal form moves and swims like a dolphin and we have the joy of the dolphin within us. We play here in these living crystal waters, where light flows from all around, illuminating forms and colors through which we flow.

After a time, we see a bright spiral light, a great glow pulling us towards it, and we flow to it. As we near it, we shine brighter and we feel even more alive. We flow into the light, entering it in a blaze of radiance. We have entered the sacred Heart of Earth. In the presence of such love, we bathe in the bliss while we feel ourselves transform into a purer form of light, a living flame.

I hold you closer. You shine within me.
You will not be lost again, you will not be forgotten.
We will play and celebrate life in our gardens of the heart.
We will grow in each other. We will rise together, we will emerge in true light.
We will rebirth as one.

There comes a moment in the flow when a golden spiral finds us and wraps itself around us, drawing us back. We move now into our crystal form, swimming through currents that are cooler and slower. We see a circle of light ahead and we swim on towards it, feeling stronger in our crystal body. Soon we feel ourselves flowing out of the water and have the sensation of something solid beneath our feet. We are being held closely in a warm embrace. In this embrace of love, we discern a face within the light. The face of a being looking at us with such depth of love that our heart opens even more, and we shine even brighter. Then this being steps back, yet we are still held softly within her love. She moves back to join the circle of other beings, who shine as brightly as her.

We see them in a ring around us; we form a Circle of Thirteen Crystal Beings. We stand at the center of the circle of brilliant light, surrounded by a ring of unbreakable love. We delight in this experience, as we turn to see all the faces and forms around us, and enjoy their loving presence. We feel the healing they are giving to us in the circle of Rainbow Light flowing around us. We feel that our joyful heart could not open any wider, but it does. Our heart opens deeper to the flow of crystal love and the light increases, flowing around us brighter and higher. Light spirals faster around us until, beneath our feet, we feel something rising…

We look down to see a rising Rainbow Flame, flowing upwards from the Heart of the Earth, bathing us in glowing rainbow fire, filling our crystal body with the Earth's love and her golden light. We are bathing in this loving rainbow light; the living expression of the Earth's love for all Creation. Until suddenly we feel ourselves transform into rainbow fire. We feel ourselves grow taller, stronger and brighter in this fire with deep roots, reaching down into the Heart of the Earth from which we flow as a living expression of her love. We rise higher and higher, yet still connected to the Earth's Heart.

We reach up our arms to see they are wings of rainbow flames! We stretch them out as we feel ourselves reborn as a winged being of living flame, with a heart of rainbow fire burning within us. Our wings stretch broader while higher we rise, as the flames rise higher and we move with them. Our wings are beating strong and opening wide, and we are rising in a spiral of golden light, flying upwards on our rainbow wings. We rise up through the Earth, showering our love and our light through her realms, lifted by the warmth of love from the Earth's heart rising beneath us. She pushes us higher and higher still we fly higher, up through the layers of fire and water, rock and crystal, and we are rising so fast that soon we are nearing the surface of the Earth. Our wings and our heart open even wider as we rise and we know soon we will reach the clear air. We open our hearts still wider and burst through, out into the air and light.

Now we are in the clear air, still rising up from the surface on our rainbow wings. Our fiery wings cool a little in the calm air around us as we slow our ascent and look down to behold the Earth below us. The air holds us steady as we gaze down with love on the face of Mother Earth, in whom we have been renewed. We glide over her surface, floating on the warm currents of love rising from her, which catch our broad rainbow wings and fill our heart anew in every moment.

The Earth has graced us with new life through her love. She has given us new form and expression through her passionate love for us and our true love for her. We feel deep peace within us. We glide gracefully over the loving Earth, reborn.

Our Rainbow Arc has risen high. And now, like every rainbow, we return to touch the Earth. In human form, we reveal the light of the divine. In new awareness, we move through the worlds.

We return in our true light, reborn as the One we are. The One I Am.

ONE

The Butterfly Awakens

There was once a Rainbow butterfly whose wings shimmered in every color that could be.

Though her wings were delicate, they were broad and open. When she opened her heart, her wings opened wide to the world, and her colors were displayed for all to see in their unique patterns. Those who saw her felt gladness in their hearts for she was beautiful and bright, and, in her wings, they saw colors they did not even know existed. People were fascinated by her, and enjoyed her miraculous display, as she flew by them in the fields or in the streets. For, when she opened her wings, she seemed to scatter color through all the world, and brighten everywhere she went. Even to the darkest, grayest places she brought her gift of colors.

In these places, her wings would shine out brighter, her colors would seem clearer and stronger, and the faces of those that saw her would brighten up with surprise and pleasure.

She loved, most of all, to fly into these gray places for she knew in her heart that she was showing the people a mirror; that her glittering wings were a mirror to the beauty that was hidden inside them. Each saw only their own beauty within her, and those that did not notice her could not see their own beauty. So she loved to fly far and wide, opening her heart and her wings to all, so that more would remember their beauty.

She would flutter and fly until her wings grew tired, and she would close them and rest for a while. Then she would enjoy the sights around her, the colors of the world, the shapes and textures of everything. She hungered for beauty, herself, at times. You see, she could not see her own wings, so she never saw the beauty that others could in her. There was no one to mirror her beauty back to her, and there were times when she forgot it herself. These were times when her heart seemed tired and heavy. She would go then to the high places and the open spaces, where she could look out at the flowers and the plants, at the blossoms and the trees, the glistening of the waxy grass. She would watch the creatures for a while and observe how the light played on everything and how everything played in the light. She would enjoy the beauty of all around her and soak it into her heart. Soon she would feel herself revived, for she would be filled with love for the beauty of all that she was part of. Her energy would rise again, her heart and her wings would feel lighter, and she would set off into the air, once more, holding her mirror up to the world, to show its forgotten beauty. She would flutter around anyone who was heavy-laden or sad, whose face was downcast; anyone who had lost their color, who seemed dulled to the beauty around and within them. These, she would seek out, to brighten their eyes, if only they would look up.

Yet she knew well how they felt for, not long before, she had known a dark time, a gray phase without any color at all. Most of this time, she was held in a heavy slumber from which she could only awake with difficulty, and then only for brief moments. Her only relief was that sometimes in her sleep, a dream came, and she came to long for this dream. In her dream, her eyes were suddenly flooded with color, and she saw colors flooding out from her, pouring out of her, flowing out of her heart, which had been so heavy and dark. She would watch beautiful patterns appear, wonderfully lacy and delicate. Colors appeared one after the other, each more gorgeous and glowing than any she could have imagined. They flowed together into wonderful patterns of mirrors, shimmering like rainbow scales, and as they flowed out to each side of her, she saw that each side was mirroring the other exactly. So that she saw before her, two images in perfect symmetry, each mirroring the other, in their breathtaking patterns of color and light.

She would enjoy this image, drinking in the colors for as long as it lasted, because she knew, each time she had the dream, there would come the moment she dreaded. That moment when the mirror would shatter, the colors would crack, and both mirrors would fragment and fall, to disappear into the darkness. She would be left alone again and sad. Alone, but for the memory of this magical image, which had come to her in the dream. Again and again, she had this mysterious vision, and again and again, she was plunged back into darkness. Only the vivid memory of this vision of perfect symmetry sustained her; its beauty and color kept her hopes alive.

Until once, when she was there held in the shadows, the grayness itself suddenly seemed to shimmer and shift. She shook herself, to see if she was dreaming. For it seemed that there were subtle colors appearing in the dim, gray light. Then she saw a bright line begin to appear in front of her, like a single thread of light. She watched, entranced, as this thread of light grew thicker and thicker and brighter and brighter. It was dividing the grayness! And even the grayness was now filling with iridescent colors and marvelous patterns that shimmered and shone. This ribbon of light grew still wider until it almost filled her whole field of vision. Slowly her eyes adjusted to the light so that she began to see colors and shapes emerging; wonderful patterns and forms began to appear. She felt light and air flood into her and surround her. She could feel her body moving, and it felt freer now. She began to wriggle and move, writhe and dance. She could feel that her little legs had become longer and more graceful, for now they stretched out in front of her. These long, long legs she had never seen before were reaching out into the light, as if to touch its source.

Then she remembered that she had woven this gray casing around herself. She had first slowly wriggled high up into a tree, while its leaves fell about her. She had climbed out onto a limb, and spun a thread to attach herself to the branch. The world was growing cold and its light seemed to be fading, and she had felt compelled to weave this gray chrysalis around herself. But had found herself then in darkness. After a time, she had even forgotten how she got there. She had spent her time in dreaming and forgetting, waking up always in the dark, wondering if this time would ever end. Now her cocoon had opened, she found she was free of the gray threads that she had wrapped around herself. The whole world had opened up, and she felt renewed, just as her body felt new to her.

She stepped out into this world with her new legs, and found herself walking along the branch, high up in the tree, which was now in full leaf. Bathed in golden green light, she gracefully made her way along a slender twig onto a wide green leaf. She walked along its body, testing out her new legs, for she was a little dizzy with joy and intoxicated with these new colors and experiences. At the edges of her vision, she kept seeing colors shimmering, but, though she looked around, she could not see where they came from. Yet this light shifted and shimmered in colors that glowed just like those she had seen in her dream, so clear and strong. The sunlight was holding her in its rays warm in the sun, which was strong and bright on her body. She drank in its light and she felt herself grow in love for all that she could see. After a time the colors around her grew stronger and brighter, so many colors she could see all around, but whose source she could not see. Suddenly she felt something stir in the back of her heart, and something opened. She felt a great rush of air and light into the back of her heart, and she felt it racing and pumping with joy, for something was stirring into life there.

She knew now that something was opening around her, and this something was the source of these wonderful colors; this rainbow of myriad colors that surrounded her. Although she could not see it, she could feel all the colors surrounding her. She felt within her a knowing begin to stir within her, something that seemed too wonderful to believe. For this knowing told her that she could leap now from this leaf and fly out into the world, just like the feathered ones she had often seen flying so freely. She doubted this for much more than a moment. How could she, who had once had such a stubby and heavy body, now fly into the air, like one of the feathered ones?

Yet something inside told her that she had changed so much in the time of darkness that now she, too, was ready to fly. Her transformation was complete. So she made her way to the edge of the leaf, her heart racing with excitement at all the possibilities that would open up to her, if this inner knowing were true. But when she looked over the jagged edge of the leaf, there seemed a very long way to fall. Still she knew she must test these wings of her heart. So she took a great leap of faith and dived from the leaf. She found her heart opening to the light and the air…and, yes, she was flying! She could feel the great formations of color and pattern were fluttering around her, allowing her to fly, to be free. She could not see them, but she knew these were the shimmering visions of perfect symmetry and color from her dream. Now her dream had come true, her vision was made real, and she flew on and on, enjoying her freedom. She flew to greet every flower, tree and creature she could find and then she flew on over the changing landscape, until she found herself hovering over a busy city.

She fluttered down and began to fly through the canyons of brick and stone. So many of the people, she noticed, were worried and fearful, wrapped in thick, gray veils. Others walked with heavy clouds hanging over them. Yet some of them noticed the brilliant butterfly, flickering like a Rainbow Flame, and their faces lightened with delight. She realized that she brought them joy. She knew then this was to be her joy; to bring her light and color to those who had forgotten their own. She would find those who had forgotten their own true beauty, who were still in the shadows.

Like an Angel of love, she would share her beauty with the world, and shine her heart of love into the darkest places. In the flash of surprise of those who saw her, was a flicker of the memory of who they truly were, revealed in a flash of her wings. In the flicker of color and light from her mirrored wings, each saw their own light reflected. Her mirror showed a glimmer of the true faces that they had forgotten, and their joy was the joy of remembering themselves.

And it was one dull day in the city that she saw herself reflected for the first time. She had been flying through a shaded place, past high cliffs of brick, when she came to a wall made of many clouded mirrors. She hovered in front of one of the man-made mirrors, noticing a bright being dimly reflected there. When she realized the reflection was hers, the surprise set her heart fluttering! She could see the eyes of her own wings, with their rainbow colors, and their patterns that pulsated in lively rhythms though the air. And she could see beyond these... Meanwhile, on the other side of the mirror, a down-turned face looked up. The one who raised his face saw a beautiful butterfly hovering before him, with the colors of a perfect dawn. He felt like he had awoken suddenly, and his heart fluttered a little. He felt like he had been half-asleep a moment before, and through the grayness of the window, he watched his awakener dance in the light breeze, as if she was celebrating something.

The happy butterfly then saw a smiling face in the mirror, with twinkling eyes that watched her every move. She understood this was no reflection, so she danced a special sign in the air, just for him, to show that she had noticed him. Then she fluttered on, along the row of mirrors, until a pair of eyes was raised up, and a face opened in surprise. This one felt her heart lighten in a moment of joy. The Sun had finally opened the heavy clouds, and the butterfly fluttered in front of his face, so the woman felt like the Sun was winking at her. She relaxed back in her chair, and watched this winged one dance her patterns, so carefree. And she remembered this sensation from moments she had known. She saw her own smiling face reflected back in the mirror of the window, and she was reminded of her right to feel this happy every day. As the butterfly flew on, the feeling stayed with her. She looked around and saw her joy reflected in another smile nearby, on the face of one who knew what she was smiling at. And, in that tower of clouded mirrors, two lights met, heart to heart.

The butterfly fluttered on, with her flickering wings. And on, through the world of shadow and light, she flies.

Epilogue

Earth's Tree of Life will be reborn.

Her Tree of Light will rise again. Its seeds have lain dormant in her core, but they are opening, and from each seed, a thread of light emerges. The love of the Sun has been warming the Earth, to germinate the seeds and feed the roots; this solar love will help the Polar Tree to rise. The New Tree of Life will grow up through the poles, the trunk emerging in vibrant fibers of light. And the branches will reach out to the stars, with buds unfolding and the flowers releasing their light. Every twig of the tree, every fiber of energy, will be aligned perfectly to the web of starlight, as every living pattern of the tree will be in divine alignment. For this Earth Tree will also be a Star Tree, connected to the Starry Web and the Star Heart of the Earth.

The Weavers of Crystal Light are busy, and the Deep Weavers of the Earth are hard at work, reweaving the very fabric of the crystal web and the living matter of Mother Earth. We are united in the weaving of this Crystal Tree, whose roots will run through the Earth as a root-web through her body. From the womb of the Earth, life is renewing as the roots are rising. Within their web-work flows the sweet sap, these juices of renewal. The Earth herself will nourish this blessed tree and every bud that emerges and opens will release great light, so that the very air of the planet will shine as the atmosphere is enlivened, and the soil beneath your feet will be enlightened.

This sacred tree will have the power to renew life all over the Earth. It will tower over the lands of the planet, north and south, east and west. A trunk of this polar tree will reach up from each pole and grow as one, roots and branches united. It will become the new axis of the world, drawing in love from the Sun, Moon and stars, Light from all over the Cosmos. This Tree of Rebirth will be like a giant spindle, spinning out its threads of light, and these living filaments will reach into the weave of life on this planet and revive it.

Its broad, strong branches will stretch overhead, and people who are free in their hearts will be able to climb this tree, to fly through its branches, to explore its many levels, to travel through its wonderful trunk, to glide up to its myriad branches and appreciate its flowers and taste its fruit. Or they can slide down the light-fibers of its trunk, deep into the core of the Earth, into her heart of love.

New life will arise from the seeds of this sacred tree, from its abundant love, new forms of living love will arise. Humanity will hold hands around the planet and encircle this Crystal Tree. In its Light, as it rises, ancient links will be revealed, and fresh connections of love will be made. Its guardians will emerge, the Crystal Keepers of the New Earth Tree. And we will taste the sacred fruit when it falls, to nourish all the children of the New Earth, and we will share it, in love, with All.

In Name of the Creator, in the Name of the One.

Afterword

Cosmic Clues and Helpful Hints

When the channeling began, I had read very few spiritual-themed books, so I didn't realize how many references to ancient symbols, concepts and so on were contained in the material. Since then, I've had a very steep learning-spiral! Though this has mostly been about remembering what I already knew at some level. We discovered later that many of the symbols and references throughout the book, especially in the stories have meanings in Star lore, and you might have fun checking these out. Here are a few of the clues and hints we found....

The "Procession" and the "Circle of Animals" both seem to have references to the phenomenon known as the "Precession of the Equinoxes." To put it clumsily, it is based on the fact that the Earth is quite egg-shaped and "wobbles" around the Sun, creating the illusion over many centuries that the constellations – the Animals – are precessing across the sky. There are much more elegant descriptions of this process available in books on astronomy and astrology, and it has a major significance in timings of long-range calendars like those of the Mayan tradition. The word "Zodiac" actually translates as "Circle of small animals"...

It is well worth looking into Sacred Geometry and the "Flower of Life," which relates to a lot of the patterns in the book. There are numerous fascinating books and websites on these subjects.

There are references to the processes of Alchemy, whose aim is the transmutation of impure or dense elements to gold or, more deeply, the clarification of the human spirit.

Two websites with information on these and many other subjects are www.spiritmythos.comand Ellie Crystal's, www.crystalinks.com.

We have more information on our website: www.oneheartweb.com. If you have any discoveries you would like to share, or would like to get in touch, you can contact us at: info@oneheartweb.com.

Marc Maramay

O

is a symbol of the world,
of oneness and unity. O Books
explores the many paths of wholeness
and spiritual understanding which
different traditions have developed down
the ages. It aims to bring this knowledge
in accessible form, to a general readership,
providing practical spirituality to today's seekers.
For the full list of over 200 titles covering:

- CHILDREN'S PRAYER, NOVELTY AND GIFT BOOKS
- CHILDREN'S CHRISTIAN AND SPIRITUALITY
- CHRISTMAS AND EASTER
- RELIGION/PHILOSOPHY
- SCHOOL TITLES
- ANGELS/CHANNELLING
- HEALING/MEDITATION
- SELF-HELP/RELATIONSHIPS
- ASTROLOGY/NUMEROLOGY
- SPIRITUAL ENQUIRY
- CHRISTIANITY, EVANGELICAL AND LIBERAL/RADICAL
- CURRENT AFFAIRS
- HISTORY/BIOGRAPHY
- INSPIRATIONAL/DEVOTIONAL
- WORLD RELIGIONS/INTERFAITH
- BIOGRAPHY AND FICTION
- BIBLE AND REFERENCE
- SCIENCE/PSYCHOLOGY

Please visit our website,
www.O-books.net

The Good Remembering
Llyn Roberts

I stumbled into The Good Remembering and felt compelled to read it from cover to cover. Now I recommend it to anyone searching for insight into spiritual growth during these intense times. Responsibly and well-written, it is a magical, powerful little book that transcends words and speaks directly to soul.

Melody Beattie, New York Times Best Selling author of *Co-Dependent No More*
1846940389 196pp **£9.99 $19.95**

Let the Standing Stones Speak
Natasha Hoffman

Destined to become an evergreen...a book that deserves to become a permanent point of reference for the serious seeker. This is a book not to be missed by anyone with either a heart, a mind, or a soul, let alone all three.

Ian Graham author of *God Is Never Late*
1903816793 288pp **£9.99 $14.95**

The Letters of Paul
A new interpretation for modern times
Sylvia Moss

Publication of The Letters of Paul, with revisions and commentary by the original author is an historic event. Above all, there emerges the universality of the teaching by the Christ, of love as the dictum for all ages to come. I was delighted and uplifted, and am pleased to commend the book to you.

Donald Keys, founder of SANE and co-founder of Planetary Citizen
1903816947 336pp 254x718 **£14.99 $24.95**

The Vision
Out of-body revelations of divine wisdom
Jaap Hiddinga

What a refreshing treasure I found this book to be. I felt like I had my own beliefs and intuition validated, and in others I felt challenged to look beyond my scope of comfort and to re-evaluate what I had come to know as true. This simple yet very insightful book can be a great help to many on their path to enlightenment.
StarzRainbowRose
1905047053 144pp £9.99 $14.95

Back to the Truth
5,000 years of Advaita
Dennis Waite

A wonderful book. Encyclopedic in nature, and destined to become a classic.
James Braha, author of *Living Reality*

Absolutely brilliant...an ease of writing with a water-tight argument outlining the great universal truths. This book will become a modern classic. A milestone in the history of Advaita.
Paula Marvelly, author of The Teachers of One
1905047614 500pp £19.95 $29.95

Beyond Photography
Encounters with orbs, angels and mysterious light forms
Katie Hall and John Pickering

The authors invite you to join them on a fascinating quest; a voyage of discovery into the nature of a phenomenon, manifestations of which are shown as being historical and global as well as contemporary and intently personal.

At journey's end you may find yourself a believer, a doubter or simply an intrigued wonderer... Whatever the outcome, the process of journeying is likely prove provocative and stimulating and as

with the mysterious images *fleetingly captured by the authors'* *cameras - inspiring and potentially enlightening.*
Brian Sibley, author and broadcaster.
1905047908 272pp 50 b/w photos +8pp colour insert **£12.99 $24.95**

Don't Get MAD Get Wise
Why no one ever makes you angry, ever!
Mike George
There is a journey we all need to make, from anger, to peace, to forgiveness. Anger always destroys, peace always restores, and forgiveness always heals. This little book explains the journey, the steps you can take to make it happen for you.
1905047827 160pp **£7.99 $14.95**

IF You Fall...
I always thought I'd rather be dead than paralysed: One slip, one moment, and everything changes…
Karen Darke
Karen Darke's story is about the indomitability of spirit, from one of life's cruel vagaries of fortune to what is insight and inspiration. She has overcome the limitations of paralysis and discovered a life of challenge and adventure that many of us only dream about. It is all about the mind, the spirit and the desire that some of us find, but which all of us possess. **Joe Simpson**, mountaineer and author of *Touching the Void*
1905047886 240pp **£9.99 $19.95**

Love, Healing and Happiness
Spiritual wisdom for a post-secular era
Larry Culliford
Larry Culliford has a remarkable gift for making connections between psychology and spirituality, and for linking our basic human needs with divine love. This is a wonderful book for those who are searching for 'life in all its fullness'. It draws on secular and

religious wisdom to speak to men and women who are looking for a spirituality that meets them where they are.
Rt Rev Dominic Walker, Bishop of Monmouth.
1905047916 224pp **£10.99 $19.95**

The Marriage of Jesus
The lost wife of the hidden years
Maggy Whitehouse

The "missing years" in the Bible are those he spent as a husband, raising his family. Given that the average life-span of a woman 2000 years ago was 27 years and two out of three women died in childbirth, Jesus was probably a widower when he began teaching. So what happened to Jesus' wife, this most forgotten of women?
1846940087 260pp **£11.99 $19.95**

Punk Science
Inside the mind of God
Manjir Samanta-Laughton

Wow! Punk Science is an extraordinary journey from the microcosm of the atom to the macrocosm of the Universe and all stops in between. Manjir Samanta-Laughton's synthesis of cosmology and consciousness is sheer genius. It is elegant, simple and, as an added bonus, makes great reading.
Dr Bruce H. Lipton, author of *The Biology of Belief*
1905047932 320pp **£12.95 $22.95**

Rosslyn Revealed
A secret library in stone
Alan Butler

Rosslyn Revealed gets to the bottom of the mystery of the chapel featured in the Da Vinci Code. The results of a lifetime of careful research and study demonstrate that truth really is stranger than fiction; a library of philosophical ideas and mystery rites, that were heresy in their time, have been disguised in the extraordinarily elaborate stone carvings.

1905047924 260pp b/w + colour illustrations **£19.95 $29.95** cl

The Way of Thomas
Nine Insights for Enlightened Living from the Secret Sayings of Jesus
John R. Mabry

What is the real story of early Christianity? Can we find a Jesus that is relevant as a spiritual guide for people today?

These and many other questions are addressed in this popular presentation of the teachings of this mystical Christian text. Telling the story of this gospels loss and recent recovery, readers will learn how Jesus' original community was eclipsed by followers of Paul, and how Jesus' true teaching was subverted and buried under centuries of fabricated history.

1846940303 196pp **£10.99 $19.95**

The Way Things Are
A Living Approach to Buddhism
Lama Ole Nydahl

An up-to-date and revised edition (three times the length) of a seminal work in the Diamond Way Buddhist tradition, that makes the timeless wisdom of Buddhism accessible to western audiences. Lama Ole has established more than 450 centres in 43 countries.

1846940427 240pp £9.99 $19.95

The 7 Ahas! of Highly Enlightened Souls
How to free yourself from ALL forms of stress
Mike George

7th printing

A very profound, self empowering book. Each page bursting with wisdom and insight. One you will need to read and reread over and over again! **Paradigm Shift**

1903816319 128pp 190/135mm **£5.99 $11.95**

God Calling
A Devotional Diary
A. J. Russell
46th printing
Perhaps the best-selling devotional book of all time, over 6 million copies sold.
1905047428 280pp 135/95mm **£7.99** cl.
US rights sold

The Goddess, the Grail and the Lodge
The Da Vinci code and the real origins of religion
Alan Butler
5th printing
This book rings through with the integrity of sharing time-honoured revelations. As a historical detective, following a golden thread from the great Megalithic cultures, Alan Butler vividly presents a compelling picture of the fight for life of a great secret and one that we simply can't afford to ignore. From the foreword by **Lynn Picknett** & **Clive Prince**
1903816696 360pp 230/152mm **£12.99 $19.95**

The Heart of Tantric Sex
A sourcebook on the practice of Tantric sex
Diana Richardson
3rd printing
One of the most revolutionary books on sexuality ever written. **Ruth Ostrow**, News Ltd.
1903816378 256pp **£9.99 $14.95**

I Am With You
The best-selling modern inspirational classic
John Woolley
14th printing hardback
Probably the consistently best-selling devotional in the UK today.

0853053413 280pp 150x100mm **£9.99** cl
4th printing paperback
1903816998 280pp 150/100mm **£6.99 $12.95**

In the Light of Meditation
The art and practice of meditation in 10 lessons
Mike George
2nd printing
A classy book. A gentle yet satisfying pace and is beautifully illustrated. Complete with a CD or guided meditation commentaries, this is a true gem among meditation guides. **Brainwave**
1903816610 224pp 235/165mm full colour throughout +CD **£11.99 $19.95**

The Instant Astrologer
A revolutionary new book and software package for the astrological seeker
Lyn Birkbeck
2nd printing
The brilliant Lyn Birkbeck's new book and CD package, The Instant Astrologer, combines modern technology and the wisdom of the ancients, creating an invitation to enlightenment for the masses, just when we need it most!
Astrologer **Jenny Lynch**, Host of NYC's StarPower Astrology Television Show
1903816491 628pp full colour throughout with CD ROM 240/180 **£39 $69** cl

Is There An Afterlife?
A comprehensive overview of the evidence, from east and west
David Fontana
2nd printing
An extensive, authoritative and detailed survey of the best of the evidence supporting survival after death. It will surely become a

classic not only of parapsychology literature in general but also of survival literature in particular. Professor Fontana is to be congratulated on this landmark study and I thoroughly recommend it to all who are really interested in a serious exploration of the subject. **Universalist**
1903816904 496pp 230/153mm **£14.99 $24.95**

The Reiki Sourcebook

Bronwen and Frans Stiene
5th printing
It captures everything a Reiki practitioner will ever need to know about the ancient art. This book is hailed by most Reiki professionals as the best guide to Reiki. For an average reader, it's also highly enjoyable and a good way to learn to understand Buddhism, therapy and healing. **Michelle Bakar**, Beauty magazine
1903816556 384pp £12.99 $19.95

Soul Power
The transformation that happens when you know
Nikki de Carteret
4th printing
This may be one of the finest books in its genre today. Using scenes from her own life and growth, Nikki de Carteret weaves wisdom about soul growth and the power of love and transcendent wisdom gleaned from the writings of the mystics. This is a book that I will read gain and again as a reference for my own soul growth. She is a scholar who is totally accessible and grounded in the human experience. **Barnes and Noble review**
190381636X 240pp **£9.99 $15.95**